finding rhythm

finding rhythm

AN INTERNATIONAL DANCE JOURNEY

ALIÉNOR SALMON

APOLLO PUBLISHERS

Finding Rhythm: An International Dance Journey
Copyright © 2021 by Aliénor Salmon

Apollo Publishers books may be purchased for educational, business, or sales promotional use. Special editions may be made available upon request. For details, contact Apollo Publishers at info@apollopublishers.com.

Visit our website at www.apollopublishers.com.

Published in compliance with California's Proposition 65.

Library of Congress Control Number: 2020935820.

Print ISBN: 978-1-948062-72-5
Ebook ISBN: 978-1-948062-73-2

Printed in the United States of America.

*To my mother, Nadine, for encouraging
me to always believe in my dreams.*

1　**NEW YORK:** Salsa On 2, Cha-Cha, Pachanga, and Boogaloo

2　**MEXICO:** Jarabe Tapatío, Regional Folklore, and a Guelaguetza

3　**CUBA:** Cuban Salsa, Son, and Cubatón

4　**DOMINICAN REPUBLIC:** Bachata, Merengue, and Dembow

5　**PUERTO RICO:** Reggaeton and Puerto Rican Salsa

6　**COLOMBIA:** Cumbia, Porro, and Salsa Caleña

7　**BRAZIL:** Samba No Pé, Forró, Samba de Gafieira, and the Lambada

8　**ARGENTINA:** Tango and La Chacarera

Contents

May we dance in the face of our fears.
—Gloria Anzaldúa

1

THREE LOVES LOST

"If you could do anything without the worry of time or money, what would you do?" I ask Naoko.

"Swim with whales in Papua New Guinea!" she exclaims with absolute certainty. Naoko is obsessed with sea creatures, dependably quirky, and always willing to entertain my line of inquiry. "What about you? What would you do if you could do anything?"

Somehow I hadn't expected my own question would be asked of me too. *Why haven't I asked myself this before? As an emerging happiness researcher, shouldn't I know what would make me most happy?* I turn to stare blankly at the limestone cliffs dropped like sugar lumps into the Andaman Sea, which I admire from our hotel's terrace in Thailand's Krabi Province. A series of sad events has left me with a broken heart, the first signs of burnout, and a cloudy mind, making it difficult for me to think or see clearly. *In what situation am I happiest? In what kind of environment and with what kind of people? What would make me feel free and alive?* I desperately want a break from work to learn something new, even if for just a few months. I want to liberate my body from my desk.

Over the years I have pushed myself to do more, produce more, in the hope of being more. But my achievements have come with a growing work-load and a flooded in-box, leaving me with little space to quietly reflect on my creative outlets and countless ideas. It dawns on me that I am much more than my profession. I am a person whose inner child has dreams yet to be fulfilled. The answer comes to me.

"You know what? I would learn to dance."

Living in the tropical metropolis of Bangkok with a budding career in the United Nations and a bustling social calendar, my life may seem like the pinnacle of success. But the loss of three great loves—my mentor, the man I'd considered my soulmate, and my grandfather—has left me devastated. It turns out that there are three ways men can abandon you: a diplomatic recall, ghosting, and death.

I had worked for a visionary, a man whose integrity and tireless dedi-cation to building a happier and more peaceful world made me feel like I was part of something bigger than myself. He was my mentor, my *maestro*. When you live and work far away from home, your colleagues and friends become your family. I'd been fortunate to be part of a remarkable team: we bonded over frequent happy hours, embraced the work hard, play hard culture, and won every office competition. We were an eclectic bouquet of human beings led by a person whose daily presence, inappropriate sense of humor, and genuine interest in our work motivated us to innovate, create, and strive to be better.

When my mentor called an impromptu team meeting and announced he was leaving in just one week, it was like a stab to my chest. My throat tightened and I turned my face to hide the tears that were streaming down my cheeks. His absence even for a few days would have been strongly felt. Now our team didn't know if we would see him again. It was like a collective trauma, and a heavy sadness and loss filled the room. Over the weeks and months to come, the sharp pain in my chest would occasionally return, causing tears to roll down my cheeks without warning. I would sometimes start to email him out of reflex, only to remember that there would be no reply. What made it worse was that we had no contact with him whatsoever, and no news. We knew nothing. He seemed to have vanished—incommunicado.

A few months after losing my mentor, I met Cristián. It was the height of Thailand's monsoon season, and I'd made it through the rainstorm to a Latin party at Above Eleven, my favorite Bangkok rooftop bar. As the rained poured down and lightning flashed across the city's sparkling sky-line, we took shelter. By the bar I caught his gaze and instantly felt a force drawing me toward him. It was like we'd known each other before, and when we spoke, his eyes pierced through my soul. He placed his hand on my heart and brought my hand to his cheek.

A tuk-tuk ride and twenty-four hours later, I knew I was in love. The next day he was bound for the airport to return to Europe, but within weeks we met up again in Spain. We went to Seville, where we lost ourselves in the labyrinth of the Alcázar Palace, strolled across the Triana Bridge, and shared secret kisses on patios surrounded by fragrant orange blossoms. People would stop to admire our glow, one old man even crying, *"¡Que viva el amor!"* (Long live love!) During a romantic horse-drawn carriage ride through Maria Luisa Park, we passed the statues of three young women representing the three phases of love: hopeful love, possessed love, and love lost. Mine was certainly the first. Cristián was my first great love, and I pinched myself looking up at him and wondering if I would endure through the three phases.

Within a few days of my return to Bangkok, I was back at Above Eleven, a place full of memories, for their weekly Latin night. When one of my favorite songs started to play, I asked the DJ what kind of music it was, and he told me it was bachata, a genre from the Dominican Republic. The soulful voice singing to the lament of a weeping guitar mirrored my own emotional state. I found solace in the wistful longing. My heart was open, bare, and beating. I was allowing myself to feel. I decided to sign up for beginner bachata classes at rumPUREE, Bangkok's leading dance studio, that week.

Cristián and I were separated by distance, but I had hope—what we felt seemed too precious to let go. Because of the time difference, I would read his messages every morning as I woke up. They felt like heartfelt letters sent from the front, amorous declarations. But over time his texts became less frequent. I would increasingly wake up to an empty screen, leaving me trembling and distressed. One stormy evening, while admiring the deep purple clouds above Bangkok, I surprised myself by praying to the moon that he would come back to me. I almost never pray. I was possessed.

Weeks of silence, sudden manifestations, and excuses passed, sending me into an agonizing roller-coaster of emotions, until he disappeared completely. I had waited twenty-nine years to feel this love, and now it was lost.

When December arrived, about six weeks after I last heard from him, I was no less heartbroken, but it was impossible to resist the cheer of Christmas celebrations and that universal "holiday feeling" that emanated despite Bangkok's eighty-degree heat. For me the holidays are very special because I've lived on a different continent than my family for almost seven years, but the holidays are a time to be together. My French mother raised me in England, where I was born. But I grew up between both countries, with frequent ferry rides across the Channel to France where I spent time with my grandparents, with whom I am incredibly close.

As I got into my mother's car at London's Heathrow Airport, which I always fly into en route to France, she sighed from behind the wheel and then slowly said, "Your grandfather is dying. This is probably the last Christmas we will have all together."

My grandfather was the most important man in my life. He was my mother's stepfather, but he cradled me as a baby and loved me as if I were his own child. I even danced my first steps with him—when I was little, he would lift me up so that I could put my feet on top of his. It was no secret to anyone in the family that I was his favorite. He'd even figured out how to set my photo as his computer screen saver.

In postwar France, my grandmother, who had lived through the Nazi occupation, would often attend the village ball. She was known to dance like a butterfly, light in the arms of potential suitors. It was at the ball that she met her first husband, my biological grandfather, and they later left their home in rural Brittany to move to Paris for a better life. They were deeply in love and lived simply but happily in the Parisian suburb of Asnières-sur-Seine, where they had three daughters.

At the age of forty-two, my biological grandfather died from an incurable illness, leaving my grandmother widowed and heartbroken. She returned to Brittany with her daughters and worldly possessions and went to work in a telecommunications factory, where she met her second husband, whom I know as my grandfather. They shared a passion for dance, and after discovering a local dance club for pensioners, my grandmother became its president and my grandfather its treasurer.

"A waltz has nothing to do with a tango," she would tell me whimsically. "A tango is tender and amorous, but a waltz is magnificent. They are the most beautiful dances that will ever exist, and they will exist forever." And so I grew up joining them at the dance club every week during my summers in France. Over the years my grandfather and I twirled through seventieth and eightieth birthday parties, weddings, and anniversaries. I twirled into a teenager and then into a woman who reached his height.

Losing my grandfather struck me as something my heart couldn't endure. Arriving at their home that Christmas break, I was in denial about his condition until I saw his sunken face. He had lost weight from his illness, and he looked frail. My father had never been fully present, and died when I was just sixteen, so my grandfather had been my father figure my whole life. Now it hit me that he was dying. I put on a brave face, not wanting to show my emotion in order to make his last holiday season as nice as possible, and in the days that followed I made every effort to be cheerful. I would throw my arms around his neck at the dinner table and bring him his daily apple and handful of walnuts—his favorite dessert. He was weak but determined to see the new year, 2016, and I was determined to see it with him.

On New Year's Eve, in keeping with our family tradition, we laid out an exquisitely decorated table prepared for several courses, including indulgence in the annual luxuries of champagne and oysters. Seeing my grandfather so joyful and so frail at the same time filled me with a mix of contentment and pain, and they clashed into each other.

As I was setting the table I heard my cell phone ping. It was a text from Cristián, after several weeks of silence.

"Hi Aliénor, how are you? I'm thinking about how I'm ending the year, and I feel bad about the way things have been left with you. I thought our love was something light and fun, but then it became intense, and I don't think either of us wanted that. You're a great woman! I hope that you are very happy. May all your dreams come true."

The rage was fast, uncontrollable, and all-consuming. *How dare he try to rid himself of his guilt, and probably while en route to a New Year's Eve party*. Once our celebration was over and everyone had gone to bed, I cried violently in the bathroom, not recognizing my own eyes in the mirror. They change colors with my mood, and they'd become an emerald green from grief, contrasting against scarlet cheeks burning red with fury. Cristián had illuminated my life—it may have been short-lived, but the light he brought in had shined bright. Now that it was clear that it had only been a fleeting romance, I felt burned.

The next morning, on New Year's Day, I sat in the kitchen and drank coffee out of a small bowl, as is common in France and as my grandfather had always done. Through the doorway I watched him get up, turn on his computer, and play traditional accordion music. He danced alone in the living room. He knew he was dying. It was almost like he had to dance his last steps.

"WHAT DANCE WOULD you learn?" asks Naoko enthusiastically.

I took my first dance class at four years old, beginning a childhood stint as a ballerina, but my rebellious nature took pleasure in defying my ballet teacher's traditional (and somewhat abusive) methods, and I found myself often ignoring her demands to plié at the barre, choosing to pirouette across the room instead. My obedience could only ever be summoned by love, not by fear. She wanted to turn us into the Royal Ballet's next little swans. I simply wanted to dance because it brought me joy.

But my ballet class only allowed a glimmer of this. I needed an environment that allowed bountiful freedom. As I grew up, I began to believe that this freedom was intrinsically bound to Latin dance. I'd had a fascination for the Latin way of life ever since I started to learn Spanish at the age of fourteen, and thinking of it conjured up images of smoky dance salons and mystical tango halls, shiny brass bands, and bustling crowds of people dancing and singing in the streets. Vivid colors, sounds, and movements came together like a kaleidoscope as I imagined myself dancing across Latin America.

If I could have it my way, and truly live my dream, I would go to Buenos Aires for a few months and learn to dance tango. Maybe I would also go to the Dominican Republic where I could dance bachata. (I've taken a few beginner classes already.) And then there is Rio de Janeiro, home of Carnival—a nonnegotiable. I have always dreamed of dancing samba in the Rio Carnival. And I couldn't leave out salsa, but which style and where to learn it? New York? Cuba? Colombia? Scenes begin to play in my mind, from polished wooden stages and bright lights to white-sand beaches, concrete urban settings, and candlelit colonial homes. It strikes me that I could make a video of each dance I would learn, and record precious memories from a journey of colors, costumes, and countries. The fact that I am a beginner won't put me off.

Practically speaking, it would be unrealistic to try and master each of the dances I want to learn. I don't have an endless supply of free time and travel money. But I also wouldn't want to just show up for a few classes and then move on. I want the adrenaline rush of truly dancing the dances, and I want to be diligent, focused, and motivated in my learning. A performance would be terrifying, but I love the idea of intensely rehearsing and losing myself in my practice with the kind of determination that comes with preparing for a show. I assume I could perform in the Rio Carnival, since it is both a performance and a parade. It seems easy to enter, but how would I find other opportunities as a beginner? For a moment this seems impossible, but then, just as quickly, it *is* possible. I feel a flame ignite inside of me.

Naoko and I make a pact to resign from our jobs within the year and focus on making our dreams come true. I fix a date in my head: nine months from our conversation.

In the days that follow, I feel a mix of emotions. There is continuous excitement and determination, but there are also waves of doubt and anxiety. I am choosing to leave behind a life that many would kill to have: an important career in a prestigious international organization, a fabulous group of friends, and a lifestyle that I couldn't afford elsewhere. I truly adore my life in Bangkok—sidesaddling on motorbike taxis in stilettos and pencil skirts to whiz between yoga classes, Latin parties, and ministerial conferences. And professionally, I am quitting my job just as my career is taking off. My portfolio of research publications has started to gain recognition over the last few years, along with my speaking engagements. I'm even set to be a keynote speaker alongside the world's most prominent happiness experts this summer. I'll also be turning thirty in just a few months, and society still seems to expect women to have accomplished certain goals by this age: in addition to a stable job, a mortgage, marriage, and perhaps a baby. I won't have any of those.

In the worst moments, my head spins with questions. *What will my colleagues think when I tell them I am quitting a dream job to dance? Does that sound crazy? If I quit my job, will I ever be employed again? How will I finance the trip? Is my dream even realistic? Will I really get to dance bachata*

on a sun-drenched Dominican beach or glide effortlessly through tango, as I
imagine myself doing? Can I actually parade down the sambadrome in Rio
de Janeiro and perform in the process? Is Rio even safe? What if something
happens to me?

I also wonder how dance will affect my relationship with my body—if it
will make me feel happier in it and increase my self-esteem. In recent months
I've started to understand the connection between movement and mental
health. I've been attending classes at a yoga studio for a few months, and with
my practice I have slowly noticed the stiffness in my body start to soften. The
class is where I go to meditate on my potentially life-changing decision.

Not long after I began taking yoga classes, I'd considered approaching Minh, the instructor and one of the owners of the studio, to ask her
about the tightness in my chest, but I was hesitant to do so. One morning,
however, when I was feeling particularly heartbroken, she beat me to it. It
turned out she could read my soul.

As we lay on our mats toward the end of our practice, she instructed us
to place a block between our shoulder blades.

"As you stretch your back over the block, feel your heart opening,"
she said.

The block painfully dug into my back, and I was so tense that it felt like
my chest was about to break violently, like a concrete slab would. But while
breathing through the pain, I started to feel an unexpected release.

"Sometimes we don't want to open our heart," Minh said, looking at
me as she noticed my resistance, "because somebody hurt it."

With my shoulders rolled back, I was exposing my wounded heart.
Tears rolled down my face as my cheek fell to one side.

At the end of the class, I tried to walk unnoticed past Minh, who was
sitting near the changing rooms. She stopped me anyway.

"Come take a seat," she said and motioned me to join her on the bench.
I sat down and tried to remain composed without letting out the tears I
held inside.

"You know I look at you sometimes in class. You have such beautiful energy. Did anyone ever tell you that?"

At the time I'd wondered if she was talking about me or who I used to be. I'd always been described as "so full of energy," but I had felt like my soul had been lost to sadness and paralyzed by fear.

Now, months later, I can feel that energy returning. Every Thursday morning, I enter the studio and pick my favorite spot next to the window. There I can feel rays of sunshine glowing against my face and filling me with light. I feel strength in my arms as they spread wide and in my legs as I stretch deep into the postures. While I flow from one sun salutation to another, I relish the connections between movement and emotions. It is a testimony to the fact that yoga, like dance, is a union of body and soul that can bring peace and contentment. *This is what I'm going to feel every day*, I tell myself as I think about my upcoming journey.

THE LOSS OF my maestro, Cristián, and my grandfather forced me to reevaluate my life, myself, and what it means to truly live. It made me question everything, including what I want to do and who I want to become. I'm not looking to fill a void left by the loss of these men, but rather, to see myself more clearly. I want to know what it feels like to be free of the kinds of responsibilities and obligations I've been weighed down by. I want to know what it feels like to find contentment in simple things, to embrace the power of human connection, to be a kinder, more tolerant, and more empathetic version of myself, and to live a truly joyful and successful life.

Now, the awareness of what I might gain flutters inside me like a fledgling bird. I can't quiet the burgeoning notes of possibility: exploring a continent that has fascinated me since I was a child, where my fluency in the language could allow me to embed myself in the culture and capture precious stories and discover new ways of life. Even if I'm there for less than a year, I will be free from my desk, living authentically and experiencing destinations that I have so far only dreamed of immersing myself in. I have just nine months, and then I'll be on my way. I'm not sure it's the right decision, but it's a risk worth taking, and now that I've decided, there's no turning back.

2

_____

BANGKOK

Yoga, Latin Parties, and Ministerial Conferences

Since the dawn of the Ayutthaya period, in the fourteenth century, a legend has been told throughout Thailand and across generations about a princess named Manorah who lived in the mythical Mount Grairat kingdom. Manorah was the youngest of King Prathum and Queen Jantakinnaree's seven Kinnaree daughters, graceful creatures who were half woman, half swan. Known for their excellence in music and dance, they had the celestial ability to remove and wear their wings whenever they wanted so that they could fly between the human and mystical worlds.

One night, under a full moon and starry sky, the seven Kinnaree were bathing in crystal pools of water in a lake surrounded by towering bamboo trees and pink lotus flowers deep in the kingdom's Himmapan forest. A huntsman named Prahnbun walked past, saw the Kinnaree, and thought that if he could catch one and present her to Prince Suthon, the prince would fall in love with her. An old hermit told him that it was not so easy to catch a Kinnaree because they would simply fly away if he tried. But seeking the help of the Great Naga, a dragon who lived in the forest, Prahnbun obtained a magical rope, captured Manorah, and took away her wings.

Prahnbun presented Manorah to the prince and was rewarded generously for his "gift," and the prince and Manorah married soon after at the palace. Over time, the beautiful Kinnaree grew to love her handsome and kindhearted husband. But what is sometimes left out of Manorah's story is that before she could live happily ever after, she had to get her wings back for one last dance.

The legend of Manorah, the dancing princess, lives on in the form of a classical Thai dance and the golden Kinnaree statues that watch over Thailand's glittering temples.

My story isn't about finding a prince. It's about finding my wings so that, like a Kinnaree, I could dance. In the face of adversity, emotionally drained from the loss of my three loves, my sadness turned to anger, building a fire inside me that fueled an indomitable spirit capable of blazing sadness and shame.

KHUN GUÏ, THE caretaker at my office, stops by my desk to pick up the trash as she does every afternoon. She has seen my face, and perhaps my soul, slowly break over the last few months, and the exhaustion that I now carry must be transparent.

I returned to Bangkok just a few days ago, after my grandfather's funeral and just in time for a ridiculous Hello Kitty–themed race. I'd signed up just for fun, but running with my best friends, Lauranne and Emily, proved to be a cathartic experience. My mind has felt clearer since then, and I'm excited for my future now that I've chosen to create a different path for myself. I now need to plan carefully, as my journey is only six months away.

"*Su su!*" Khun Guï exclaims, throwing her fist up in the air and nodding her head reassuringly. It's as if she can read my mind.

There is no perfect English translation of *su su*; the best equivalent is "fight fight." It is a quintessentially Thai expression used to cheer someone on and encourage them to keep going, to keep fighting, and to never give up. Sometimes I feel like Khun Guï is smarter than the rest of us. She has an intuition, kindness, and humanity that make her my hero and one of the most popular people in the office—a small victory in the face of institutional hierarchy. If she's telling me to keep fighting, she knows that there are good things ahead if I can summon the strength. Khun Guï doesn't know my plan, but I know she believes in me.

A minute after Khun Guï leaves, my phone rings. It's my Colombian friend and colleague Juan asking if we can meet in our usual place, an archway leading to the building's gardens. As one of my closest confidants, he has patiently counseled me over the last few months, listening to me talk about heartbreak.

"How are you feeling?" he asks, hugging me tightly.

"You know what?" I respond slowly. "I have a plan." It feels good to tell someone. It starts to make it more real.

The other person I'm most eager to share my plan with is Arianna, a colleague from Mexico who, along with Juan, has formed part of my insight into the Latino approach to life and with whom I practice my rusty Spanish. Her vibrant energy and steady stream of party invites have helped me immensely.

I make plans to see Arianna and wait for her on the platform of the BTS sky train, Bangkok's overground metro that snakes through the city's skyscrapers. Eventually, she flies out the doors of the sky train carriage and takes my hand to lead me to Soi 11, Bangkok's party street. We have a night of tapas, wine, and dancing ahead of us, and for the occasion I'm wearing a red silk dress that I bought in Luang Prabang, a mystical and ancient city in northern Laos. The dress is crushed crimson-red silk composed of a floating red skirt and a wrapped bodice. From the moment I saw it hanging in the window of a boutique on Sakkaline Road that was reminiscent of French Indochina, I knew this dress was meant to dance.

Over dinner I tell Arianna my plan: "The idea is to dance from New York to Buenos Aires, with a few stops along the way—I'm thinking the Caribbean, Colombia, and Brazil."

On hearing this, Arianna immediately throws up her hand to wave over the jovial Spanish owner of the tapas bar and request wine to celebrate the news.

"*¡Amiga linda!* (Beautiful friend!) I love it," she exclaims, her eyes widening. "But you have to add Mexico to the list. I insist."

Arianna insists I include Mexico, Juan had insisted I include Colombia, and after initial research on the different dances of Latin America, I had my own countries, too. I'd drawn up a wish list of dances that I plan to learn in their countries of origin. A few months would never be enough time to master the dances. For the more complicated ones, I would probably need about six to eight months in one place just to master the basics. But the longest I am willing to plan the entire trip for is eight months. The itinerary I eventually decide to go with will take me through eight destinations from New York to Buenos Aires by way of Mexico, Cuba, the Dominican Republic, Puerto Rico, Colombia, and Brazil, to learn a total of eight dances in eight months. Of course, plans often work out differently than expected, and my adventure will lead me to learn a total of eighteen dances in these eight destinations over the course of ten months. But I don't know that yet.

Arianna suggests that I arrive in Mexico in time for their Independence Day in mid-September and leave in early November, just after the Day of the Dead, where I can expect to enjoy an abundance of excellent tequila-fueled parties. She also says that I absolutely need to get to Rio by February for Carnival, and under no circumstances should I miss that. I'm not sure if all my dance dreams are achievable, and the trip will definitely be intense, but it's certainly not impossible. I'll have to pick and choose how much time I spend in each country, but I'll never miss the opportunity to dance. These are places where people dance all year round!

As we finish our tapas, we consider where to go next. We are only a few steps from a popular wine bar that hosts a weekly salsa night. Arianna doesn't dance salsa, but inspired by the idea of my dance pilgrimage, we decide to stop by. I've never taken a proper salsa class, so I try to improvise and follow my partner without really knowing what I'm doing. "Bailando" by Enrique Iglesias plays as we approach the bar. The simple translation of *bailando* is "dancing," but in Spanish it has the grammatical connotation of being something continuous—an approach to life. Bailando will now be my approach to life.

My beginner bachata classes have been going well. I'd wanted to take Latin dance classes for years, but something always held me back. I'd been afraid to go alone and failed to convince friends to join me. I'd also thought that somehow the "right moment" to sign up would show itself. The wait was based on a fear of making mistakes and looking stupid. Now I am less forgiving of the excuses I gave myself.

In my bachata classes I expected to be surrounded by competitive dancers, but instead I find myself surrounded by beginners like me. Some people came straight from the office. They all have their own story of how and why they ended up here.

When our teacher slowly guides us through the basic bachata steps, I realize that anyone who knows how to walk would be able to follow. A thought hits: *Maybe dance is more accessible than I thought. After all, even professional dancers have to start from zero.* Maybe the ability to dance well isn't a mystifying talent that you're either born with or you're not; maybe it's something that anyone can learn.

LIKE ANY OTHER self-respecting person in Asia who is facing a major life decision, I consult a fortune-teller, Mr. Geng, who tells me I should forget Cristián (apparently, I'll meet a "man of uniform" in the next few years), watch out for my hip, and leave my job.

Although I take this with a grain of salt, it adds to my confidence that I'm making the right decision. I begin spending my evenings and weekends researching and planning my trip. Juan has warned me that flights in Latin America are steep; it's not like Asia, where there is a wealth of low-cost carriers that offer cheap one-way flights in clean, comfortable aircrafts.

Thankfully, I've been religiously (and aimlessly) saving air miles for the past seven years with the same airline alliance. I always thought the miles were pretty useless, but they end up covering most of my flights. I'll also use the savings I've set aside, including the benefits of a modest bond I invested in stocks that has since doubled in value. I decide I'll release the lot and keep saving each month until I leave. I could also sell most of my things.

It's hard to figure out how much money I'll need for each place. I've heard that Mexico and Colombia are similar to Thailand, but Rio seems to be really expensive, and Argentina's rampant inflation might be a problem depending on currency fluctuations. These are factors beyond my control, but with my best guesses I sketch out a monthly allowance that should see me through most places. I'm just a few thousand dollars away from what I'll need.

I take a deep breath, knowing I can get there. This week I handed in my notice, giving the reason that I wanted to work remotely to experience living in different locations for a set amount of time. Everyone knows that I love Latin culture and have taken every opportunity to speak Spanish with Juan or Arianna in the office corridors, so when I said I was moving to Mexico, nobody flinched. It wasn't a lie—the first Latin American country that I will be living in, after a brief stint in New York to visit a friend, is Mexico. But what I didn't publicly announce is that my plan revolves around learning how to dance. It doesn't square with the polished workaholic demeanor that I believe I give off at work. I'm concerned my colleagues might judge me for choosing to do something fun rather than continue my vocation to support the development of global policy. I'm worried people might not take me seriously anymore.

WITH ONLY ONE month until I'm set to take off, there is just one more group from whom I need to seek validation: the dancers of Bangkok.

Luiz, my bachata and salsa teacher, had immigrated to New York from Mexico at twenty-two years old. After a car accident left him with a hunch, a friend recommended he try dance as therapy for his posture. He ended up learning the Horton technique, a drawn-out method of developing strength and flexibility to improve performance and lengthen the spine, at New York's famous Alvin Ailey dance school, and entering the world of dance. It connected him to his culture and himself. "Every time that you dance you discover something new," he told me.

Karn, my Thai zumba instructor, was spotted by a dance trainer at an outdoor aerobics class. She was overweight at the time but moved well. Her dazzling smile assured him of her potential. She went on to become a Thai salsa champion. Natural, radiant, and full of energy, she doesn't conform to Thai beauty stereotypes and lets her wild lion's mane fall over her bronze shoulders while bouncing around town with giant headphones. She has been a key part of lifting my spirits over the past few months. When I tell her my plan, her eyes widen. She shows me her arm, covered in goose bumps. "You have no idea what your dream makes me feel," she says.

For my samba teacher, Nino, dance was his ticket out of poverty. He had grown up in the favelas of Recife, Brazil, dancing caboclinho with his family, a dance named after the marriages between black and indigenous populations, of which he is a product. He had no toys or playground as a child, just his body and his friends. He ended up teaching capoeira, B-boy break dancing, and samba. For Nino, dance is a natural expression where there's no right or wrong. His belief is that dance should be fun rather than forced: "Some people dance to impress, and some people dance to express."

I also speak to Gabriela, an Ecuadorean dancer I met at a Latin party who started dancing at home when she was just three years old. She evolved through ballet lessons and learned to samba by watching a Brazilian group on Ecuadorean TV. After moving to Bangkok at the age of eighteen, she was spotted by a Brazilian woman who asked her to be part of her show, and that's when her adventure began. She felt like she had entered a dream from which she never wanted to wake up: "When I dance I feel like I'm flying toward the sky and touching the stars. I feel a happiness so immense that it's bursting out of my chest, and a freedom so great that I feel I can conquer the world," she told me.

The dancers I've encountered in Bangkok have confirmed to me that dance is about learning, feeling, and dreaming in a way that is authentically human. Society has taught me to be strong, hold back my feelings, and keep it together. But what's the point of being alive if I can't express what I feel? Now I acknowledge the humanity of my feelings, which fills me with a new kind of strength. I summon Manorah the Kinnaree and plan to find my own happily ever after. But first I need to flutter my wings and take flight.

3

NEW YORK

Salsa On 2, Cha-Cha, Pachanga, and Boogaloo

As I board the flight to New York's John F. Kennedy International Airport at London's Heathrow Airport, I feel a rush of excitement. The journey I have imagined, planned, and dreamed of for months is now happening and will kick off in New York City—the birthplace of salsa and the city where so many people come to pursue their dreams, leaving everything behind to follow the promise of a new life. For me, New York is my launching pad. I envision myself dancing with divas and searching for the past in Spanish Harlem, also known as El Barrio (The Neighborhood).

Incidentally, one of the world's biggest salsa events—the New York International Salsa Congress, known as the NYISC—coincides with the very weekend I arrive. The question of where salsa originates from is one of the most contentious issues in the dance world. The general consensus is that its roots are mostly Afro-Cuban, with many genres of dance leading to its creation, such as Cuba's son and rumba, Puerto Rican folkloric dances like the plena and bomba, and Dominican merengue.[1] The word "salsa" was used to refer to the dance coined in New York in the 1970s. *Salsa* means "sauce" in Spanish, and the dance was given its name to reflect the fact that salsa is also a blend of many ingredients.[2] With the dance, it's a fusion of genres developed by New York's Latin immigrant population.

In the 1930s, musicians from Cuba came to New York for work.[3] They brought son and Afro-Cuban rumba, which they later blended with jazz influences.[4] But following the Cuban Revolution in the 1950s came the end of diplomatic relations between Cuba and the United States and the stopping of all travel and cultural exchanges between the countries. The surge in emigration from Puerto Rico in the 1950s led New York's thriving Puerto Rican community, known as Nuyoricans, to take over the city's Latin dance scene.[5] Spanning from the 1940s to the 1960s, the Palladium Era, or the Golden Age of Dance, was already in full swing. The name comes from the Palladium Ballroom, which opened its doors at the corner of Broadway and West 53rd Street in 1946 and started featuring Latin music in 1948, including the "Big Three" big-band orchestras—Machito and his Afro-Cubans, Tito Puente, and Tito Rodríguez.[6] Home of the mambo craze, the Palladium Ballroom attracted some of the most exceptional dancers until it closed its doors in 1966.[7] Somewhere between the walls of the Palladium and the lights of the streets, between the trembling vibraphones and tantalizing tones of mambo in the late 1940s, the cheerful shuffling of cha-cha in the 1950s, and the swiveling leg moves of pachanga and the funky head bopping of boogaloo in the 1960s, salsa was born.

Among those credited with the founding of the salsa movement are the Fania All Stars, a legendary orchestra that included some of the greatest salsa artists of all time, such as Héctor Lavoe, Celia Cruz, Willie Colón, Roberto Roena, and Jimmy Bosch.[8] For months before beginning my journey I listened to their music and could feel the fusion of styles, especially between jazz, soul, and funk in one song that I love called "Ella Fue" (She Was the One). Fania and other Nuyorican artists sang about life in Spanish Harlem and the discrimination, crime, and inequality that the Latin community faced. To make fun of stereotypes of Latinos at the time, the cover of the 1970 album *The Big Break – La Gran Fuga* shows an FBI posted warning that "Willie Colón and Héctor Lavoe have been known to kill people with little provocation with their exciting rhythm."[9]

Salsa's popularity kept surging back, with the "new wave" in the 1990s bringing artists like La India and Marc Anthony. Here in New York in August 2016, salsa feels as popular as ever, with people from all different countries and cultures taking up salsa classes as a hobby. No wonder—the music is infectious, its sultry beats spreading happiness around the world.

AT THE AIRPORT I step out of Arrivals, grab my luggage, and head to a classic New York City yellow taxi. "Brooklyn," I tell the driver and hand him a paper with my friend's address. I will be staying with Hannah, one of my oldest friends. We've known each other since we were sixteen and in high school together in England. She recently moved from London to New York, and I'm on my way to crash on her air mattress.

Peering out the windows to look at the buildings, I think of the people before me who came to New York to find fame and fortune or to escape misery for a better life. The different waves of immigration: people arriving at Ellis Island over a hundred years ago, those escaping war and violence, those hoping to become a star or looking to reinvent themselves like Holly Golightly in *Breakfast at Tiffany's*. Some of these people brought their instruments, music, and dances. *What brought me here, and what am I searching for?* We humans are colorful and complex characters with so much to offer. For so long, I defined myself—my worth and my very being—by my profession, so who am I now?

Finally, after making our way through heavy traffic, I arrive at Hannah's recently renovated redbrick building. On her rooftop terrace, we clink glasses of rosé and watch the equally rosé sunset flood Manhattan's iconic skyline. It's a view that I won't get bored of, but I can feel the jet lag kick in and I need to go get ready. Tonight is the launch party of the NYISC at a club called HAUS and it's not something I want to miss. I was so excited to be arriving in time for NYISC that I bought tickets to it and related events almost immediately after finding out. Included in my itinerary is a nine-hour "Diva Challenge," where I'll learn cha-cha and boogaloo choreography to perform onstage, led by a dancer named Griselle Ponce. I'm new to the dance world and haven't heard of Griselle, but a quick Google search informs me that she is famed as the "Mambo Diva" and is one of the most renowned salsa dancers in the world. My beginner's journey will start with me surrounded by dancers of a semiprofessional level and higher, in a city that inspires competition and excellence.

When we arrive at HAUS, we pass a step and repeat in front of the backdrop featuring the logos of all the sponsors, which reflect the richness of New York's Latino community. The space is relatively empty but quickly starts to fill up. The club feels like it could have been an old cabaret theater, with velvet seats and small tables lined up in rows leading up a set of stairs.

As dancers fill the floor, I stand in awe at the sight of them twirling and spinning in the dark, their outlines made visible by the clash of the club's violet and pink neon lights, and the sparkle of the giant disco ball that hangs from the ceiling above them. *They're truly dancing like nobody's watching*, I think to myself. They dance relentlessly, expressing themselves freely and seemingly without a care in the world.

I'm dying to join in, but I'm still so new to Latin dance. Despite having a natural feel for the music—at least in my heart, perhaps not so much in my feet—I don't feel ready to dance socially with strangers or able to anticipate any steps or moves without knowing where I need to step next. *I'm a beginner, and that's okay*, I remind myself. *This is just the beginning of my journey; I shouldn't be so hard on myself. Maybe in a few months, I'll dance like them.*

We don't end up staying very long, leaving after two cocktails. I feel disappointed in myself for not having had the courage to join in. As I walk out the door, I take one last glance at the dancers. There's a woman in a floaty sheer skirt that opens up and shimmers as she twirls. The expression on her face is of pure joy. *One day, that will be me*, I decide.

WHAT DOES ONE wear to a salsa congress? I go with a black crossover leotard that I bought for the event and patterned yoga pants. I feel like I'm going back to school, nervously fidgeting as I check that my bag is packed and make sure not to forget my subway card or my dancing shoes.

Through Times Square I make my way toward the venue, a huge hotel just off Broadway and West 46th Street. It's still early, nine thirty in the morning, and the bright lights make me feel slightly nauseous but excited at the same time. Crowds of commuters and tourists cross one another's paths through the square, while two men dressed as the Statue of Liberty, perfectly painted in pale turquoise, contrast against the colors of the bright billboards.

At the venue I trade in my ticket for a tote bag and take out the schedule to scan the various workshops. I decide on four: the aptly named session "Welcome to New York. Fundamentals of NY On 2," a beginner class organized by the Balmir Latin Dance Company that I can just about follow; an "Introduction to Kizomba" class, where we study a dance originally from Angola that I note down on my list of prospective dances to learn in the future; "NYC Mambo Shines" with Jimmy Anton, whom I had heard about from my teacher Luiz in Bangkok and whom I struggle to follow as he teaches us "shines," a sort of adornment or decoration danced individually or as a sequence to glamorize the basic step; and a workshop on body movement that I don't follow at all and that makes me realize that it's time for a much-needed break.

I have three hours until the meet and greet for the Diva Challenge, followed by three intense hours of class. I take a deep breath and try to remember to be kind to myself. We all have different levels and abilities, and I shouldn't expect to start as a pro. Even if I don't dance well, at least

I'm doing it. After all, Woody Allen once said that "80 percent of life is just showing up." And I'm really showing up! Seven hours of dance class in a single day is a massive undertaking for a beginner. I decide to take a walk and stop in Bryant Park to have lunch in a leafy terrace restaurant where I soak up the late-summer sun, enjoy a glass of sauvignon blanc, and celebrate my experience thus far.

In my first workshop, I had been greeted by three glamorous and elegant instructors, each dressed in black and wearing her hair in a large, tightly pulled back bun. They were women of different shapes, ages, and looks, and seeing this variety of women broke the stereotypes that I had about the dance world.

One of the reasons I was kicked out of my ballet school at ten years old was that I was considered not thin enough—a childhood trauma that left me with the impression that the world of dance is cruel and only for people with "perfect" bodies. At the congress, professionals of all ages, shapes, sizes, and ethnicities prove that you don't have to be young or skinny to be a fabulous dancer.

When I walk into the studio where the Diva Challenge will be, I try to keep a low profile. I feel ashamed that I was unable to keep up with the others in the workshops I took earlier. *Am I just faking it?* I ask myself. I find an empty spot at the back of the room next to an alluring woman with dark feline eyes and thick chestnut brown hair. Her name is Teodora, and she's a Canadian originally from Serbia. When she discovered Latin dance a few years ago, she traded Serbian folklore dancing for salsa, and she's been learning, performing, and teaching salsa since then. She asks me the same usual questions, including why I'm there, and I surprise myself by sharing my story for the first time, hearing myself say it aloud.

"Actually, I don't really know how to dance and don't live anywhere right now. I used to live in Thailand, but I left my job to learn how to dance." I absorb the beautiful craziness of my words, which most likely only make sense to me. I love that here nobody asks each other what they do for a living, just where they're from and how long they've been dancing.

"Oh my God, you are so inspiring!" exclaims Teodora. "I don't think I've ever met someone like you. It makes me dream!"

I'm shocked, though flattered, that an advanced dancer could feel inspired by me. It strikes me that I was so focused on preparing for my journey that I hadn't quite realized the magnitude of what I've done.

Suddenly Griselle Ponce walks in, wearing big sunglasses and a dazzling smile—diva style. I'm so curious to learn more about this woman, who is one of the most decorated and recognized salsa dancers in the world and has her own unique presence. Griselle was born in Puerto Rico to a musician father and mother. She dreamed of one day becoming a movie star or fashion model. She was thrilled when she got a job cohosting a TV show, and she worked there for six years. But dance found her, and she quit her job in television because she knew that dance was what she had to pursue. She was meant for the stage.[10]

Griselle asks us to introduce ourselves. Many of the women here are of Latin origin, but people have come from all over the world to learn with Griselle. She listens attentively to each person as they speak. A very friendly girl named Petal whom I had met in the kizomba class introduces herself and announces that she will not be performing onstage at the end of the challenge. She says she just wants to do the boot camp for fun.

"If you're going to rule out performing at the outset, you won't give 100 percent because you won't have the pressure," says Griselle encouragingly. "Act as if you're going to perform and then make the call at the last minute before the performance."

I'm impressed that Griselle wants all the women in her boot camp to push themselves to be the very best they can be, regardless of their level. She must give so many of these workshops, but she genuinely seems to care about us.

"If the person next to you is faster than you, who cares?" she asks. "It doesn't matter what level you are. What matters is that you work hard and keep going, no matter what."

What she says strikes a chord with me. *Why compare myself to others if it's only going to make me feel discouraged?* Her words become my mantra for the rest of the congress.

We stand in rows and go through some of the steps of the choreography that we will learn over the next few days. As I stumble my way clumsily through the steps as the others seem to glide, I keep Griselle's words in mind and keep going. At the end of an intense three hours, Griselle demonstrates what the choreography, a mix of cha-cha and boogaloo, will look like as a sequence. The steps are unlike anything I've ever seen before, with sweeping legs, head rolls, and little jumps that comprise a complex pattern that I can barely understand. A few of the students decide to drop out.

They are much more advanced than me, and yet they are ready to give up. I can barely dance, but nothing will stop me from going up on that stage and trying, no matter how hard I need to practice or how many blisters I have on my feet. At the end of the workshop, I get a moment alone with Griselle and share my dance journey with her. She clearly believes in grit, and I do, too. We may not share the same dance level, but we share the same passion and perseverance that drive people to achieve their dreams.

At the end of the Diva Challenge, I make my way to the hotel's Westside Ballroom and arrive just in time for the first live concert: Jimmy Bosch and his orchestra. Bosch, or "El Trombon Criollo" (The Creole Trombone), is known for his hypnotic rhythms and soulful trombone. Some people consider him the most talented trombonist in contemporary Latin music, and he has played with some of the greatest Latin artists of all time.

Right in front of the stage, an older gentleman, probably around eighty years old, who is wearing a panama hat, dances with a woman of about the same age. The man has clear skill and *sabor*—a word meaning "flavor" that is often used to describe a way of being: savoring music and dancing with soul. I later find out that this gentleman is mambo legend Carlos Beltran, who some people say is "the best Palladium-era dancer still alive."[11] He is considered to have paved the way for future generations. They remind me that dancing is not limited by age. It's about feeling and passion. If you have those, then you can dance for the rest of your life.

After the concert ends, I don't dare to dance with anyone at the social because I'm nervous my level is not high enough. I feel like I should force myself, so I gravitate to the side of the dance floor, but only to watch other couples. I decide to leave, feeling sad that I can't bring myself to participate. As I walk toward the door, I hear one of my favorite salsa songs start playing—"Allegría" (Joy) by the Fania All Stars. The song is purely instrumental, led by the pretty melody of a classical guitar and raw percussion. Just before I reach the door, the song's piano solo—my favorite part—begins. My heart skips a beat, and I turn around to see an ocean of couples salsa dancing across the ballroom in smooth, suave spins.

THE SECOND DAY of the congress, before Griselle's class begins at noon, I have time to fit in two additional workshops. I choose "Secrets of Spinning" and "NYC Salsa," both of which leave me feeling dizzy. After, I peruse the stalls selling sparkling salsa shoes, clothes, and accessories at the congress and decide to buy a pair of Griselle's favorite GFranco shoes: black satin with a silver metal heel. When I arrive at the workshop, I see that a few of the other women have also arrived early, including a Chilean woman named Karen, with whom I practice my Spanish.

"Hello, divas!" Griselle greets us. She flashes her dazzling smile as she walks in, and her ponytail sways along with her hips. She really knows how to make a fabulous entrance.

We quickly go through all the steps and then begin to work on them as short sequences. Disoriented, I try to follow the woman in front of me and Karen, who's on my left, but I stumble around breathlessly. I can't even make the individual steps, let alone follow along. My brain just can't understand the steps and sequences—it's a disaster. *What the hell was I thinking?* I had no idea that the routine would be this advanced. I start to dread the idea of performing onstage tomorrow, and part of me wants to back out, but I'm not going to give up. I just need to practice more.

Karen tells me she'll help me and stays with me for three hours, helping me manage some of the trickiest parts. I've never before even heard of some of these dance styles, like boogaloo and pachanga, and thankfully she breaks them down for me. Boogaloo challenges me with coordinating the basic structure of cha-cha steps while stretching out my arms to the side and adding a funky head nod. I'm out of sync and convinced I look like I'm suffering from some kind of spasm. Pachanga adds a whole other level of complexity, requiring me to keep a bend in my knees and lean my chest slightly forward while stretching out each leg behind me in shifts that repeat continuously. My brain cannot make sense of the movements, but we repeat them again and again, until, suddenly, I can at least do them without seeming pained.

"*¿Ves? ¡Lo tienes, lo tienes!*" (See? You've got this!), exclaims Karen.

The sequences are finally starting to make sense, and I'm so grateful to her for helping me. As I move on to practice a part of the choreography that looks like a walk, one of the other women in the boot camp—a very young, moody woman with striking blue eyes and a strong Bronx accent— stops me.

"Try and walk more like this," she says, demonstrating a supple sideways gait. I give it a go, but she's clearly unimpressed with the outcome. She raises her eyebrows and tells me I look awkward, "Like a robot," she says harshly. "Just try and walk normally."

I fight the urge to quit and walk out. I can't tell if she's just mean, or trying to help, or both. I decide to give her the benefit of the doubt. While I'm hurt, I realize that if I want to learn how to dance, I'm going to need a thick skin. People are going to be a lot more blunt than she is. I continue to practice, and as a class we go through the routine a few more times, gradually speeding up our moves to match the quickening tempo of the music, which grows increasingly faster with the help of an iPhone app. I can't keep up. Despite the progress I make, I'm unable to meet the pace of the song, which feels like an unshakeable setback.

Eventually Griselle calls out "Ladies!" and the class comes together. "I'm going to ask you a question and I want you to answer honestly. Those of you who feel like you've got it, stand to the right. Those of you who aren't totally confident, step to the left."

Griselle could have picked out the best dancers herself, but instead she lets us decide how we categorize ourselves. Even with my terrible skills, I could dance in the front row if I wanted, but I'm grateful not to have to. The less confident group will perform but leave the stage before the most difficult part. This is exciting for me. I can accomplish my goal of performing onstage, but I don't have to worry about hindering the choreography. Griselle works out the dance to have an alternating formation, a design that means that those of us who aren't as good as others won't detract from the dance but add to it. I feel relieved.

As we practice the full routine with the alternating format, Griselle faces us and kneels attentively, one elbow resting on her knee and hand curled up under her chin as she looks at us pensively. She is very observant, checking everyone's movement. She guides us where we need help and corrects our position and timing so that the formations are perfect—something that she refers to as "cleaning." She tweaks our moves by pulling imaginary threads with her slender, manicured fingers.

At the end of the workshop, she calls us to gather at the front of the room for some final words of advice. She tells us how important it is to believe in ourselves and to be present onstage, and not to give up no matter what our dance level or background is. "You can do this whether you're a professional dancer or," she looks at me, "it's your first time onstage and you're doing this as a personal project."

As class wraps up, my new friends Teodora, Lisa, and Nic squeeze my arm, cheer, and give me high fives, and the whole room claps. I have tears in my eyes and am overwhelmed by the kindness and encouragement of others who spent time to help me even though I was a total beginner (and in my opinion a total waste of their time). I think of how far I've come. My feet are covered in blisters, my neck is sore, my whole body hurts, and my routine isn't perfect, but I think I've got about 80 percent of the choreography down. I almost feel worthy of going onstage, and now the performance is about to start.

Backstage is another world altogether—one of excitement, adrenaline, and sparkling costumes, where sequences are practiced and last-minute adjustments are made. When people begin to shout for the next performance to start, it feels like time slows down, even stops. For a moment, all I hear is the sound of my own breath and my heart pounding. And then: "Ladies and gentlemen, put your hands together and give it up for the Griselle Ponce Diva Challenge!"

It's showtime. The crowd cheers as I walk up the steps to the stage. I'm apprehensive, but I set my nerves aside to enjoy the moment. I've never seen such a huge audience in my life. I'm more accustomed to presenting PowerPoint slides than a cha-cha and boogaloo dance routine. I'm positioned in the second row, just behind Teodora, which reassures me because if I get lost I can always follow her.

The music starts and my mind goes blank, but instead of freezing, I go into a strange sort of autopilot. I give the dance everything I have, and I can tell that the other women do too. The feeling of collective effort is powerful. I'm still not comfortable enough with the choreography to be able to smile and add my own style to the moves, but I manage to get through the whole routine with just two tiny mistakes (for which I decide to forgive myself).

After, Nic finds me and taps me affectionately. "You did it!" Her words mean the world to me. We regroup backstage with the other performers, hug one another, and take a photo with Griselle before she goes to get changed for her solo performance. I can't believe this has really happened. I've just performed in the same show as one of the world's best salsa stars in New York—and to an audience of around a thousand people!

I change out of my costume and walk my raw, blistered feet to an area in front of the stage where I sit with Nic and her boyfriend to watch the next act. At the table next to us, Carlos Beltran, the Mambo Legend, is conversing with the trombonist Jimmy Bosch.

A Pitbull-esque MC with a shaved head and an earring announces the band up next, a group of young musicians. In typical Nuyorican fashion, they address the audience in a mixture of English and Spanish. "*¡Mi gente!* (My people!) The way we relate to dance is here," says the singer as he places his hand on his heart. The audience applauds. We feel the same.

"Ladies and gentlemen, tonight joining us we have the one and only Señor Bongo, Roberto Roena!" announces the singer.

The crowd roars with excitement. Although I'm ignorant of many people in the dance world, Roberto Roena is one name that is very familiar, and my heart flutters as he takes the stage. Roena was the percussionist of the Fania All Stars. In preparation for my bailando journey, I had listened to the Fania All Stars almost every night, and by now I know many of their songs. There's something about listening to salsa music that, whatever your mood, makes you instantly happier. Fania's songs make me happier.

Roena wears a shiny black suit and eyeglasses. He seems almost shy—or at least modest, despite having been part of a group who shaped salsa history and whose songs people still dance to religiously. Onstage, he joins the band and sits on a small stool placed in front of two bongos and smiles. He gently lifts one palm and slams the bongo. The room fills with an explosion of sound—a whirlwind of percussion and piano, trombones and trumpets.

When the song finishes, a couple of male dancers who are dancing onstage invite Roena to join them in some basic salsa steps. An older gentleman in the VIP section, who appears to be in his eighties and sports a neat mustache and a smart suit, also approaches the stage. He struggles to climb up and I'm relieved when one of the men helps him. But once onstage, he erupts into rhythmic and cheerful salsa footwork.

"He's another mambo legend," Nic whispers in my ear. "His name is Carlos Arroyo, but he's known as Mr. Cha-Cha Taps." I couldn't think of a more appropriate nickname for this man. Just looking at his infectious smile and tapping feet makes me happy.

After a few more dances, Roena returns to his bongos and the band launches into one of Fania's most famous songs. The crowd goes wild— cheering, shouting, and declaring their love. I see a woman throw her arms up toward the stage, reaching out as if to touch him.

As the song comes to an end and Roena uses a clave—the key to salsa's rhythm—to tap his final beats of percussion, he turns to face me, looks me straight in the eye, and mouths, "pa, pa, pa—pa pa!"

I WAKE UP feeling like I'm recovering from a battle, and the soon-to-be scars on my feet are my evidence. I danced for twenty-one hours in just three days, and mostly while wearing my new salsa shoes instead of a worn-in pair. It was a clear rookie mistake, as my feet are now bloodied and covered in blisters.

With the congress over, I start planning the rest of my time in New York. I want to make the most of it and decide to take a few more classes with the incredible artists who teach here. I also want to dig deeper into the city's salsa history, but I'm finding it harder than I'd expected to find my way into their world. After several attempts to contact the organizers of a history-of-salsa tour, I'm met with a brash rejection that feels stereotyp-ically New York and quickly shooed off the phone. I try the number for a salsa museum next, but the line is disconnected. Some dance instructors or schools don't even reply to my emails. I don't understand why. I know that traces remain of salsa's past; I see posters of Héctor Lavoe in subway record stores, and I hear his soulful voice trailing in the distance when I walk down the streets. New York has a rich salsa history, so why is it so difficult to get information about it? Or rather, why doesn't anybody want to share it?

I consider ending this frustrating treasure hunt, but there's one line left to call. The number connects me to a record shop in Spanish Harlem that my teacher Luiz in Bangkok told me about. It's amazing that it still exists. Luiz said he thought the store owners knew all the members of Fania and even suggested they might be able to help me get in touch with them.

I dial, and a man with a thick New York accent picks up. I ask him if I can ask about the store, but he barks, "I don't give interviews!" His voice softens, however, after I explain that I'm not a journalist but on a personal journey to learn Latin dances and their history.

"Everything has changed here!" he says. "Even in the last ten years it's different. I don't know what you expect to find here. It's not the Spanish Harlem of the 1970s anymore. Everyone moved away from El Barrio."

IF YOU MENTION New York salsa to almost anyone in the dance world, there's one name that is always mentioned: Eddie Torres. Legend holds that it was Torres who brought the street into the studio, imbuing the salsa that flooded barrios and clubs in New York with a new sophistication. The classic salsa step usually breaks on the first beat, but Torres's variation of it—known as "On 2" or "mambo"—breaks on the second, with the follower stepping forward on the second beat instead of the first. The variation made the New York salsa world-famous, celebrated for its complexity and suave expression.

Though Torres never claimed to have invented "On 2," he is credited with having popularized it, as his students spun out classes and studios of their own throughout the city and used it in them. He came to be considered the "Mambo King" and is certainly uniquely qualified to comment on salsa dancing's evolution in New York. I once read an article in the *New York Times* where he was quoted as saying, "It's gotten so sophisticated. Before, we'd give the girls a little turn here, a little turn there. Now we start her off with fourteen spins in the first bar."[12] This is someone I could learn so much from.

I locate Torres's email online and optimistically, albeit naively, email him to ask if he might give me a private class or be interested in helping me with my project, to which he replies that he only offers group classes. I look up the class schedule and find that he gives intermediate classes, but his wife, Maria, a salsa queen in her own right, gives beginner classes and I decide to give it a go.

Maria is an excellent teacher and an entertaining one. She greets everyone who shows up late or whose attention dwindles with a bright "Good morning!" even though it's evening. She gives high fives when someone gets something right, and jokes in her thick Bronx accent. I like her style of teaching. Under her guidance I let my guard down and loosen up enough to really enjoy the learning process.

"Gentlemen!" she cries, "give me more oomph! Ladies, move your arms like *mantequilla*, like butter!"

My dance partner compliments me with a "Good spin!" and I finally feel like I'm getting something right. I'm able to grasp what Maria is teaching much faster than some of the dances in the more advanced workshops I've taken at the congress. We continue to switch partners as we dance through a basic sequence interrupted only by Maria's hilarious one-liners. Occasionally I look over and see her dancing too. I notice that her curls bounce freely on her shoulders as she moves.

At the end of the class, I ask Maria for a photo of us together. She seems a little hesitant but ends up putting on a classic dancer's pose. We hug and she invites me to watch Eddie's class with her (the level would be too high for me to participate), but it's getting late and is time for me to go back to Brooklyn. As I begin to leave, I see a man in a hat sitting cross-legged in an armchair, surrounded by a few admiring students. He gets up suddenly, stands in line with the students, and starts to demonstrate some of his shines. I hover in the doorway in awe of his movement. *This must be Eddie Torres*, I think to myself. I want to introduce myself—there's so much I'd like to ask him—but I hesitate. I'm presented with an opportunity, but fear overtakes me and I keep to myself. Instead I quietly watch him as he spins alongside his students and then breaks into elaborate footwork. *Today isn't the day I'll meet Eddie Torres*, I tell myself, *but maybe one day I will.*

I'D WANTED TO deepen my knowledge of "On 2" by going back to the basics and had asked Griselle during the workshop whom she would recommend as a teacher. She'd had no hesitation in her response, and told me Ismael Otero, also known as the Million Moves Man. Today I have a one-hour private class with him.

I'd heard from some of the women in the workshop that Otero has a unique approach to teaching and is especially good at working with beginners, breaking down the steps and helping them find the rhythm. I'd also heard that he puts a lot of emphasis on *feeling* dance as opposed to just memorizing the steps and believes that every dancer should bring his or her own personality to the dance. This makes sense, given that he's said to be the secret force behind a large number of talents, though you can't tell he trained them because they each dance differently. His approach really appeals to me, and when he replied to my email and accepted being part of my journey, I couldn't believe my luck.

When I arrive at his studio in New Jersey, the percussion instruments in the window tell me I'm in the right place. The door is ajar, propped open by a metal rod, which I immediately trip over. Then I wait around awkwardly until Ismael emerges from the back of the studio.

After a hasty introduction he lets me know that there isn't much we can cover in an hour and we should get right to it. He takes me to the front of the studio, invites me to take a seat, and then sits behind a bongo where he starts to tap out a rhythm with his palms.

"Let's see if you get the rhythm," he says, looking at me with great concentration. "What are you doing?"

"What do you mean what am I doing?" I ask, confused.

"I mean, what are you doing in your head. Are you counting or are you feeling?"

"I think I'm counting," I reply hesitantly. "Well, first I was feeling the pattern of the rhythm, but then I thought maybe I should count, so I started counting."

"You see," he says, "some people are 'left-brained,' meaning the left side of their brain is dominant. They count because they need logic and technique. 'Right-brained' people are creative and need to visualize things in order to feel the rhythm."

It's weird because I had tried to do both—feel the rhythm but also count. *Is there such a thing as "both-brained"?* I wonder. Or had I simply tried to crush my naturally creative side with the logical side that has dominated most of my adult life? I wonder if I'm killing my creativity out of fear. The truth is that I started counting because I assumed the way I was feeling the pattern was going to be wrong.

"Okay, now I want you to stand up and just dance however you want," he says as he continues to tap away on the bongo.

There is nothing more terrifying to a beginner than improvisation. No instructor to guide you, no steps to follow or sequence to hide behind. The sad part—and I've seen it in myself and in others—is that maybe we wouldn't look that stupid if we let ourselves improvise wildly, disregarding technique and instead letting the *feeling* of dance lead us. But our lack of confidence and experience in dance leads us to assume that everything we do is wrong, so we instead end up painfully dancing like we are in a small box, tensing up our shoulders and making ourselves as small as possible, which ends up looking worse. As Ismael watches, I dance just the basic step and do a couple of turns to stay safe. I can't help but feel stupid just standing up and dancing like that.

After a while Ismael stops tapping on his bongos and sighs. "Okay, that's terrible," he cackles, barely holding back a laugh.

My face drops. I'm disappointed with myself—crushed, actually. After dancing a total of twenty-one hours during the salsa congress, and all the beginner classes in Bangkok, do I really dance a basic step terribly? My cheeks flush and I feel a sharp pain in the pit of my stomach.

"It's okay!" says Ismael, chuckling at the mortification my expression gives away. "It happens to everyone. People go straight into learning choreographies rather than learning to understand rhythm. This is why some students say that I'm some sort of wizard. But actually, it is all about learning the rhythm first. Figuring out what dance makes you feel."

I begin to understand his approach. It's definitely not an easy way to learn, at least not in the short run, but in the long run I would rather be able to feel what I'm dancing than just follow along. According to Ismael, understanding the rhythm is the solid basis required for all dances, not just salsa.

He stands next to me in front of the mirror. "Just walk," he says. In salsa, you're supposed to let your shoulders, arms, everything, be loose. "Now look at your arms." I look in the mirror and notice that my arms are swaying from side to side without my intentionally moving them.

"You see the direction your arms move as the opposite leg steps forward? That's how your arm movement should be—they naturally sway as you walk." I had always struggled with the arm position while dancing salsa and never quite knew what to do with them. He picks up the metal rod that I tripped over on my way into the studio. "Here, hold this."

I hold the metal rod horizontally in front of my chest, bending my elbows to make sure each hand is placed to each side of my chest. As I start my basic step, my posture starts to straighten. My torso shifts, I engage my shoulders, and I can better see the coordination between my upper and lower body. We do this for the rest of the class, and then he invites me into his office to show me some of the music he's been working on.

"You might be interested in this," he says and hands me a printout of a couple of interviews he has given.

I skim through the papers and read out one of his answers: "If you understand what you are doing, then you are more confident, and confidence is a big part of learning and dancing."

"It's true!"

I tell him that I can relate, and I think back to the horror of having to freestyle. If I understood the rhythm better, I would be much less hesitant. I ask Ismael how he got into salsa.

"When I was young I thought salsa was for old people," he says, laughing. "I was more into hip-hop and break dancing, but then I went out to clubs and saw that all the guys who danced salsa got to dance with girls, so I decided to learn. I also secretly loved the music."

Ismael added his own spin. "Everyone was dancing Eddie Torres style, but I added hip-hop to salsa. I was just some guy from the streets, but I guess people saw something original in that."

He goes on to confirm for me what the women in my class had said, that he likes to help his dancers channel their personalities as they dance.

"I ask people what dancing makes them feel. Dancing has to bring out the best in you and your potential. Many *salseros* [salsa dancers] dance to any song today, even if they don't like it, because they don't feel the music. It's like it's become a social network that I can't connect with anymore. Most people's routines look exactly the same. People are scared of being original, scared of criticism and what other people might think."

I take in all of these thoughts, impressed by his commitment to authenticity.

"I'll give you an example," he says. "I was once dancing with a woman who did everything technically wrong. But she had the biggest smile on her face and was really enjoying herself, so I just followed her rhythm and had a great time."

We continue talking about New York as the birthplace of salsa, and I ask him about its origins, which seem to be highly contested.

Ismael tells me that Cubans get credit for salsa, but it was the

Latino—and mostly Puerto Rican—community in New York who brought salsa to the world stage. He begins to list various salsa artists and asks me if I've ever heard of them.

"The names sound familiar," I reply, almost apologetically.

I have my work cut out for me, he tells me. There is so much I need to learn about salsa history. In New York, there's a huge range of salsa styles danced, from Dominican uptown to midtown Eddie Torres style to the style of the ABAKUÁ Afro-Latin Dance Company with Frankie Martinez.

Ismael agrees to allow me to film a video of us dancing some basics of New York–style salsa together—the first in the series of videos that will record each style I learn along my journey. We find a spot at the edge of the Hudson River in Hoboken, with Manhattan's towering skyscrapers as our backdrop. After I set up my camera and tripod, he puts on a flashy smile and we dance. Surprisingly, I don't feel that tense. I love dancing in a public place with people walking past us, stopping to look. At one point a kid on the boardwalk stops and joins in to dance himself, freestyling in the background of our video. I now have a video of myself at the Diva Challenge and a video with a partner.

"That wasn't so bad," Ismael tells me after we finish filming.

I'm relieved, filled with a renewed hope that maybe I'm not an absolute disaster.

GRISELLE HAS AGREED to give me an exclusive interview, and we arrange to meet just before her "Mambo Diva Tuesdays" class at a studio just a few steps away from the Empire State Building. She invites me into the studio and we sit on the bench, accompanied by her mother. As the daughter of a single mother, I identify with their closeness and admire that her mother is so present in her passion, joining some of Griselle's dance classes and other activities.

Griselle tells me how she grew up with dance in Puerto Rico; she would see her mom dancing in the kitchen and would join the dancing at family parties. When she moved to New York at just sixteen years old, she started taking classes to learn in a more structured way. One day, the sight of a man doing spins piqued her curiosity. He was Ismael Otero, and he would become her teacher.

I tell Griselle about my class with Ismael the day before, and we each share our experience of learning his unique approach to dance.

"The way I learned with Ismael was very hard—it wasn't the easy way," she tells me. "It's the way that he teaches. For example, I would ask him, 'So how am I doing?' and he would say, 'How does it feel?' I thank him for that type of training because he made me look inward, to start working on myself, not just follow someone else."

Griselle's personality undoubtedly shines when she dances. She has her own style, and I can see how her training with Ismael encouraged that.

"What do you feel when you dance?" I ask.

"Freedom. Freedom is the best word I can use to describe what I feel. When I dance I'm free—no worries, no aches. Nothing goes to my mind other than feeling free. This is also why I dance very freely. I don't stick to being technical and 'It has to be this way,' because that limits me from doing what I'm feeling."

It's true that she evokes freedom when she dances: she stretches her arms wide and open, like a bird, or perhaps a Kinnaree, taking flight.

I tell Griselle about the next countries on my journey and ask if what I've learned here in New York will relate to the other dances that I'll be learning on the way. After all, the dance styles I've chosen are all so different. She assures me that when dancers learn to move from feeling, the fundamentals of expression translate into myriad forms and styles. If all movement emerges from feeling, all movement is connected, personal, and possible.

We talk for twenty minutes, and then it's time for Griselle to start her class. It's pretty advanced, but I join anyway. This is one of my last nights in New York, and I need to soak in what I can. As I predicted, I'm not able to follow much and stumble my way through while admiring the dazzling moves of the other women: whipping their hair, shimmying their shoulders, rolling their hips.

"Ladies, if you don't smile, you stop breathing. If you stop breathing, it stiffens your neck and then you look like *this*." Griselle points to her neck while making the face of someone who's either terrified or has overdone Botox.

"Ladies, I feel like you're holding something back. You've got to focus on what the music makes you feel!" She stops the music. "What are you feeling—good or bad? Tell me!"

I don't dare speak up. The truth is that I'm feeling stressed, and when I can't grasp the footwork, I feel blocked. It's as if all I can I focus on is standing up and basically staying alive. I wish I could reach that feeling of total freedom and happiness when I dance. But I'm more used to feeling it in a club after a tequila shot. That's when my muscles relax and I can finally let go—but it's no longer the way that I want to achieve that feeling. I want an intrinsic freedom, one that comes from within.

"Unfortunately, we all have moments where we think, 'Oh, no! The other girls are so much better than me.' Don't think about that!"

"At exactly what angle should I tilt my head?" asks one of the students. Her question reminds me of my conversation with Ismael.

"Don't worry about the technique. Do what feels natural and comfortable. I only do movements that are comfortable."

When the class ends, I thank Griselle and say goodbye. I'm touched by her kindness and the time she spent with me. She's so humble and hardworking. On my way back to Brooklyn, I think about her call to do only what feels nature and comfortable. *Who cares if I'm doing it all wrong and I look stupid? If I want to dance well, I'll just have to go through doing it wrong until, one day, I start doing it right.* I tell myself that as I continue my journey, I should carry Griselle's words of encouragement, and my inner diva, with me.

4

———

MEXICO

Jarabe Tapatío, Regional Folklore, and a Guelaguetza

In the early hours of September 16, 1810, Miguel Hidalgo y Costilla, a Catholic priest turned revolutionary leader, rang the bell of his church in the small town of Dolores in the state of Guanajuato, giving the call to arms that led to Mexico's independence.[13] Ever since then, the sitting Mexican president reenacts *El Grito*, or the Cry of Dolores, by ringing Hidalgo's bell from the balcony of the National Palace in the Zócalo, the main square in Mexico City, at eleven o'clock at night every September 15—the eve of Independence Day.

I will arrive in Mexico, the land of mezcal and mariachis, on September 15, 2016. I'll get there just in time to celebrate the country's independence, and perhaps also my own.

This is my first trip to Mexico, and as I take in a bird's-eye view of the land from the airplane window, I spot the Sierra Madre's grassy mountain range, the snow-capped volcanoes surrounding Mexico City, and countless square, rainbow-colored houses. On our descent into Benito

Juárez International Airport, I also see what from above looks like a blue training ground with six white spots twirling on it like spinning tops. As we get closer, the white spots become larger and twirl faster. It dawns on me that they are Mexican folklore dancers. Viewed from above, their wide skirts appear to open like flowers as they swirl in perfect synchronization. Usually I would immediately pull out my phone to snap a photo for social media, but it's the last thing on my mind. I want to witness this beauty with my own eyes. It strikes me that this must be a sign, welcoming me to the chapter of my journey in which I'll learn *folkórico Mexicano* (Mexican folklore dance).

I will be staying in Roma Norte with my friend Farah, a Scottish American, and Twiggie, her recently adopted dog. Farah and I have known each other since university, where we both dreamed of living abroad with careers that would allow us to help others. Now, almost ten years later, it seems that we've both accomplished this. Farah is like an Amazonian woman, strong and striking, with piercing blue eyes and choppy blond hair. She is the youngest and only female regional director in her company, a woman leader in a continent ruled by machismo. I plan to stay with her for two months and dog-sit Twiggie when she travels for work, as she does frequently.

My taxi pulls up in front of a gray and red building, and a large man opens the door. It's Enrique the *portero* (doorman). "You must be Farah's friend. She left the keys for you," he says, smiling. To my surprise he immediately carries my suitcase up the stairs.

"*Gra-c-ias,*" I say with a Spanish lisp on the word's *c*, wondering if I should change my accent now that I'm in Latin America.

I step inside and find Twiggie, who eagerly joins me in a nap on the sofa. I have just a few hours to rest before meeting up with Arianna's family to celebrate Independence Day.

Later there's a knock at the door, and through the peephole I see a guy in his mid-twenties shifting his feet awkwardly. He sways a bit when I open the door.

"*Hola*. I'm Daniel, Arianna's brother," he says and greets me shyly with one kiss on the cheek—different from the two that we give in France.

Daniel suggests that we walk across the city to the affluent neighborhood of Polanco so that we can take in some sights on the way. From the Paseo de la Reforma, one of the largest and most important avenues in Latin America, we spot the Torre Latinoamericana (Latin-American Tower), a skyscraper completed in 1956 that resembles the Empire State Building.

"And this is the Angel of Independence," says Daniel, pointing to a neoclassical stone column of simple grandeur. It stands in the middle of Paseo de la Reforma and is topped with a majestic bronze angel covered in twenty-four-karat gold that holds a broken chain in one hand and a crown of laurel in the other, a representation of freedom and victory. It was inaugurated in 1910 to celebrate the centenary of the Mexican independence and is one of the most emblematic monuments of Mexico City.

At a crossroad on the posh Avenida Presidente Masaryk in Polanco, we meet Arianna's mother, Susy. It is comforting to be with relatives of a close friend from Bangkok, and I am struck by how much Susy looks and speaks like Arianna.

At a traditional Mexican restaurant, they encourage me to order a *chelada*—beer with squeezed limes in a salt-rimmed glass—along with guacamole, beans, and other traditional foods. A group of mariachis arrive at our table and start playing traditional songs. They wear embroidered black velvet hats, jackets, and trousers studded with shiny brass buttons. They play their instruments, including a violin, trumpet, and three types of guitars, while singing. To me their words pour out *desde el corazón* (from the heart). I wish I could sing along too, but I don't know any Mexican songs yet.

After a second round of cheladas it's almost time for El Grito. A waiter switches on a big TV, and we see a crowd of people standing in the Zócalo. The camera then zooms to the balcony of the National Palace, and President Enrique Peña Nieto and his wife emerge.

"You know this president isn't loved at all," says Daniel. "He accepted a meeting with Trump even though Trump wants to build a wall."

"They say that he had his first wife killed so he could be with the second one," adds Susy, her smile fading.

The president rings the bell. "*¡Viva México!*" (Long live Mexico!)

"*¡Viva!*" everyone in the restaurant shouts.

"*¡Viva la patria!*" (Long live the motherland!)

"*¡Viva!*" we shout, raising our glasses.

Despite the politics and rumors, the pride and patriotism run high. People in the restaurant cheer, blow party horns, and throw confetti the colors of Mexico's flag: green, white, and red. The mariachis break into song, and I can faintly hear the sound of glass breaking in the back of the restaurant.

I have a sense that I'm going to fit in well in Mexico.

AFTER I WAKE up from a comatose-like sleep, Farah, who is back in town for a few days, takes me on a tour of her favorite places in Roma Norte. I'm not sure what I had in mind when it comes to Mexico City, but instead of knife-wielding criminals and narcos, I find beard-bearing hipsters and stylish women walking their designer dogs. I'm surprised by this leafy neighborhood, with its vibrant Art Deco houses, terraces, and cafés. It's so cosmopolitan! Why does Western media make Mexico City sound like a death trap?

Farah leads me into what appears to be a trendy town house with an oak staircase and plush velvet chairs, and we enjoy a fine Mexican twist on eggs Benedict.

I ask Farah for advice as a newcomer and if there is anything I should watch out for.

She gently dabs her mouth with her napkin and then says: "One thing you absolutely need to know is that people are always late and sometimes cancel at the last minute. They come up with excuses that usually begin with '*Es que . . .*' or 'Well, it's just that . . .'. The sick mother is a classic, but they can get pretty creative with their '*Es que*' excuses. It's not out of any bad intention; they just don't want to hurt your feelings." She takes a bite of her eggs. "The other thing is that some guys can be a little creepy and possessive, and quite *machista*." Her word refers to a machismo, often chauvinist attitude. "Watch out for those."

After brunch we stop by Mercado Medellín, a local market, to buy fresh fruit and flowers for the house. I end up selecting different pastel shades of roses to make a soft-colored bouquet.

"*Aquí tienes, mi reina*," says the flower man as he hands me the bouquet. "Here you are, my queen." His eyes crinkle kindly.

We pick up a freshly squeezed juice of tropical fruits, which are common and shockingly affordable in these small markets, and stop at an organic farmers market on the way home. *I could really live here*, I think to myself.

THAT AFTERNOON I meet Daniel outside Chapultepec Forest. It is home to some of the city's most important museums and sites and is one of the largest city parks in Latin America. I stop by a food stall to get something to eat and settle on a quesadilla with nopal, a type of cactus with flat, oval-shaped pads. It's one of Arianna's favorite Mexican delicacies.

After lunch, we stop to admire a sculpture of the symbols from the Mexican flag in the distance: an eagle with a snake in its mouth, and the nopal cactus. We then continue on, passing archaeological sites, including tombs, altars, and water structures. Some of them date back to pre-Columbian times or were built by the Aztecs or the civilizations that preceded them. After a stop in the baths of Moctezuma, a sacred retreat for Aztec rulers, conquistadors, and royalty alike, we head up to Chapultepec Castle, perched on top of a hill in the forest.

"This was the residence of the monarchy, when we had one."

"Mexico had a monarchy?" I ask, surprised.

Daniel tells me that Mexico was an empire twice, although the second time lasted only from 1864 to 1867, when the country was ruled by Emperor Maximilian I, or Maximiliano, an Austrian archduke, and Empress Charlotte, or Carlota, daughter of Belgium's King Leopold I. France's Napoleon III helped coronate them following the second French intervention.

"The French had already intervened before," Daniel continues, referring to La Guerra de Los Pasteles, which literally translates into English as "The War of the Cakes."

My knowledge of Latin American history is lacking. And despite being French, I have never heard of this French empire by proxy. It has always bothered me that history textbooks at school were so narrowly focused on selective national events rather than providing a broader view of the world. Now I am learning events from my country's history while I'm on the other side of the world.

"The empire ended with the execution of Maximiliano. Carlota became known as *Carlota la loca* (Carlota the crazy). She was already mad but went even madder after losing her husband. She was so in love with him that she kept all his belongings until she died," explains Daniel. "We named our dog Carlota after her because she's crazy and hides in the closet all the time."

What a story, I think to myself as we stroll through the castle grounds, admiring its architecture, gardens, and sculptures. The castle is similar to those in Europe, but its gardens have more cactuses than flowers.

Daniel points to a plant that is shaped like the top of a pineapple and has wide, prickly leaves. He tells me it's blue agave, the plant that tequila and mezcal are made from.

Inside the castle, we watch an exhibition on the Mexican Revolution, and after we walk out of the park through a winding path and come across two folklore dancers. The man is dressed in white pants and a white shirt, and the woman wears a white top and a large white lace skirt. She has a red sash around her waist and flowers in her hair. As their song plays, they each step on a long red sash, known as a *listón*.

The song sounds familiar, and Daniel tells me it's "La Bamba," an international hit based on a traditional folk song from the State of Veracruz on the Mexican Gulf. In the accompanying dance, which is popular at weddings, the couple uses detailed footwork to create a bow out of the listón. In this part of the world, people dance in the street, in parks, and in squares for pleasure, nothing else.

I HAD WRITTEN to a number of dance schools, with no knowledge or reference to help me determine which one was best, but I have a positive feeling about where I've landed—Instituto de Danza Mizoc—a dance school on Calle Héroes (a street named after the boy heroes who defended Chapultepec Castle from American invaders during the Mexican-American War) in the Guerrero neighborhood. They told me that they have an adult beginner class on Monday and Wednesday evenings and suggested I try one class to see how I like it. After signing up, I found out that Guerrero, just northwest of the historical center, is one of the most dangerous parts of town, but luckily with affordable car service, I can get there safely.

When I arrive I spot a building with large, colorful posters showing the dances of Mexico. The school's slogan reads, "El Sitio del Folklor Mexicano" (The Home of Mexican Folklore).

I walk inside and a cheerful secretary, Brenda, greets me. She tells me that they have a skirt that I can borrow for today and leads me to a back room.

I had no idea what I was supposed to wear. Clueless, I had brought my salsa shoes just in case. The other women are all wearing long-sleeved black tops and, fortunately, I'm wearing the same type of top, but I only wore it to keep me warm on the way here, not to dance in. When I ask if I can dance in my strappy pink sports top, Brenda gently shakes her head no.

"It's better that you wear sleeves," she says as she helps me into a huge, bright orange skirt, tying bows at the sides of my waist. "The shoes are okay for today, but you will need real folklore shoes." Brenda measures my feet. "We have a local lady here who makes the shoes by hand, so they would take about a week. Is that okay?"

More than okay. I'm thrilled at the opportunity to wear handmade shoes. I walk up to the classroom on the third floor and find that I am the youngest person here—the other students appear to all be over sixty. Knowing I'll be dancing with them brings back memories of learning to dance with my grandparents and their friends in France.

A woman who looks to be in her seventies and is wearing a line of dark blue eyeliner and an interesting double-fringe back comb combination approaches me. She introduces herself as Bety.

"*¡Mucho gusto!* I'm Eleonor," I reply, telling her it's a pleasure to meet her and introducing myself with my Spanish name to make things easier. We start chatting but are quickly told that class is beginning. Bety puts her hand on my shoulder and guides me inside the classroom, in a way that I find so welcoming and reassuring for a young gringa about to take her first folkloric dance class.

Bety leads me to the teacher of the class and introduces him as "our maestro." The teacher is the son of the school's founders and named Zadoc, but we are to call him "*maestro*," teacher, not by his first name. He's very friendly and professional, speaking clearly and smoothly, and making sure that I get the steps. I throw myself into the practice and attempt to follow choreography to a song called "sones de Betaza." "Son" or "sones" refer to various traditional styles of songs and accompanying dances from different places around the country. "Sones de Betaza" is from San Melchor de Betaza, a small town in the state of Oaxaca in southwestern Mexico. Some of the steps involve a natural walk, while others involve rhythmic skips and hops.

I am also introduced to the *zapateo*—percussive footwork reminiscent of flamenco that creates a complex, patterned sound. We form a line, with the women facing the men, and dance in small zigzags before shimmying toward our male partners while holding our skirts at our hips. When we approach the men, we let go of our skirts to take their hands into ours for a few romantic skips, before letting go to twirl back to our line. Our skirts swirl just like those I saw from the airplane window.

Bety seems to be the most playful one in class, always joking around, but she's also the best student. You can see from her impeccable posture, with shoulder blades perfectly aligned, that her body moves like a dancer's.

"Maestro! Am I a girl or a boy today?" she asks.

I laugh, but it turns out that by "girl" and "boy" Bety means follower and leader. Her ability to dance in both roles clearly shows that she's advanced.

Maestro Zadoc asks us to do a basic skip diagonally across the studio, each of us going one at a time. I hear a loud thud in each of the steps as everyone dances, which I find strangely satisfying—it adds emphasis to the energy in their steps. But when my turn comes, my steps are silent. I don't have the right shoes. Folklore shoes have metal studs hammered into the heels and toes, almost like tap shoes, that create a metallic stomping sound.

"¡Derechita!" says Maestro Zadoc, telling me to hold myself straighter. He motions for me to lift my chin and flashes an encouraging smile. My posture really needs to improve. I tend to hunch over and look at the floor. It might have something to do with shame or the years I spent glued to an office chair. I hope that I will overcome this when I become more confident dancing in front of others.

To my surprise, I can follow the basic steps. They remind me of the folklore dances of my native Brittany in northwestern France. The smiles and cheerfulness that fill the room spark a burst of energy that makes me forget the significant age difference between the other students and me. As I've learned, age really doesn't matter in dancing—dancing is ageless.

THOUGH I LOOK forward to learning many different dances from Mexico's regions of Oaxaca in the south and Jalisco in the west, I have one paramount goal—to learn the national dance of Mexico: the *jarabe tapatío*, also known as the Mexican hat dance. Developed in colonial times from the interplay of popular Spanish music and indigenous dances, the jarabe tapatío is a partner dance that mimics the courtship of doves.[14] In some versions, the man, in hot pursuit of his mate, throws his sombrero on the ground as if tossing down a gauntlet. His partner, teetering on the delicate balance of coy and suggestive, hops, slides, and kicks around the brim of the hat—her footwork showing her deliberating the merit and allure of his advance and the tenor of her own desire. As she bends to retrieve his hat from the floor, he kicks his leg over her head. Warmed, finally, to his giddy advances, she shields their faces with the hat. The audience is left to imagine what the couple is doing that is hidden from their view.

To truly learn this intricate dance, I need to have private classes. I had contacted several dance schools, including the most prestigious one in the country: the Ballet Folklórico de México de Amalia Hernández, whose dance troupes perform not only in Mexico City's Palacio de Bellas Artes (Palace of Fine Arts), its cultural center, but all over the world. Their prestige didn't warrant any kind of response, but I wanted to try them anyway, counting on luck more than anything else. If you never try, you'll never know.

When I call, Renato Levi García Moreno, the school's director, answers the phone. He says he can arrange for me to learn the jarabe tapatío. My first class will be with La Maestra Gabriela tomorrow at five thirty in the evening. Renato even offers to provide me with the traditional costume and a dance partner for the final class so that I can have the full experience. As he notes the tone of surprise—and delight—in my voice, he says, "We want to help you achieve your dream, to get to know Mexico and our traditions!"

When I arrive at the school the next evening, Renato welcomes me and leads me to the classroom where the class will take place. It is a group class, not a private class, as I'd expected, but they are covering the jarabe tapatío in the second half. The first half is some sort of tribal dance, the origin of which I can't pinpoint. He invites me to take a seat in the corner until they finish rehearsing.

When the students take a break, a stunning, magnetic, Mexican version of Rihanna who had been dancing at the front approaches me. She introduces herself as "Gabi, La Maestra." I had envisioned La Maestra Gabriela as a woman in her late forties, thin, with gray hair in a bun, and strict. I can't believe how wrong I was. She's probably younger than I am and sports a black knitted bodysuit over lace tights, deep black lipstick, and a septum nose ring. She breaks every stereotype of a maestra and contradicts the idea that all teachers at the National Ballet are strict and austere. Gabi invites me to join in with the others for the second half of the class, even though I don't have a skirt or proper shoes to practice in.

As the jarabe tapatío music plays, my new classmates launch into a series of intricate footwork and sweeping arm movements that are simply incomprehensible to my brain. I stumble from one foot to the other, turning moments after the others and probably the wrong way. By the time I've processed the first three steps, they're already twenty steps ahead. I survive another two songs and then return to my chair in the back of the room, defeated and distressed.

At the end of the class Gabi comes over to check on me.

I apologize for stopping early and tell her that I couldn't even follow. "I need to be taught in baby steps. This is just way over my head."

"I understand," she replies calmly. "Let's go and talk to the director."

We head into Renato's office and he seems equally understanding. He offers for Gabi to give me private ninety-minute classes. All the rooms are occupied at this time, but he says we can book them for earlier in the evening, just before the group class, which will allow me to avoid going home when it's dark out. At this early evening hour, it's already pitch-black outside, and the neighborhood is a little concerning. There is a heavily armed police presence and nearby lookout tower. My driver had clearly been a bit uncomfortable and even insisted on walking me to the door when I arrived.

Now as I wait for a car to pick me up, I hang around nervously behind the metal bars of the school's front door. New surroundings, like new dances, can feel terrifying. But as quickly as night falls, they can begin to feel familiar and routine.

TO MAKE UP for missing Wednesday's class at Mizoc, the school where I'm studying Mexican folklore, because of a huge storm (and a hangover), I join its longer Saturday morning class. The altitude still has me easily out of breath, but I'm finally reaching that amazing feeling of pure happiness when I dance, expressing my joy and pushing my emotions into the steps. The older students from the weekday classes all recognize me now. At one point, when I get the moves right, I even get a wink from Gonzalo, one of my favorites, who has become an *abuelo* (grandfather) figure for me. With his curly white hair and kind face, he reminds me of my own grandfather.

I thought I would be getting my new shoes today, so I have come in the hiking shoes I've been wearing since I walked Twiggie earlier, but the shoes haven't arrived yet, and I once again feel ridiculous dancing with a wardrobe malfunction. This time I'm wearing hiking shoes with my big orange skirt.

We learn a new dance from the state of Jalisco, the home state of the jarabe tapatío, and then practice the same dance as last time, sones de Betaza. It fascinates me how even when you "get it," you can still get the moves wrong after having completed the entire routine perfectly four or five times in a row. The patterns of the footwork are like mathematics. It hurts my brain to see them all together at first, but if they are broken down into tiny pieces, one foot at a time, I can put the pattern back together to make sense of it, memorize it, and dance it. Learning to dance is almost like learning the alphabet for the first time or studying a foreign language and racking your brain for specific words, until one day the letters and words come out naturally. The effort is painful, but the reward is bliss.

"*Chicos*, today we will learn about *el camino del saludo*!" says Maestro Zadoc, referring to the greeting walk. We are organized into two lines, one for women and one for men, and then we, the women, walk up to our partners while opening our huge skirts, holding them at the edges, then folding them back in by bringing our hands into fists at our waists. The move is accompanied by a little jump.

Maestro Zadoc is, as usual, in top form and explains another move, where we have to slowly wiggle our hips from side to side while walking toward our partners. Women have their hands on their hips, and men clutch their *cintura,* the front of the belt.

"*¡Mueve todo lo que tienes que mover!*" (Move everything you've got!), he exclaims, before letting out an adapted version of the traditional cry: "*¡Yeehaah, ow-ow-ow!*"

In the next move the dancers lean in toward their partners, almost cheek to cheek, first to their left and then to their right, with arms open to the side.

"And this one is to make your partner fall in love with you," says Maestro Zadoc, encouraging us to lean closer to each other. His passion for his work inspires us, and he occasionally jams by himself, smiling and looking at the floor while doing some sort of happy shrug movement as if he's ridding himself of his problems. At the end of the class he invites us to stand at the barre and take a breath.

Maestro Zadoc welcomes the new students in the class and thanks them for joining the dance family. It seems that in the Saturday class there are a few women around my age or younger. Then he announces that there will be a huge dance festival in honor of the school's anniversary—to take place at the end of October. We'll rehearse four traditional dances onstage over the coming weeks and perform in a big theater with a capacity of eight hundred seats, which are likely to sell out. I start daydreaming of the color-fully embroidered folklore dresses that we'll wear, their embellishments and cakelike layers swirling onstage.

Maestro Zadoc asks which students will be able to join and turns to ask me. "Yes!" I yelp, unable to contain my excitement.

I HAVE FALLEN victim to what they call the Mexican diet, or Montezuma's revenge: food poisoning. An unfortunate incident involving shrimp ceviche at a rooftop barbeque forces me to leave the party early, something that I never do. Farah nurses me through the night, gives me soup and bread, and sets me up with an unlimited supply of Netflix for the rest of the weekend. After a monumental twelve-hour sleep from which I wasn't sure if I'd ever wake, I find the strength to peel myself off the sofa and make it to my class at Mizoc.

The others seem to notice that I'm not quite well, and after I explain the situation to Maestro Zadoc, he looks at me sympathetically:

"Bad tacos?" he asks.

"Ceviche," I mumble.

"Ouch." He nods his head, indicating that this is a common occurrence.

My body feels so weak and my shortness of breath is worse than normal. On the bright side, my shiny new shoes are here. Carefully handcrafted, with black patent leather glazing around the toe, and thick heels and tips embedded with metal pins, they will allow me to finally stomp relentlessly. When the rest of the *abuelitos* arrive, they all seem happy to see me wearing proper shoes. Gonzalo even congratulates me.

We line up, and I'm ecstatic to hear the metallic tapping sound of my shoes as I stomp around the class. We learn another new dance (or at least it's new for me) called *jarabe mixe* (dance of the Mixe people) and go over sones de Betaza, which I'm now grasping quite well. My favorite part is when the accompanying music slows down dramatically before launching into short, continuous trumpet bursts as we zigzag and skip back and forth past our partners in our rows. We keep switching partners, but I most enjoy dancing with Gonzalo. He's reassuring and encouraging and always gives me a look that says *you've got this*. Whenever we go over the opening of the song, Gonzalo clutches his cintura and lets out a joyful cry as he happily skips around.

"That ceviche really worked out well for you!" says Maestro Zadoc, seeing me sweating and panting as I grip the wooden barre that lines the side of the room, trying to recover from all the jumping. "Next time you should have a shot of tequila!"

"Ah, yes, tequila kills everything!" says Roselo, another student, as she fans herself with a hat while clutching the little silk bandana around her neck.

A PHARMACIST ASSURES me that I have nothing more than severe altitude sickness and arms me with an inhaler, aspirin, and some anti-nausea medication, but by the time I arrive to my first one-on-one class at the Amalia Hernández, I am weak, teary, and full of doubt. *Why did I ever take this trip? I don't dance well. I'm barely seeing anything outside of Mexico City.* I stop myself. I have to suck it up and be stronger. This was always meant to be a struggle.

I can't find my teacher, so I head into the eerie changing rooms. Empty sinks, benches, and mirrors are everywhere. Gabi sits in front of the makeup mirror, applying her dark, almost black lipstick. When she sees me, she smiles and walks with me into the lobby where she asks me to wait patiently.

Twenty minutes pass, and I begin to want to drop everything. I even practice in my head in Spanish how to tell them that sadly this isn't for me and I won't be taking any more classes.

Finally, Gabi comes out and we head upstairs. One of the students from the group class hadn't been informed of the time change, and Gabi asks if I mind if he joins my private class. We'll still only focus on jarabe tapatío.

Then everything changes. We start from zero, and with my new shoes I start to tap away, the metallic sound guiding my steps as I paint patterns with my feet. I then launch into an energetic zapateo, and my feet strike the ground to create a rhythmic sound, almost like in tap dancing. When I first witnessed the movement, the tempo was so fast that I felt I'd seen tornadoes instead of legs and feet. Only at a slower pace could I see and hear the whole pattern. It's just beginning to make sense when Gabi calls for us to increase the speed. She uses an app on her phone to make the music go faster.

I'll probably get it wrong, but I'm focused and determined. My footwork is getting faster and faster as I beat out fury, disappointment, and sadness with my feet. A sudden mistake trips me up, but I'm astonished I made it as far as I did.

Gabi tells me to stop looking down at my feet or at them in the mirror. "Just fix your eyes onto a random blank point as you dance," she tells me.

It actually works. Just like in yoga, where standing on one foot and staring at something neutral helps maintain balance, keeping my focus on a fixed point (and not my reflection in the mirror) keeps me on track. I wonder if looking at my reflection in the mirror makes me self-conscious, causing me to lose my steps, my balance, and my confidence. It's like when you fear that you will fall, you fall, and when you fear that you will fail, you fail. Maybe learning to dance is as much about overcoming fear as it is about mastering intricate choreography. With renewed strength and confidence, I keep dancing. I can't believe the speed of my zapateo. It's like my feet are not even part of my body anymore. Gabi seems pleased.

But so far we just have the footwork, and there's a lot to practice— not to mention the arm work, direction, and movement to add in. I'm struggling with a step called *el lanzado*, a name that comes from the verb *lanzar*, meaning something between "throw," "launch," and "release." The step involves stamping one foot while sweeping the other, lifting your knee to gracefully draw a circle in the air with your leg, before sliding to a gentle tap on the tip of the foot followed by a double stamp. I need half an hour to repeat that step by myself before I can master it.

This repetitive movement is almost meditative. I can feel the connection between my brain and body. It's like they're working together as one huge machine.

We work on another zapateo that calls for striking our feet eight times before ending with a double stamp. I seem to be getting it right, but I'm not counting to eight. Instead, I'm following a pattern and rhythm in my head. This is what Ismael Otero meant, and it's clear he was right. If you want to learn how to dance, you need to find the rhythm first.

I leave class in high spirits, having decided to set the negative self-talk aside. The drive home takes me through narrow backstreets of the historical center, and I see vendors selling everything from tacos to secondhand phones and manicures. As daylight falls I feel a sudden sense of insecurity. This is a part of town that, as a woman, I've been conditioned to not feel safe walking alone in. I wish I could walk off the beaten path to experience life as the locals do. I get an adrenaline rush just thinking about it. If I weren't so obviously foreign, I would plunge myself into the nighttime culture. I'd explore the bustling night market kept upbeat by the bouncy sound of blaring *cumbia* music.

MEXICO CITY IS known for its terrible traffic, and I'm already late for my class at Mizoc. People are generally relaxed with time in Mexico, as Farah told me to expect, but the world of dance is surprisingly punctual. I, however, am not, and I clamber up the stairs so rushed that I almost trip over my orange skirt. I'm gasping for breath as I enter the classroom and find that our teacher today is not Maestro Zadoc but Mizoc himself, the founder and director of the school. He is comparatively formal and strict, commanding both respect and admiration. I apologize, feeling ashamed, and run to the last row. He asks us to demonstrate the basic steps of waltz and then introduces a number of folkloric steps. Before I would just copy everyone else, but now I'm learning the names of the steps and the different ways of moving the skirt.

"Don't fold your elbows!" Mizoc warns. I hadn't known that our arms have to be straight. He instructs us to make figure eights to create a continuous ripple through the different layers of the skirt, like waves, guided from my wrists up to my shoulder blades.

"No jumping!" Mizoc says to me. A typical beginner's error in all dances—I'm trying to get rid of my tendency to bounce rather than ground my weight into my feet.

We continue through our repertoire of four dances. I can't believe I can actually follow all of them now.

"*¡Por el amor de Dios! ¡Escuchan las frases de la música!*" cries Mizoc. (For the love of God! Listen to the phrases in the music!) His face radiates passion for music and dance, and with great enthusiasm he calls out the name of a dance I don't know. "You must know the names of the dances, so that when we call it out you know exactly what to do!" he announces.

Bety, Gonzalo, and I share a few *I'm in trouble* glances.

"We need to move beyond these simple dances from now on," Mizoc says kindly but sternly. "*¿Están chicos?*" (Are you all with me?)

"*¡Estamos, maestro!*" (We are, sir!), affirms Gonzalo.

MY LEGS, SHINS, and thighs are killing me from the number of classes I've taken in the last few days, especially yesterday's class where Maestro Mizoc made us dance the entire repertoire.

I force myself to go to the Amalia Hernández, and after I wait twenty minutes aimlessly in the stairwell, Gabi comes running breathlessly up the stairs. The usual room isn't free, so she waves me to an attic-like room that's filled with props and costumes. There are no mirrors in the room, so in a way it's a better space because I'm free from the judgment the mirror reflects.

Today we are going over all the footwork, but I keep having trouble figuring out where the first step starts. I'm distracted by the melody rather than listening to the beat.

"Listen to the *guitarrón*," Gabi says, referring to the notes of the big guitar. "It's your guide." I'd seen the instrument played by mariachis. It looks like a large guitar but sounds more like a bass. Its sound will be a signal telling me when to start my zapateo.

As we go over the whole choreography, my body starts doing very strange things—moving to the wrong side and turning on the wrong foot. My brain knows it's wrong, but for some reason my body struggles to keep up. I try to tell my body to stop making the same mistake, but it seems it doesn't want to listen. How can Gabi bear having to keep repeating the same moves with me? Patience is definitely one of the great virtues of Latin Americans. I keep repeating the same errors, at times painfully, but she stays with me and slowly breaks me out of my bad habits. By the end of the class, her smile tells me it was all worth it.

"That's so much better," she says. "You got it!"

I'm beaming from the feeling of accomplishment after working so hard to master something that feels completely unnatural and difficult. She invites me into the main studio, where the students are, so I can run through the choreography once in front of the mirror and with my shoes on—the fragile attic floorboards couldn't handle the force of the shoes. I dance the entire song, giving everything I have in front of the other students. Miraculously, I have almost all of the footwork nailed down.

THE SOUND OF the zapateo has become part of my dreams, and even my thoughts come in patterns of metallic thuds and taps. I've only gotten three hours of sleep, and I don't know how I will survive stomping around for the next two and a half hours at Mizoc. It's our last rehearsal before the performance.

Last night my friend Pablo, whom I met through a friend from Bangkok, showed me some of Mexico City's nightlife. We started with cutting-edge cocktails in one of Roma Norte's hipster bars, then went to a strange reggaeton club with a purple interior and a smoke machine, and finished with an electro party in Condesa, a short drive from my home, at three in the morning.

Gonzalo looks at me suspiciously, and I confess to him that I spent the whole night partying. He places his finger over his lips, vowing to keep my secret. In the back of the studio, my hands hold the barre for support at every chance for a short break. I'm struggling to do even the most basic zapateo, and I push through the migraine as we jump and skip.

At the end of the class Gonzalo winks at me: "*¡Ya aguantaste!*" (You held on!), he says with a little nudge, chuckling that I've managed to survive the class.

Maestro Zadoc motions for all of us to take a seat on the floor and briefs us on our upcoming performance. It will be a re-creation of a Guelaguetza, an annual indigenous festival in the state of Oaxaca usually held on the last two Mondays of July. It's also known as Los Lunes del Cerro (Mondays on the Hill). He says we will be dancing traditional dances including sones de Betaza and sones de Pochutla, and ending with a dance called son Istmeño. He also introduces us to the last dance of the show, which goes with a song named "Tangu Yu," meaning "small clay doll," and we will have to dance to it with a doll balanced on our heads. He tells us that next week we should bring a bandana and a bottle and says something about cinnamon, which I don't understand.

"Our show will be in the evening, and we'll be going there by coach. So be ready to leave the school at midday." He names a destination city with a long name that I can't pronounce, and after class I have to ask him to repeat it. Maestro Zadoc shows me a sheet of paper and points to the city's name: Ciudad Nezahualcóyotl. Then he asks all of us to go downstairs and into one of the school's back rooms for one of my favorite activities: a costume fitting. Mizoc's wife, Noemi, eyes me attentively before selecting a white cotton outfit with a skirt of the right length for my height. I'm used to being the average height in Europe, but I'm considered tall here. She gives me a red sash to use as a belt and clip-in hair braids made out of wool woven with silk ribbons. Long braids are one of the traditional hairstyles of indigenous women across Latin America, from the Maya to the Inca; we'll be dressed in the traditional attire of the Zapotec people of Oaxaca. I recall having read that the long braids represent the mind and heart woven together. For the other song I'm given a colorful outfit with intricate layers of flower patterns, along with elaborate jewelry and flowers to pin in my hair.

Receiving my costume hammers in the reality of the situation: I'm going to be performing onstage with a Mexican dance troupe.

Once home, I share the news of my upcoming show with Farah and her boyfriend, Hugo.

Hugo spits out his drink in shock. "Ciudad Neza?" he confirms, using the nickname for Nezahualcóyotl.

"Yes," I tell him. "We'll be performing at the Pluricultural Center—with a capacity of eight hundred people."

"May God protect you," he says, his eyes widening. "Forgive me if I don't come to the show."

Perplexed by Hugo's reaction, I search for the venue online. Ciudad Nezahualcóyotl, named after the pre-Hispanic philosopher and poet, translates as "fasting coyote" in Nahuatl and is apparently one of the most dangerous places in Mexico. It's to the northeast of Mexico City, and while it was once known as the world's largest slum, Neza transformed into an industrial hub and is now a self-made suburban municipality. Most of Neza's residents are migrants from other parts of Mexico who face poverty, a high crime rate, and *cholo* (gang culture). Still, some people champion the city as "*Neza York*," drawing a parallel to New York because of the constant flow of people between these two urban cities and the fact that they are both cultural melting pots—each drawing immigrants bringing hardships and dreams.[15]

TODAY IT'S MY turn to show up twenty minutes late for my class at the Amalia Hernández with Gabi. My driver got lost, going past the street twice and then making a wrong turn in the wrong part of town. A woman, visibly high on drugs, charged like a zombie toward our car and pounded her fists on the window. Thankfully, the driver remained calm and very gently steered the car out of the one-way street. I think about listing my excuses to Gabi, but she is completely unfazed and brushes my tardiness off as she calls me into the room.

We spend half the class working on a single step: *el lanzado*. I learned it last week but still can't get it right—it's like a puzzle that I can't put together. I practice it hundreds, if not thousands, of times before it finally comes out correctly. My mind and body need to understand it, and it only takes a tiny step out of place for me to lose the whole sequence.

I've just about given up when it suddenly comes out right. Researchers and theorists have gone back and forth on the merits of long practice hours (Malcolm Gladwell even popularized the since-debunked theory that it takes ten thousand hours of practice to become an expert in anything[16]). If my battle with el lanzado teaches me anything about practice, it is that mastering what seems impossible doesn't always require innate talent; determination, effort, patience, and perseverance can allow us to achieve our goals. Given how we can access so many things at the snap of our fingers, summoning these can be especially difficult—but for me, it was worth it.

"What about the graceful skirt movements?" I ask Gabi, referring to the *faldeo*, the tempestuous waves steered by arduous arm and shoulder work. I'm sure my upper-body weakness will make this the most difficult part, even harder than the footwork, which I'm barely able to do—and I'll have to coordinate them! We only have a few days and two more classes before we film our video, the next one in the series I'll be making during my journey. Self-doubt and negative thoughts plague my mind once again.

"We'll get to the arms and the faldeo now," she says. "We've also been dancing 'flat' until now, meaning that we're dancing almost only on one spot and facing only one direction. You'll have to also learn how to do it all while moving around the room."

I don't know if my mind or body can handle such an overwhelming amount of new information. But Gabi tells me not to worry and that via text message she's arranged all the details of the video filming. (This is how everything seems to be arranged in Latin America.) Without having to worry about that, I focus on trying to not be demoralized. After all, I've come this far—there's no giving up now.

THE DAY HAS finally come for me to dance the jarabe tapatío in full costume with my new dance partner, Osvaldo—and all on video. In my last class with Gabi, I learned how to move my arms using my shoulder blades. The movement requires so much upper-body strength that I can't manage it for more than a few minutes at a time. It's both physically and mentally exhausting. I've learned, though, that moving one's arms in dance reflects confidence—and the more confident I feel, the bigger and bolder my arm movements.

I've rehearsed as much as I possibly can, and although I'm still not completely at ease with the dance, the pressure of filming a video means that I'll give it everything I have.

I find Gabi in the lobby, wearing a cute red dress and a matching red bow in her hair. She suggests we begin by going through the whole song with Osvaldo, and I immediately start to panic. *Already?* I have barely practiced the arms and feet together or the direction of movements with a partner.

Gabi shows me how to hold the skirt correctly, and I feel an ache in my shoulder blades as I try to hold up its heavy layers and move my arms. Osvaldo starts moving in so many directions that I can't follow and get totally lost.

"*¡Bien!*" says Osvaldo. Good! He gives me a high five. He must be joking.

"I was terrible!" I reply, mortified.

We try it a second time. I've slightly improved but am now completely exhausted.

"Breathe through your nose!" Gabi reminds us. "And don't forget to smile!"

I have a terrible habit of breathing through my mouth when I dance, which makes me tired and dehydrated. I do everything I can to smile, remembering how Griselle said that a big smile is worth so much more than perfect footwork. Even a dance full of mistakes can look beautiful simply because a smile fills it with emotion and joy.

On my third try I'm feeling even more confident and sure of myself—until halfway through, when I slip on my skirt and twist my foot.

Gabi and Osvaldo run over in panic. Fortunately, I didn't twist my ankle.

On my fourth try I make it through the entire dance. My skirt undulates as I move in loops around the room. Osvaldo throws his sombrero to the ground, and after teetering around its rim in intricate steps, I kneel down to pick it up, praying I won't be kicked in the head. Victorious, I hold up his sombrero in triumph. My dancing was far from perfect—it was never going to be—but it is almost perfect to me because I overcame so many obstacles, so much self-doubt and physical pain, to be able to perform the full routine. As we finish, tears of gratitude fill my eyes: for Gabi, for Amalia Hernández, for the possibility of any dream to become reality through sweat, struggle, and song.

I SPENT AN amazing two weeks discovering Mexico's states of Chiapas and Oaxaca, learning about indigenous cultures and admiring the jungle-covered pyramids and rugged Pacific coast. Now I'm back in Mexico City just in time for Day of the Dead celebrations.

Farah's boyfriend, Hugo, has invited me to join him at a party in the home of a famous DJ in Polanco. I don't really have a costume and settle on a simple black dress with a crown of red roses set over my hair, which I've styled in waves. As we step inside the party, I feel like I've entered an issue of a tabloid magazine. A DJ in the corner of the main room spins electronic music, while the Polanco set lays across sofas and spills out onto the balcony, where there's an improvised bar. A girl with skeleton makeup and long blond hair dominates the room, shouting orders at people.

"I think she's the queen," says Hugo, raising his eyebrows. We decide to head onto the terrace instead.

I chat with two guys—one dressed as Superman and the other as Alex from *A Clockwork Orange*. They seem amused by my love of Mexican folklore and my demonstration of a basic zapateo. I suppose folklore isn't "cool" to everyone. It certainly isn't to these posh Polanco kids, an elite variety of *fresas*, as the Mexicans call them in slang, literally meaning "strawberries." And really, who's to blame them? It's not often that someone immerses themselves in the folklore of their own homeland. Even I haven't—I've been drawn to the culture of a different continent. I think we don't always value what is ours and are even amused by the fascination foreigners have for things we take for granted. It might take an outside view to see the richness and beauty in elements of our culture that we overlook.

From the terrace we can see the expanse of Polanco and the rest of the metropolis shimmering in the distance.

"You know," says Superman smugly, "my family owns half of this."

I frown, searching for how to respond, but nothing comes. A great uproar breaks the silence—the police have arrived, followed by a torrent of Ubers to carry us into the night.

Hugo and I head to a club in Condesa: the Leonor—my name in Spanish.

After a tequila shot at the bar, I make my way to the dance floor. I'm stumped by how enthusiastically people are dancing to the music playing. *How can you happily dance to electronic music?*

I sway to the music instead of dancing, and eventually I succumb to a haze probably brought on by an ill-thought-out combination of a cocktail and tequila shot. Out of curiosity to know if it's even possible, I try to dance some of the folklore steps to the music, which switches between electronic dance music (EDM), disco, and funk. My body enters a sort of zapateo autopilot. It looks weird, sure, but somehow it works. I start throwing my hands up in the air, twirling around the center of the dance floor.

A few potential suitors dare to approach, carefully prescreened by Hugo, but I'm in my own world and barely notice them. Feeling free of inhibitions, I close my eyes and liberate my body as I dance.

Applying folkloric steps to electronic dance music is undoubtedly unorthodox, but it makes me free—unrestricted by any one style. Instead, I adapt and combine styles while trying to stay in sync with the rhythm of the music, performing a mix of zapateo and cha-cha and invoking dramatic ballet leaps—all while spinning an imaginary skirt with my arms. After a while I stop thinking about my steps at all, giving way to feeling instead.

Soon it is six o'clock in the morning. We need fuel after a night of dancing, so Hugo and I make our way to one of the twenty-four-hour taco restaurants on Avenida Álvaro Obregón and order tacos *al pastor* ("shepherd style," with spit-grilled pork and often pineapple). Hugo orders another drink with his and drunkenly wails of his affection and longing for Farah. I warn him not to mess it up or he'll have to deal with me, wagging my finger at him threateningly for emphasis.

Hugo asks if I've ever been in love and I tell him, "Only once." Then, sighing desolately, I add, "Just over a year ago."

"Tell me."

I take a deep breath and tell him my romantic tragedy, and as I do so, tears begin to stream down my face and eventually into my tacos.

"Ah, summer love!" says Hugo knowingly. "I've had one of those." He orders another round of Corona beers. "It took me years to get over mine. All you need is time, and new people. You'll get there eventually."

I SLIP INTO my black dance rehearsal outfit, pull my hair into a tight bun, add a dash of red lipstick, and then head out for Mizoc, carrying my heavy bags of costumes, props, and a box of accessories that has my name written on it in thick black marker. I wait outside the school with the other students until it's time to load everything into the coach. The retro bus has a tiny old-school TV and a giant crucifix in the front.

Today is the big day, and we make our way to Neza with a feeling of oneness, traveling as a team on our way to our performance. We sing and clap to old Mexican folk songs, until Maestro Zadoc interrupts to announce that the tickets for the show have sold out. The theater will be at full capacity—meaning there will be eight hundred people in the audience. I'm going to be performing two of the dances: sones de Betaza, which has become my favorite, and son Istmeño, which the whole group will perform together at the end of the show.

The excitement and adrenaline of going onstage mitigate my nerves, but I also feel unprepared. I've recently returned from two weeks of travel during which I had no time to practice. I'm also missing a few elements of my costume: white tack, a hairnet, and the same brown sandals the others have. The tack is for lining the rim of my doll's skirt so it can balance on my head without falling during son Istmeño. The hairnet is to hold my bun. The requirements are strict. Luckily, one of the advanced dancers, a younger student named Tanya, helped me procure brown sandals from an obscure market and loans me some of her white tack.

"I don't want to see one hair out of place!" Maestro Zadoc had briefed us. "All of you with exactly the same shoes, hair, and makeup!"

As I look through the bus window, I notice that the people of Neza look and dress differently than the people of Mexico City; that old Volkswagen Beetles, once immensely popular in Mexico and affectionately named *vochos*, line the streets, including one entirely covered in graffiti. I can see that old furniture fills local restaurants, and stores look different too. Rows of dead chickens hang upside down in one window, and huge bags of potato chips fill another. As we pass through town, the houses appear to become smaller, older, and rougher. Everything seems to get grayer and more unassuming. We pass a mural that reads, "No to gas, electricity, and water price increases for our economic life." It occurs to me that there is likely a quiet majority here that is often forgotten.

Our coach pulls into the parking lot of a huge, cube-like building, and we go inside and into the changing rooms. There is a booth with a mirror for each of us, and I choose the one next to Bety. I hang my costumes and line my shelf with my box, props, and makeup. I could almost feel like a star, were it not for the malfunctioning light bulbs that leave us in the dark.

My new friend Tanya helps me prepare my props: a hand-painted bowl crafted from a gourd in traditional pre-Hispanic design, and a colorful clay doll, which has little flags that surround it. The doll's arm sadly broke in transit, but we manage to discreetly fix it with the white tack.

During the technical rehearsal I feel a rush of excitement. The mariachi band tunes its instruments and tests its trumpets, and Maestro Zadoc and Brenda start putting tape on the stage floor to lay out segments for the dancers. I'll be center right of the main line.

While we make our way through the steps, testing out the stage and formations to make sure that we will use the space correctly, I breathe in an incredible feeling—today I can showcase the Mexican folklore I've learned. It feels like a milestone in my journey.

During our final rehearsal, Gonzalo pinches my arm and gives me a wink to wish me luck. He has been paired with his wife, Sandra. They always seem so happy dancing together, and I catch them exchanging a hug as they practice. Their affection moves me—a powerful reminder that love too is ageless. Meanwhile Bety rehearses with her dance partner, her grandson Armando. Dance not only brings people together but also reinforces bonds between generations. This is not just a show but a family and community experience. Generations of grandparents, parents, children, and grandchildren are coming together to dance.

As we head back into the changing rooms, Bety asks if I need any help. I have so many questions—*How high should my bun be? Should I wear more makeup? How do I add the sash around my waist?* I have a million things I want to ask, but I keep my questions to myself. Instead I let her help me with the final touches of my costume, fixing a hairpiece with the long, ribboned braids and setting the red sash around the white cotton outfit. Erika, one of the teachers and lead dancers, paints my face with makeup. In other circumstances it might seem like too much, but the harsh stage lights require a heavy hand in order to distinguish facial features.

We open the show with a parade to greet the audience. Heading out to the back of the auditorium, in lines, we go down the steps, through the audience, and onto the stage while smiling and waving, all in our different costumes with our colorful props. We continue waving until the opening dance, and then it's showtime!

I wait in the wings and watch the advanced women's group, which is mostly made up of teenagers. They perform a colorful and complex dance, balancing pineapples on their heads while twirling their skirts in an explosion of bright blues, pinks, and yellows. *How do they manage to do so many things at the same time while keeping the typical radiant smile of Mexican folklore?*

Next up: sones de Betaza. I've been paired with a young girl named Angelica. We are the only female pair in the group and dance directly behind Gonzalo and Sandra. As we prepare to go onstage, Sandra does a sign of the cross and kisses her curled fingers, which represent the trinity, and then kisses Gonzalo softly. Maybe couples who dance together stay together. Maybe it helps keep love alive.

I take a deep breath, roll my shoulders to straighten my back, and smile at Angelica. We step onto the stage, and time stands still as I'm blinded by the bright lights. I'm not nervous but instead exhilarated by the adrenaline. I'm determined to enjoy every second and do my best to honor Mexican folklore. I owe it to my school and my classmates.

The music starts, and as I skip and twirl through the steps, gliding and smiling the whole way through the dance, I feel incredibly alive. I stamp and thud in rhythm with the blast of trumpets, and my braids fly through the air as I move. This performance is a precious opportunity to bring out the best in myself, and there's only one opportunity for it. I can't do another take, edit, or put a filter over it.

With immense concentration, I make it through the entire second dance while successfully balancing the little clay doll on my head, something I hadn't managed to do in any rehearsal. Thankfully the dance moves aren't too strenuous and instead are mostly small steps back and forth, toward and away from our partner, as we open our skirts gracefully. At the end of the dance, we all gather onstage to sing "Tangu Yú," the song about the little clay doll. I didn't have time to find the lyrics online and memorize them, so I mouth my way through it instead, and rather convincingly, I think—which isn't too difficult given that the chorus is mostly a repetition of *"tangu yú."* I don't really understand any of the words in the lyrics, and halfway through the song, it dawns on me that the song isn't even in Spanish. It's in Zapoteco, one of Oaxaca's main indigenous languages. I stifle a laugh at my own ridiculousness, feeling both ashamed and amused that I'm pulling this off.

After the song, we cheer "*¡Viva México! ¡Que viva Oaxaca!*" (Long live Mexico! Long live Oaxaca!), and I cheer with all my heart, as if cheering for my own country. Gonzalo, who stands one row ahead, turns around impressed and gives me a discreet thumbs-up. Though I may be an imposter, a foreigner infiltrating a Mexican dance troupe to perform with them onstage in celebration of a culture and tradition that aren't my own, I feel part of something special.

When it is time to say goodbye to my friends at Mizoc, I do so with a heavy heart.

Gonzalo places his hands on my shoulders and looks at me so tenderly it reminds me of how my grandfather used to look at me.

"Please take very good care of yourself, Eleonor. I'll really miss you." I choke back tears while he hugs me. I don't want to leave what reminds me of my grandfather's embrace.

5

CUBA

Cuban Salsa, Son, and Cubatón

El cocodrilo—the crocodile. This is what they call Cuba when seen from an aerial view. I peer out the airplane window and see why, gasping at the emerging sight of an almost crocodile-shaped peninsula rimmed in breathtaking turquoise waters. It's my third visit to Cuba, but this time is going to be different. The communist island changed so much between my visits in 2002 and 2010, and I wonder what it will be like now.

On my prior visits I stayed in tourist resorts, sheltered from the realities of local life. This time I'm going to live in a *casa particular*, a homestay with a local family, and have a packed schedule of daily dance classes in Old Havana's nostalgic salons and on its sunlit rooftops. After considering many of Cuba's leading dance schools, I'd discovered a school with a social project that works to empower Cuban dancers to be self-employed with fair working conditions. Reforms to labor laws have allowed Cubans to be self-employed, including as dance teachers. The school is managed by a German woman named Renate who is also organizing my accommodations and airport transfers. From our email exchanges, she seems to be very efficient. I suspect that the course organization will be flawless.

Although I'm aware that Cuba has changed, I have confidence that comes from having been here before and having planned meticulously for the trip. When it's my turn in the enormous immigration line, I greet the officer in a fluent Spanish that does not match my British passport. He asks what I'm doing in Cuba, and when I tell him I've come to learn how to dance, he nods approvingly and waves me through.

I booked a taxi to wait for me outside the airport and am arriving armed with a stash of Cuban Convertible Pesos (CUCs) acquired in advance. "One country, two currencies" is the slogan attributed to Cuba's dual currency system: the CUC, which is pegged to the US dollar and used by tourists, and the Cuban peso, or *moneda nacional* (national money), used by the locals. But the dual currency system also creates a dual consumer system—with different services, establishments, and transportation made available in each currency for locals and foreigners.

As I walk outside, I feel the warmth of the Caribbean air on my cheeks. I scan the crowds for my driver and check all signboards for my name, but I can't find my driver anywhere. I shake my head sadly to a few drivers who approach me with signs displaying Russian names. (It must be the blond hair or the cheekbones.)

It takes me half an hour, but I finally accept that the driver isn't coming and head to the airport information desk, thinking that they surely must be able to help.

"*Hola,* good afternoon!" I say enthusiastically to two middle-aged Cuban women with over-gelled pulled back hair and heavy makeup. They look at me with annoyance. I must be interrupting an important conversation.

"My taxi didn't show up, and I really need to make a call. Could you tell me if there's a phone anywhere?" I ask calmly, hiding my desperation.

"No, there isn't," replies one of the women harshly as she turns back to the other woman.

"Would you maybe have a phone I could use just to make a quick call?" I start to panic, and she slowly turns back to consider me as she loudly snaps her gum.

"You can. But it's going to cost you." She smiles.

"Fine. How much do you want?"

"Three CUC, or three dollars," she snarls, her smile widening as she chews her gum louder in satisfaction.

I grudgingly hand over three one-CUC bills, and she dials the number into her phone before passing it over the counter. After several rings I hear a faint voice lost in background noise.

"Hello? Renate?"

"Aliénor, is that you? What happened? We were waiting for you yesterday at eleven for coffee!" says Renate, her voice fuzzy. There's been a misunderstanding. I was planning to arrive today, November 11.

"Look, all the taxis into town are thirty CUC—that's thirty dollars and—" the phone call cuts off.

Great. Not exactly the perfectly planned arrival I'd envisioned.

"Hey, lady, I can help you!" says a man with a strong Cuban accent—Latin America's equivalent to an East London cockney twang, where half the syllables go missing. He's with a significantly younger and attractive Cuban woman, and they seem to know the two women at the desk, as they'd been chatting with them while I was on the phone. "Where do you need to go? If it's Old Havana, we'll take you for thirty CUC."

Well, at least he isn't ripping me off. "Okay, then," I reply, "I'm going to a casa particular on the corner of Aguiar and Teniente Rey."

"I'm Jorge, and this is my daughter," he points proudly toward the young woman.

"Hi. I'm Yenny," she says with a warm smile and leans in to kiss me on the cheek.

I love this about Latin America. Even strangers touch, hug, and kiss each other.

"*¡Vamos!*" (Let's go!), she says.

We walk out of the airport terminal and toward a battered blue car. I wonder for a moment if I should be worried about getting into a car with two strangers, but I remind myself that Cuba is one of the world's safest destinations for tourists, especially women. Lonely Planet labels Cuba as a dream destination for female travelers where a very low rate of violent crime means a woman should be safe walking the streets of Havana at night.[17] The bigger risk, the travel bible claims, are *piropos* (pickup lines) given as compliments and catcalling—and relentless courtship.[18]

Jorge is leading the way but glances back and sees me struggling to lug my suitcase, and I wonder if he's going to offer to help. I was spoiled by the polite *caballeros* (gentlemen) of Mexico and became used to being treated like a *dama* (lady), spoken to softly, having doors opened for me, and having my bags carried. Though I consider myself a feminist, it doesn't mean I can't enjoy chivalry. Who doesn't enjoy being treated nicely? Cuba wakes me up like a slap in the face.

We arrive at the car, and Jorge struggles to force the trunk open. He then finally waddles over to take my suitcase, wincing at its weight. "Whoa, what do you have in here, stones?"

"It's only fifty-five pounds, and I'm traveling for almost a year so . . ." I stutter, unable to think of any additional excuses.

"And tell me, why do you speak like a Mexican?" asks Jorge.

The question makes me proud. It's been my goal to adopt a softer Latin American accent, and I'm thrilled to know it's convincing. "I was in Mexico for a couple of months. I guess the accent rubbed off on me."

I clamber onto the dusty brown seats in the back of the car. Yenny smiles reassuringly while Jorge starts up the engine, which rumbles and coughs out fumes as if it's living its final days. Finally we are off. The car is rattling, stalling, and steaming, but it makes it onto the main road and keeps going. I can see Jorge eyeing me in the rearview mirror and can sense the standard taxi driver questions coming.

After I try to explain my name, origin, and nationality, which inevitably brings more confusion, he looks at me unconvinced. I'm grateful when he changes to the next standard taxi question: "So what are you doing here in Cuba?"

"I'm learning to dance around Latin America. Cuba is my third stop."

"*¡Ay!* I love dancing!" exclaims Yenny, suddenly engaged in the conversation. She rustles open a map of Havana and looks at me seriously. "Look— this is where you need to dance," she says, pointing to a block in Old Havana. "Your *casa* is here," she says, pointing at my house, "and you need to go out dancing here, and here, and also here. Oh, and you have to go here!"

I'm growing fond of Yenny. She tells me that she studied philology and worked at the Cuban Book Institute until recently, but getting by in Cuba is difficult.

I nod, understanding. I have read that Cubans working on a state salary often need to work two or three jobs to survive.

"Can you imagine that what I used to earn in a month I can make in a day just by helping my father with his taxi?"

"I didn't realize it was that bad," I reply, stunned.

"Yes, the state salary is thirty dollars a month—the cost of your ride into town. Imagine if we do a few trips a day. Even after all the commissions, we still earn more."

"The commissions?" I ask.

"Everyone charges a commission here," she says flatly. "Those women at the information desk at the airport, we pay them a commission. That's how we got to take you into town. And so do the security guards at the entrance to the airport and everyone else. It's just how it works." Yenny points to a modern glass building along the Malecón, the stone wall that surrounds the city. "Look! That's the boat terminal they just built."

I recognize the Malecón. Built at the turn of the twentieth century to protect Havana from the sea, it has become a coastal promenade thriving with Havana's social life and colorful characters.

The car turns to enter Old Havana and onto a small street lined with crumbling colonial buildings. There's always a melancholic feeling when you come back to a place that you have been to years before. You wonder if it's the place that has changed or if it's you.

"It looks like we can't get there by car."

I start to wonder if they will actually bring me to the right place.

"We'll have to walk for a bit," says Jorge, parking his car at a random spot.

I battle with the door latch, which had become stuck, and then scramble out of the car with Yenny. The three of us walk down the cobblestone streets followed by my loud, rattling suitcase until we reach a pale-yellow building.

Jorge looks up at the building and cups his hands around his mouth to shout: "Yaqueline! Orlando! Are you there?" It seems he knows the casa.

A woman with rollers in her hair pops her head out from one of the balconies and shouts up to the balcony above hers. "Hey, Yaqueline, a new guest for you!"

A head pops out from the other balcony. "Who are you?" asks Yaqueline.

Intimidated by this balcony shouting, I shift around hesitantly before cupping my hands around my mouth and shouting as loud as I can: "I'm Eleonor! Renate booked me a room here."

Yaqueline's head disappears, and a few moments later, two men almost mechanically march out of the building's thin metal door and quickly take my bags. I thank Jorge, handing him the thirty CUC, and then give Yenny a warm hug. The taxi ride with them had been a crash course on Havana life.

Inside I walk up the staircase and look around at the paint peeling from the walls, and at the antique, decorated doors. Yaqueline waits for me outside an apartment door and introduces me to a woman with large brown eyes and curly dark blond hair.

The curly-haired woman introduces herself as Lia and gently shakes my hand. "Welcome! Please come in!" She then introduces me to her husband and three-year-old daughter and shows me to my room.

The decoration is a little outdated, but I quickly realize that this apartment is not typical at all. The room is very comfortable, and the bathroom is modern and spotless. A no-smoking sign and coasters lie around the room, labeled with names of different hotels. On my previous visits I'd heard that there's a huge black market in Cuba in which housekeepers from tourist resorts sell random hotel amenities. I had also been approached by people to ask if I had a spare bar of soap, a pen, or sweets. Not only do these basic items seem hard to get ahold of in Cuba, they seem to be currency. Maybe Lia wanted her home to be perfect for a foreign guest to stay in, but it would be lovely without those items anyway.

"Eleonor!" calls Lia, "Renate is here to see you."

I open the door, relieved. "Renate, it's so good to finally meet you!" I wonder if she's going to go for a German-style handshake or a Cuban-style hug. She goes for a hug.

After unpacking, I wrestle with the wooden shutters and then go out onto the balcony. Leaning against its railing, I spot a few people on the street and imitate them by watching the world go by: street vendors pushing carts, tricycle taxis blaring music, people chatting from one balcony to another.

The next morning, I find Lia in the living room setting the table for breakfast. I'm shocked at how vast the offerings are and wonder if her family will join me. The table is covered with items: fresh coffee, milk, an omelet, a smoothie, fruits, a sandwich, and yogurt. But there's only one place mat. It's so difficult to get ahold of some of these items in Cuba that I almost want to protest, but I also don't want to hurt her feelings by rejecting her generosity.

It's too much for me to finish, but it pains me to waste food, so I wrap up the sandwich and fruit to save them for lunch. Then I go back to my room to get ready.

Today is my first day of dance class. I'm starting an intensive course where I'll be cramming in five hours a day of dance training over the next five days. It sounds hard, but I'm excited about the challenge. What can my body learn to do in less than a week?

My dance teacher has come to my casa to pick me up. In the living room I find a handsome man in his early thirties with olive skin and brown eyes. He wears a blue T-shirt and a thick gold cross around his neck, and when he sees me he gets up timidly from the sofa to shake my hand, while out of instinct I go for a kiss on the cheek, which seems to surprise him.

"Nice to meet you. I'm Yosnel," he says in a serious voice. "The dance salon is just a ten-minute walk away. Let's go."

We walk down Aguiar, and I soak up the atmosphere and sights around me: the cobblestone streets, the music playing, the people sitting in their doorways, the sun glowing on my face. I haven't heard the name Yosnel before, but Renate had explained an interesting phenomenon in Cuba: the rise in popularity of names beginning with *Y*, such as Yenny, Yaqueline, Yoangel, and Yuri—and now Yosnel. This so-called Generation Y was mostly born toward the end of the Cold War—just like me. Some people say that the parents wanted to find original or different names, while others argue that the use of the letter *y*, uncommon in Spanish, came from the influence of the Soviet Union. I've also heard people explain that in a highly controlled system, naming their children was the only creative freedom they had.[19]

I focus my attention back on Yosnel and ask how he got into dance.

He tells me that he's an engineer by profession, but dance has been his passion since he was fourteen. Recalling my conversation with Yenny, I presume that he earns a far better living as a dance teacher than as an engineer.

We arrive at a building with a chipped wooden entrance, a barely visible address, and an old man sitting in the doorway smoking.

"*Buenos días, mami*" (Good morning, baby), says the old man. He scans me from head to toe while puffing on a cigarette.

I awkwardly squeeze past him and walk up a narrow staircase surrounded by turquoise walls. Just as I begin to wonder what kind of place this is, a man with a kind face opens a dark wooden door with a loud creak.

Salsa music blares, and my breath is taken away by the sight of a vintage salon that makes me feel like I've stepped into a different time.

"So, you told me that you've danced New York–style before, right?" asks Yosnel, trying to figure out my level.

"Yes," I reply nervously, watching the other students dancing fluidly and confidently with their teachers.

"Well, it should be a good foundation, but it's quite different than Cuban salsa. In New York–style, you dance in a line, but in Cuban-style you dance in a circular way around the man. Let's dance a song together and see." He takes my hand and leads me to the middle of the salon.

I try to feel confident. Surely all those hours of back-to-back classes in New York have amounted to something. But as we begin dancing, the awkwardness sets in. Yosnel keeps making direct eye contact, and it's making me paranoid—I don't know where to look. When he tries to guide me into a move, I can feel my body tense. I'm so afraid to make a mistake that I can't let myself go—instead I freeze. At first, Yosnel politely ignores my discomfort, continuing to lead me through some of the basic steps and inviting me to focus my eyes on a fixed point to maintain a "visual line." But I can tell his patience is already starting to run out.

"Okay," he says with a faint smile. "You have a problem with the rhythm. We need to go back to the basics."

I nod, defeated.

Yosnel leads me to the mirror at the back of the room. He checks my posture and positions my hands and arms in the right place. "Remember," he says, "when you're walking down the street, your arms swing naturally from side to side; that's the arm movement when dancing salsa."

When Yosnel says, "Let's do a basic step, five, six, seven, eight, and . . .," he takes my hand and we begin. I slowly start to feel more comfortable, adding my own style to the steps by rolling my hips almost in a figure eight. Something lights up inside of me, while a puzzled frown forms on Yosnel's face.

"No, no, no. Please stop."

"What's wrong?" I ask, feeling slightly hurt.

"Don't make that movement." He winces.

My cheeks start to burn. I feel like my entire femininity has been rejected.

"That swaying hip movement you see in salsa, it doesn't actually come from the hips," says Yosnel.

"It doesn't?"

"No. It comes from the feet and the knees." He puts his hands on my hips to stop them from moving. "Now do a basic step, but lift your feet higher off the floor."

Following his instructions, I can see that as my feet lift higher, my knees bend, causing the opposite hip to naturally move out toward the side.

"See!" says Yosnel. "Your hips can move naturally because of a different step."

I nod and go back to the basic step—this time taking his advice.

It feels strange to intentionally move one part of my body and then see another part move by itself. I feel like I'm starting to gain creative control over my body, learning how to make movements that had seemed impossible. The steps become more defined, and the movement more supple. In the mirror I smile at Yosnel, and he smiles back as we dance in perfect synergy. I feel like I've entered an almost meditative state where a new kind of energy seems to be releasing from within me. I'm in a state of flow.

Suddenly, an unidentified object flies through the balcony window, sharply grazing my arm as it lands at my feet with a loud thud.

"What was that?" I cry, horrified.

"Oh, that's just the newspaper," Yosnel says casually. He and the other teachers laugh, amused by my reaction. "It's how they deliver it here. They throw it through the balcony window to avoid having to climb the stairs."

I pick up the newspaper, which has been folded twice to create a block-like mass. It abruptly interrupted my nascent dance confidence, but I've faced far worse obstacles than this before, not only in dancing but also in life. To me, this local custom is both bizarre and amusing. What is a mundane action for Cubans is a manifestation of Havana's spirited balcony life, bustling with gossip, trade, and, apparently, the newspaper delivery service.

After three hours intensely practicing the same steps, I'm exhausted, but Yosnel doesn't even have a drop of sweat on his forehead.

Renate has already arrived and has been waiting patiently. I tell her the class went well, but I'm still learning the basics.

"Don't worry, you just need a strong foundation and then you'll be dancing in no time," she tells me in an encouraging voice. "Tonight we're all going out to a concert. It's quite far out of town, but it's somewhere the tourists don't know about. If you're up for it, we're meeting at eight in front of Hotel Inglaterra at Parque Central."

When people here make a plan, they set a time and place to meet and stick to it. To me it's old-fashioned but wonderful—a reminder of how things were before technology made us so flaky. Now you can just send a message from your cell phone to cancel or say you're going to be late, but they don't do that here—in part because service is spotty, but also because phone credit is considered a currency that is to be spent preciously.

"Of course I'm up for it! I'll see you there," I reply.

After a short lunch break, my second teacher arrives for two hours of class focusing on "lady styling."

"Hi, mami. I'm Esmeralda," she says and gives me a kiss on the cheek. Her all-white outfit contrasts with her rich black skin.

We continue the basic step, to my disappointment. Though I am dying to progress, I will have to repeat it for hours, maybe even days, until I get it right. Dancing requires immense patience and determination—in other words, grit.

Shortly before embarking on this journey, I met the psychologist Angela Duckworth at a happiness conference where we were both set to speak. In Angela's research, she determined that grit—defined by the combination of passion and perseverance that fuels deliberate practice—is a significant predictor of success.[20] Little did I know then that her insight would ring so clearly and profoundly true in the context of a Cuban dance salon.

Esmeralda suddenly stops and turns down the music, interrupting my thoughts and flashing a smile so bright it might be whiter than her outfit. "Congratulations! You are dancing salsa!" she says and takes my hands in hers. I feel a connection to Esmeralda already, moved by her warmth and encouragement.

We take a seat to recover, and she tells me about Santería, her religion, which is a syncretic belief. It was banned throughout most of Cuba's history, first by enslavers, then by imperialists, and finally by the revolution in 1959. Santería, meaning the "Way of Saints," dates back to the slave trade,[21] when it developed as a fusion of the traditions of Roman Catholicism and the rituals and beliefs of the African Yoruba tribe, which, though forced to convert to Catholicism, managed to keep the worship of its orishas, its gods, secret under the guise of devotion to saints. Since the ban on religion was lifted in the early 1990s, Santería has flourished, gaining widespread popularity among Cubans. Many Cubans incorporate Santería practices, rituals, and orisha devotion in some ways into their lives.[22]

Each orisha is associated with a color and a dance, whether deep blue and the movement of waves for Yemayá, the revered goddess of the oceans, motherhood, and moonlight,[23] or a golden yellow and the movement of stirring a pot of honey for Ochún, the sweet and sensual goddess of rivers, love, and beauty.[24] In some ways, I feel like these two goddesses represent an inner conflict between my relentless independence and powerful presence, and the delicate and feminine energy that I've been holding back. On this dance journey I can feel that beneath the fierceness and protection of my Yemayá-inflected shell, I carry Ochún: quiet and soft. The Ochún part of me is desperate to breathe. Maybe it is dance, which forces me to be vulnerable, that will allow this inner part of me to come forth. So far, I'm able to put all my energy and effort into the movements, but I struggle to allow myself to smile, to make delicate movements with my arms, or to flirt with my male dance partners.

Esmeralda has almost finished her yearlong initiation as a *santera* (Santería priestess), during which she has had to be fully clothed in white as a symbol of purity and rebirth before she can start practicing rituals and ceremonies. I have a feeling that her spirituality might explain the connection we share and that with her I might feel safe enough to let my inner Ochún shine.

I WALK ALL the way up Teniente Rey until I reach Parque Central—a hub for transport, hotels, and Wi-Fi. The Hotel Inglaterra stands next to one of my favorite buildings in Havana, the Gran Teatro de la Habana (Grand Theater of Havana). When illuminated at night, the theater looks like it's covered in white lace.

I find Renate with a group of German students at the hotel. The six of us scramble into a vintage car after haggling a decent rate and make our way to the concert. The driver seems annoyed—either about our success in getting the price down or that there are way too many people in the car, or both. He drives us an hour out of Havana and then pulls up to the concert venue, which looks like a town hall.

A long line of locals are waiting to get in, but instead of going to the back of the line, Renate says, "Follow me" and saunters to the front, where she approaches the bouncer. She whispers in my ear that if I pay an extra ten CUC, I can skip the line altogether. I don't like bribing my way to the front or cutting past locals, but I follow her lead. It's clear that there are two entrance fees—one for locals and one for foreigners. We go inside and find a table by the side of the dance floor. The venue feels different from other salsa clubs, which are often filled with professional dancers or dance tourists and their dance teachers. Here we are the only foreigners, and the place feels genuinely local. Young couples dance salsa together, friends celebrate birthdays, and families enjoy quality time together. I feel a distinct energy—one fueled by a sense of community.

"Let's get a Cristal," says Renate.

It's so hot in Havana, and after a long drive, an ice-cold beer sounds heavenly. We head to the bar, and while waiting to order our beers, I notice a rather austere-looking woman in a bow tie and jacket who sits at a desk placed a few yards behind the bar. She seems to be hand-writing pages and pages of accounts, presumably the orders from the bar. In a world where everything has become automated and digitalized, it's hard to imagine running an establishment with pen and paper alone; it requires diligent record-keeping and presence of mind that are reminiscent of another time. This is bar bureaucracy at its best, fit with a communist cashier.

Slowly the dance floor fills with couples and other dancers twirling and spinning into the night. A group of Cuban girls around my age shake their hips, their large hoop earrings dangling from their ears as they dance. I want to dance with them, to be like them, but I am an outsider here, still a foreigner. I feel like I am infiltrating their world; I am able to see them, but invisible to their eyes. The authenticity of this place cuts both ways, entrancing and alienating me at the same time. I have found a hidden gem, a place so local that it can never be mine.

DESPITE A SHORT night of sleep, I wake up motivated for my second day of class. Lia lays out the breakfast spread on the living room table—it's identical to the one from yesterday. She goes out of her way to make sure I feel comfortable in her house, but I feel uncomfortable being served all this food that Cubans rarely get to enjoy. I wish she would keep some for herself.

I take a bite of my omelet, my senses awakened, and hear four songs flood the room. A salsa song blasts from the streets, but I can also hear the pounding beat of a reggaeton song, a son song that plays on one of the balconies, and faintly, I can make out Marc Anthony's distinctive cry to his iconic song "Vivir Mi Vida" (Living My Life). It's not even nine o'clock in the morning, and this unrestrained, cacophonous mess is testimony to the fact that Cuba is a country bursting with life.

On my walk to class, the houses on Aguiar start to look more familiar. I struggle to find the school's wooden door, which has an illegible sign, but thankfully I recognize the old man sitting on the step smoking. He was there yesterday and will be my landmark from now on.

Yosnel leads me to the middle of the room.

"Today we're going to try to learn some of the *figuras* (figures), but the basic ones," he says as he starts to show me different moves. He dances each of them while saying their names: *pa'ti, pa'mí, paseala, sácala, exhibela, dile que no...*"

I try to stifle a giggle, but he catches it.

"What's so funny?"

"Well, this might sound silly to you because you use these terms all the time. But for me, if you translate them into English they mean 'for you, for me, take her for a walk, take her out, exhibit her, and tell her no'—literally," I explain. The steps tell a story of courtship and rejection, just by virtue of their names.

"I'd never thought about it like that," says Yosnel pensively.

We practice the steps for a good hour and a half before I take a seat at the back of the room, gasping for breath and desperate for water. Intricate framed pieces of Japanese art cover the walls of the room, geishas with fans surrounded by cherry blossoms. *How did this art make it here?* It seems so out of place but somehow adds to the nostalgia of the salon and goes well with the colorful star-shaped patterns on the floor tiles.

On the salon's balcony, I spot a cardboard sign with faded writing painted so neatly that it almost looks like it was typed: Comité de Defensa de la Revolución No. 4 (Committee of the Defense of the Revolution No. 4). These committees (CDRs) form the core of "revolutionary vigilance"[25] and are responsible for reporting any counterrevolutionary behavior or activity that could threaten or destabilize the Cuban political system.[26] Founded in Havana in 1960 by Fidel Castro, CDRs exist on every *cuadra* (block) and depending on your outlook can be considered either a neighborhood watch group or a tropical KGB.[27] CDRs gained power from spies and informants, but their utility went beyond the sinister pursuit of "collective surveillance."[28] The social welfare work of the CDRs, lesser known internationally but officially promoted domestically, includes activities such as providing vaccinations, cleaning streets, maintaining buildings, and keeping neighborhoods safe from crime.[29] Today these committees seem to be shadows of what they once were,[30] and it appears that at least one of their branches has been converted into a dance salon.

AFTER CLASS I have dinner at one of Old Havana's most iconic hotels: the Hotel Ambos Mundos, which is on the walking street of Obispo and was Ernest Hemingway's first residence in Cuba. As I walk inside, I feel like I'm entering Hemingway's world, complete with high ceilings and Art Deco pendant lights that tower over cream couches, green plants, and the mahogany bar where he probably enjoyed a few too many daiquiris. Three days without internet access has refreshed me in many ways, but it's time to reemerge in the digital world, even if just briefly.

When I first visited Cuba, the internet was highly restricted, with tourists limited to one or two old desktops in the resort's internet room. But that was back in 2002. Now in 2016, the internet is freely available—you just have to buy a card, with a cost that is often beyond the means of an ordinary Cuban, and then enter indecipherable login details wherever you can find a connection, which is usually limited to big hotels and, oddly, parks. The Wi-Fi is currently out in most parts of town, but through word of mouth I've heard that the Hotel Ambos Mundos has a signal today and sells internet cards at its reception desk. (They're double the price of the cards at the telecommunications office, but I wouldn't even consider going there given its lines.)

After taking an antique birdcage elevator to the top floor, I take a seat at one of the tables in the hotel's rooftop restaurant, which has iconic views of the buildings and bay of Old Havana. The arduous process of connecting to the internet must block Cubans at each step and limit their access. Even though it is available, how could they afford an internet card given the meager salary that they earn? Why do only foreigners squat on the sofas in hotel lobbies to use the internet, even though they aren't hotel guests? Considering this striking inequality makes me queasy.

The waitress approaches and asks if I would like something to drink: "*¿Quiere tomar algo?*" She's neatly dressed in a classic black-and-white uniform befitting a Parisian bistro and seems solemn.

I quickly scan the menu and order a mojito, Cuba's classic cocktail.

While I wait for my cocktail, I walk to the edge of the terrace and admire the sunset and golden rays flooding Old Havana, painting it sepia. The hotel's name, Ambos Mundos, means "both worlds," and I wonder if this is indicative of it having been a favorite of gringos when the island was their playground. I feel like I live in two worlds sometimes—in part because I'm both English and French, and in part because I'm a European who spends most of her time in other cultures, often feeling more at home in them than in my own. I don't feel like a tourist, but it hits me that I will never be a local, either.

Between taking in the sunset and busying myself with my thoughts, I still haven't logged on to the Wi-Fi. Cuba is one of the only places left in the world where you can truly disconnect. For all of the lifesaving assistance and efficiency that the internet offers, and the opportunity to interact with the world that it provides, it also has negative consequences. Our online existence can cause a notification overload that leads to stress, anxiety, and sleeplessness.[31] Easily accessible work emails or event invites can lead to a diminished capacity to concentrate, a loss of deep engagement with real life, and a lack of faith in others.[32] Social media can cause us to compare ourselves to others, and cause feelings of narcissism or self-doubt.

Technology has also changed the way we interact, reducing intimacy and human touch. When we are hooked to our devices, we neglect our surroundings and the present moment.[33] The result is that the promise of ease can lure us into loneliness. Although the restrictions that Cubans face with access to technology and the internet are wrong, having a break from them is making me feel more connected than ever before, but to people, places, and experiences—not to my smartphone.

YOSNEL REACHES OUT to take my hand and I anxiously down a few sips of my Cristal as he drags me toward the dance floor.

"Just relax," he says. "You have a lot going on in your mind. Try not to think so much."

We're at Club 1830, a salsa bar along the Malecón that feels like an enchanted garden. Trees illuminated with sparkling lights meet the ocean breeze, and as the waves crash against the sea wall, people spin from the dance floor to the bar and between the tables. I've come here with teachers and students from my school. The whole point is to practice, but I don't feel ready to dance salsa in front of everyone else yet. While everyone else seems at ease, I feel awkward and nervous that I will make the wrong move.

Yosnel starts to lose his patience. "*Sin miedo, sin miedo,*" he keeps repeating, telling me to dance without fear. He can repeat it as much as he wants, but sometimes the fear is too strong and I feel only stress. I just can't seem to find the rhythm. My cheeks are burning. I want to cry.

The MC announces the beginning of the club's show, and I breathe a sigh of relief. Yosnel takes me to the front so I can get a good view and gives me a running commentary of what the dancers are doing.

One girl, very pretty and petite, with freckles, a wide smile, and long, wavy dark hair falling around her shoulders as she spins, dances near our table. She's from our group, and when the song ends, she comes over and in a strong south London accent introduces herself as Sophie, and then gives each of us a hug and a kiss. (Clearly handshakes are rare in Cuba, and I'm okay with that.)

Half English and half Chilean, Sophie can identify with the feeling of belonging to two cultures and is also interested in dance as a social phenomenon. To Sophie, touch, which is ever present in dance, is the most important of the senses. After chatting for a while, I ask her about the influx of German tourists that I've noticed in Cuba, including the many women in the bar right now who are German. When I arrived earlier I asked myself if there was a secret German connection with Cuba.

"Think about it," Sophie says. "German and Cuban cultures are pretty much polar opposites. One is organized and planned, while the other is spontaneous and basically all over the place. It's like Germans come here to liberate themselves and live a totally different experience."

In contrast to many popular conceptions about German rigidity, the Germans around me are dancing and smiling and look to be having the time of their lives. I suggest that perhaps dance affords those who grapple with the stresses of modern life—managing people, homes, decisions—a break from their anxieties. Renate concurs.

"I'm a very independent woman. I have to make tons of decisions every day, and sometimes I want a break where I don't need to control everything. When I dance, someone leads me and I just have to follow. I can let myself go and be carried away by the music."

As I watch the dancers, I think about how dance is such a powerful medium, traversing diverse cultures. Toward the end of the show, the MC invites people from the crowd to join some of the dancers for a *rueda* (wheel). I ask Yosnel what this means. Although I've heard of rueda, I haven't seen one yet.

"So the couples form a circle. See that male dancer over there? He's the caller. His job is to shout out the moves."

So it's almost like he's a dance conductor.

The music begins and the couples start to move around the room. "*¡Dame!*" (Give me!), the caller shouts, and all the men move to the next partner in the circle; then after a few more steps, he shouts "*¡Dame dos!*" (Give me two!), and they move up two girls in the circle. Meanwhile the girls are twirling their skirts and shimmying their shoulders. From above, the scene would look like the view through a kaleidoscope: complex, bewildering, but enchanting. I hope that one day I can dance rueda too.

"TODAY WE'RE GOING to work on improving your rhythm," says Yosnel when I arrive at the salon the next morning.

"You don't have it yet, and you won't be able to dance without it." He takes out his smartphone. "I have an app that can help. I'm going to play each of the main instruments in salsa, and we're going to count together."

There really is an app for everything.

"First, the most important: the clave," he says while pointing to an icon of two small wooden blocks on his phone that looks like the percussion instrument.

He presses play, and I know I've heard this distinctive pattern before, in concerts and recordings. The singer or someone in the audience often starts to clap it, and then everybody else joins in. I've even heard people sitting outside their houses in Old Havana playing it with the wooden blocks as they gaze at passersby.

He taps each icon, one by one, and gradually adds the instruments together. We listen to the full song, and I mentally follow each of the instruments, putting the pieces of the puzzle together.

"There's a clue to figure out when it's the first beat," says Yosnel. "It's the voice of the singer. When they finish a phrase and take a breath, they then come back to sing in full force with all the instruments together. The more you listen to music, even when you're not dancing, the more you're improving your rhythm, and your dancing too."

Much later I will understand what he means. You can practice a dance not only by physically moving through it but also by listening to the music and focusing on it, deconstructing its mysteries like a puzzle until you can paint the sounds in your mind and then use your feet to bring it to life.

After lunch it's time for another class with Esmeralda. She's more willing to acknowledge my progress than Yosnel is, but I don't hold it against him. Every teacher has their own method.

"I can see your rhythm is much better!" she tells me.

"Actually, that's what I worked on today with Yosnel," I reply.

"Ah. The *blanquito*?" she asks, literally referring to him as the white boy.

It seems that people here casually refer to each other with slang based on the color of their skin. In my experience, *blanquito*, *negrito*, *mulato*, and *jabao* (white, black, mulatto, and "jabao,"[34] which is used for a type of mixed-race person) aren't used as degrading terms in Cuba; they're simply used to determine who's who, and even used with affection and pride. I've often heard them in salsa songs, including one of my favorites from Celia Cruz: "La Negra Tiene Tumbao" (The Black Woman Has Rhythm). I had been shocked at first but came to understand that it was being used in a positive manner.

I ask Esmeralda if we can try dancing son. I want to go deeper into my understanding of salsa's Afro-Cuban roots, which I can do by learning the quintessentially Cuban dance son. It's a predecessor of salsa and blends Spanish guitars with Bantu bongo beats.[35]

"Ah, son!" she exclaims, framing her arms around an imaginary dance partner as she closes her eyes. "I love to dance son with my husband. It's such a romantic dance." She changes the music playing from the stereo.

As Esmeralda demonstrates the steps, I see why it's so romantic. The dance includes long pauses during which she sways her hips and visibly savors the moment of each step before shifting her weight to take the next one.

"Okay, now join me."

I'm hesitant, but I follow her, shifting from side to side, allowing my hips to sway like a pendulum. The music calls me—I can feel the rhythm more easily than in salsa, even though many people consider son to be harder. The dance feels almost meditative to me, so I close my eyes and allow my body to naturally flow in sync with Esmeralda's, slowly grounding my feet into the patterned tiles and stretching my body to oscillate from side to side. As I luxuriate in the soft caress of each step, I no longer feel afraid of my femininity.

TONIGHT, RENATE, A few of the teachers from the school, Sophie, Magda (a timid Polish girl whose casa is in the same building as mine), and I will be going to Asturias, a club hidden in a nearby hotel lobby, to dance reggaeton, Cubatón, and other forms of Latin hip-hop.

"Just be a bit careful," says Renate. "The guys in there will probably try something, and they can be quite persistent."

"If that happens, I'll just turn my back to them," I reply.

Renate and the teachers laugh. "You know," she says, "turning your back might be seen as an invitation when you're dancing reggaeton!"

I had forgotten that one of the ways to dance reggaeton is *perrear*, which means to "twerk" or dance "doggy style"—presumably due to the position in which it is danced—a carnally inspired move in which the man bumps and grinds behind his bent-over partner.

I blush. I pride myself on being a very free and open-minded person, but this kind of dancing makes me cringe. I just can't bring myself to dance this way.

Security confiscates our bags at the entrance, and we step through black velvet curtains to find the club packed with people dancing intensely—mostly men, and mostly local, but a few tourists too. Emboldened by a round of mojitos, we head to the dance floor.

A couple of Spanish men approach Sophie and me. They seem charming, but Sophie quickly shoos them away.

"You know I'm a *jinetera,* right?" Sophie blurts out in Spanish.

They raise their eyebrows and retreat awkwardly.

"Why did you say that?" I exclaim. Jineteros—or jineteras for women—are prostitutes or talented street hustlers who use their multiple charms to make money off tourists.

"It's funny. Tourists are so worried about getting harassed or ripped off by a jinetera; I use it to make guys go away." She laughs.

I'm relieved that no one tries to perrear with me. Our group dances with enthusiasm, releasing our heaving energy onto the dance floor. Even Magda has some badass moves. Beyond her short hair, oval-shaped eyeglasses, and khaki pants is an excellent dancer—a girl who dances with *sabor* (literally, "flavor"). I'm reminded to never judge people; we're all filled with surprises.

Eventually, dripping in sweat, feet burning, Magda and I call it a night. At what appears to be a taxi stand, we come across a few tricycle drivers—no cars.

"It's a twenty-minute walk and pretty safe," a teacher from the school had assured us. "But just in case, you should get a tricycle. We never used to have any crime, but lately people seem to get mugged from time to time."

The double-edged sword of Cuba's reforms is that not everyone has benefited equally, leading to widening disparity and desperation. Two girls walking around at four in the morning with smartphones in their hands worth a year's salary or more could be a tempting target. We approach a tricycle driver and give him our address as we climb into the back seat.

"You two remind me of some French girls I had the other night," the driver says in a thick Cuban accent. "They'd had a few too many mojitos!" he cackles loudly, revealing a toothless grin. He laughs so hard that we can't help laughing along with him all the way to the corner of our casa on Aguiar and Teniente Rey.

He points to the sky. "*Mira.*" (Look.)

It is the night of the supermoon, and silver light bathes Old Havana, shimmering over each rooftop and cobblestone. We stand still for a moment, in silence, and absorb the immensity and splendor of the large, round moon. According to NASA, this is the closest a full moon has been to the earth since 1948.[36]

"THERE'S BEEN A change of plan," Renate tells me when I arrive at the dance salon. "Esmeralda can't make it to class this afternoon; she has a Santería ritual."

Renate's expression seems to indicate that this happens often.

"You can either reschedule with her for another day, have two more hours with Yosnel if he's free, or . . . " Renate's face lights up. "What about a reggaeton class?" she asks. "I thought you might like it given how you were dancing last night."

I think it over but tell her I'd planned to learn reggaeton in Puerto Rico. "How about Cubatón given that it's Cuban?" I ask.

Renate makes a quick call and comes back. "Confirmed. You'll do two hours of Cubatón with Daiana. She's a dancer in one of Cuba's best dance groups, Tierra Kaliente." Renate leans in toward me as if about to share a secret. "And in my opinion, they are *the* best dance group."

Later that afternoon I return to the salon after a short lunch break and meet Daiana, a doe-eyed girl with her hair tied into a high ponytail. Despite her youth, her demeanor is professional and impressive. I ask her about Cubatón—I'm not clear what kind of music it is or how it's danced.

"Well, Cubatón can be danced just like reggaeton, but it's more about the music, which is a mix between salsa and reggaeton. If you want, we can go through a basic sequence I made to 'Shaky Shaky,'" she says, referring to Daddy Yankee's latest hit. She takes me through various movements, including popping my chest in an unnatural and uncomfortable way.

I try to follow her, but my chest and back are totally blocked. "Seriously,

Daiana, I can't do it. My brain just doesn't get it. It's like I'm made of stone!" I'm used to dancing reggaeton in clubs, and rather well I think, but now I feel awkward and clumsy.

"Look, I had a German student who took classes with me every day for a week. *¡Dura, dura, dura la mujer!*" she says, recalling how hard and inflexible the woman was. "It just takes a lot of practice."

This is what I have learned so far: practice. It requires patience, perseverance, and passion, but with practice, anyone can learn to dance. And there's no optimum level. Dancing is a skill that can always improve, no matter how advanced one is.

We practice until I'm exhausted from trying to roll my hips and pop my shoulders in all different directions, and then we take a break during which I tell her about an idea I had for Cubatón.

There was a song that was often played at Latin parties in Bangkok, "Hasta Que Se Seque el Malecón" by Jacob Forever, that is about partying "until the Malecón dries" (the title of the song). The song used this Havana landmark to describe a party and a sense of youth that will never end. For the majority of young Cubans, who can't afford to pay an entrance fee to a club or buy a cocktail in a tourist bar, the Malecón is the main place to hang out, usually with a bottle (or two) of cheap rum, and just as the Malecón will never dry—its salty breeze and waves will always crash against its walls—the party must never end.

"I would really love to dance along the Malecón with a group of Cuban friends, just how locals do," I say hesitantly, feeling suddenly inspired by Jacob Forever.

"You know what?" says Daiana. "One of the dancers from Tierra Kaliente created a quite simple routine to go with that song. We use it as part of our shows, so people can follow along to the steps."

I note the coincidence silently, sure that they would never want to perform with an amateur, but then she says she can arrange for us to dance it along the Malecón.

My jaw drops. "But you guys are so famous, and I don't really have the financial means to—" I protest.

"Leave it with me," she says with a smile.

YOSNEL HAS INVITED me to watch him perform in a show in the Vedado district, and Magda doesn't have plans, so she joins me. We have to hunt to find the venue, but eventually locate it: a large dance hall hidden behind unimpressive gray metal doors.

When we arrive, a man at the entrance asks my name and leads me to the second row facing the stage, where Yosnel has arranged for us to have our own table. Yosnel can be hard on me at times, but I find this gesture very kind. We take a seat and order two Cuba Libres, the local version of a rum and coke.

With jumping and popping to Cubatón all afternoon, there had been no chance to eat, and now I'm starving. Leaving Magda at our table, I head to the bar to find out if they have any food.

As I wait at the bar, Yosnel comes up behind me and gives me a big hug.

"Thank you for coming! Is everything okay? Are you happy with the table?"

He seems genuinely happy that I've come to his show and is so warm that it's almost like he's a different person than he is in class. I thank him for the invitation and warm welcome, and then he goes backstage to get ready.

After I put away a small but mighty corn masa *tamal* (tamale), on the house courtesy of a generous man behind the bar, Yosnel and his group members go onstage dressed in bright and colorful costumes. The group represents Cuba's diverse demographics. Yosnel is the only blanquito in the group, as Cubans would say, and they are each dressed in a different color; I presume each represents a different orisha. They start to dance Afro-Cuban folklore, and each dance tells a story or a ritual. Yosnel dazzles onstage, electrifying the audience with his flamboyant style and effortless moves.

After his performance, he comes up to our table with a postshow flush that exudes radiance and pride.

A live band has already started playing, its musicians dressed in refined suits and hats, and a few couples have taken to the dance floor.

"You see that abuelita over there?" asks Yosnel, pointing to a black woman with a short white Afro who appears to be in her seventies. "She's dancing son to salsa music. Look!"

She must have danced son for years—since before salsa even existed. She barely sits down the whole night and seems to be known by the locals, as so many stop by her table to greet her. I hope that at her age I can still go out to a Latin club, alone like her, and dance along to live music.

"Just look at the couples dancing," says Yosnel, pointing to a slightly older couple dancing son, while two others dance salsa to the same song.

A woman appears onstage to introduce the musicians, dance group, and notable personalities in the audience. Then she addresses the foreigners: "You know, we Cubans have so little. We've faced so many hardships. Life here is difficult. We're not rich, but we have the richest thing—our music and dance—and this is what we are sharing with you tonight."

The band breaks into a new song; trumpets blow, and a deep voice bellows from the stage. Only in Cuba. The quality of the music is next-level—I feel like I've been transported into a movie with the Buena Vista Social Club playing the soundtrack. Some of the locals approach our table, including an eccentric old man who alternates dancing between me and Magda, showing off funny faces and moving his feet so fast it's almost like he's hovering above the floor. His craziness makes us feel alive, and we continue to dance with him until we're left breathless from laughing and dancing.

When Magda and I head out, we search for a taxi but can't find one. We stop at a small pizza shop and ask a young man behind the counter if he knows where to grab one.

"There are no taxis around here, but I can drive you home. I'm finishing my shift. Just pay me whatever you paid to get here."

I have come to admire the flexibility of the people I've encountered in Cuba. It's part of their philosophy of *manejar*: to manage when things are difficult. It also doesn't cease to surprise me that getting into a stranger's car is normal and generally considered safe.

As the man drives us, he tells us about his cousins who live in Miami and what a different life they have compared to his own. He wants to leave the island, like so many other Cubans, in search of a better life. I've heard this before. In Europe we take for granted our access to food and upward mobility, but dancing and music are not valued as essential facets of a fulfilling life. I wonder if there is a place that offers safety and promise but also access to joy, revelry, and dancing. Why should a comfortable life and one where we can dance whenever we want be diametrically opposed?

IN MY LAST class with Yosnel, he tells me that I've advanced a lot but then quickly hardens his face as if he wants to make sure that his compliment doesn't stop me from continuing to work hard. To say that he's been tough on me would be an understatement. He makes me feel like I'm doing everything wrong all the time no matter how hard I try. But it's also good to feel that my efforts are recognized, even though I still have a long way to go.

There's no time for a lunch break between my class with Yosnel and my class with Esmeralda, just fifteen minutes to relax on a dusty green couch in the hallway. When my second class starts, Esmeralda and I go through the steps of son again. I feel so at ease with her; we have fun dancing to the music—our hips swaying from side to side with our eyes closed. I can feel that son has taken over all my senses and become a part of me.

"You've got it," says Esmeralda. "Now just enjoy it. Savor it."

I tell her about the night before, and how I saw people dancing son and salsa to the same music.

"Of course it's possible," she says. "And what's more, I can even show you the ten main dance styles of Cuba in one single reggaeton song."

She changes the music on the stereo and dances one style at a time, calling out their names and adapting the speed of her steps. Esmeralda shows me that it can be possible to dance many different styles to the same song—each a different thread to form a rich tapestry when combined. It leaves me with a harmonious picture of how our differences as people, regardless of our backgrounds or origins, can be woven together by a single melody.

When Esmeralda suggests a break, I realize that my energy is suddenly extremely low. I'm craving something refreshing to give me a boost, something like a Coca-Cola. It's officially banned and illegal to buy or sell in Cuba,[37] but you can sometimes get ahold of it in tourist shops, bars, or restaurants—but only to be consumed by foreigners, not Cubans. Outside the United States, Cuba was actually one of the first countries to have a Coca-Cola factory, when Coca-Cola expanded its operations abroad in the early 1900s, but it was banned shortly after the revolution and later restricted by international sanctions.[38] I ask Esmeralda where I can find a Coca-Cola close to the salon, assuming there might be a tourist restaurant or bar nearby.

"Try the blue shop opposite. I'm sure they have it," she says.

I go out onto the stone balcony and lean over the railing to take a closer look. I walk past that shop every day and always see lines of locals, many of them holding small white papers. I've pegged it as a ration shop where people exchange coupons for food—surely, they wouldn't have Coca-Cola.

I should trust my own instinct, but Esmeralda insists, and given that she is a local, I assume she knows best. I head down to the blue shop and join the line, which is really more of a mass of people waiting around and waving white papers, gesticulating and talking loudly at the women behind the counter who sell fluorescent cakes baked in bulk. One of the women behind the counter looks at me suspiciously, probably wondering what I'm doing there. Finally it's my turn.

"Do you have Coca-Cola?" I almost whisper, embarrassed.

"*¡¿Que?!*" (What?!) replies the woman, looking at me like I'm insane.

"No. We don't have any of that here."

I nod, ashamed. "Any cold drinks maybe?"

She points impatiently to the fridge.

"I'll just have a bottle of water," I say, taking out bills of CUC.

"No. We don't accept CUC here, only moneda nacional," she says, rolling her eyes.

Of course the ration shop only accepts the local currency. I leave the shop and walk around the next few blocks feeling like a stupid gringa desperately looking for her imperialist soda.

Eventually I come across a small shop, which has no more than three items neatly laid out under a glass cabinet, and a fridge.

"We have tuKola," says the woman behind the half-empty cabinet, pointing to a red and blue can. This soda is made in Cuba and is its most popular. Its name translates to "your cola."

I buy one and feel relieved by the metallic sound of the cap snapping open. A sip reveals that it tastes almost the same as Coke.

Once back at the salon, I tell Esmeralda and the other teachers what happened. They howl with laugher, and despite my embarrassment, I end up laughing with them at my search for a symbol of capitalism in a communist ration shop.

Back at my casa, I entertain Lia with the story of my Coca-Cola debacle. I pride myself on being sensitive to local life, and this felt like a slip-up. So I ask Lia to tell me more about the rationing system.

"Every family gets a book every month called the *Libreta de Abastecimiento* (Supplies Booklet), or *Libreta* for short. It has coupons to exchange for coffee, eggs, beans, and rice, and also other items like cooking fuel and even cigarettes. But to be honest, the quality is really quite low. The coffee, for example—it's barely drinkable so I buy a better one on the black market."

Suddenly, a voice shouts from outside, interrupting my thoughts.

"Hold on a minute," says Lia. She walks into the kitchen and comes back with some sort of apparatus made out of a plastic bag, laundry clips, and a rope, which she then takes out onto the balcony. I follow her, curious to see what's going on. She puts a few notes of moneda nacional into the bag and lowers it down to the street, where a man takes the notes and replaces them with bananas.

"What is this?" I ask, fascinated.

"This is how we do things here. It avoids us having to go down the stairs to the street or them having to come up." She pulls the rope back up.

I nod, impressed by the balcony economy.

THAT EVENING I treat myself to *langosta*, a small rock lobster from local waters. It's so inexpensive for me, but I know the average Cuban may never have the chance to taste it, which leaves me with a feeling of unease. I discreetly head out alone and pick a chic terrace restaurant not far from Plaza de la Catedral, one of Old Havana's most magnificent squares. Musicians play romantic boleros and son, filling the balmy evening air.

All of a sudden, the dramatic sound of trumpets and drums floods the plaza; it isn't salsa—it sounds more like a procession. I look back and see a number of priests and members of the public marching and holding up banners and candles. The music sounds solemn, as if it is grieving a loss. I ask the waiter what's going on.

"Today is the anniversary of the founding of the City of Havana," he replies.

Every November 16, the traditional procession marches to the Templete—a monument that symbolizes where the city was born—and then walks three times around the ceiba tree where the very first mass in Havana was held.[39] Tradition calls for every participant to ask for three wishes as they walk around the tree, throwing a coin into a fountain each time.

After paying the bill, I walk home in the moonlight, losing myself among the crowd in the solemn procession, and for a moment, I feel like I am part of it.

AT THE LOBBY bar of the Hotel Florida, set in an iconic colonial building on Obispo, the salsa dancing never stops—and neither do the mojitos. The room is small, but what it lacks in space it makes up for in atmosphere. Tonight a group of us have come to drink in the scene and join the bustling crowd. The moment we arrive, a young man approaches Magda and whisks her off to dance.

Renate fumes. "She can't be dancing with him! He's a jinetero!"

Living in Thailand, I grew accustomed to seeing older foreign men with very young Thai girls, but here I see so many older women with young Cuban guys. One woman in her late sixties and a guy young enough to be her grandson are making out like teenagers on the sofa. *At least they're using each other*, I think to myself. But then I spot a woman in her early forties who seems quite innocent and blindly enamored by her Cuban boyfriend. I hope for her that she won't fall victim like all the others, but it's probably too late. Luckily, we are out dancing as a group, and I can reduce the risk of falling victim to a jinetero by dancing only with our teachers.

Yosnel takes me to the dance floor, and for the first time I dance without feeling mortified. I drop my shoulders and let my hips loose, transported by the blasting trumpets and the sweaty atmosphere—until he releases my hands to burst into a provocative rumba solo. As he rapidly circles his hips and grins widely, I stand alone awkwardly deciding what to do with myself. After a flash of panic, I start to add my own touches to a timid basic step, giving way to my own nascent style. I'm actually having fun. When he takes my hands back into his, he leads me through my first ever double spin. The moment is incredible, like I'm almost reaching that feeling of elation I've been searching for—liberated from my thoughts and carried by my heart, the music, and my feet.

Yosnel and I arranged to meet up to practice dancing son together and film a video of it. So far I've only practiced the basic step alone, with guidance from Esmeralda. Now I want to dance it with a partner, and Renate booked us one of the school's best spots—Maria's rooftop. There's nothing extraordinary about it at first glance, but it has the magic of a typical Havana home with a tiny staircase, sheets hanging on the surrounding balconies, and the neighboring buildings glowing from the rays of the setting sun.

Maria rented her rooftop for just one CUC an hour. Sadly, in her eighties, she has started to become frail and is slightly losing her mind. She interrupts us a few times while we are mid-dance, trying sell us bags that she has knitted and insisting on offering us lemonade so sweet that you could become diabetic in just one sip.

We begin by rehearsing some of the steps I learned with Esmeralda.

"She's got it, don't worry," Esmeralda had assured him when he asked her skeptically if I had the basic step down. Her encouragement allowed me to flourish, while his doubt fuels the doubt that I have in myself.

"We'll try *el tornillo*," says Yosnel. *Tornillo* means "screwdriver," but in son it's a move where the woman takes the entire weight of the man in her forearm with grace, slowly circling him while he turns and balances on one leg while the other reaches up in the air.

I inhale the femininity, confidence, and grace gained from my classes with Esmeralda. I know I can dance son on my own; now I have just one hour to learn how to dance it with a partner, and a demanding one at that.

Unfortunately, throughout the practice, Yosnel becomes more severe, tapping my back if I move the wrong way and stamping his foot loudly if I miss the beat. I'm trying as hard as I can, but there's no doubt that I'm disappointing him. All I feel is shame and an ache in the pit of my stomach that tells me that I'm just not good enough.

"You know what? I don't think we should even include this step. You can't do it properly," he says dryly.

"Please, Yosnel, it's such a classic move." I plead, devastated. I feel like I have failed.

He tells me sternly that he doesn't have time for this.

We practice all the steps one last time before we film. After, I take a deep breath and go to get changed into a floaty white dress that almost matches the bedsheets hanging from the surrounding balconies. I'm so distraught that I emerge with one strap over my shoulder and the other under my armpit.

Halfway through the first take, I accidentally step forward, colliding into him rather than flowing backward with him. It's something I kept getting wrong in the earlier practice. Even though it is a logical step, my subconscious just doesn't want to follow. He stops abruptly and takes a step away from me.

"I already told you not to do that step that way!"

I feel my patience dwindling. His perfectionism is invalidating, and there's no one to stand up for me except myself. A sudden strength rushes through my body like lightning; it feels fiery, golden, glowing with will and determination. I roll my shoulders back and hold my head high. I calmly remind Yosnel that I'm a beginner. I'm never going to dance perfectly, and that's okay. I will make mistakes, and I need him to let me make them until I can get it right.

"Let's just dance to the entire song without stopping," I beg him, exasperated.

"Fine," he snaps.

I brush his reaction aside and let myself be carried away by the song "Venenosa" (Poisonous Woman) by Alexander Abreu and Havana D'Primera—one of Cuba's finest bands.

Verdad que cuando caminas, se enciende la carretera.
Y si estás llegando al baile, se alborotan tus caderas.

(It's true that when you walk, the highway lights up.

And if you're coming to the dance, your hips start up a storm.)

The woman of the song might be venomous, but my God, is she empowering. I decide to channel my *fuego* (fire) to become more *venenosa* myself.

As we move, a couple watches us from one of the nearby balconies. For a moment, I see us through their eyes as a sort of romantic apparition: dancing son on a golden rooftop dressed in white, among the sheets floating in the breeze. Before the song comes to an end, the couple heads up to their own rooftop and joins us in the dance.

THE FÁBRICA DE Arte Cubana (Cuban Art Factory) perfectly embodies Havana's growing hipster scene. Housed in an old cooking-oil factory in Havana's modern Vedado district, it's an impressive cultural center with exhibitions, bars, concerts, and events. To get there, I take a *colectivo*, a shared taxi, that runs from Old Havana to other districts along three main avenues, which you can wave down and then get off at the closest street. People usually pay for this in moneda nacional, but having not been able to get ahold of the local currency, I pay one CUC, just over the fare, and get off to walk and meet Sophie on the corner of Calle 24 and Línea.

"This place is packed on the weekends," she says. "It's where all the young hip Cubans come, and sometimes it takes forever to get in."

Luckily there's no line, and as we walk inside, I'm taken by the bright paintings, abstract portraits, and modern light installations that bathe the room in a scintillating glow. This is the new and emerging Cuba, and it is creative and colorful.

We step onto a patio and fall upon a group of tango dancers. It's surreal to watch how delicately they glide, like ghosts. We watch them in silent wonder and then head back inside through a corridor covered in paintings. It leads us to a large room with images projected onto the walls and, finally, to a bar.

After sitting and chatting into the night over three rounds of enormous piña coladas, I call it a night. It's already 2:00 a.m., and thanks to Daiana's efforts, Tierra Kaliente has agreed to dance Cubatón with me on the Malecón tomorrow.

WE WILL MEET in front of Hotel Inglaterra at Parque Central and have planned to dress in the colors of the Cuban flag, but I still need to figure out what I'm going to wear.

I fuel up over brunch with Renate at a new hipster Havana café, which, according to Sophie, is one of only two in the city where you can find a decent latte. The coffee and food are not what I had expected; they are what you would find in a hip part of Brooklyn, and we enjoy a freshly pressed juice, perfectly poured latte, and avocado toast. I'm fully aware of my privilege to be able to eat out half the time in tourist restaurants. My experience with local people has made me appreciate this kind of food, which I have taken for granted until now. Even for foreigners who live in Cuba, the food shortages mean that getting ahold of the simplest items can be very complicated.

Sophie had told me that she spent five days looking for eggs, and when she finally found them she was asked to buy them in bulk. "It was thirty-three eggs or no eggs," she'd said with a shrug.

A man with a trolley bag walks into the café and toward the kitchen. Renate follows him with her gaze. "He's one of those guys who find stuff," she says hurriedly. "That's how these restaurants get all these ingredients. Even your casa, they have someone who supplies them with bottles of water, toilet paper, and other things. I need to find out where he found this milk. Can you believe that I've been looking for fresh milk for a week? I've already been to four supermarkets in Vedado!"

While staying at Lia's casa, I've never needed to go to the supermarket and buy things. The breakfast was enough food to last me until dinner, and the fridge in my room had been stocked with water bottles for purchase. But I've had to move to a new apartment, so I decide to stop at one of the small shops on Obispo. It's probably the most touristic street in town, so I assume they will have more supplies than other places. But what I find is the familiar sight of a few lonely items lined up neatly below glass cabinets and just one bottle of water on a shelf behind the counter. I rush to the cashier, praying that the tourist couple in front of me isn't going to buy it.

"You go ahead," says the woman. "We're still looking." After a sigh of relief, I walk home cradling my bottle of water preciously in my arms. This is only a glimpse into the reality that people live here.

Breakfast completed, I need to figure out my outfit for dancing on the Malecón and pull myself together; this will be another day of filming. I am confronted, however, with the unfortunate truth that my hair is a mess. I also have to deal with the hole in my shoe that I've been walking with for days. It's something that a Cuban wouldn't be caught dead doing; the scarcity of goods, including shoes, means that Cubans take extremely good care of the few things they have. I ask Lia to borrow a thread and needle to repair the hole and almost feel ashamed that where I'm from, things are treated as disposable and replaceable.

I get back to Lia's and ask her if I can borrow her hair-dryer for the next couple of days, but a new tenant, a Hungarian guy, has claimed it. She suggests that I get a *peinado*—a wash and blow-dry—and recommends a place nearby.

"Ask for Aldea," she tells me, "and tell her that Lia sent you—they'll probably do it for five CUC."

I like the idea, so I head down Calle Muralla to find the hairdresser, rejecting a marriage proposal from an old man along the way. Arriving at the salon, I ask for Aldea, who eyes me suspiciously.

"Ten CUC," she says firmly.

After I try to negotiate, she won't budge. I hesitate. She might be ripping me off, but I'm also running late and need to wash my hair and get going. I'm also intrigued and would quite like to experience a Cuban hair salon.

Inside, women gossip over manicures. Towels with strange purple stains cover the floor, and bottles that smell like bubblegum sit on the counter. Aldea takes me to the shampoo sink, also covered in stains, and I start to fear for my blond hair. I recall Sophie telling me that she comes with stocks of her own shampoo in her suitcase, given the lack of quality products.

I sit down in the shampoo seat. A man crouches at the feet of the client next to me. He opens a canvas sack to reveal a stash of onions and a local fruit, perhaps mamey, which grows red in Cuba and tastes like something between an apricot and a sweet potato. The experience is already interesting.

After the shampoo, my hair is thankfully still the same color. Aldea then sits me down and gets to work with her brush.

A visitor stops by, a lady wearing a beige *aduana* (customs) uniform who seems to be good friends with Aldea.

"Ah!" Aldea screams, her face lighting up. She tells me, "One moment," as if she needs to take an important phone call.

They scuttle arm in arm over to the reception desk, excited to catch up as they go to scribble something down on a piece of paper that seems like a recommendation of a place or person, and they continue chatting for more than ten minutes.

Aldea finally returns. But just moments later the next visitor arrives— this time a woman selling smuggled products. The irony! A visit from customs followed by the arrival of contraband. She pulls out family-sized boxes of Colgate toothpaste, mouthwash, and Palmolive soaps. The staff, including Aldea, who has ditched me once again, begin scrambling over the products while the contraband lady frantically passes a notebook around for people to record their selections. She announces the products she will be receiving next week. An ordinary trip to the hairdresser has become a window into Cuba's black market—where soap is currency and mouthwash is imported by mules.

WHEN I GET to Hotel Inglaterra, I see that Daiana has already arrived and is waiting for me. I rush toward her. The whole hairdresser experience took much longer than I'd expected it would, but at least my hair looks pretty good. The other members of Tierra Kaliente arrive one by one, except for la maestra, the leader of the group, Karelia Despaigne, who is famous in the world of salsa. "She has another thing now, but she's going to join us later," says Daiana reassuringly.

After negotiating with multiple vintage car drivers around Parque Central, we settle for an old Cuban taxi and head to the Malecón. The perfect spot faces the US embassy, a horseshoe-shaped part of the wall that will shelter us from the breeze. "*Ay, amiga*" (Uh oh, friend), says Daiana, worried. "I'm not sure if we can film here. There's a lot of security at the embassy, and they may not like it."

"Look, we're not filming their building, but the Malecón, which is a public place. If anything happens, I'll take the blame," I say decisively.

We go through the dance routine that I learned with Daiana. I really enjoy the change from partner dancing to taking my own steps, popping my chest, and shaking my hips. We jump on top of the Malecón and follow the same steps as we dance in a line, the waves crashing behind us.

Karelia arrives, her dark curls falling around her face as she runs to join us. She has a unique look—being half Cuban and half Ukrainian—and an energy that is both powerful and delicate at the same time. We jump off the wall to join her, and she leads us through a whole routine. Every move looks different when she does it—it's like her body interprets each step with her own tantalizing style, accentuating it to be more raw, sensual, and fun. I struggle to keep up, dancing with a two-second delay behind the group.

With each song we dance, the sun sets a bit further and the wind blows a coat of salty mist, or dew, onto my face and hair. My hairstyle is destroyed by the crashing waves and wind, which makes Aldea's work a victim of the Malecón. I embrace the experience anyway. *When again will I get the chance to dance on the Malecón with Cuba's best dance group?* I allow myself to just dance—with or without mistakes. We wave our hands in the air, stomp our feet, and pop our chests as we jump in 180-degree turns.

After a while of group dancing, we gather in a circle and take turns dancing one by one. Karelia shakes her ass with isolated movements and a level of diligence that I have never witnessed before, and one of the male dancers starts to break-dance. It hadn't even occurred to me that I would have to perform a solo. I dread it as I wait for my turn, but then I allow my hips to grind and lift my arms above my head to roll my body like the waves and wind. Something blocked inside me starts to shatter, allowing me to break free of an oppression I have been holding. I couldn't feel more alive.

AFTER QUICKLY STOPPING at an ATM and Hotel Florida to squat in the lobby and use its Wi-Fi, I head to Parque Central to find a colectivo to take me to the Museo Nacional de la Danza (National Museum of Dance), which I've read is the only dance museum in all of Latin America (a fact I find surprising considering the importance of dance in the region). Only private taxis seem to stop as I frantically wave my arm out. Some tourists ask me if I'm at the taxi stand, and I politely motion them to cross the street to the tourist taxis, explaining that where I'm flagging a car is for locals only (as if I were one). A few colectivos come by, but none headed down Línea—the avenue I need to get to. At last a rusty old car stops, and the driver looks at me through the window with raised eyebrows.

"Línea and Calle 11," I say confidently.

He nods, motioning for me to open the door and sit in the front next to him. He's young, with a Cuban accent so thick it's barely comprehensible between the blasting reggaeton music and the sound of the grumbling engine.

"So what do you think of Cuba?" he asks, turning down the music slightly.

I reverse the question and tell him I'm curious to know what he thinks of Cuba. It is obvious that things are changing, but in what direction are they going? Toward what future?

"Life here is hard. People struggle to find food sometimes. Can you imagine me, as a colectivo driver, nothing fancy, I make more in a day than most people do in a month." He shakes his head desolately. "Something's gonna change. I don't know what Fidel and Raúl have in mind, but we can't continue like this."

No other passengers join us on Línea, and we come to a stop opposite the museum. I find no change left in my wallet and resort to pulling out a twenty-CUC bill awkwardly from my bra.

"I'm so sorry, this is all I have. Any chance you have change?"

The driver smiles. "Don't worry, it's on me. Enjoy the museum."

I can't believe what has just happened. Nothing in Cuba is free; they need every CUC or peso they can get. I'm not sure if it's the revolution, the regime, or manejar, but Cubans seem more generous to me than many people who live in abundance.

The Museo Nacional de la Danza houses collections dedicated to Alicia Alonso—a Cuban icon and cultural figure of the revolution. She founded the Cuban National Ballet in 1948 and was later given funding by Fidel Castro, who wanted to expand the country's cultural programs.[40] She was Cuba's *prima ballerina assoluta*, a title indicating her status as Cuba's top ballerina, and has been hailed as one of the best ballerinas of her time across the globe.[41] Alonso suffered from partial blindness her entire life, and her dance partners had to whisper cues to her while invisible strings and blaring lights guided her onstage.[42] Though her health and vision deteriorated, her spirit remained undeterred; she could accept her failing eyesight, but she couldn't accept a life without dance.[43]

In interviews, Alonso would say that she danced not only with her body but with her mind as well.[44] My dance journey has so far been a love-hate relationship between my mind and body. Mastering a step requires intense concentration and deliberate practice, and sometimes distracting thoughts or self-doubt hold me back from dancing in a relaxed, authentic way, or even smiling while dancing. Sometimes my mind and body feel out of sync—fighting each other to reach different goals. As I learn increasingly complex sequences, the necessity to meld my body and mind feels more urgent. I need to first visualize myself dancing the steps if I want to have any chance of performing them with a sense of ease or flair. To do so takes practice, time, and care. The blisters on my feet might be more visible to outsiders, but the shifts inside my head—the clarity, confidence, and focus—feel just as important. They allow my body and mind to be in tune with each other, and when they do, I find that I reach a rare, momentary bliss.

"WE DON'T HAVE much time," I say to Yosnel seriously. "If I make mistakes, just let it go and let me dance."

It is my last night in Havana, and we're going to celebrate by dancing salsa into the early hours at the Hotel Florida. After sweet-talking the manager, I managed to convince him to let us inside for half an hour before they open so we can film a video of us dancing together.

Yosnel nods, seeming to acknowledge my trauma dancing son with him a few days earlier on the rooftop.

We dance an entire song without interruption—a salsa version of a popular song called "Pelearnos un Ratico" (Let's Fight for a Little While) by the Cubatón group Divan. The first time I feel uneasy, the second time I start to get into it, and the third time I finally find the rhythm and flow. My dancing is starting to feel natural, and the feeling of mortification is giving way to lightness and elation.

The doors open and the crowds that have been queuing outside pour into the bar. We head to our table to join Renate, Sophie, her friend Yoendrys, and a few other students and teachers. When a salsa version of Ricky Martin's new song starts to play, Yosnel and I look at each other and then rush to the dance floor. I feel less pressure now, and with each song

I'm not only more relaxed, but I also improve. Now that the classes and videos are over, we can really let go. This is one of our favorite songs, and we spin and twirl while singing along. In a way it's a shame that this dance isn't recorded, but that's why it's so special—without cameras around it's natural, joyous, and spontaneous. We hug at the end of the dance. I'm going to miss him. Despite his harshness and tough love, thanks to him I have advanced from being barely able to do a basic step to being able to dance confidently in just a week. I look around and see that many of the couples aren't doing even half the moves and steps that he has taught me.

He asks me when I'll be coming back, and I imagine that some salsa tourists return every year, but I tell him that I truthfully have no idea. I hand him the internet cards I have left and promise to send him the videos when they're ready.

He nods, gives me one last hug, and steps out into the night.

Sophie and Yoendrys offer to walk me home, and I feel sentimental as we walk on the cobblestones, following the shimmer of the silver moon that has guided me home each night.

I look up at the clear night's sky and spot a shooting star.

"Do you think that Havana is the only capital city left in the world where you can still see the moon and stars so clearly?" I ask. Something as simple as seeing stars has become rare in most big cities. In Havana, you can see them because of how little pollution there is.

We stop and stare up at the sky with respect and admiration. This, to me, feels like a luxury.

"I think it is," says Sophie pensively.

"But for how much longer?" asks Yoendrys. "We're really worried about the election of *el Trump* and how it's going to affect Cuba. We have no idea what our future will look like."

Five days after I leave the island, Fidel Castro will die. Nine days of national mourning will prohibit music, alcohol, and dancing in bars and restaurants. But behind the blacked-out windows of secret salons, Havana will continue to dance.

6

DOMINICAN REPUBLIC

Bachata, Merengue, and Dembow

Someone I danced with in Bangkok once told me that your dance journey begins when you first fall in love with a dance style. Mine began with bachata.

Traditionally played on a patio over a bottle of rum, bachata features weeping guitars that sing tales of lost love and despair known as *amargue* (bitterness). Until the 1980s,[45] it was shunned by the elite as the music of the poor and confined to the countryside, later accompanying rural migrants to the suburbs of Santo Domingo, the capital of the Dominican Republic, before gradually emerging as one of Latin music's most popular genres.[46]

I first fell in love with bachata when I heard "Propuesta Indecente" (Indecent Proposal), the hit song by Romeo Santos that continuously played at Above Eleven's Latin nights in Bangkok. I'd had a vision of dancing to this song in one of Santo Domingo's historic five-hundred-year-old colonial buildings, dressed in gold beneath a warm, glowing backdrop.

But in the Dominican Republic, bachata was repressed for decades—despised, for its rural connotations, by the dictator Rafael Trujillo, who adopted merengue as a national symbol of modernity and a tool for self-promotion and propaganda.[47] After his death in 1961, bachata began to spread on patios and over airwaves. By the 1990s, it had broken social barriers and reached across all sectors of society and even into the United States.[48] Bachata went from censored to celebrated as new artists brought its melancholic style to the world stage.

FLICKING THROUGH THE in-flight magazine as my plane descends into Las Américas International Airport, I find an article dedicated to the global rise of bachata, showcasing photos of three famous artists who popularized bachata on an international level: Juan Luis Guerra with his Grammy Award–winning *Bachata Rosa* in the early 1990s, Romeo Santos ("The King"), and Prince Royce. It feels like a sign.

Francesca, my host, waits for me outside the airport, holding up a board with my name. Her warm demeanor draws me in, and as she drives us, she talks about bachata and merengue and how important dance is to Dominicans, and then she gives me an introduction to the country.

"First and foremost, you need to know about the *colmado*," she says, and begins to describe the small, local convenience stores that are a bastion of Dominican society. You can find colmados on most street corners in the Dominican Republic. They sell everything from household items to mobile phone covers and, of course, alcohol. Their counters double as bars, and people sit on high stools or stand beside them sipping Presidente beers or Chivas whisky. Sometimes the drinks are wrapped in brown paper bags, presumably to cover the store's lack of liquor license.

"But most importantly," Francesca continues, "the colmados play bachata and merengue all day long."

She explains to me that the rise of the colmado as the ultimate social and dancing locale was a reaction to a surge in bars and clubs opening. They would not only charge people for entry but also screen them based on their appearance.

"There's a lot of racism here, you know. If your hair was too curly or your skin was too black it was really difficult to get into a club and go out dancing. So people started to go to the colmado, where they wouldn't be judged, there's no entrance fee, and the drinks are cheap."

We pull up by a colmado that appears on our right so that I can buy some water and also get a glimpse of the scene. At first, I'm intimidated. It's dark outside and the rain is pouring. But I barely get a glance from the locals, who are busy dancing. Although the raucous music blaring from the jukebox and the scratched counter lined with empty bottles of Barceló rum leave me feeling slightly on edge, the establishment feels beautifully raw and honest.

I get back into the car, and Francesca and I continue our conversation. What she told me about racism in the country struck me with surprise. As a white person, I had an understanding of racism that lacked nuance, assuming that the perpetrators of racism are always white. But racism is not confined to a person or people; it is a fervent and deadly virus that breeds, repopulates, and devastates within communities, and within systems at large. In the Dominican Republic, as in other Caribbean nations and the United States, the painful legacy of colorism—the "hierarchy" of color—is so entrenched within the culture that despite the shared and broad African ancestry that exists on the island, people with darker skin often have a harder time finding work and face discrimination.[49]

The legacy of colorism and anti-black racism in the Dominican Republic stems in part from an uneasy relationship with Haiti, the nation that shares the island of Hispaniola. There is a sizable Haitian population in the Dominican Republic, many of whom have crossed the border to escape poverty, political upheaval, and natural disasters. These Haitian migrants, mostly black, have faced discrimination and violence, as well as accusations of taking low-wage jobs from Dominicans.[50]

"Here people don't like to say that they are black," she says with a sigh. "You say you are *café con leche*" (coffee with milk)—she points to her own skin—"or Taíno Indian," a reference to the indigenous inhabitants of the island. "For some reason Dominicans think that the only black people are Haitians."

We drive past an establishment with bright blue glittering lights and bachata music blasting. She tells me it's the car wash, another popular place to dance.

"A car wash?"

"Yes. You bring your car to be washed, and while you wait you have a beer or two. They play bachata and merengue, and you have a little dance to pass the time. It's not the most responsible idea though. It's caused lots of accidents."

The idea of dancing in a car wash blows my mind. *What if people start dancing in other everyday places? In the line at the supermarket, waiting for the bus, or at the coffee machine. Actually, why don't we do that? Dance is an innocent expression of joy, so what's holding us back?*

After driving circles in Santo Domingo's Zona Colonial (Colonial Zone), we finally find a parking spot. We arrive at a quaint colonial house on Calle Sánchez with rooms set around a patio with a small pool and outdoor kitchen. For the first night I'll be staying in a smaller room without air-conditioning, but the cool weather makes it bearable. The problem is the heavy rain, which has caused a terrible mosquito infestation. I'm also worried that I'm coming down with something—I can feel my body starting to stiffen and my bones aching.

But I refuse to be disheartened and decide to go for a walk to get to know the area. I walk past my local colmado, watch the locals dancing, and then head to an Italian restaurant that Francesca recommended. It's a cute place, and I order a Presidente beer and pizza before settling into a sofa to people watch, observing the Dominicans who come in and out of the restaurant.

After I've eaten, I head off to explore the streets of La Zona, as it's called for short, starting with a walk down El Conde, the main pedestrian street, which is lined with shops, cafés, bars, and speakers blaring merengue. Music pours onto the streets, filling every corner of La Zona. I start to worry that I'm getting lost, but after finding my way down Calle Isabel la Católica, I hear merengue playing again and decide to follow the sound.

I turn right and see a little street leading uphill with crowds of people and lights of all colors illuminating the colonial structures that I can't quite make out from a distance. They are the ruins of San Francisco, a monastery built almost five hundred years ago. Every Sunday night the Ministry of Culture hosts an open-air concert here with music by a group called Grupo Bonyé, old friends with a passion for dance and music, especially son. They also play salsa, merengue, bolero, and bachata rhythms into the night.

I walk closer and discover a huge crowd dancing merengue among the ruins. Watching them dance so full of life makes me want to find the courage to ask someone to dance with me. I take a deep breath and walk through the crowd.

I'm surprisingly comfortable being here alone, and I move forward with confidence until I accidentally stumble into a group of men. One of them grabs my arm and aggressively pulls me toward him. I break free and run back the way I came, feeling vulnerable and terrified.

SOMETHING IS WRONG. My bones hurt, my mind is hazy, and I have to drag myself out of bed. Luckily at the end of my cuadra, right opposite my local colmado, is a hipster brunch café. The barista notices that I'm not well and suggests that I get a juice made from *chinola* (a locally grown passion fruit).

On my phone I research dance classes so that I can accomplish my goal of immortalizing my bachata experience with a video. Francesca is confident that I'll find a dance school and teacher very easily because bachata is everywhere. She's also given me the number of a dancer, Carlos, who might be able to teach me. I save his number in my phone, causing a profile photo to pop up of a man with huge muscles wearing nothing more than white (and slightly skimpy) underwear. I cringe slightly—maybe it's a cultural difference? In Latin America, messaging is the main mode of communication, used to organize everything from work events to social activities and bookings, and your profile picture is a showcase of yourself.

I can't resist taking a screenshot and messaging it to Juan, who I know will appreciate the six-pack.

"¡Jesús mío!" (Sweet Jesus!), he exclaims. "That's going to be your teacher?"

Unfortunately, with Carlos's packed schedule, he can't fit me in. I don't have any other clear leads and begin to worry that I won't find a teacher in time. I pay the bill and notice that I'm starting to run out of the modest stash of pesos I'd acquired at the airport's currency exchange counter. I've got to find an ATM, but it's raining and that, in combination with my cold, flu, or whatever it is that I have, doesn't help my miserable mood. To make things worse, every ATM I try declines my cards. I run home through the rain to call my bank, am put on hold for an hour, and then have to explain to them that no, my card has not been cloned. I tell them that I am alone in a foreign country and if they don't unblock my cards, I won't be able to eat tonight. They assure me that they are now unblocked, so I head back out into the rain and end up walking around La Zona in a rampage to try all the ATMs again, at least four times each. None work. I'm desperate and exhausted, fighting to not be demoralized, as the rain pours harder.

My trip has had a rocky start, but I won't be defeated and push myself to continue in my search for a dance school. I begin by stopping by a small dance studio a little farther down my street than I went when I first walked around. It's in one of the square colonial houses, all of which seem to have metal bars on the front door, perhaps so they can be left open for air to flow in but still guard against intruders. I'm asked to wait behind the bars, which I cling onto dramatically for support. It all feels slightly sinister.

The manager finally arrives to let me in. I pitch her the challenge of how to teach me to dance bachata like a Dominican, with substantive sequences, in record time. The result would be captured on video in an iconic local setting. This is the first time that I've actually had to sit down at a desk and pitch my project to someone. She likes the idea (especially because it would promote her studio) and tells me that she has a teacher in mind who might be able to help.

"Have you chosen a location to film your bachata routine?" she asks.

I shake my head no.

"You should go and have a look at that house," she says, pointing across the street at a white colonial house. "They've filmed movies in there and it could be what you're looking for."

I step outside and hear the voice of a woman coming through the bars of the house opposite: "Are you the *joven* (young person) looking for a place to film a bachata video?"

Nodding, I approach the window to distinguish her face in the shadows.

"Come in. I'll show you around!"

I enter the house through a heavy wooden door adorned with elaborate bronze embellishments and step into a hallway paved with Bordeaux tiles and filled with exquisite antiques and delicate candleholders, all lit up by a breathtaking chandelier. It is exactly the kind of old colonial house that I've envisioned dancing in. The woman introduces herself as Sayra and explains that this is a family home where everyone—cousins, aunts, uncles—is always around. She takes me to a lavish but classic dining room with family photos in intricate silver frames and rare objects before leading me out onto a moonlit patio sheltered by deep red bougainvillea.

"*Buenas tardes, señorita*" (Good afternoon, miss), says an older gentleman who has come to join me on the patio. Sayra tells me the man is her cousin.

I'm enamored by the energy of the house, how the relatives interact with one another with kindness and love. The rain seems to have calmed down to a distant drizzle, as has my mood. I wave goodbye to them feeling positive and confident. Little by little.

I'm SIPPING ON another chinola juice at my local café, which has become my new morning routine, when an unusual couple bursts in, giggling. The man is pink-faced, perhaps due to the sun or the DR's abundance of Barceló rum, with fine blond hair and small blue eyes, and appears to be in his fifties. The woman, who is clearly Dominican, has a head full of bouncy curls, wears a tight, strapless pencil dress, and seems to be half his age. They act like teenagers, whispering into each other's ears as they sip their lattes.

It's started to rain heavily again, and I try not to let it make me miserable, though it's far from the tropical sunshine I had expected to find. Turning back to my phone, I continue my search for a bachata teacher. The woman from the small studio on my street tells me that her teacher has disappeared and can't be tracked down, and many other schools don't reply. In the middle of my search, I serendipitously receive a message from Carlos, recommending another dancer, Natanael, from the same school where Carlos teaches.

I add the new contact into my phone and am relieved to find that Natanael's profile picture shows him posing next to his motorbike, and a religious phrase in his status shows him to be pious. I send him a few messages, and it isn't long before he confirms that he can teach me, enthusiastically thanking me for inviting him to be part of my journey. As with most teachers so far, his excitement doesn't seem driven by the extra income these classes will bring—he seems genuinely interested. He tells me to meet him at the dance studio, Centro de Danza Belkis Sandoval (Belkis Sandoval Dance Center), tonight at six.

At the door of the studio, a banner reads: "Dancing can change your life, discover it!" When I find Natanael, he is already surrounded by his students and about to start a class, but he takes the time to chat with me before they begin.

"What kind of bachata do you want to dance?" he asks.

I don't know. How many types of bachata are there?

Sensing my confusion, he puts on a bachata song and calls over one of his students. She demonstrates the variants, including a new and popular style that adds some cha-cha-cha triple steps.

"Now let me see about you," Natanael says, taking my hands and whisking me to the center of the room to dance with him in front of the others.

He takes me by surprise, which makes me stiff, and I timidly sway my hips from side to side before we break into impromptu step syncopations that give a certain swagger to this sensuous, wave-like dance. Dominican bachata is faster and more precise than *bachata sensual*—the style I'd been introduced to in Bangkok and that holds worldwide popularity. But the steamy body waves, pelvic grinding, and neck rolls of bachata sensual sometimes feel terrifying and unnatural to me. I feel drawn to the Dominican style, which has a healthier distance between partners and a more staccato, fun, and playful side. Dancing with Natanael helps confirm this type of bachata is for me. Our small steps add a cool, sharp edge to the roundness of the movements, like punctuation giving structure and panache to long, voluminous strophes.

"Great. You've got the basics. We can start tomorrow. Now go and negotiate with the secretary on the details. When the boss is away, she's in charge." He winks.

I sigh in relief at what felt like an impromptu audition and find the secretary, who offers me a slight discount and agrees to let us use the room when it's free.

I thank her gratefully and perhaps with a bit too much enthusiasm.

"You know," she says hesitantly, "I had a dream once too... When I was young I wanted to go to Tibet alone with nothing more than a backpack. Now I'm married with kids and I'll probably never get to do that. If I can help you with your dream, that's meaningful to me."

UBER DRIVERS HAVE become my best informants, providing me with precious insight into local life, including the sense of humor and way of being. I'm on my way to my first bachata class with an older gentleman in his seventies named Miguel Angel. It's pouring again, and he can't find my school's address as he battles with his GPS. I'm going to be late.

After the typical questions, we get to talking about Dominican music and dance, and I tell him I'm on my way to a bachata class. He tells me that he loves bachata but was always more of a merengue dancer. "But I'm a *viejo* (an old person) now. I stopped going out to the *discotecas* a long time ago! And besides, these days all these young people seem to play is rock, or whatever it is that it's called."

"Reggaeton?" I ask.

"Urgh, yes," he says in disgust. "It's so vulgar." He skips through the radio stations, and we play an impromptu game of "guess-the-tropical-beat."

"Ah, bachata . . . " he says dreamily, settling on a song. "You know I started listening to Juan Luis Guerra over twenty years ago. The lyrics are about bitterness, rejection, and *desamor*."

It's the first time I've heard the word "desamor." It translates literally to "un-love" and is used to define heartbreak, neglect, and love that has come undone. My desamor sent me on my journey, and in a way, dance is a form of processing it, battling it, and shattering it into pieces to allow me to find happiness. My experience with bachata in Santo Domingo thus far has lent itself to reliving heartbreak: the tropical rain weeps just like bachata's classical guitars, and the lyrics weigh heavily on my heart like the gray clouds, massive and unwieldy in the Caribbean sky.

WE PULL UP in front of the school and I rush up the stairs, quickly saying hello to the secretary before joining Natanael, who's already waiting for me in the studio.

"There you are!" he says.

He puts on a song and we dance through all the basic steps.

"Good," he says. "Are you ready to start to build a choreography now?"

Already? In Cuba I'd become used to doing everything wrong. *Is it possible that for once I am finally doing something right? Or maybe it's just that Natanael has a different approach to teaching?*

He sits on the floor cross-legged and plays Romeo Santos's "Propuesta Indecente." A frown forms on his forehead as he listens. I stand in front of him, trying to figure out what's wrong—but he's just quietly imagining the steps in his head. He suddenly jumps to his feet and demonstrates the basic box step, front and back and side to side, before launching into an intricate grapevine step where his feet trace a chain and end with a buoyant cha-cha shuffle. He ends by dancing on the spot, opening his arms in a bird-like floating movement.

This is the first time on my journey that I'll get to join in creating the choreography rather than being told it. I love the creative process—listening to the sound of the melody and imagining its shape, finding a flow in the movement of the different instruments and changes in the musical phrases.

At the end of the class, Natanael offers to share some books on the history of bachata and Dominican dances. His knowledge is as impressive as his professionalism and positivity. The word "bachata" denotes loud, messy, and fun patio revelry and was an insult before the genre became widely accepted. Its origins are in bolero and son, with elements of guaracha (a quick-tempo, almost comic Cuban music) and *guaguancó* (a style of Cuban rumba that combines percussion, voices, and dance), and the latest trend puts emphasis on the cha-cha-cha. What makes it instantly distinguishable is the plucked melody of the guitar that guides the sliding steps, allowing the hips to sway before rousing them to finish the four and eight counts with isolated pops.

When I stop by the receptionist to pay for the class, she comments on what a good teacher Natanael is, confirming my initial judgment. I later find out that Natanael is part of the Ballet Folklórico Nacional Dominicano (National Dominican Folkloric Ballet), and with his wealth of dance knowledge and experience he often gives lectures and seminars on Dominican dance history. He's so humble, kind, and encouraging, only alluding to evidence that he is so accomplished.

TONIGHT I'M GOING on a Tinder date with Fernando, a Venezuelan of Italian heritage who works in the beer industry. Based in Germany, he's in Santo Domingo with the mission of setting up a brewery within just three months. I accepted his invitation based on the premise that he knows how to dance merengue—a Dominican dance style that is popular in his native Venezuela.

Like many other Venezuelans, he had left a spiraling economic crisis in search of better opportunities. Severe food shortages, a lack of medicine, rising delinquency, and inflation put Venezuelans in a desperate situation. I suppose that people like him, with higher education and a descendance that allows for a second (often European) passport, can obtain work in Western countries. For others, the Dominican Republic has become a haven; it has seen an exodus of Venezuelans coming to work in everything from highly skilled industries to bars and, as desperation has increased, prostitution. The people of the Dominican Republic have shown great solidarity with Venezuela by accepting a large number of migrants, which some claim is fueled by a "historical debt."[51] Under the dictatorship of Rafael Trujillo from 1930 to 1961, waves of Dominicans sought exile in Venezuela. Today, Dominicans' welcome of Venezuelans is considered an act of historical gratitude.[52]

I walk up to Parque Colón (Columbus Park), a UNESCO World Heritage Site and the main square in La Zona, wearing skinny jeans and stilettos, and find Fernando in front of the statue of Christopher Columbus. He suggests that we go for drinks at a bar named Beer Market, which seems appropriate given his profession. The bar has high stools on its terrace, where we sit and order local craft beers while this year's top reggaeton hits play in the background. Fascinated by this blond Venezuelan, I ask what his impression of the DR is, how it looks through the eyes of a Latino living in Europe.

"Well, everything works in Germany, but when I'm there I miss the spontaneity of Latin America. Even us meeting tonight for example, we planned barely a day in advance to go out for drinks. In Germany we would have had to plan this weeks in advance for it to be socially acceptable."

Spontaneity. Perhaps that's something that has attracted me to Latin America, or even to living in far-flung locations for the past seven years of my life. Being surprised by something new every day, and stimulated by a different culture, inspires me and makes me feel more alive.

He asks why I'm fascinated with Latin America, and I notice him subtly trying to edge his seat closer to mine.

"Well, when I first started studying in Spain as a teenager, I always felt that Spanish people knew how to live. They take every opportunity to celebrate life and connect with others, regardless of age or background. Then I lived in Bangkok and had a lot of Latin friends who showed me that this was even more true in Latin America. They value close social relationships and cherish them through the expression of love and joy. I find that one of the ways they do this best is dance."

"You know," he says, "in Venezuela we dance at funerals."

We pay the bill and walk around La Zona in search of a merengue bar. Despite his many not-so-subtle attempts to move his stool closer to mine, I had managed to keep just enough distance to be comfortable. I'm confident in many areas but very shy with men. I'm attracted to him and this makes me feel nervous, on edge.

We find a club that's bursting with people and tropical beats and head to the bar to get a round of beers. When the DJ begins to play merengue, Fernando takes my hand in his and leads me onto the dance floor. Our hips shift rapidly from side to side, and our feet grind into the floor. He turns me around and puts his arms around my waist, and I can feel his face getting close to mine. This isn't a dance for him, this is a game. I feel powerless to his advances, and as he spins me, I surrender.

The intensity of being conquered through dance is an almost mystifying combination of romantic domination, subjugation, and triumph. I'm seduced over three merengues and unable to think of a single reason why I shouldn't make a decision that I know I'll regret.

I SLOWLY TIPTOE down the stairs of his hotel—just like the Pink Panther, whose theme song plays in my head. I knew that this was a bad idea. When we'd arrived last night, the security guard had asked for my ID and asked Fernando whether he even knew me. I'd been horrified, assuming he must be bringing back a different girl every night, but with the promise of a budding romance, he'd managed to convince me to stay.

This morning his tone had changed, and he had turned cold. To avoid further hostility and awkwardness, I've slipped out before the break of dawn. Now I try to discreetly get past the reception desk, hoping that the security guard is asleep. But as I get to the door, I find the handle bolted by a bicycle lock. I have to call the security guard for help, and he eyes me disapprovingly. I need to get out of here.

I step one single stiletto out of the building, and I'm wolf-whistled before I even have a chance to step my second foot outside. *Come on! It's only six thirty in the morning!*

I set off on my walk of shame through the Parque Colón and onto El Conde and am accosted three times on the way home. I wish this walk could be called something without the word "shame" in it, a "victory march," perhaps. I wish I felt a sense of empowerment—but I don't.

The sun is starting to rise behind me, and it strikes me that this time of day should be sacred. It should be illegal to harass women at dawn—or ever.

Once outside my guesthouse, I quietly open the padlock around the metal bars of the front door, trying not to make any noise, and tiptoe my way across the patio and into my room. I feel humiliated and empty. Trembling slightly, I climb into my bed and close my eyes.

That night, in an effort to shake off the bad feelings from Fernando, I head to a dance social in an industrial part of town. After dancing a few rounds of bachata, the instructors call for us to dance rueda, as I'd seen people doing in Cuba. My determination to eliminate the lingering negativity gives me the courage to throw myself into the circle, and I twirl from one partner to the next.

In partner dancing, respect is codified. Your partner is not to harm you, make you feel uncomfortable or degraded. Within the boundaries of dance, I can find an intimacy that leaves me enriched, not wrecked. My encounters with the Fernandos of this world make me feel worthless, humiliated, and empty—like an object that can be used and tossed away—and make me want to withdraw into myself. But in dance, or at least most dances, I can lose this inhibition. I can open my heart for the length of a song. With teachers like Natanael, whose integrity and professionalism are indisputable, I feel protected.

AFTER DAYS OF rain, the sun emerges from the clouds, and warm rays of sunlight shine through the window of the dance studio. I'm in an intense morning bachata class, and thanks to Natanael's encouragement, I've progressed to working on more complex spins and sequences for our choreography. We've even managed to complete a short sequence where I fold into him with a double spin before allowing myself to fall backward toward the ground as he catches me firmly at the waist. It demands a huge amount of trust for me to let go and let someone catch me.

I'm not used to relying on anyone else for anything, and this sudden vulnerability feels strangely satisfying. Relieved from the punishing pressure I put on myself and freed from my fear of imperfection, I let myself fall.

Once home, I open a packet of Santo Domingo coffee in the outdoor kitchen and pour it into an Italian espresso maker. The sun finally floods the patio, and the lack of rain seems to have granted a temporary reprieve from the mosquitos. I take my coffee to a bench and breathe in the warmth of the sun.

The phone rings—it's Juan.

"I have a Dominican staying in my house," he says. "He wants me to connect you with his friends so you can meet them!"

I suddenly have three new Facebook friends and a party invitation. One of my new friends, a woman around my age named Leomaira, lives just a few cuadras away and has offered to meet me beforehand to take me to a concert and then on to the party.

There's a huge festival filling El Conde with music and dancing, and I walk through it on my way to meet Leomaira in Parque Colón. Leomaira is a political journalist for an online magazine and leans toward the revolutionary left. She is a natural beauty and wears no makeup; her braided hair is pulled up casually into a half ponytail. Within minutes of talking with her, I feel a connection. I'm relieved to have made a female friend.

We arrive at the entrance of the concert venue, the Spanish Cultural Center, but Leomaira suggests we first grab a beer from the colmado opposite. They're served to us in brown paper bags, and we proceed to drink them on the steps before going into the venue.

The inside of the cultural center is stunning; the colonial building's golden stone walls seem like they are made out of sand. Leomaira introduces me to a group of her friends, who all appear to be intellectuals and social activists, and gives me background on tonight's event.

"The concert tonight is about promoting our African heritage and our links with Haiti," explains Leomaira. "The problem is that Dominicans don't really like to acknowledge their African roots or to see themselves as too black."

The history of racism and colorism in the Dominican Republic is rooted in colonialism and is complex. The DR is the only country in Latin America that didn't gain independence from European powers—it was liberated from Haiti, a black country, which ruled the entire island of Hispaniola after defeating the French colonizers. When the Dominican Republic finally eked out its sovereignty from Haiti twenty-two years after Haiti's takeover of the island, Dominicans had negative associations with anything Haitian—including, and especially, blackness[53]—and many people continue to feel this way today. The 1937 Parsley Massacre, where Trujillo ordered the killing of anyone who was, or even looked, Haitian, was seen as another grave turning point cementing the idea that being Haitian was incompatible with being Dominican.[54] Today, a socially constructed stigma fuels an exclusion that still manifests itself in various nuanced forms.

As the music starts to play, I hear a rawness in the beat of the drums and sense an energy among the audience that seems to be a mix of social activists, humanitarians, and hipsters.

Mid-song, the singer suddenly calls out for unity: "We are one island! Love to our Haitian brothers!" he cries, championing a geographic and cultural communion for the island.

We stay for a few more songs and then head to a house party in the modern part of town.

I WAKE UP tired. I'd enjoyed the party, but it had been rather subdued, with people preferring to get stoned and talk philosophy, when all I wanted to do was dance. I'd come home in the early hours, and the accumulation of the events, alcohol, and exhaustion has left me feeling melancholy.

To battle this sudden feeling of sadness, I put on a cheerful pink dress and enormous sunglasses before heading down El Conde in search of coffee.

The gray sky doesn't stop the speakers from blasting out merengue, and the pounding beat mirrors that of my headache. I take a seat on the outdoor terrace of a café and sip a coffee, beginning to feel relief as I watch the locals and tourists roam up and down El Conde.

An attractive guy in his early thirties with blond hair slows down as he walks in my direction. He turns his head and stares hungrily, looking me up and down with an arrogant smirk. I glare at him from behind my sunglasses, and then all of a sudden his eyes widen in terror and he abruptly turns his head back and power walks away from me. It's Fernando, the Venezuelan. I almost spit out my coffee. He'd walked past me, stopped to check me out, recognized me, and then run away without even saying hello. *¡Idiota!*

Why do men behave like flagrant philanderers and then refuse to confront the consequences of their actions? Why am I even a consequence? A few moments later, he walks back, this time keeping his eyes fixed on the road as he marches past.

Part of me wants to ignore him, and another part wants to get up and slap him. He doesn't even deserve any more of my attention, but I also don't want to let him get away with it. I opt for a compromise and text him.

"Did you seriously just walk past me without greeting me?"

The act of *saludar* (greeting people) embodies a sacred ritual in Latin America, often accompanied by warm eye contact and an affectionate kiss on the cheek. Ignoring someone might be normal in other countries, but here it's brutal and unacceptable.

Revolted, I pay the bill and walk down El Conde in search of stronger coffee. I pick a leafy outdoor terrace on the Parque Colón, with a nice view of the Basílica Catedral Santa María la Menor de la Encarnación, the oldest cathedral in the Americas,[55] and the statue of Christopher Columbus. I order a double espresso. My headache has turned into a sharp migraine, and I sit, massaging my temples.

"Hungover?" asks a male voice coming from the table behind me.

I turn around to see a preppy but chic gringo in a checkered Ralph

Lauren shirt, his legs crossed and his hair slicked back. His eyes are hidden behind a pair of black Ray-Ban Wayfarers. I return his smile and nod politely before turning back to my coffee.

"Tell me about it," he says and stands up to pull out the chair next to him in invitation.

I hesitate, given my current distrust of men, but decide that this will take my mind off things. He asks me about my life and what led me here.

We pry into each other with questions over another round of double espressos. His name is Clarke, and he describes himself as a former CIA officer turned tobacco trader, with a passion for politics and on the lookout for the next business idea that will make him rich. Reserved and slightly forlorn, he was drawn to Latin America for its expressive character, which is so different from his own. His abhorrence of innocent civilian deaths caused by little-documented air raids where he had been stationed had led him to decide to leave the agency. When he was taken hostage by an armed militia, who chose to throw him out of a car by the side of the road, bound and gagged, rather than end his life, it had been the last straw.

I observe him incredulously. Only at a terrace in a tropical haven, where one can simply disappear and live anonymously, do we share such aspects of our lives with complete strangers over double espressos. He had narrowly escaped torture and death and chosen a continent that best knows how to feel alive.

Behind Clarke I spot Fernando once again awkwardly roaming up El Conde. I find the sight of him so unbearable that I dramatically pull my sunglasses from the top of my head back over my eyes. I don't want to make a scene, but he hasn't responded to my text, and I'm dying to call him out and say hello to make him squirm in embarrassment at his own cowardice. But I'm not a fan of confrontation, and instead I look on in amusement as he nervously scuttles past my table, pretending not to have seen me. I'm so sick of all the Fernandos I've seen in Santo Domingo. *What are Clarke's intentions?*

"Clarke, can I be honest with you? What I really need right now is a friend."

He smiles, quietly puffing on a *puro* (cigar), and nods understandingly as I explain the harassment, sleaziness, and loneliness of the last few days.

"Don't worry, we can be *amigos*," he says and orders a round of Aperol spritzes. Clearly we've evolved beyond our hangovers by now.

"Maybe we could even say that we're *socios*—business associates," I laugh. "We seem to have a similar approach to life."

IT'S SUNDAY NIGHT and my last chance to experience dancing in El Bonyé in the ruins of San Francisco. I'd joined an online group to find people to go with, but it had resulted in my receiving a multitude of private messages from unknown numbers—all men offering to meet me "privately" beforehand. Although I tell them that I'm meeting other people as a group, they keep insisting. Thankfully Clarke has agreed to come with me, and what better personal security could I ask for than a former CIA officer?

"So where are all these men?" Clarke asks as we meet at Parque Colón for beers and street food, apparently amused by the situation.

We go to the meeting point in front of the Christopher Columbus statue, where the four men come to find themselves nose-to-nose with one another and Clarke. They look at me with a mixture of incredulousness and anger, but there is nothing they can reasonably protest. I'd told them that this was just a group outing with friends.

Two of them make excuses and leave, and the other two accept the challenge as we head to El Bonyé. Clarke and I exchange a few glances and walk ahead of them to be out of earshot.

"Be wary of the one on the left," he says in low voice. "He won't give up easily."

Determined to enjoy the night, I try to ignore the awkwardness of our group dynamic. The band Grupo Bonyé is playing. and masses of people are dancing on the golden ruins, bursting with energy and sweltering as merengue beats thud under the stars.

I dance a few merengues with my "friends" while Clarke watches and sips on a glass of Chivas whisky, and the night begins to wind down. We head to the plastic chairs to take a rest and get a round of beers. A couple dances salsa next to us with so much sabor that it attracts my attention. They're the giggly couple from the café who I'd seen a few days ago. I decide to introduce myself and invite them to sit with us.

While squeezing the man's arm, the woman tells me, "He's the *emperador* of bachata!"

The emperor of bachata? I ask myself, watching them curiously as they jump up to dance, still giggling. Later, even though we've only spent a few minutes talking, we exchange numbers and plan to meet for breakfast the next day to talk bachata. Meanwhile, my new friends have successfully approached a group of female backpackers, and we've all decided to head together to Parada 77, a bar nearby where they play bachata. After a few too-close-for-comfort dances with locals and some leering looks from a volatile-seeming suitor, I call it a night and slip into a car with Clarke.

SALVATION: FRESH COCONUTS. One hangover turned into another, and today Clarke and I have met to search for the cure on El Conde.

The days have flown by. I still haven't found my dream venue to film my bachata routine, and it is happening tomorrow. My several calls to the "cousins" from the colonial house have gone unanswered since they became aware of my limited budget—a far cry from what they get paid by Hollywood studios.

"Socio, I don't know what to do," I say to Clarke, almost whimpering. "How will I find a venue by tomorrow?"

He offers to drop me off at a small colonial hotel that might work, just opposite his place, on his walk home.

The operation becomes a treasure hunt. The hotel sends me to another hotel lobby, which appears to be perfect, and I'm ushered into the director's office only to have my request politely declined. Afterward, I meander around La Zona, dropping into every hotel, art gallery, shop, museum, and building that seems like it could have potential. Nothing is right, but I'm told there's one place I have to see—an art gallery.

I arrive and knock at the door, but there's no response. A woman yells, "He's not here today!" Her voice comes from behind the metal window bars of the colonial house next door. She waves me over and insists that I come inside her house. Next thing I know I'm sitting awkwardly at her dining table, threatened by three angry poodles barking at my feet while she shouts at them to leave me alone. It's a strange situation, but I'm used to those by now.

"Ay, *mi amor*, how I wish I could help you," she says affectionately while attempting to tame her angry poodles.

It seems like "mi amor," my love, is used casually in conversations in Latin America, a testimony to its people's fearless expression of sentiments. Unfortunately, I've seen it frequently used before someone breaks bad news.

She asks for my number and offers to call me if she sees the gallery owner, before she waves me off and returns to shouting instructions at her husband.

As I arrive at my last bachata class, I take comfort in the fact that despite my achy feet and lack of venue for the video shoot, the choreography has been going really well and I'm pretty confident that I have it down. I share my woes about finding a space with Natanael, who suggests that I try Lucìa 203, the most famous live music and dance venue in La Zona. I hadn't even bothered trying it. Given its fame, I figured its owners wouldn't be interested.

In the mirror, I can see how fatigued my body looks. I've pushed myself too hard again. I let the exhaustion float me through the steps and surrender to the bird-like arm movements. They make me feel like I'm spreading my wings—wings I hoped to find during this journey.

Suddenly, in the middle of an intricate cha-cha sequence, drops of blood drip on the floor. My dance shoes have rubbed the bottom corner of my big toe until my skin became raw, leading to a tiny but surprisingly deep cut. The sight of the blood, now almost pouring out of my shoe, makes me feel faint, and Natanael rushes to get a wad of toilet paper.

But even after using up half the roll, the bleeding doesn't stop, and the blood stains my favorite green and gold shoes—the first pair of dance shoes I had bought back in Bangkok. I want to cry, but Natanael cheers me up with his positivity and sense of humor.

"Try to get some rest," he says at the end of the class, draping his arm around me. "Don't stress so much."

ON THE WAY home, I call Lucìa 203 out of curiosity, but expecting nothing. To my surprise they tell me that the owner can meet me there in half an hour.

I arrive at the building's silent entrance and thick bolted blue door, which must be sheltering a stream of sound. A woman with long, silky hair approaches me with a large bronze key in her hand. She introduces herself as Iza, the owner, and invites me in.

As I step inside, I'm taken away by the golden colonial stone arches that frame a large outdoor patio adorned with vines and shimmering lights. *This is the place*, I think to myself as I stand silently in admiration. Iza shows me around and explains that the venue is hundreds of years old and often used for film sets, including for a recent Netflix original series.

"Can I get you something to drink?" she asks. She seems to be very friendly but also very direct, and I assume that she would appreciate my honesty. I'm too tired to sell myself or pitch my project to her. I almost want to give up.

"I have to be very honest with you, Iza. This project is a dream that I made true using my life savings. I don't have a Netflix-sized budget for a place like this and don't want to waste your time—"

"I don't want anything," she cuts me off, shaking her head. "The world is made of small things, and sometimes we need more balance in the world." It seems that for her, small gestures of kindness are what balance out success and Netflix deals. I make a mental note to balance out any good fortune that comes my way with my own small gestures.

I want to hug her, but I restrain myself. We end up sitting at the bar and talking for hours about dance and how it shapes society. She offers me the place for the following night and only asks that I tip the security guard.

I'm overwhelmed by her kindness. Like so many other people on this journey, she has no reason to help me, but she does so anyway. Sometimes a decision we make that demands so little from us can mean so much to others. For me, dancing in Lucìa 203 allows me to live another dimension of my dream.

A BLUE SKY greets my last full day in Santo Domingo, making it perfect for exploring. I walk down El Conde and make my way to the cathedral. It has thick coral limestone walls and is filled with ornate religious art, from oil paintings to intricate baroque engravings made of precious metals. The gothic architecture and golden reverberant arcs speak to a long and complex history; the basilica is over five hundred years old, with construction that spanned over two decades from start to finish.[56] [57] These walls have witnessed the pain and suffering of this continent since the moment Christopher Columbus dropped his anchor off the shores of Hispaniola in 1492.[58] They have been a silent bystander to exploitation, injustice, and abuse.

Until now I've only admired the cathedral's imposing exteriors from the Parque Colón, but I knew that it would be full of stories inside.

Treasured by popes and pirates,[59] it has been visited by a variety of guests. It was also once the home of Francis Drake—knight and naval commander to Elizabeth I of England, and a bandit nicknamed El Draque (The Dragon) by the Spanish.[60] [61] He held the city at ransom, ordering its looting and destruction, before sailing away and leaving wide swaths of Santo Domingo in ruins.[62] Now people dance in those ruins.

After the cathedral, I head down Calle Las Damas. On my way I walk past the Panteón de la Patria (Pantheon of the Fatherland), a church converted into a national mausoleum by Trujillo. I stop in a huge square named Plaza de España that sits at the edge of the Ozama River.

In front of me, a group of students line up to visit the Alcázar de Colón (Columbus Palace), built for Diego Columbus (Colón in Spanish), the son of Christopher Columbus who became the fourth governor of the Indies in 1509.[63] Teenagers skate across the square on their skateboards, flying past an enormous Christmas display courtesy of Coca-Cola. It's approaching the end of November, and Christmas is coming. Even the music that blasts out of the big speakers along El Conde has switched to merengue renditions of "Jingle Bells" and other Christmas songs. Commercialized Christmas songs remind me of propaganda, and these renditions have an eeriness that evokes Trujillo's shameless merengue-infused political campaigns.

Contrast breathes everywhere. Behind the stunning stone edifices lie centuries of suffering. Ancient monuments, striking and stalwart, stand next to modernity. A warm Caribbean breeze blows through palm trees adorned by Christmas lights. Somehow, a painful chapter of a continent's history gave birth to an abundance of music and dance that provide happiness and peace. But, of course, the joy is not without complexity—parts of it are vengeful, rebellious, and defiant. Dance was always a form of expression that allows us to find joy in times of despair.

At the Museo de las Casas Reales (Museum of the Royal Houses), which is home to the first administrative headquarters and courthouse of the Americas and Trujillo's former office,[64] I make my way through different rooms that cover the Americas' violent and painful history of colonization, evangelization, and slavery.

Standing in front of an enormous map of the different slavery routes, I take in the sheer scale of the slave trade and the suffering of the people who brought the rhythm of Latin dance from the African continent. The force of it all strikes a blow to me. I have come to learn, and take joy from, traditions such as dance that are born from cruelty, struggle, and resilience. Underneath the sensuality and jubilation of bachata and merengue are centuries of hardship and perseverance. Each dance tells the stories of those who built and fostered it, feeding it with night, music, and sweat. Each dance yearns for home, for freedom, and for the possibility of joy in a world that denies it. Each dance paints the arc of pain, beauty, oppression, and freedom, of home and away, of great sorrow and enduring joy, within a song. As I continue on my journey with these dances, I must honor the arc of their own journeys—through centuries, conflicts, and continents—and with that comes a responsibility to always endeavor onward with hope.

I RETURN HOME feeling humbled and lift my spirits by rehearsing the bachata choreography as many times as I possibly can until Romeo Santos seeps out from my ears.

Rosanna, a professional photographer and keen dancer, offered to help me film the video and has arrived early with her friend and a huge amount of equipment. I make my way down the street and find Natanael standing outside his car. Rosanna recognizes him immediately and, slightly starstruck, tells him she's seen him onstage. It turns out that Natanael is quite famous.

Iza has come to unlock the door and watch us rehearse, and I get changed into a gold two-piece I bought at the salsa congress in New York. It's a shimmering crop top and high-waisted pencil skirt, and possibly the tightest outfit I've ever worn.

Under the golden colonial arches, I find myself stiffening. Natanael makes jokes to try to get me to laugh and relax, but my body tenses up and I feel terrified.

We go through the routine, and I dance with static steps. I'm not even able to smile—my face is frozen in mortification. Rosanna offers me a shot to help calm me down, but I opt to do some deep breathing instead, which doesn't work. *What's happening?* I feel like I can barely move.

"You were fine in the studio. I don't even recognize you," Natanael tells me.

It must be the fear of being watched or judged. There's a camera in front of me that might as well be named the Lens of Judgment, and it's proving to be a powerful barrier. Dance requires reflex and rapid-fire decision-making; fear, with its annoying habit of freezing our brains to the point that we're unable to think or make decisions, makes an unusual bedfellow. I take a deep breath. *I'll never dance this again*, I think, *so I should really try to enjoy it.*

On the third take, I finally soften into my steps, dipping into the delicate tango-infused footwork to add sweeping leg moves and pivots to my basic bachata. I surrender to the music, allowing myself to fall into Natanael's arms time and time again. I find the courage to take the risk, to be vulnerable.

When we wrap up I realize that it's taken far longer than I'd promised Iza it would. In the end I don't even care how the video turns out. It's two dreams accomplished: to dance bachata in a legendary colonial venue in Santo Domingo and to learn to let go.

Natanael gives me a warm goodbye hug, thanks me for trusting him, and asks Jesus to protect me.

I WALK INTO my local café for my last breakfast in Santo Domingo and find Clarke hiding behind his Ray-Bans. He greets me with an air that implies his life is unbearable.

"I need a vacation from a vacation," he says as he kisses me on the cheek and pulls out my seat.

He appears to be slightly hungover after a night at a shady bar in La Zona run by a man known as El Halcón (The Falcon), and muses over what he describes as the bar's strange air of intrigue, seediness, and depression. The truth is that Clarke is becoming a regular there, and now El Halcón and his business partner are texting him with promiscuous propositions. Suspecting an illicit human trafficking operation bringing in Venezuelan prostitutes, Clarke has taken it upon himself to investigate.

"It's 100 percent a trafficking ring. I'm sure of it. And it's a top-down operation. Some people are making a lot of money to let this happen."

I will miss the colorful characters of Santo Domingo, even the more clandestine and sinister ones. In a strange way, I feel like I have become a prisoner of La Zona, wandering aimlessly up and down El Conde like a zombie to the beat of merengue.

It has rained pretty much the whole time I've been in the DR, and there hasn't really been a chance to explore the country. With a few days left before leaving for Puerto Rico, I have decided to escape to the small fishing village of Bayahibe, where I plan to slow down and recover.

"Goodbye, socio," says Clarke. I lean toward him to give him a hug, but he awkwardly steps back, telling me that he doesn't "do hugs." Forever forlorn, he instead offers a solemn wave as we part and go our separate ways.

In the car on the way out of Santo Domingo, "Hijo de la Luna" by Mecano plays on the radio. Its melancholic melody overwhelms me with a wave of nostalgia. The song was released in 1986, the year that I was born. I heard it for the first time at fourteen, when I started learning Spanish. It speaks of the "Child of the Moon," and its sadness never fails to pierce my heart.

Y las noches que haya luna llena,
Será porque el niño esté de buenas.

Y si el niño llora menguará la luna,
Para hacerle una cuna.

(And on nights when there's a full moon,
It will be because the child is in good health.
And if the child cries, the moon will be diminished,
To make him a cradle.)

Raindrops freckle the window. We drive past a few car washes with multicolor disco lights playing bachata as people dance. I want the driver to stop and let me out for one last dance, but this will have to wait for another time.

"**THERE YOU ARE!**" squeals Laura, a marine biologist working at my eco hotel. She takes my hand and leads me inside the local colmado to order a round of Presidente beers. It's my last night in the Dominican Republic. I've been making the most of my time in Bayahibe over the last few days, taking a break from dance to connect myself with nature. I visited the paradise of Isla Saona (Saona Island) in the East National Park—home to crystalline waters, white powdered beaches, and baby hawksbill turtles. (I somehow ended up there with a boatload of Italian girls from a nearby all-inclusive resort and a tour "photographer" who encouraged them to place large pink starfish over their breasts for an Instagram opportunity. Naoko would have hated every second.) I also spent time walking around the village's narrow streets lined with colorful houses, went horseback riding in the jungle to admire bright birds and butterflies, and explored caves glowing with dark blue pools of water. In the evenings, I sat on the hotel's rooftop, watching the sunsets bleed over the ocean and letting the breeze blow through my hair.

Tonight I change into a black dress, swipe on my red lipstick, and venture out to meet Laura at the colmado. I want a night out, to enjoy, make friends, and dance.

The colmado is tiny, and people squeeze inside to order drinks and dance bachata under a mechanical fan that hangs from the ceiling. Its bare walls enclose a scene so energized that it would rival that of any hip club in most cosmopolitan cities. The bar is simple, but the crowd is vibrant. It's the people that make the place.

"It's amazing what you'll find in the colmado," says Laura. "Everything happens here."

The bachata switches to a different kind of music. It almost sounds like reggaeton, but is faster and has a rawness to it, with electronic synthesized sounds and rapped lyrics. Laura tells me the music is dembow, the "Dominican cousin of reggaeton."

I recently found out that the word "colmado" translates to "full," and the scene tonight lives up to its meaning, as the patrons literally spill out onto the pavement and people dance outside. The variety of people ranges from locals to foreigners, retired expats to prostitutes, Argentinian hippies to American backpackers. In a small village like Bayahibe, the colmado is the central meeting point and it seems to attract everyone.

Laura points to a European woman who looks to be in her fifties and is dancing bachata with one of the locals. She tells me the woman lost her husband and children in a terrible accident but refused to leave the country and dances bachata here every week.

I wonder if the dancing heals her. *When you've lost everything, is dance something that can help you come back to life? Can it help you find joy again?*

We spend the rest of the night in a blur of discotheques, dembow, and merengue. Laura introduces me to Igor, a kindhearted Spanish man in his late thirties with a long ponytail, a slapstick sense of humor, and an inclination for rum lemonades and rolled cigarettes. After a nightclub foam party gone awry and a run-in with a tarantula, he kindly offers to drive me home on his motorbike.

I don't know if I should be more worried that I have no helmet or that Igor seems to have enjoyed his fair share of rum lemonades, but I jump on the back of the motorbike anyway, and we swerve out of the Pit Stop discotheque to find our way back to my hotel.

The bike rattles down the road lined with huge palm trees. A sea of stars glistens above me. I let go of the back of the bike and throw my head back as I lift my arms over my head. I can feel my heart beating and my adrenaline pumping. It dawns on me that even if we crash, I'm no longer afraid that life will pass me by without my having lived fully. I've experienced a freedom and meaning that I wasn't sure was possible. My journey allowed this to happen, but not because of the far-flung destinations I've visited. The reason is simpler: I've authentically connected with people, with music, and with myself in a way that has allowed me to truly be present.

I'VE BARELY SLEPT three hours and am enjoying some final moments on the rooftop, soaking up some sun, when my phone buzzes. It's Fernando the Venezuelan, and he's full of regret.

"Please don't tell me I'm idiot," he writes, "but I would die to see you one more time."

I take great pleasure in breaking bad news the Dominican way: "Mi amor . . . " I type, savoring the sweetness of my revenge. "You're too late!" I find a flattering bikini photo and hit send. "I'm sorry to tell you that you are, in fact, an idiot. *Ciao!*" This feels like a victory for women everywhere.

I wrap up the afternoon with a plate of fried chicken and plantains at Mamajuana Café, across the street, and then a car speeds me back to Las Américas International Airport.

I'd arrived in the Dominican Republic sick, miserable, and in the rain. I leave enchanted and empowered. Bachata plays throughout the airport, and I discreetly sway to the weeping guitars as I board the flight.

7

PUERTO RICO

Reggaeton and Puerto Rican Salsa

I'd read in travel guides that Puerto Rico is what Cuba would have looked like if there hadn't been a revolution—a parallel world of capitalism over communism, annexation over embargo, and restoration over disrepair.

I peer out the airplane window and am struck by the bright, glistening lights of cruise ships, highways, and high-rise buildings. San Juan is a short flight from Santo Domingo, but even from above, the contrast is striking.

I feel a sense of having escaped, and a relief that comes with it. *But from where and to where?* I've now been traveling for four months and it's not like I'm on my way home. Upon landing, I text Clarke, who replies with words of wisdom within minutes.

"Don't worry, socio. This is how globe-trotting nomads like us feel—the constant relief of having escaped. Even though it's an escape from another place that we had escaped to."

What are we running away from? Responsibility, a mundane lifestyle, the nine-to-five matrix? I'm now escaping within the realm of my own escape. Is it because we'll never find our home in the world? Or because we're spoiled by our many options? Or maybe, as dreamers, we are always running toward something—toward beauty, freedom, and a way to take hold of the reins of our own lives. If that's so, this journey is about discovery, not escape.

I step out of Arrivals and head straight to the taxi line to get into the first car I find. I'm out of cash and they don't accept cards. The driver refuses to stop at an ATM on our way and instead kicks me out and leaves me on the curb outside the airport with my luggage. I lug my bags up to the top floor of the airport to get cash and wobble back down to try again. This time armed with a wad of dollar bills, I get into a second taxi.

In the car, my driver asks me where I've come from, and I tell him Santo Domingo.

"My country! *¡Soy Dominicano!*" (I'm Dominican!)

He tells me that there are a lot of Dominicans in Puerto Rico, many having come here illegally in search of a better life, but also as a springboard to make it to New York or Miami.

"We thought that once on US soil there wouldn't be as many controls domestically. But security got much stricter after 9/11, and many of us Dominicans ended up staying here."

He asks what I'm doing in San Juan, and I tell him my story: the life I left behind to dance, the countries I've been to so far, and the dances I've learned. I've told a version of this story so many times that it feels like I'm reciting a script that I keep adding on to. When I say I've come to dance reggaeton—Latin America's answer to urban hip-hop—with locals, he frowns disapprovingly.

"You know, reggaeton was huge in the early to mid-2000s. But now people are more into salsa. Salsa always stays in fashion. Be careful if you're going out to dance reggaeton alone here. It might be seen as advertising. You know, that you're looking for something not totally innocent."

We enter Old San Juan, and drive past the Capitolio—Puerto Rico's capitol, where its legislature sits. The building is known as El Palacio de Las Leyes (The Palace of the Laws) and is currently illuminated with sparkling Christmas lights and a colorful nativity scene. And then we pull up to the hotel. I've decided to split my budget between two extreme opposites: three nights at El Convento, a seventeenth-century Carmelite convent turned luxury hotel, and seven nights in a twenty-dollar-a-night hostel. I can sleep pretty much anywhere from a pasture to a palace, but I'm happy to be here. It's the perfect place to relax and reset.

The hotel's cream-colored facade and imposing arched doorway have welcomed guests such as Truman Capote and Ernest Hemingway.[65] The lobby has black-and-white tile floors and a radiant chandelier hanging from the ceiling's dark wooden beams. Potted poinsettias, with their festive crimson blooms and star-shaped leaves, line the entrance of the lobby, where a magnificent Christmas tree, draped in dazzling lights and delicate silk baubles, stands. Soft classical music guides me up the polished marble steps and into a lounge filled with mahogany antiques and religious artifacts from the Conquistador age. An arched patio off to the side stuns with its dangling ivy and patterned Spanish tiles.

A porter accompanies me through the courtyard and up a stone staircase that leads to an imposing wooden door, which he unlocks with a huge bronze key. Behind it lies a world of comfort and luxury. I drink in the splendor of the room: the dim lights and soft music; a set of antique wooden furniture that hints of history, intrigue, and a storied past; and a regal queen-sized bed with Egyptian cotton sheets and soft pillows cradling a rose and chocolates. I shiver in satisfaction and then take off to the lounge to enjoy a glass of wine and gaze at the lacquered oil paintings, rustic wooden sculptures, and baroque bronze lamps. An older gentleman wearing chic chino pants and a checkered shirt sits in a velvet armchair reading the paper and puffing on a cigar. *That could be Clarke in thirty years*, I think to myself. *He would love this place.*

I make myself a hot peppermint tea and take it back to my room, where I enjoy a steaming bath in the marble tub before slipping into the soft monogrammed bathrobe and slippers. I order room service. I have to enjoy every second of this while it lasts.

An hour later, a handsome waiter arrives with a silver tray. Starving, I rush to sit down and eat, but he lingers in my room.

"Can I do anything to make your stay more comfortable?"

I'm salivating at the sight of avocado. "It's really quite okay," I reply, hinting that he should go. But he insists on staying a minute to shake my hand and introduce himself.

"My name is Mateo," he says in a velvety voice. "*Mucho gusto.* (It's nice to meet you.) Is there anything else I can bring you, anything you might need during the night?"

Maybe I've become hypersensitive from the events of the last few weeks, the frequent catcalling and the disrespect from Fernando, but this sets me over the edge. I had run away, quite literally, to a convent to escape catcalls, men dancing too closely, and sketchy guys who see me as an object to use and intimidate. Now I can't even get room service without a side of a suggestive proposal.

I sigh, getting up to open the door and show him the way out, politely saying goodbye. It's possible that he was just doing his job and offering excellent customer service, but he also could have been hitting on me.

Once alone, I devour my dinner and then slip into the luxurious bed.

THE HOTEL HAS a colonial-style patio restaurant on which I enjoy a late breakfast, hiding behind my enormous black sunglasses. Sometimes I have this ridiculous feeling that I'm a female, dancing version of James Bond, waiting for a villain to take a seat at the table next to mine.

I can't help feeling like I'm on the run—living life out of a suitcase, which I unpack in different destinations. It's like I'm several different people at once, with costume changes to help me adapt to each new character and scene. To adapt to my current role, I'd chosen a black dress over a red bikini to match my red nails and lipstick for a simple but dramatic look.

A waiter pours black coffee from a silver jug as I sip a grapefruit juice and remind myself to savor every second of this place before I go back to shorts and flip flops.

In the lounge I make a green tea, and then I head up to the rooftop to soak up the sun and start researching dance schools. From here I can see the Catedral Metropolitana Basílica de San Juan Bautista (Metropolitan Cathedral Basilica of St. John the Baptist). At more than five hundred years old, it's the second-oldest cathedral in the Americas. It's almost as if I'm following the cathedrals in chronological order.

I want to find a place to learn the fundamentals of reggaeton. I'd had so much fun dancing to reggaeton in Bangkok, especially at DJ Pepe Pepelucho's infamous parties at Havana Social, where the dance made me feel voluptuous and empowered. But my desire to learn reggaeton runs much deeper than wanting to dance along to some of my favorite hits in a nightclub. It's a way to learn about San Juan's urban underground life from the early 1990s through today and a worldwide phenomenon that has affected ideals of beauty, body image, and feminism.

I've watched quite a few reggaeton music videos, and while initially horrified by the objectification of women in them, I'm curious to know what they mean in terms of these ideals. I also want to learn steps that will improve the way I move my body and push me to new physical limits. After drafting a message in Spanish, I send it to ten schools over social media.

My phone beeps, and to my surprise it's a reply from my top choice among the ten dance schools I've reached out to. They can give me a reggaeton class this evening. The school is too far to walk to, but I can get there in about twenty minutes by car.

Victor, my driver, a refined and handsome man who looks to be in his forties, asks me the standard taxi questions, and I give him the rundown of my journey so far. Then comes the awaited question: "So what dance did you choose for Puerto Rico?"

I shyly mumble that I'm here to learn reggaeton. For a moment he seems bewildered, but then he starts to laugh.

"It's very *popular*," he says, referring not only to its popularity but also to the other meaning of the word "popular" in Spanish: that something belongs to the masses, or those from a less privileged socioeconomic background.

"Everyone likes it, even if they say they don't," he says, looking at me in the rearview mirror. Then, as if confessing, he whispers, "I love reggaeton. *Se te mete por los pies*."

In English this means "It gets under your skin." But the literal translation is "It gets under your *feet*." I wonder if the difference has anything to do with how much Latin culture values dance.

There's no clear sign to indicate that we've arrived at the dance school, but I spot people hanging around on a balcony and see lights coming from a dance studio through the window. I head up the metal outdoor staircase, and a man named Benito, with a short peroxide-blond Afro, opens the door. He gives me a form to fill out, and to my amusement, alongside the generic health and safety disclaimer is a list of boxes to tick with a dozen dance styles—but not reggaeton.

"So what is a Mexican doing here in Puerto Rico to learn reggaeton?" he asks curiously.

I laugh and explain that I'm not Mexican, though I might have picked up a convincing accent.

"La maestra is just in the other studio," he says, calling to her.

Keila, la maestra, is a striking woman with waist-length silky black hair, and she gives me a smile as she emerges into the studio lobby. She seems like the protagonist of a reggaeton video, her long-sleeved, cropped plunge top holding up an impressive set of implants and her low-cut tight jeans sitting below her perfect abs. As she approaches, I can see that her face is caked in makeup, and her breasts, teeth, and eyelashes are all fake. Is this the ideal of beauty here? La maestra will be the perfect case study in my quest to understand how the dance affects perceptions of beauty.

We go into one of the studio rooms, and Keila takes me through some basic reggaeton steps. She teaches me how to step from side to side while synchronizing my arms and how to turn in a circle while stamping the ground and making a circular motion with my hips. Despite all my dancing at DJ Pepe's parties in Bangkok, my body struggles through the hip sways, body rolls, and chest pumps. I have to coordinate my chest, shoulders, hips, and waist all at the same time. After doing this slowly for a hundred or so times, I gradually start to increase the speed.

"Yee-aah!" says Keila, in a stereotypical American accent. "Sometimes you just need to repeat the same thing over and over."

After class we take a photo of "Team Reggaeton" in front of a sparkling display of medals, trophies, and diamanté dance artifacts, and exchange social media accounts.

DURING THE DRIVE home, I send our photo to my Bangkok friends, which unexpectedly launches a heated debate on feminism and plastic surgery.

"She looks like a fucking candle," writes Dya, my fierce French-Thai friend and lingerie model whose natural style and love of cats have made her popular among animal rights activists. "Why can't she embrace her natural beauty rather than cake herself in makeup like that?"

"But if this is how she wants to look, she should be free to look however she wants without caring what anyone thinks! It's her choice!" insists Lauranne.

I understand both perspectives. It's true that Keila should be able to make her own choices when it comes to surgery and makeup, but it also feels important to consider what influenced those choices. The lyrics to reggaeton songs are hypersexual, and arguably misogynistic, and in the music videos, women seem completely objectified. One music video in particular, tied to the song "Como Yo Le Doy," by Pitbull and featuring Don Miguelo, left me equally revolted and fascinated. While neither of these artists is Puerto Rican, the song and video are arguably representative of the genre. The title, which translates to "How I Give It to Her," is even more explicit in Spanish. The song is about a woman making a booty call, where she sexualizes men to meet her desires and needs. Yet somehow, the video seems to focus on the men. In the video, Pitbull rubs his hands together in satisfaction while surrounded by a lingerie-clad harem and boasts of his ability to meet their needs when they call at three in the morning. Some women parade their assets at the poolside, while one woman in a pencil skirt sports a sexy librarian look and bites suggestively on her eyeglasses. With more than 360 million views on YouTube, the video clearly has a mainstream audience. Even I like it. On multiple occasions, I requested that DJ Pepe play the song; its rhythm gets under my feet, even though I have to block out the lyrics to enjoy dancing to it.

If the women in reggaeton videos—who are often scantily clad and do nothing more than represent a sexy, pulsing landscape for the male solo singer—always appear sexualized and heavily made up, this nearly unattainable look becomes not only aspirational but expected. These videos play everywhere—in cafés, malls, and gyms—and are fueled by social media. Being constantly exposed to this imagery in day-to-day life can only place undeniable pressure to conform. With heavy makeup, augmented body parts, and risqué clothing ubiquitous, is there any space left in reggaeton for a woman's natural beauty?

I GET BACK to the sun-drenched daybeds at El Convento after a midday reggaeton class, my second of the trip. We went beyond some of the basics and built a choreography to a mash-up of my favorite reggaeton hits. I'm now exhausted, but satisfied, and indulging in a quintessential Puerto Rican treat: the piña colada. The rum, coconut, and pineapple concoction is so beloved here that it was declared the official drink of the island in 1978.[66]

As the sun starts to set, I step out onto Calle del Cristo to explore the blue cobblestone streets of Old San Juan. In Havana the crumbling colonial houses added a sense of time-worn nostalgia, of decay, to my experience on the island, but in San Juan the houses are bright, pristinely painted, and perfectly preserved.

I walk past an intriguing cocktail lounge by the old city walls that doubles as a spa. In a final bid to enjoy my temporary extravagance, I go in to book myself a nail appointment. They can see me right away.

My manicurist, Claudia, offers me a bottle of Medalla Light beer with a slice of lime. She seems quite reserved, but we chitchat. While I speak in Spanish, she insists on replying in English. I learn that she's half Cuban, half Mexican, and lived in Las Vegas for most of her life but recently moved to Puerto Rico for her husband. She seems to be in her forties (even though she's already a grandmother) and has waist-length black hair, an upturned nose, and no small amount of facial fillers.

As trust grows between us, we open up about our lives. She mentions her various husbands, but I can't keep track and eventually she clarifies that she's been married five times. She pushes my cuticles back and tells me her latest husband is fourteen years younger than she is, and cute! She says they married last year.

I'm fascinated by Claudia, a manicurist and man-eater who turns out to be a former groupie who has rubbed shoulders with every major Latin artist from Ricky Martin to Enrique Iglesias.

"So how's Enrique Iglesias?" I ask, curious. "I actually have a huge crush on him. He'll marry me someday," I joke, suddenly realizing that most men I've dated have a slight air of Enrique in their face.

"Ha! Enrique, well my friend slept with him and . . ." she leans in to whisper a secret into my ear, and I narrowly avoid spitting out my beer in shock.

"He was a total caballero—a real gentleman—and super-respectful with me, but a totally different story with my friend. He's a *mujeriego* (womanizer), you know? The kind of man who cheats on his girlfriend all the time. I would never tolerate that. I would slap him first and then I would kill her!" she shouts, her words echoing through the empty salon.

Sometimes I think my constant avoidance of conflict means that I don't stand up for myself when being disrespected, neglected, or abused, especially by men. There's a lot I could learn from Claudia, and I can instantly think of a few romantic deceivers who would have better deserved a slap than my seemingly aloof silence—something I use to cloak my true feelings of abandonment, rejection, and betrayal.

I struggle to contain my laughter as she files my nails, completely unfazed, and continues to spill the beans with her Latin pop star gossip.

She shows me photos of her with the celebrities she's met, and photos of her with her current husband. "Look, this is me at forty-three, before I had surgery on my back and got fat. I was so hot!"

She looks incredible in the photo, flaunting a flat, toned stomach—the product, she tells me, of cosmetic surgery. "After four kids the body needs a little help. It's all lipo." She slaps her ass and then lists off a litany of procedures she's had.

"Come on, mi amor, have you seen all those celebrities who say they work out and naturally have the perfect body after having kids? It's all lipo. They're all doing it!"

I find Claudia's candor refreshing. Life could be more fun if we cared a little less.

"I'm so glad I met you," I say, feeling almost speechless at her revelations. This conversation has been more informative than any gossip magazine. The unexpected encounters with people I would never usually meet have opened my mind to new dimensions, in this case of beauty, body image, and a general openness toward people's life choices. Claudia's face may be full of fillers, but in many ways she's more authentic than most.

I STRETCH OUT on the queen-sized bed feeling like a princess. It's my last morning at El Convento, and I'm planning to maximize my R & R before heading to hostel life. I spend the entire morning lounging in my room until checkout, reading, taking a hot bath, and ordering breakfast before I pack my suitcase.

After checking out, I head up to the rooftop. I have a change of clothes in my bag to help me go incognito again, though this time I'll be disguised as a backpacker. Music plays from the phone of the gardener who diligently trims a rosebush as he quietly sings along to the romantic song "Bésame Mucho" (Kiss Me a Lot) in a smooth, soulful voice. His playlist then shifts to a brutal reggaeton song, to the horror of some of the gringos sitting nearby, while I tap my feet against the lounge chair, relishing it. It then switches to salsa, and I start to shift my shoulder blades almost instinctively. Clearly the gardener and I share musical tastes. I can't help but react, even physically, when I hear this music. I'm not sure if it's a sort of hyperreactivity or a lack of restraint in emotional expression, but I'm convinced that shimmying in my lounge chair is a rebellious act of joy driven by the fact that I simply don't care what anybody else thinks.

I'M PLEASANTLY SURPRISED that the Mango Mansion, my hostel and home for the next week, is actually very nice and clean. But when I arrive, the staff is whispering in hushed tones. Something scandalous seems to have gone down. From what I can tell, they are debating among themselves about whether to kick out a guest who brought drugs into the hostel and was discovered naked and asleep on the sofa in the common room the next morning.

I couldn't be farther away from the Convento. I dread what might be in store over the next week as I hide in my room and dress for reggaeton class.

In the common room I had met a few of the guests, ranging from young spring breakers to a man who looks to be about seventy. I had also noticed a board in the common area where you can list any activity you want to do with others, and I had swiftly taken a marker to advertise my search for someone who would like to go out dancing reggaeton with me.

When I return to the hostel from class, the older man approaches me excitedly.

"There she is!" he exclaims, pointing at me. He introduces me to a petite blond girl around my age and tells me she's Raquel from Alaska, and she's also looking for someone to dance reggaeton with.

I can't believe my luck. She seems slightly timid and unassuming for someone who wants to dance reggaeton, but I later discover that she's not new to Latin dance. She spends half the year living in a van and working as a road construction supervisor in Alaska and the other half dancing in various Latin American countries. She is also a big fan of salsa and tells me there is a salsa scene here in Puerto Rico that is not to be missed.

We head to Old San Juan together and check out the Nuyorican Cafe, a legendary salsa institution. The security guard draws a smiley face on the back of our wrists as an improvised entry stamp, and we grab a round of Medalla beers before taking a seat to watch people dance. This small, intimate place feels like it could be part of a film set with its live band and glamorous dancers. I still feel too shy to approach anyone to dance, but Raquel has no hesitation and makes her way up to a man who looks like a good dancer. Later she will tell me that she hadn't danced salsa in over a year and a half and warned her dance partner that she was a bit nervous.

"With me," he said to her reassuringly, "you don't need to worry."

I watch them dance, entranced by their smooth spins. Raquel's partner picks her up and twirls her as the song ends. He was right—she didn't need to worry; he's such a good leader that he can make anyone look good. But Raquel is also an incredible dancer.

Felix, her partner, is an aerobics instructor for the elderly and proves to be kind, patient, the perfect gentleman. He encourages me to dance with him too, and despite my initial protests, I eventually give in. I don't feel ready to dance in a new bar like this, especially because they dance salsa differently than what I had practiced in New York and Cuba. But I'm in good hands. Felix is an excellent leader and carefully covers up my mistakes; he's clearly concerned with making sure his partner looks good and taking care that she isn't smashed into the neighboring dancers. But he also doesn't hesitate to flaunt his suave moves. It's not him showing off; it's him having a good time because he really loves it.

"That's the way it should be," says Raquel after we've both had a chance to dance with him and are analyzing his style. "Some guys show off to make themselves look good and the girl look stupid, but Felix, he's a true caballero."

IT'S GOING TO be a strange day. I barely slept through the night thanks to ice-cold industrial air-conditioning. I get out of bed and head into the communal area for a surprisingly generous buffet of fresh waffles, pineapple, and peanut butter, and Bob Marley's "Buffalo Soldier" is blaring on the speaker. I get in line behind a slew of friendly traveling zombies, and everyone from the girl with the tattoo kit to the bearded hipsters and a pair of Scandinavians tries to give me advice on what to see and do. But I'm already agitated by distractions and need to coordinate my packed dance schedule.

When I arrive at the reggaeton studio, a huge lock chained around the door at the bottom of the stairs indicates that it's closed. I wait around in the harsh heat until I receive a voice message from Keila. Apparently, she's stuck in terrible traffic.

I seek refuge in a tiny patch of shade under the stairs, pressing myself against the wall to avoid the scorching sun. Usually I love soaking up the sun, but today it feels unbearably strong.

Several voice messages and one hour later, Keila finally arrives. She gets out of her car wearing ripped jeans and another cropped long-sleeve plunge top, but under her thick layers of makeup I can see that she has dark circles around her eyes.

When she sees the padlock, she shrieks, throwing her hands up in the air. She forgot to bring the key.

She waves me into her car, and we drive through monumental traffic back to her home over an hour away to get the key. If earlier in the day I had felt unproductive, then this wasn't going to change that. Thankfully, my time in Latin America has allowed me to work on my patience.

She parks in front of a modern villa in a gated community, runs into her house, and rushes back carrying a huge pink, fluffy key ring—which I find nauseating in this stuffy heat.

"I didn't sleep last night," she tells me, her eyes bleary, as we drive back to the dance studio. "My *nena* (baby) was in the hospital, and now my mom is looking after her. I'm exhausted."

I should be more compassionate. I may have lost a few hours of my life in the back-and-forth debacle to get the key, but someone having their kid in a hospital puts things into perspective.

On our way back to the studio, we start talking about the choreography and what would be an authentic setting and outfit to use for the video. We drive past a huge billboard advertising a Daddy Yankee and Nicky Jam concert. *Los Cangris*, it reads.

She tells me that "Los Cangris" roughly translates to "The Greats" and is what the duo were called back in the early 2000s when they sang together—because they were the greats of reggaeton. She perks up a bit. "You know their concerts are a really big deal. They sold out so fast they had to add more dates. They had a huge falling out years ago and reunited onstage after more than a decade."

I look at the date on the billboard. The concert happened just two days before I arrived.

We fall silent as we sit in traffic and listen to slow reggaeton playing on the radio. We're moving so slowly. At some point a car swerves right toward us from our left. I cover my face and scream as Keila jumps from her seat and we crash into it.

"I closed my eyes! *¡Dios mío!*" (Oh my God!), she shrieks. "I'm going to cry! I'm shaking." She shows me her wavering hand.

The guy from the other car comes over to our window and Keila rushes out, covering her face with her long, claw-like nails. I'm terrified he'll shout or freak out at us, but instead he comes over with a smile. Thankfully neither car even got scratched.

Eventually we make it back to the dance school, where it's baking hot and we get to work on a segment of the choreography to "Shaky Shaky." It requires rather intense and robust dance moves.

We've already advanced a lot with a routine full of side-to-side step taps, shoulder pops, and risqué lower-body isolations. When you first start putting a choreography together, everything is light and slow; you could go on for hours. But as the routine becomes set and you go through the whole thing in time to a song, you can exhaust yourself in a matter of minutes. My energy level, however, is explosive today. I'm going through the routine over and over again, dripping with sweat from the chest pumps, punches, hip circles, and stomps, and yet I'm able to keep going. I've almost transcended into an addictive, inescapable fury that I'm unleashing over and over again. My body doesn't want to stop.

Keila, however, who has not eaten all day, seems truly shaken to her core and leans against the window to hold herself up. She looks like she might faint. Maybe the intensity of my goal in addition to everything else is too much for her—teaching choreography in such a short amount of time is more demanding than teaching normal classes. Although I could continue, it's clear she needs to stop. We end the class early.

TONIGHT REGGAETON RAQUEL and I are going to La Placita de Santurce, a market square that doubles up as San Juan's party hub. According to our sources, this is *the* place to find reggaeton.

After a round of piña coladas in a quiet bar, we head to the center of the plaza. The kiosks are selling plastic cups of Medalla beer.

Raquel shares tips and tidbits of her favorite dance destinations, and I tell her that I dream of joining the parade for Rio's Carnival. She has already done it, of course, and tells me that it's completely possible but that being in the parade is entirely different that watching the parade. Given that different samba schools parade over the course of four days, I make a mental note to do both and find out the difference for myself.

Music is blasting around us, but no one is dancing, so we begin walking around the square, searching for a place to dance. Earlier that day, Keila messaged one of her reggaeton-loving friends who suggested a club named Vibra.

Once there we walk up an empty staircase and enter a large and mostly empty open room. After a short while a group arrives and gradually begins to dance a mix of salsa, bachata, merengue, and reggaeton. I pay close attention, eager to understand the dynamic of their reggaeton dancing. Two girls dance with their partners behind them—it doesn't seem completely innocent, but it isn't scandalous either. One of the girls grinds her ass into her partner's pelvis in a way that's so perfectly timed to the rhythm of the music that it makes it look like a skill. I assume they are two couples, so I'm confused when they suddenly swap male partners and continue the same move.

Out of pure ignorance I'd imagined reggaeton danced solo, like the shoulder pops and body waves I'm learning with Keila in the studio. That's how I always danced it in clubs. But as with every dance, there's always another layer that you discover only in local clubs and on the street. Reggaeton's official dance, *sandungueo*, is a provocative front-to-back dance that emerged in the late 1980s and involves heavy grinding and pelvic thrusts in an almost twerk-like manner. It's also known as *perreo*, the noun to the infinitive verb *perrear*, related to doggy-style dancing. The style created so much controversy that Puerto Rican senator Velda González launched a national crusade against reggaeton and perreo in the early 2000s, claiming it was morally corrupt, quasi-pornographic, and degrading to women.[67]

A middle-aged couple enters the room. The woman, who has short hair and oval reading glasses, seems quite ordinary—the type you might imagine working quietly in an office. Within seconds, however, she starts to shift from side to side, swaying to the music. Suddenly, she bends over and starts to grind into her partner's crotch as he proceeds to thrust his pelvis back and forth. Then the woman bends over even farther and places her palms on the floor. Her partner grabs her ass and gives her a few gentle spanks.

I'm practically hiding my face behind my hands as I watch—fascinated, shocked, and with admiration for their total lack of inhibition, but also feeling uncomfortable.

"This is just too extreme," I say to Raquel, who seems completely unfazed and expresses surprise at my shock.

I feel like such a prude. Why does this way of dancing make me so uncomfortable? I can't shake off the feeling that it's demeaning to women, even though they are clearly enjoying themselves. I look around the room and find something in the dynamic that uproots my initial impression. Women choose the intensity of the dance. Women choose how close or how far they dance from their partner. Women take the lead. They seem to have no reticence, dancing provocatively without caring what anyone thinks.

When "Shaky Shaky" starts to play, I decide to throw myself into the center of the dance floor and allow myself to dance. I'm not quite ready for perreo, but body rolls and chest pumps are a start. A big, eccentric guy in a pink shirt starts to dance next to me. During a part of the song that requires simulating an earthquake, he throws himself onto the floor and twerks, jiggling everything he's got.

I WAIT ONCE again outside the dance studio, in the small corner of shade under the staircase. As Benito and Keila pull up in their car, this time only twenty minutes late, I'm almost relieved.

Keila seems to be feeling much better. Her daughter is now out of the hospital, and she's dressed to match her sunny mood, wearing tropical print leggings with a strappy bright fluorescent yellow crop top. To make up for the time we lost the other day, we'll have over three hours of class today, intensely shaking and popping every muscle in my body. We even manage to finish our choreography, but some of the moves are still impossible for me.

"I can't do a body wave," I pout, looking in disgust at my stiff back in the mirror.

"Never say you can't do something!" Keila warns me, tapping her temple with a long, gem-studded fingernail. "You know, *la mente es bien poderosa.*" It's true—the mind can be very powerful.

After class, Benito and Keila drop me off at the enormous Plaza Las Américas shopping mall with a list of boutiques Keila recommended I check out for reggaeton apparel. I'm tasked with finding some denim hot pants and a crop top, items that I've never dared to wear before.

I leaf through the rails of skimpy crop tops, shorts, and tight dresses in fabrics ranging from faux leather to lace. *Can I really pull any of this off?* I bring a huge wad of clothing into a changing room, take a deep breath, and try on whatever I can squeeze into.

The reflection in the mirror startles me. I thought I was too chubby to wear this kind of clothing, but I don't look half as bad as I'd expected I would. It's strangely liberating to allow myself to wear clothes that show off my thighs, my breasts, and what I've avoided revealing my entire life: my stomach. *What has always stopped me from wearing clothes like this?* Fear of judgment, harassment, or worse—being attacked. But revealing, sexy clothing isn't the problem—clothing itself doesn't incite these actions. While I'm still not familiar with the social context here, there are two things that

I've noticed. First, women of all sizes walk around in skimpy clothes, and second, nobody seems to care. In fact, the more you reveal, the better. If they can feel safe and confident dressing this way, why shouldn't I?

Feeling empowered, I shortlist a black strappy crop top that wraps around my rib cage and high-waisted, ripped denim hot pants. I hesitate for a moment and send a photo to Keila in search of validation, my old habit of self-doubt creeping up on me once again, but she replies with a line of hearts and heart-eyed emoticons—a seal of approval. I head out of the dressing room with a wave of confidence and even pick up another crop top on the way to the register. I don't even bother trying it on. My newfound crop-top confidence tells me it will fit.

I don't have time to go back to the hostel before my night out with Raquel, so I slip into one of the mall's public bathrooms to get ready. The crop-top fits perfectly, and armed with my new reggaetonera attire, I transform myself, painting my bare face with dramatic makeup. I feel like I'm on the run, taking on a new identity and embracing the freedom that comes with it. Public bathrooms have become my dressing rooms, and bags have become my closet. I begin to enjoy this incognito existence—entering as one person and exiting as another.

When Raquel sees me she squeals with approval. I share my theory about empowerment through revealing clothing, and she tells me that she had the same thought earlier that day. She saw a girl FaceTiming on the street in Condado who was popping out her chest to "Shaky Shaky." She says the girl didn't have the perfect body but was confident and didn't care what others might think.

I have a lot to learn from girls like her. We all have a lot to learn from girls like her.

Our plan for tonight begins with trying to get into Marc Anthony's sold-out concert. Earlier today I spotted a huge billboard for the concert, and we've decided to see if there are any last-minute seats available or someone is reselling tickets outside. On our way there, we crash the police headquarters' Christmas party—with a live salsa band, fireworks, and a helicopter circling above us blasting horns and salsa music.

In front of the Coliseo, the largest indoor arena in Puerto Rico, we can't find anyone selling tickets, so we nervously rush to the ticket counter and join the others also hoping to get in. With so many people waiting in line like us, I don't expect much. But we wait for our turn and hope for the best.

The cashier says he has tickets for standing at the back of the disability area and to "Take it or leave it." We don't even hesitate to take them and then scuttle toward the entrance holding our tickets preciously. As soon as we break through the doors, we immediately sign up for a charity raffle offering the chance to meet Marc Anthony.

People have come really dressed up. Some women wear glamourous two-pieces composed of silk crop tops with wide-legged pants or long skirts for the occasion. Others have arrived in ball gowns.

The view from the disability area is actually excellent, and even though we are the farthest and highest up from the stage, we can see everything. I spot a vendor carrying a carton full of frozen piña coladas over his shoulder and rush to buy a round to celebrate.

Marc Anthony—the best-selling salsero of all time[68]—was born in Spanish Harlem to Puerto Rican parents and grew up listening to Héctor Lavoe, Willie Colón, and Tito Puente.[69] As he walks onstage, the entire audience, filled with thousands of excited fans, falls silent, anticipating what's to come. "*¡Mi gente!*" (My people!), he shouts, calling to us, and the crowd roars with excitement. Then, "*¡Boricua!*" The term is of indigenous Taíno origin and is used to refer to someone from Puerto Rico or of Puerto Rican descent. It elicits an uncontrollable applause.

The percussion takes off, and trumpets burst as he launches into his greatest hits. He sings with a voice so powerful that even from our section in the back, I can feel goose bumps on my arms.

Everyone in our section is dancing, including the couple next to us—a glamorous woman with a boyfriend who barely reaches her implants. From up here we can see, hear, and feel the entire arena and dance salsa at the same time.

When Marc Anthony breaks into his final song, it's clear that he's overcome with emotion—and I am too. His song "Vivir Mi Vida" (Living My Life) is the soundtrack to my new life and captures what life is about—laughing, dancing, and, most importantly, being present and fully engaged. As he begins to sing, an old man who has until now been sitting in his wheelchair suddenly gets up, supporting himself on his wife's arm, and starts to sing, cheer, and, as much as he can, dance. When Marc Anthony belts out the final bars of the song, someone in the audience hands him a Puerto Rican flag, which he proudly holds up in the air.

"Boricua!"

The audience goes wild, and covering his back with the flag, Marc Anthony makes his exit through the audience. His soulful voice continues to ring out from backstage, leaving us breathless and completely starstruck.

"I NEED YOU to be punctual," Keila tells me in a rather severe voice message. I've only had a few hours of sleep, and she sounds almost threatening. Today we'll be filming my reggaeton routine, dancing in a basketball court with a group of girls in Guaynabo, a municipality in the outskirts of San Juan.

I'm not usually the one who's late, but I let it go. It must be nerves. I rush to get my things together, without even taking the time to eat breakfast, and of course end up in front of the closed gates of the dance school, waiting in my patch of shade again. After she eventually shows up, we practice the routine while we wait for the other two dancers to arrive.

"Have the others had a chance to practice?" I ask.

"Don't worry, they'll get it fast," says Keila. "They dance all the time."

The two other girls arrive, and we rehearse some more. I can feel the stress in the air, and although they're able to learn the choreography impressively fast, we're far behind schedule. DJ Sonar, who, according to his T-shirt, is the 2012 Puerto Rico DMC DJ Champion, has shown up with his wife, Ina, who will film us. Ina is German, and it's interesting to have a Western perspective on everything. Even though we are delaying them, she seems unfazed. "It's Puerto Rico," she says with a shrug.

"Okay, we need to get ready now!" shouts Keila, who has brought a number of small suitcases filled with makeup. She's also a professional makeup artist and will style us for the video with a modern, feminine twist on reggaeton glam. She tells me to put on a base of foundation and blush and then rush back for her to do my eyes. When I return, she's not impressed. "You call this base? It looks like you have nothing on!" She seems scandalized and sighs in exasperation, and I stand silently as she uses various tools and products on my face. She works so fast that she's done in a matter of minutes.

I change into my tiny black crop top and ripped high-waisted hot pants and place a black velvet headband over my head to keep my hair away from my face. One of the girls lends me a pair of black boots, which I slip on quickly before going to look at myself in the mirror.

I don't recognize my reflection—flawlessly airbrushed skin, huge cat eyes, and black lips that make the blue in my eyes pop out so dramatically that they're glaring. Despite the confidence I grew to wear these clothes, I can't help but feel insecure about dancing in front of a camera wearing so little, and some of the dance moves are a bit risqué. One move involves rapid tapping of the feet that jiggles my womanly assets.

"Can we do this move facing the camera?" I ask the others shyly, thinking this might be more appropriate than showing my posterior.

They look at me in indignation. One makes a dramatic pout and says, "That move looks ugly from the front. The whole point is to see your ass shake."

And she's right. Often seen in reggaeton music videos, this dance step is inspired by a folkloric Puerto Rican dance called *la bomba* (the bomb), which given its name and boisterous movement perfectly matches with the *terremoto* (earthquake) portion of "Shaky Shaky."

"The thing is," I say hesitantly, "I work in gender equality, and I'm worried it might send the wrong message dancing like that and dressed like this." Fear has led the words to almost slip out of my mouth.

"Hang on a minute," intervenes Ina. "Have you ever thought that you might be more of a feminist for wearing whatever and dancing however you want?"

She's right, of course. There's nothing wrong with my outfit and dance moves. What's wrong is my fear of judgment, and stereotypes of being slutty, easy, vulgar, or nasty. These are sexist labels women have long faced, used as shameful justifications for harassment, assault, rape, and even murder. In a world of true equality, women can dress and dance however they wish, without fear that they might face consequences.

The attacks on reggaeton as violent, vulgar, and degrading of women might be ignoring the real problem. In discussing this paradox a while back with my Mexican friend Paola, she shared a quote from Jenny Granado, a Brazilian dancer based in Mexico City:

"To reaffirm this idea that a woman dancing to reggaeton encourages the objectification of her body is like reaffirming that a girl who steps out in the street at night in a short skirt is encouraging rape."[70]

Paola and Jenny are feminists who love reggaeton, and I am too. I can choose to ignore the lyrics and instead enjoy the rhythm, dancing along to it in a way that makes me feel confident and strong. And the pleasure I feel dancing reggaeton doesn't contradict my values.

As the legendary Ivy Queen, one of the founders of the feminist reggaeton movement, sang in her 2003 hit "Yo Quiero Bailar" (I Want to Dance), "*Porque yo soy la que mando, soy la que decide cuando vamos al mambo*" (Because I am the one who commands, the one who decides when we're going to mambo). With this understanding, reggaeton provides a space for the woman to calls the shots. She is in charge of her body and decides when and what she wants to do with it, and men should not expect anything from her. For me, just like for Ivy Queen, reggaeton is a form of empowerment—not of objectification.

WE HEAD OUT of the dance studio and make our way to a nearby basketball court, strutting down Avenida San Patricio in denim hot pants and boots, each of us with dramatic black eyes and lips. We look fierce.

At the basketball court, we position ourselves in a *V* shape. If there was ever a reggaeton version of the Spice Girls, it would definitely be us—a group of very different women, dressing and dancing however they like. Unlike the dancers in most reggaeton videos, however, and in the spirit of girl power, we're not dancing around men.

The speakers and camera are set up, and we begin to dance, at first putting all our energy into it. But after several technical issues, the music cuts off—the speaker isn't working. The atmosphere begins to grow tense, and I can tell that Keila is losing patience. We give it another attempt, the speaker finally working, until we are interrupted by an old man who claims to know Daddy Yankee personally.

"I don't want to do this anymore," says Keila, exasperated.

To my relief, another girl pleads with Keila to let us go one more time, and finally we dance through the entire routine. I step onto the basketball court, hesitant, as they huddle together, laughing and twirling their hair. They look at me like the gringa that I am, getting up to push and shove me around, before pulling my arms from either side to sway me into the steps. We take up our positions and start to punch the air, our elbows bent like Wonder Woman—pulling across our chests as if breaking free from an iron cast of repression. Our waists swirl in unison as we stomp, and then we form a line to place our hands on the back of each other's shoulders and pop our hips. I make mistakes throughout the performance, but I don't care. I prefer to enjoy and truly live this moment in the present rather than have it be perfect.

We break into solos, each of us taking ownership of self and space in a ferocity of movement. The medley turns to "Shaky Shaky," and when Daddy Yankee signals it's time to terremoto, we give the earthquake bomba step everything we've got, our feet tapping furiously into the court's tarmac and arms circling through the air, fueling the tremble of our thighs and seismic booty shaking.

As the music comes to an end, we step closer to each other and end in dramatic poses. My heart is pounding, and my skin is glistening from sweat.

My makeup, outfit, and pose don't feel like *me*. But it feels liberating to allow myself to dress and dance in a new way. Or maybe this *is* me, but just another version of myself that I've repressed until now.

INA MESSAGES ME to let me know that Roberto Roena of the legendary Fania All Stars, whom I had admired onstage in New York, will be playing tonight at La Factoría, a small bar in Old San Juan. I call Raquel right away. This isn't something we're going to miss.

Raquel and I have been to other bars in search of the heart of reggaeton but have mostly come up short—instead encountering rowdy bachelor parties, chic mixology haunts, the dastardly bar Señor Frog's, and Club Brava, San Juan's premier nightclub, which made up for its lack of reggaeton and Latin music with the incessant droning of booty jams.

La Factoría is something else entirely: an iconic, dimly lit speakeasy that would soon become famous as the bar where the video for "Despacito" was filmed. For me, it's where I'm about to have one of the best nights of my life.

As Raquel and I finish up our drinks at the bar, I spot el Señor Bongo himself, Roberto Roena, walking toward us. My starstruck face must have caught his attention, as he comes over to greet us. I first saw this man in documentaries about the global rise of salsa, then onstage in New York, and now I'm chatting with him in a bar, joking around over mango martinis. I have some trouble understanding him, as he has a raspy voice, but he embodies warmth. He gives me a hug and sticks out his tongue as we pose for a photo together.

"I'll see you girls back inside!" he says, giving us a happy thumbs-up.

At seventy-seven, Roena is still a headline act at the world's most important salsa events, but he has a tradition of performing for free in Puerto Rico for his own people, just like tonight in La Factoría.

Onstage Roberto Roena sits behind a bongo, just as he had at the congress. I can recognize the New York jazz influences in the music.

Felix is also here tonight, and we go over to the bar to say hello. We haven't seen him since our first encounter at the Nuyorican Cafe.

Two drunk gringos from Naples, Florida, sporting blazers and loafers insist on trying to speak to us, but they don't interest me, and their voices dim as my focus shifts to the dance floor, where an elderly couple dances to a smooth cha-cha song, the man cradling his wife's head with one hand while holding her at the waist with the other. On the opposite side of the room, DJ Sonar sways affectionately with his mother and a young couple dances flirtatiously, the girl's hips swaying sumptuously. There's so much love in this dance, spanning generations and time. I feel my heart swell and a pleasant buzz, but my moment ends abruptly when one of the drunk blazer boys invites me to dance. I reluctantly accept the invitation. After all, how bad could it be?

He stumbles around in front of me and, after brutally twisting my arm, smashes his glass on the floor. I'm saved by Raquel, who pulls me out of his clumsy embrace and toward the bar, where she's standing with Felix.

I have just enough time to catch my breath before Felix whisks me back to the dance floor, where we lose ourselves in an epic salsa-jazz instrumental fusion. The crowd forms a circle around us to watch as we spin and twirl. In the past my shyness and insecurity have often stopped me from being present, smiling, or making eye contact when I dance, but I can do all of those when I'm dancing with Felix. He guides me with confidence and disguises my errors to give way to a textured improvisation to trumpets and tempo.

With him, I feel like I'm flying, reaching the majestic heights of the feeling I've been subconsciously searching for since I started this journey: elation.

The song and our dance end to a cheer, and I breathlessly make my way back to the bar, exhausted but exhilarated.

"Well, congratulations," slurs the drunk blazer boy as he struggles to hold himself up against the bar.

I'VE RETURNED TO the old town to say goodbye to its blue cobblestone streets and colorful colonial houses. I stop by a boutique whose window showcases ceramic figurines: nativity scenes on one shelf and Héctor Lavoe on another—a national hero whose image I haven't seen since New York.

At the Fort of San Cristóbal, a UNESCO World Heritage Site and the largest fortification built by the Spanish, in 1783, I admire one of its *garitas* (sentry boxes) as the waves crash at the foot of the fort. The rocky coast stretches out toward the Morro fortress at the very tip of San Juan, a smattering of multicolored houses stacked in between. Curiously, they seem to be almost piled up next to each other, not lined up neatly like the colorful colonial houses on the opposite side of Calle Norzagaray. This is La Perla (The Pearl), a shantytown neighborhood that will later be made famous as the film set for the "Despacito" music video. It had first been built to house slaughterhouses, cemeteries, and the former slaves and nonwhite servants—a form of physical exclusion meant to keep them far away from the main city center and society as a whole. For years it remained one of the poorest barrios in Puerto Rico, but it has since overcome the grip of drug traffickers and the violent crime of the last decades.

La Perla has an interesting history when it comes to music and dance and is mentioned in a number of songs from salsa to reggaeton. Carlos Pérez, the director of the "Despacito" music video, said that the artists Luis Fonsi and Daddy Yankee "had a very clear vision of what they wanted . . . culture, sensuality, color, and dance."[71] La Perla has all those qualities—and singers and bands like Ismael Rivera, Calle 13, and Rubén Blades have fought to preserve it, even dedicating songs to the impoverished cliffside community.[72] Culture, sensuality, color, and dance are what I'm searching for on my journey too.

I look up at the Morro fortress and see three flags floating in the breeze: the flag of the United States, the flag of Puerto Rico, and a military flag with a burgundy cross—this flag was used between the sixteenth and eighteenth centuries to identify loyalty to the King of Spain.

As I pass through the fort, I enter a pop-up Christmas market filled with Puerto Rican artisanal products. I then head down Calle Norzagaray to admire the colonial houses dolled up in a palette ranging from raspberry to lavender, pistachio to apricot. The white trimmings around the windows make them look like elaborate desserts. Bougainvillea and Puerto Rican flags hang from their balconies.

I arrive at the center of Old San Juan and find the colonial buildings on Plaza de Armas covered in Christmas decorations, with glistening stars and sparkling lights adorning the streets. It's strange to witness the holiday spirit in the tropical Caribbean heat, as it had been for the years I lived in Bangkok. It's a far cry from the cold, gray skies of Europe.

I briefly stop by a boutique run by Claudia's best friend, Gici, where I'm enticed into buying a pair of butt-enhancing jeans over sangria, strawberries, and an active demonstration of perreo paired with blasting reggaeton and a disco light. Gici gives me a stern warning to stop hiding my body under my clothes and to keep dancing—lipo won't last, she says.

Thus far it's been a quiet Tuesday morning, but as I continue walking I begin to hear salsa everywhere, even if it's coming from the smartphones of people trying to make the working hours go by as they paint the nearby buildings or set up tables in restaurants. I'm still exhilarated from the night at La Factoría, and I take tiny salsa steps along the cobblestones as I make my way to the Museo de las Américas to learn about Latin America's indigenous heritage.

On my way I stop by the Institute of Puerto Rican Culture's bookstore and decide to see if I can find any books about reggaeton, but I don't. I approach one of the staff members to ask but first end up briefly telling her my story.

When I tell her I chose to learn reggaeton in Puerto Rico, her face drops. "Reggaeton? But why? Puerto Rico has so many traditional dances, like la bomba or *la plena*. They're far more culturally rich." (Like la bomba, la plena is a percussion-driven folkloric dance native to the island.)

Reggaeton may not be the most traditional musical genre here, but it strikes me as being the most dominant one, and not even just in Puerto Rico, but across Latin America. Surely we can't deny its prominence, whether we like it or not. And besides, aren't the violence and vulgarity in reggaeton an honest reflection of the reality of life for the majority who live in less fortunate conditions? I tell her as much and surprise myself with my own passionate outburst.

Her face softens. "I've never seen it that way before."

I DON'T WANT to leave Puerto Rico, but my journey requires me to— beckoning me onward.

At the airport, I check my luggage and then put in my headphones and discreetly dance my way through security. There's only one thing that can make me feel better at an airport when I'm leaving a place that I love: a MAC makeup counter. Empowered by the fearless reggaetonera look I experimented with this past week, I inquire about the possibility of purchasing a black lipstick. The enthusiastic sales assistant makes me try obscene shades that almost make me shudder and convinces me to choose between a dark, almost black matte burgundy and a shiny berry color. I choose both. To my dismay, the latter is sold out.

"You won't find it anywhere," says the sales assistant, closing her eyes as if this were a terrible tragedy. "I'll be right back." She leaves me at the cash register for a minute and then returns and takes my arm, somewhat forcefully, and walks me away from the counter. "Merry Christmas," she whispers into my ear and drops a brand-new sample of the limited-edition, sold-out lipstick into my shopping bag. "Don't tell anyone, otherwise I'm fired."

I look at her in disbelief. Wary that I shouldn't make anything obvious, I give her a quick, tight hug and walk away with a beaming smile.

Salsa plays in the souvenir shop, and I shamelessly shift my hips from side to side despite the weight of my huge backpack. I dance past the magazine stand and then pick up a bag of Peanut Butter M&Ms. I love that there is a culture where nobody even bats an eyelid at my movements, where there's no need to care what anyone thinks because bold self-expression is so normal. In my case I have taken to dancing in airports.

COLOMBIA

Cumbia, Porro, and Salsa Caleña

LA COSTA

Sometimes I feel like I'm always in transit, not just in my travels but also in life. Since leaving England at twenty-four, I have been posted in countries on temporary assignments where I couldn't nest long enough to buy a toaster. I have never really built a base, let alone been able to think where I'd be a year out. My newly nomadic life has taken my lack of roots to a whole other level. I drag my suitcase from one Airbnb to the next and find new friends, new dance communities, and new comforts in places I'll only temporarily call home. I still have a way to go on my journey and have no plan to buy a toaster in the foreseeable future, but I am starting to feel a universal sense of belonging. I am starting to build many homes in the world.

I step out through Arrivals in Rafael Núñez International Airport in Cartagena, and see Juan, my Colombian colleague and friend from Bangkok, waiting for me. In his sailing shoes and panama hat, he looks as dapper as ever.

"My Juanito!" I exclaim as I throw myself into his arms. It feels surreal to see him in Colombia, five months after I said goodbye to him in Bangkok. Always a true caballero, he insists on taking my bags, and we get into a yellow taxi waiting outside. On the drive to his family's seaside apartment in Bocagrande, Cartagena's upscale neighborhood, I admire waves crashing against the city walls. When we get to his building, we fly up in an elevator that opens directly into a breezy and expansive white apartment with an infinite view over the city. I step out onto the balcony to take in the warm breeze, and Juan comes out with two cold Aguila beers.

"We made it!" he says as we raise our cans.

We had both left our lives in Bangkok behind to follow our hearts. Juan had come home to be with his family, whom he hadn't seen in years. Leaning against the balcony, I take in the view and the sound of different songs echoing from around the bay.

"Juanito," I gasp, "I can hear music everywhere."

JUAN'S FAMILY HAS welcomed me warmly since my arrival. Alcida, their housekeeper in Cartagena, feeds me *arepas de huevo* (egg-stuffed arepas), cornmeal cakes, and fresh juices. I've also been invited to a family feast at his aunt's apartment. Over wine and stuffed crab claws, they ask about my intention to learn traditional Colombian dances.

"*¡Divino! ¡Divino!*" they exclaim, calling the idea divine and clearly enamored with the idea of a dance journey. They all begin to talk at the same time, eager to demonstrate their love for the different dances of Colombia. I watch them, absolutely mesmerized.

"The steps are tiny—it's all in the hips," whispers Carolina, one of Juan's cousins, as she shows me the traditional cumbia step: shifting her feet with tiny side steps that cause an impressive movement of the hips.

"And what about *mapalé*? I could see Juan dancing as the *caiman*!" joins in her sister Alejandra, referring to a male push-up dance move meant to represent an alligator, performed with somewhat sexual undertones.

Meanwhile their mother, Alicia, has come to stand next to me at the table to demonstrate how she would pop her chest and thrust her hips at the same time to dance *champeta*, the most scandalous of Colombia's dances. In Latin America, I've come to notice, appreciation for dance and music spans generations.

JUAN'S UNCLE CARLOS had suggested we all meet in the early evening at the dock opposite the apartment for a sunset tour of Cartagena by boat. We climb onboard and set sail toward the old town while a spectacular sunset bleeds behind the numerous skyscrapers of Bocagrande.

Alejandra calls for her uncle Carlos to put on some bachata, and a song by Romeo Santos starts to play. While the boat glides across the bay, we open up a bottle of rosé as we sing and dance. Then all of a sudden, the sound of salsa jolts me. It's playing on a nearby boat. The song "En Barranquilla Me Quedo" (In Barranquilla I Stay) is a classic Colombian salsa hit from the nearby town of Barranquilla and would later become one of my favorite songs.

As we approach the historical center, I can see one of the landmarks of Cartagena: the Iglesia de San Pedro Claver (Church of San Pedro Claver). The boat drops off the cousins (a group that now includes myself, since I've been practically adopted), and we walk through the iconic Torre del Reloj clock tower to make our way toward the Parque de Bolívar, where I see Colombian dance in person for the first time.

With cold cans of Aguila beer from a street vendor in hand, we watch a couple perform cumbia. It's the national dance of Colombia and was influenced by African, indigenous, and Spanish cultures.[73] The song represents a courtship, and the drums, wind instruments, and melody of cumbia music reflect Colombia's long history of conquest and colonialism.[74] Among the many theories debated by historians on the exact origin of cumbia dancing is one that claims that many of its steps represent the lives of slaves: the small steps represent chained feet, and the raised arms symbolize either the position of the slaves' arms as they held items on their heads or the sweeping movement of a machete to strike sugarcane.[75]

As the woman opens a colorfully layered skirt to reveal her legs, her partner tries to offer her his hat, but she coyly rejects his advances until she eventually leans her head behind the hat to accept a kiss. This sultry, amorous dance is so rich in history that I feel I'm the literary equivalent of an extra in Gabriel García Márquez's *Love in the Time of Cholera*. At the end of the song the dancers skip behind the statue of Simón Bolívar, *El Libertador* (The Liberator), the nineteenth-century hero who led the movement for independence in land that today defines six Latin American countries.[76]

A new group of dancers emerges: the women wearing short, fringed skirts, and the men wearing fringed trousers. They burst into a dance that's exuberant and erotic, with the beat of the drum and clapping so fast and frenetic that my brain can barely keep up with its intensity. One of the male dancers descends into an audacious alligator push-up.

They're dancing the mapalé, a dance perceived as overtly sexual that has a history that runs deep. Thought to have been brought over by Angolan slaves in the sixteenth century,[77] it represents the lives of fishermen on the banks of the Magdalena River, the main river in Colombia.[78] In the dance, the men depict mapalé fish out of the water, while the women represent the waves.[79] Their vigorous, tireless movements tell a story of hard labor; however, mapalé's function was one of release. It was performed as a form of amusement as soon as the workday was finished and the first pulses from *el tambor alegre* and *tambura* drums quivered in the night air.[80]

Tonight the dancers move to the beat of the drum with mapalé's famous speed and vigor—hair, limbs, and fringe from the skirts vibrating across the stage with fierce velocity. At intervals, the male and female dancers interlock their bodies, jump, fall, release each other, and then with agility and strength leap upon each other again.

"Wow, can you imagine what he must be like in bed?" says Alejandra, pointing to a male dancer and nudging Juan with her elbow.

His eyes widen and meet mine with a look of shock. It's been more than two years since he's been in Colombia, and perhaps he's forgotten the honesty and openness with which people here treat topics like sex.

We make our way to the nightlife quarter of Getsemaní, a hip Cartagena neighborhood, passing countless colorful murals and backpacker hostels, and occasionally stop for a drink and listen to teenage boys improvising rap songs. Soon we arrive at a Cartagenian institution: the Bazurto Social Club, a self-declared bastion of *la gozadera*—meaning the highest possible level of fun—and a spiritual home of champeta.

A free champeta class has already begun and is being led by three *champateros* in tropical leggings up on a small wooden stage. I rush over with Juan's cousins and join the front row in following a complex choreography that can only be described as Zumba on speed.

Champeta was born out of the slums of Cartagena, where many people displaced by violence now live.[81] Named after the champeta knife and often associated with poverty and crime, it has grown into a cultural phenomenon.[82] With its whirlwind of drums, electric guitar, keyboard, and fast, hypnotizing moves, it is one of the most popular music and dance styles in the country.

When I can no longer push past my jet lag, we make our way home, walking past shady bars lined with prostitutes, some of whom are heavily pregnant. "This is the dark side of Cartagena," says Juan sadly. "Beyond the center of the city are some difficult barrios, with populations who are so poor, they're desperate."

HOLDING A LONG grocery list provided by Alcida, Juan and I enter a supermarket where we are met with an abundance of exotic fruits and vegetables. Alcida plans to prepare some of the most typical *costeño* (coastal) dishes: *patacónes* (twice-fried plantain slices), coconut rice, and fried fish.

We stare aimlessly at the various types of bananas and plantains without knowing which ones to buy, when suddenly a Carlos Vives song plays. A cultural ambassador for Colombia and a costeño himself, Carlos Vives began his career as a soap opera star before making it as a singer-songwriter and national hero who brought *vallenato* to the world.

Meaning "born in the valley," vallenato originates from the city of Valledupar in Colombia's Caribbean region. It is a unique type of folk music that is said to have been inspired by the lyrical storytelling of Spanish minstrels and adopted by farmers who would sing out the latest news as they traversed Colombia's pastures with their cattle. Gabriel García Márquez was a big admirer of the genre and even defined his masterpiece *One Hundred Years of Solitude* as a vallenato song of four hundred pages.[83]

The song playing now, "El Mar de Sus Ojos" (The Sea of Her Eyes), is one of my favorites, and as I hold our basket, I can't help but dance. With Juan engrossed in the shopping list, I think that nobody except the plantains can see me, but a perfectly tanned playboy who looks to be in his late sixties and is accompanied by his equally perfect (and much younger-looking) wife spots me from across the fruit and vegetable section. He points to me with a friendly finger-gun action, as if to say, *Hey! You!* and begins to dance back. Now with a pile of pineapples between us, we're both dancing and he starts to sing. As his wife motions him away, he calls, "Enjoy Colombia!" and then complacently followers her, shimmying his way down the aisle and still singing along to the lyrics.

The interaction feels unique to Latin America: two people making eye contact and dancing, even if from a distance and in the middle of the supermarket, just because they both love Carlos Vives. When I look around the market, I see many people singing along, swaying, or tapping their feet as they take products from a shelf and put them into their basket. This is Colombia, a land where you can sing and dance in the supermarket without a care in the world.

Juan is a cultural heritage specialist and has agreed to take me on a tour of Cartegena's history and architecture. We rent bicycles, mine with a basket full of flowers, and take off toward the Malecón, speeding through the streets of Getsemani lined with street art.

We meander through colonial cobblestoned streets to admire the bright yellows, pinks, and blues of the houses—some draped in bougainvillea, others stamped with ornate doors. Along the way to the sea wall, we see various street vendors and artists, women carrying huge plates of fruit on their heads, and young beatboxers rapping their latest composition.

We slow our bikes when we approach Cartagena's prime landmark, the Torre del Reloj clock tower, and the main gate opening Cartagena. Commissioned by King Philip II of Spain just years after the city was founded in 1533, its walls were built over the span of two hundred years to protect the city from pirate attacks.[84] I faintly hear the sound of Carlos Vives's "La Bicicleta" (The Bicycle), and as we get closer I find an impersonator entirely covered in silver paint. He carefully imitates Carlos Vives's mannerisms and dance moves, even greeting onlookers the way he might greet his fans. I rush toward him, and he bows down to kiss my hand and spin me around. He may be a silver clone of Carlos Vives, but he's the closest thing I've found to the man himself in a city that pulses with him. His songs, after all, play everywhere from street vendor carts and supermarkets to nightclubs and portable speakers on the beach.

We continue on and cycle through the gate to Plaza de los Coches, where colorful vendor carts sell fruits and traditional sweets under bright yellow arches that conceal and contrast with the dark history of the square, where African captives in chains were sold and enslaved as part of the slave trade.[85] We run into a group of men wearing *sombreros vueltiaos* ("turned hats"), traditional Colombian hats made with intricate black-and-white patterns. They play vallenato with their accordion, a small drum called *la caja*, and an instrument known as *la guacharaca* that has a metallic sound.

Our next stop honors a lighter but integral part of Cartagena's history: the Portal de las Reinas (Hall of the Queens), the headquarters and hall of fame of Miss Colombia, located in Plaza de Bolivar and demarcated by a sign on the ground and mosaic portraits of several beauty queens. Juan points to a few famous ones, including Miss Colombia from 1996 to 1997, who is the current wife of Carlos Vives. Here, Miss Colombia isn't just a beauty pageant but the most important event hosted in Cartagena, second only to the city's independence celebrations. The previous year, the presenter of the Miss Universe pageant accidentally caused a scandal by misreading the result and placing the crown on Miss Colombia before later removing it and placing it on the head of Miss Philippines. The scandal caught worldwide attention and spurred countless jokes, but in Colombia, people were outraged.[86] In reaction, Miss Colombia was awarded numerous contracts,[87] including being the female protagonist of Carlos Vives's new music video.[88]

Across the square we find a small local seafood restaurant where we stop to replenish after a long day of cycling and walking. As we finish lunch, our waitress leans against the doorframe with her notepad in hand and apron tied around her waist. She gazes pensively, contemplating the square as she sings along to a soft bachata song by Romeo Santos.

"It's like she's in another world singing along to Romeo," says Juan in admiration, before we both join her in her daydream.

Not wanting to wake her, we discreetly call a different waiter to get the bill, causing her to jump.

"I'm so sorry. I didn't mean to—"

"No! We're sorry," says Juan. "We could see that you are completely in love with Romeo Santos. We didn't want to interrupt!"

By accompanying me on part of my journey, Juan has started to see, like me, the beauty in the Colombian and Latin American way of life and the importance placed on musicality, emotion, and expression that has fascinated me for so long.

After paying the bill, we get back on our bicycles and pedal through the historical center's narrow streets and then uphill beside the city walls. The sun shines and waves crash beneath us. A man in a sombrero vueltiao plays vallenato on his accordion while ladies in colorful dresses gracefully carry plates of tropical fruits on their heads.

We take a seat at a popular terrace bar where people come to catch the sunset. Looking one way offers a view of the historical center, and looking the other way shows the gleaming skyscrapers of Bocagrande across the bay. A threadbare Colombian flag waves in the breeze among the vanguards and canons that line the walls. Everyone is admiring the sunset. The sun seems to form a cutout circle outlining a blurry rose gold. As it sinks into the sea, we all clap.

In the historical center we meet Juan's friends Juliana and Ruben at the clock tower for dinner, drinks, and dancing. All three of them worked for the Ministry of Culture at some point. Walking around Cartagena with them feels like a narration of the city's secret spots and stories.

"I'm dying for ceviche," says Juliana, peering out at all the local kiosks before eventually settling for one that has a set of plastic chairs on the pavement.

It's the most local dinner I've experienced so far in Colombia, and I curiously admire the people behind the food truck playing their music and dancing along as they hand over plastic cups of shrimp covered in salsa *rosada*, a pink cocktail sauce that is a blend of ketchup and mayonnaise. Juan's friends trade information on the latest cultural projects for Cartagena, which includes a route in memory of the slave trade and signs and landmarks around the historical center detailing the painful past of many of its colorful plazas, streets, and monuments.

I drift off into my thoughts. You can't discuss the history of Latin American dance without acknowledging the slave trade. From the sixteenth to nineteenth century, European enslavers bought and sold millions of Africans, subjecting them to a long and perilous journey to the Americas.[89]

Forced to work in unfamiliar lands, these enslaved Africans depended on music and dance to communicate with each other, worship freely, maintain traditions, and survive.[90] They also created new movements to reflect and record the travails of their daily lives in the Americas—movements still found in many dances today.[91] Latin dance, which people today experience as a celebration of life, happiness, and freedom, stems from suffering, pain, and a dark chapter of world history.

I tell Juan's friends that I'm interested in the way that the movement of people influences culture, particularly dance. I want to know the stories behind each leap, thrust, and step.

"You should tell her what you know about champeta," says Juliana, nudging Ruben. "He's an expert on the topic."

"Well," he clears his throat, "*champeta* is slang for the knife used by fishmongers to gut and scale fish, but the term is also used to describe the guys who rob people at knifepoint, a frequent occurrence in Cartagena's barrios.[92] But actually, the music is influenced by zouk, which came from West Africa's francophone countries to the French Antilles.[93] They say that it arrived here through sailors who docked in Cartagena in the 1970s, and then in the 1980s somewhat fittingly it became really popular in the town of San Basilio de Palenque."

"Why was it fitting that it became so popular in Palenque?" I ask, referring to the town in northern Colombia.

"Palenque was the first place where the slaves revolted. They spoke a creole mixing Spanish and African languages, and when they started listening to more music from Africa, they started making up their own words. One of the first major artists to emerge from there is Charles King. He's a champeta icon. *El Palenquero fino*, the fine Palenquero, is what they call him."

Ruben tells me that when Sony came to Cartagena, its studio scouts discovered champeta singers and went on to film iconic champeta music videos, taking the champeta phenomenon to a national level. The style is exotic and sexual and sometimes laden with movements so violent that they shocked people in Bogotá. I vaguely recall Farah telling me in Mexico that if reggaeton is sexual provocation, champeta is sexual assault.

"It's sad because when Sony left the scene, many young champeta artists were left behind and fell into crime and narco-trafficking. But because the phenomenon had reached a national level, some big artists got to perform in the capital. Now they add lots of electric drums and sound effects, but Charles King is still classic. His audience isn't so local anymore. He's so well known."

Born as Carlos Reyes, which literally translates to Charles King, he's known not only as the pioneer of champeta but also as the person who took it from the streets of Cartagena's barrios to a genre broadcasted on radio stations all over Colombia. Many of his songs talk of social issues like corruption, drugs, and crime, making champeta a medium that can stimulate social change. I'm intrigued by this Charles King character, and I tell Ruben as much.

Much to my surprise, Ruben tells me that he personally knows Charles King and that we're going to see him play at the Bazurto Social Club tonight. I can't believe it—a history lesson on champeta, and I also get to meet one of its most prominent characters.

At the Bazurto Social Club, Ruben greets a man with dreadlocks at the door.

"Hola, Charles!"

It's the man himself: calm, friendly, humble, and happy to meet a gringa who's heard of him and his songs. He even lets me take a photo with him. During the concert he smiles at us while electrifying the crowd with his infectious beats.

TODAY WE'RE LEAVING Cartagena to continue our adventure along Colombia's coast. We hug Alcida goodbye and set off for Santa Marta, a city more than 140 miles up the coast that is famous for being the oldest city in Colombia and the hometown of Carlos Vives. As we speed along the Troncal del Caribe, or the National Route No. 90 (affectionately nicknamed the Backbone of the Caribbean), the landscape begins to change. Stretches of sand and cacti punctuate a quiet road. Past the industrial seaport city of Barranquilla, the hometown of Shakira and Sofía Vergara, people masked as gorillas, vampires, and ghosts, gearing up for Carnival, come out onto the road to wave at us.

We get out at an intersection and walk with our bags toward a resort of holiday apartments where Juan's friends Paula and Santiaga are waiting for us. As soon as we arrive, Paula puts on salsa music for us and, despite being six months pregnant, joins me in dancing along to the music as we prepare dinner.

I lean onto the balcony and peer down at the black sand beach that lines the bay. As sunset hits, the sea appears silver, pale between the shadows of the palm trees and the dark expanse of sand.

SETTLING INTO OUR lounge chairs the next morning, I pull out *One Hundred Years of Solitude*, a metaphorical account of Colombian history that follows a family through seven generations.

"Do you know who's related to him?" says Juan, pointing to the name of the book's author, Gabriel García Márquez. He nods his head toward Paula. "He's a relative of hers!"

Awarded the Nobel Prize in Literature in 1982, Gabriel García Márquez was one of the main practitioners of magical realism, a prominent genre in Latin American literature where the supernatural, mystical, and spiritual reach even the most ordinary aspects of everyday life. I already feel like I'm breathing in so many cultural treasures. Not only am I reading his work in his home province of Magdalena, surrounded by the scenery and villages that inspired him, but I am doing so while sitting on a beach next to a relative of his.

It's often said that magical realism explains much of Colombia, and South America, in its ability to combine the modern and the mythical. So far, Latin America has had a profound impact on me; it has allowed me to traverse into my own magical reality. Captivating my imagination and enabling me to flourish in my creativity, it has revealed a raw sensitivity that I spent years concealing beneath a shell of resilience.

Adulthood had led me to lacquer myself in a sheen of professionalism and purpose. But my diligent efforts were always driven by the same dreamy vision that led me to dance. True to the defining traits of my astrological sign, Pisces, I wanted to spread peace, love, and happiness in the world, but my need to be taken seriously as an accomplished young professional had at times also concealed my truest self: my sensitivity, my creative passions, and my yearning to live beyond the bounds of my day job.

OUR TAXI DROPS us at the entrance of a small town, which feels quiet and looks dusty—almost like an abandoned movie set. The village, we soon realize, is still asleep, recovering from the festivities the night before. In the main square, the Plaza del Centenario, we stop to admire the white neoclassical architecture of a church and a small, equally white pavilion that Juan and I climb onto to dance for an audience of two or three people.

Santiaga had encouraged us to join her in Ciénaga—a nearby town esteemed as the capital of magical realism and said to have inspired the fictional village of Macondo in *One Hundred Years of Solitude*—to explore one of the most important events of the year: Festival del Caimán Cienaguero. Celebrated every January on the day of San Sebastián, the festival recalls the legend of a local fisherman who asked his daughters, Juanita and Tomasita, to go to the market and buy rum for the village festivities.[94] Everyone in the village sang and danced cumbia and puya, but as the day grew long, the fisher-man's daughters still had not returned. Upon seeing Juanita suddenly appear in the village, her father rushed to her and asked what happened. Juanita, shouting in horror, told her father that while Tomasita was washing her feet in one of the town's surrounding swamps, a caiman came up and ate her.

The village people went off in search of the caiman and upon finding it beat it to death with sticks and harpoons. Victorious, they propped the caiman up by mangrove poles and paraded the deadly corpse around as the rest of the village danced beside it.

"Look over there!" says Juan, pointing at a float bearing a huge croco-dile head. We cross the square to find more crocodile floats ready for this afternoon's parade. They're being supervised by a man dressed as a giant crocodile while he wears another giant crocodile costume around his waist as if it were a life preserver.

We continue walking through the quiet streets and find a small, family-run haberdashery where we buy flowers for our hair and feathers for Juan's hat to get us into Carnival mood. The abuelita running the shop pins an enormous pink sparkling flower in my hair and then steps back to examine me carefully from head to toe.

"¡Derechita!" she snaps, shaking her head. "You need to stand straighter, with your chest out." She demonstrates.

Embarrassed, I adjust my posture as instructed and notice in the mirror how my reflection now shows increased confidence and what looks like a reduced dress size.

"Much better!" She smiles. "And never forget the señora from Ciénaga who sold you flowers and told you to always stand derechita."

We leave the shop with a more festive look and cross the street to a local eatery called El Republicano, where we order plates of robalo fish in shrimp sauce accompanied by patacónes, my new favorite carbohydrate, before heading back out to find seats for the parade and picking up an Aguila beer on the way.

From behind the barriers, we watch group after group parade—people of all ages, from teenagers to abuelitos who look to be in their seventies. The women have full skirts and flowers in their hair; the men have straw hats and handkerchiefs tied around their necks. They dance in two lines surrounding a dancing crocodile and sing a traditional song about how little Tomasita was taken away and eaten by the caiman.

I watch an older woman with glitter around her eyes. The layers of her dress ruffle as she twirls. You don't have to be young to be beautiful, to have your hair and makeup arranged, to wear a colorful costume, or to perform in front of an audience. It seems to me that in Latin culture, you don't fear getting older. You sing, dance, and enjoy all stages of your life.

More crocodile floats and colorful costumes pass by, with the occasional amusing Shakira or Carlos Vives impersonator on a bicycle, followed shortly by a Barack Obama. A more modern float has girls in frilly miniskirts and silicone-filled bikini tops dancing to reggaeton. The parade ends with seven shimmering Amazonian lady crocodiles, glamorous representatives of the LGBTQ community, gracefully fanning themselves with bright pink feather fans and dramatically posing for photos, who draw the parade to an end with a final rainbow float. They have elected their own Carnival Queen, who struts with a royal rainbow sash draped over her shimmering scales.

"Times have really changed," says Juan in amazement, a touch of emotion in his voice. Even a few years ago, he couldn't have imagined Colombia openly representing the LGBTQ community as part of its most traditional festivities. But now it seems to have become more inclusive, bringing together people from all walks of life.

MEDELLÍN

THE EMERALD GREEN hills of Antioquia welcome me to Medellín, a place dramatically different from the one I left behind. I'm fresh off a trip from Santa Marta and an excursion to Parque Tayrona, a national park and altogether magical place where mountain, jungle, and ocean meet that is so far only slightly spoiled by a nascent influx of tourists.

In Tayrona, and on the silver sand beaches of *la costa* (the coast), I had watched the sun melt into the ocean each evening, magnetized by the rays reflecting from the water. Walking toward the enormous setting sun, I felt rejuvenated and vitalized. I felt it in my abdomen, in my solar plexus—the chakra dedicated to power and positivity. Back in Bangkok, my sorrow had led me to take an alternative yoga class that included a pre-class "aura scan" and the alchemistic use of crystals and essential oils. Though usually skeptical of such things, I came to see that my deep sadness had led to a desperation and sadness that caused my solar plexus—the Manipura chakra that sits just above the belly button—to be blocked. Along with my throat and my heart, it was the spot where my emotional heartbreak could be felt as physical pain. This chakra is yellow, like the sun: an energy center for self-power, confidence, and self-esteem. Since then I've understood that the sun heals me, whether it be while catching rays on my yoga mat by the window as I go about my sun salutations, or in moments like those in Tayrona when I bathed in its rays.

FROM THE SIERRA Nevada's snowcapped mountain as a backdrop to the Caribbean Sea, to desert-like plains and swamps, to the jutting green hillsides of Medellín, the transformation of landscapes from my airplane window manifests Colombia's incredible scenic diversity. As we begin to make our descent, a bustling metropolis emerges from the lush slopes of Antioquia's Aburrá Valley nestled in the Andes. It is a view that, until now,

I've only seen in the opening trailer of the Netflix series *Narcos*, which in its first two seasons chronicled the life and demise of the most violent drug lord of all time, Pablo Escobar. The series has led many people to believe that Medellín is still the murder capital of the world, held hostage by drug cartels, where you can fall victim to a stray bullet if you are in the wrong place at the wrong time.

But Medellín has undergone a miracle makeover and metamorphosis into a city of modernity. A revolutionary cocktail of social and urban planning programs focused on the most disadvantaged barrios has made Medellín an example of "social urbanism." The undertaking was pioneered by former mayor Sergio Fajardo and led to a drastic reduction in crime, poverty, and social exclusion.[95] Today the city's cultural scene is thriving, testimony to the city's rising local fashion designers, world-famous reggaeton artists, and modern art scene. Juan had proudly pointed to his T-shirt displaying the acronym MAAM for Museo de Arte Moderno, Medellín's museum of modern art, whose building is reminiscent of a converted warehouse in Brooklyn. I was excited to get to know *paisas*, the demonym of people from Medellín, who are praised for their charm, creativity, and heart-melting accent.

My driver takes me from the airport past haciendas and through winding roads into Ciudad del Rio, a neighborhood where industrial warehouses give way to modern apartments, hipster cafés, and a gourmet food court. When I arrive at my Airbnb, a Chinese exchange student greets me, leads me up to a two-bedroom apartment on the twenty-third floor, and robotically hands me the key. I drop my stuff and then immediately go lie in the hammock draped across the balcony. As darkness falls, I gaze at the glittering *comunidades*, former slums and the relics of the city's poverty, that sprawl across the hills. They shower the skyline with sparkles in the night.

There's a knock at the door.

"Buenas tardes, socio."

It's Clarke. He had suggested we reunite in Colombia at some point, and he steps into the apartment carrying nothing more than a small suitcase. I almost reach to give him a hug, but recalling his awkward reaction in Santo Domingo, I settle for one Latin-style kiss on the cheek.

We had made a pact as socios to support each other to work hard, eat healthy, and eliminate alcohol during the week, but it clearly wasn't going to last. Clarke heads to the closest supermarket and returns with three beers and a bottle of rosé, which he opens for us as we catch up.

I HAD SUCCESSFULLY found a great dance school to learn Colombia's national dance: cumbia. Even though cumbia is from Cartagena and the coast,[96] Medellín is Colombia's cultural capital, and the abundance of excellent dance schools and universities with leading arts programs here makes it the perfect place to learn any Colombian dance.

I meet Mayra, the owner of the Santo Baile dance school, located in the up-and-coming neighborhood of Envigado, at the school's entrance. Her sleek black hair drapes down to her toned abs, adding panache to the dance training clothes that she rocks, which on an average woman would look ordinary. She treats me with warmth and kindness, which I will later understand are typical of Colombian *amabilidad* (kindness).

Bright and colorful signs with motivational quotes cover the school walls, one of which espouses my own philosophy toward dance: "I don't dance because I live, I live because I dance." When I dance I feel alive, and while it took the depths of sadness to realize that, I'm grateful for the journey that led me here to Medellín. "This is Felipe," she says, motioning toward my teacher, a slightly effeminate man several years younger than me. He leads me toward the mirror to start a warm-up to "Otra Vez" (One More Time), a new reggaeton hit by Zion & Lennox featuring J Balvin, one of Medellín's reggaeton stars.

I ask Felipe how he got into dance, and he tells me that he began dancing as a child to accompany his mother, who danced *porro* (a faster offshoot of cumbia). He took classes and improved considerably, eventually incorporating a porro group in Dubai. Now he studies dance at the University of Medellín and is thrilled to be making a living doing what he loves.

He leads me to the middle of the room and starts to show me the basic step. It's just like what Carolina had shown me in Cartagena—a tiny shuffle, feet grounded close together to represent shackled steps, with one clearly leading as the other gently drags behind. This miniscule movement creates an equally small but meticulously marked movement in the hips that until recently I had only seen Shakira do.

Felipe puts on a sonorous cumbia; the bare beat of the drums accompanies the impressionable vibrant sound of the *gaita Colombiana* or *kuisi*—a "Colombian bagpipe" made out of cactus and beeswax. A woman's voice begins to wail in a mix of pain and jubilation.

We both do the step, which I find uses a tiny muscle on each side of my butt that I didn't even know existed, and I follow his lead to dance in a circle. At times, we zigzag playfully around one another. He motions for me to place my hands on my hips as I shuffle past him sideways, or to circle him provocatively with open arms. Cumbia is a courtship dance, after all—one that traces its origins to the celebratory Guinean cumbe dance and evolved as a blend of African, European, and indigenous influences propelled by the beat of drums, maracas, and gaita flutes.[97]

We stand side by side and each sweep an arm toward the ground before lifting our body up to step back and sweep that arm up above our head in a step meant to represent the strike of a machete in sugarcane plains.

"Cumbia is a dance of equality between men and women," he explains. "It is traditionally danced holding a candle, representing the sexual energy and power between the couple. As they pass the candle between one another, that power is being shared. As the wax melts, burning onto their hands, it shows bravery, evidence that both of them can withstand pain until the end of the dance."

MY CUMBIA CLASSES with Felipe progress well, but I am slower than he had predicted, so I extend to an additional two-hour class. Felipe and Mayra have put me in touch with people at the University of Antioquia to get hold of a traditional cumbia costume to wear when we film our video. Across town at campus, I meet a handsome paisa named Pastor outside the school gate. He leads me to a side street filled with small shops and stands that stretch downhill. It seems to be a hidden commercial hub. One of the stores is his, and we glide in between its mannequins as he takes me to a small changing room where his sister has hung up a red-and-white cotton costume for me to try.

"*¡Qué linda!*" (How pretty!), they exclaim as I come out in the corset and full skirt. The dancers I had seen in the festivals in Ciénaga and Cartagena wore bright bold colors, but in this red-and-white checkered fabric, I feel like a Swiss milkmaid. I ask them what kind of costume this is, and Pastor assures me that red and white is the most traditional.

After rushing to the back of the store to bring out the men's costume, complete with a woven straw hat and a red neck scarf, he tells me yet another theory of the origins of cumbia.

"It's the story of an indigenous man courting an African woman, where the candles represent the sexual link and communication between the two. It's danced counterclockwise and in a circular pattern drawing from its origins as an indigenous dance ritual to worship the sun."

I've also read and heard from Felipe that the dance follows an African man courting an indigenous woman, but I wonder if the subtext is wider. Perhaps this dance depicts the larger interactions between the different groups? Perhaps courtship is a metaphor for broader quandaries of interdependence, colonialism, and assimilation?

"When the conquistadors came to the Americas, they took away all the indigenous women, and the indigenous men found themselves without any women. So instead they went to try their luck with women of another race, those from what they called back then the black race. When the woman accepts the candles, it means that she accepts the relationship. The volume of candles reflects the economic situation of the man."

Like Felipe, Pastor brings up the issue of equality between the sexes in this dance where the woman has equal status to the man, and her bravery is valued just as much as his. She must prove that she can handle the hot melting wax on her hands—or even dripping onto her face, as she dances with the candles balanced on her head.

"But it's also a battle," he continues, "where the candles are the ammunition." The man uses the candlelight to attract the woman, but the woman wards him off with her flames.

I ARRIVE AT Santo Baile early for class and walk around aimlessly with a huge black garbage bag slung across my shoulder carrying my costume. Were it not for my shimmery leggings and blue-lens Ray-Bans, I would look like an outright mess. A motorcycle beeps at me, and turning to avoid what might be another catcaller, I'm relieved to see it's my teacher Felipe.

Once Mayra lets us inside, I open my garbage bag for Felipe to inspect my costume.

"¡Divino!" he exclaims, looking at the corseted top with red ribbons and the large skirt. He contemplates his own costume, checking that he has all the accessories—a red necktie, woven bag, and straw hat—and then picks up the candles bundled together in red ribbon.

"You didn't find some sort of pot or dish to hold them together?"

I shake my head no. Back at Pastor's shop, we had tried various stalls looking for something to hold the candles together, without success.

"Okay, we have to be brave then. The wax will probably melt onto our hands."

I like the authenticity of this, like the legend of cumbia, to show my bravery and ability to tolerate the pain. As we set up our improvised stage, denoting it with masking tape, the camera balancing on top of a high chair,

Felipe leans in to light the candles. I hold them preciously in my hands, watching the flames kindling one by one and reflecting against his face.

I hand the candles to Felipe and move into position to practice the circular arm movements that make the skirt ripple. My shoulders and shoulder blades feel so weak, but I need to use all the strength that I have.

"Ready?" asks Felipe as he juggles the burning candles and his smartphone to play the music.

We launch into our choreography, but during the first two takes I feel stiff, like something is blocked. I enjoy dancing with Felipe—he knows my weaknesses but doesn't punish me for them. Instead he encourages me through the things I find difficult, like the *coqueteo* (flirting)—and yet despite his encouragement, summoning confidence is a challenging barrier to overcome. In this dance, maintaining a beaming smile while adding elements of flirtation and seduction is key. After all, most of these traditional dances portray a courtship. The woman teases the man as she rejects, then eventually accepts, his advances.

Having to embody this back-and-forth in a dance reveals a great shyness in myself, but remembering how horrible a stressed-out dancer looks on film, I muster all my strength to go at it again, this time with more personality and expression. Keeping eye contact with Felipe the whole time, I soften my plastered grin to a genuine, affectionate smile. I playfully take the candles from him as I spin to push him away with my twirling skirt, holding the candles' blazing flames above my head before handing them back to him and inviting him to follow me as I dance away, glancing behind my shoulder in provocation.

The dance ends with us joining each other side by side, leaning in toward the candles to blow out the flames and then hiding behind his hat—the moment that symbolizes a union sealed with a kiss.

JUAN'S GRANDFATHER, A paisa, had been a regular at a mystical dance venue called the Salón Málaga. Opened in 1957, it is a sanctuary of yesterday, a bastion of historical and cultural heritage of Medellín, and a place where locals of all ages go to dance old porros and tangos.

I want to experience it for myself, so Clarke and I take a car through dark and empty streets, singing along to Latin pop songs to calm our nerves through the deserted, apocalyptic commercial center. The shops and vendors have shut for the day and it's very quiet. Occasionally, a solitary figure pops out, staring wide-eyed at our car like a deer caught in headlights. Whatever you do, our driver warns us, don't walk alone here at night.

When the Salón Málaga comes into view, it looks like an island of light and music, filled with merry patrons who dance in a row and wave us in from the window. The inside has a bohemian air of poetry and longing—a result of the soft porro beats, polished black-and-white tiles, a retro jukebox filled with an extensive record collection, and vintage frames of famous regulars. The waitress, intrigued by the patronage of two gringos, invites us to a table with a prime view of the small dance floor and takes our order of Aguila beers.

"That's the *patrón*" (the boss), she says, motioning her head toward an older gentleman wearing a panama hat. He seems to have retained his vitality and gets up to dance porro with one of the waitresses.

I admire the locals. They seem to be mostly in their fifties or sixties, with the occasional younger couple, and are soulfully dancing to tangos, porros, and boleros, at times even dancing different dances to the same music. My gaze rests on one of the younger couples: a woman in hot pants, stilettos, and a bold red top with long, peroxided hair pulled into a high ponytail, and her partner, who wears a T-shirt advertising a brand of tires. They dance an elegant tango, gliding across the tiles in an amorous embrace, to the bouncy beat of porro music.

If tango were to have a second capital in the world after Buenos Aires, it would be Medellín. It emerged as a popular dance style in Colombia in the 1920s, but it was firmly cemented as an iconic form of expression here in 1935 when Carlos Gardel, the iconic tango singer, died in a plane crash in Medellín. Among the photographs that fill the walls of the Salón Málaga is a classic black-and-white portrait of Gardel. He smiles at us as if in testimony of his, and tango's, cultural significance.

As the song comes to an end, the woman wraps her leg around her partner's waist, her knee almost reaching his shoulder, and tucks her face into his neck. It doesn't matter that she's wearing hot pants and her partner is wearing a T-shirt. They could be wearing paper bags or ball gowns—it wouldn't make her any more or less poised, or him any more or less captivating. Dance, with its championing of expression and connection, makes elegance and beauty accessible to everyone. It releases you from your social classification and expectations and, for the time of a song, allows you to be anyone you want to be.

I watch another couple, this one dancing porro gracefully and joyfully, and after another Aguila beer, I find the courage to approach their table. I tell them that they are the best porro dancers I've seen tonight, and although the wife seems slightly cold at first, when I politely ask her permission to borrow her husband for a dance, her face softens.

The man takes my hand and leads me to the dance floor under the amused watch of the locals. He tells me that the important part of dancing porro is to keep the movement in my hips smooth and light. He says to let my hips sway as I dance.

Following his lead, we step from side to side, nearly zigzagging across the dance floor. His wife and her friends cheer from their table as I follow my partner in lifting my arms up in a *V* and slowly twirling around to face him again. He's a sweet señor whose almost fatherly affection will reflect in the faces of many more dance partners and figures along my journey.

Meanwhile, the owner has fallen asleep at his table behind a bottle of Chivas Regal whisky, which Clarke and I take as a cue to move on with our evening.

To escape from the narco stereotypes of TV shows and films, Clarke and I embark on a "cultural day" to witness the real Medellín, a city of modernity and social transformation.

We enter a spotless metro station and follow the crowd onto the platform. As an outsider, I observe the people and sights around me, and I can't help but breathe in a feeling of hope, aspiration, and energy that radiates progress.[98] The train snakes through Medellín's major landmarks and neighborhoods, and once we reach Acevedo station, we transfer to one of the city's proudest achievements: the cable car that now connects people from what used to be the roughest comunidades to the center of the city. The cable car flies over tall buildings and small houses, some in plain red bricks and others in bright colors. Some houses seem makeshift, with bricks holding down thin metal roofs, and others have been maintained with care, beautified by colorful flowerpots on tiny, three-foot-long terraces. I can see people hanging their laundry to dry on their roofs and others painting advertisements or political messages targeting the commuters that hover above them. Children play, teenagers flirt, and an abuelita sits in a plastic chair on her porch and watches the world go by.

Graffiti murals greet us on arrival at Santo Domingo Savio station. What was once Pablo Escobar's operational playground and one of the most violent places in all of Latin America, the Comuna Popular neighborhood, is now, thanks to urban planning and social investment, an innovative space with a library, park, and incredible city views.

Our self-guided tour takes us back downhill to the city center and to the botanical garden, where we observe its vast collection of orchids in an architecturally impressive orchidiarium and butterfly house. From there we're off to the Museum of Antioquia. Built in 1881, it was Colombia's second museum and is home to one of the world's largest collections of artwork from Fernando Botero, a Medellín-born cultural icon, painter, and sculptor famous for his round-bodied sculptures and for a painting featuring the death of Pablo Escobar.

Although Botero's signature style was driven more by a fascination for volume than body types,[99] the voluptuous figures in his artwork invite a reflection on the ideals of beauty found throughout Colombia. A recent visit to Medellín's Oviedo shopping mall had served as an informative social incubator for my observations. The legacy of *narco-estética* ("narco aesthetics"), as a Colombian friend once called it, remained evident in the enhanced curves and exaggerated feminine figures that I had seen.

On visits to the United States, Colombian drug lords had discovered silicone-endowed prostitutes, *Playboy*, and *Hustler*,[100] bringing back the concept to make Medellín the plastic surgery capital of Latin America. If you wanted a rich boyfriend, you had to get with a narco. And to get with a narco, you needed implants. It wasn't uncommon for young paisas to be gifted with implants from their fathers for their *quinceañeras*—the landmark fifteenth-birthday parties that resemble debutante balls.[101] Those less privileged sometimes pulled together their savings and risked their lives in illegal "garage clinics,"[102] with the conviction that liposuction or silicone was the key to their self-esteem. This popular belief, unfortunately, continues to impact younger women.[103]

As the sun begins to set, we head to our final stop, Pueblito Paisa, a reproduction of a traditional Antioquian village. It sits atop the Nutibara Hill and is home to a turn-of-the-century town square, church, and barbershop. The small white houses with red-tiled roofs and colorful painted balconies with hanging flower baskets give way to a panoramic view over Medellín. We buy a couple of Aguila beers from a local stand and head to the viewpoint to watch the sunset. With the exception of an intense American man on a Google Translate Tinder date with a pretty young paisa, everyone is quiet, watching the lights scintillate across the Aburrá Valley at dusk.

CALI

CLARKE AND I land in Santiago de Cali—or Cali for short. The sugarcane plantations of Valle del Cauca we saw from the plane are a stark contrast from the emerald hills of Antioquia that we've just left behind, stretching out into infinity, transporting me to the painful past of colonial times. They witnessed the suffering of thousands of slaves—transported from nearby Buenaventura, Colombia's largest port—striking their machetes in the punishing heat.[104]

The legacy of the infamous Cali cartel, which by 2001 controlled 70 percent of the cocaine market in the United States and 90 percent in Europe, has contributed to Cali's often ranking among the most dangerous cities in the world,[105] and the vibe here seems different from that of other Colombian cities. There's a buzzing energy in the air as people bustle about the sizzling concrete-clad streets. Cali is an inland tropical city—gritty and a less common attraction for tourists. Foreigners stand out. We stand out.

According to legend, a demon named Buziraco once lived on a hill overlooking Cali and plagued the city with disease and debauchery. In 1837, two friars set up a cross on the hill to protect the city. It protected the city against Buziraco but was destroyed by the 1925 earthquake. In 1938, it was replaced by three crosses, and those are still propped up today.

But while Buziraco was defeated, Cali couldn't escape its demons and became ridden with danger and depravity.[106] But now, as it emerges from the stigma of its dark past of narco-trafficking and assassinations, it bustles with a new kind of explosive energy: salsa.

Cali has gone from kidnapping capital to salsa capital. Where it was once home to one of the world's highest homicide rates,[107] it now boasts the highest salsa dancing rate per capita.[108] It has more than two hundred salsa schools officially registered, as well as countless unofficial schools, and a wealth of salsa clubs, venues, and discotheques. As we speed into the center of the city, we pass an enormous brass monument in the shape of trumpets and trombones merged into one.

Maycoll, our taxi driver, points toward the eighty-foot-long structure, a monument dedicated to Jairo Varela, the founder and director of Grupo Niche, one of the most important salsa groups of all time and the most famous to come out of Colombia. Seen from above, the huge structure spells out the word "Niche." It's a declaration of love for salsa, and inside each instrument's bells are lyrics from some of the band's most famous songs and audio of an instrumental ensemble of "Cali Pachanguero," the iconic song that pays homage to the city's sizzling salsa scene.

The car stops on a cobblestone street in San Antonio, a traditional barrio with small colonial houses and a bohemian tranquility where we have rented an apartment brimming with books and artifacts from a Cali-born artist. Today is my first day of *salsa Caleña* (Cali-style salsa) and I've put on my black shimmery leggings for the occasion.

"Where are we going, señorita?" asks Alejandro, my Uber driver.

Even though my destination will inevitably appear on his smartphone, like most Colombians, Alejandro prefers to communicate with a person rather than an application.

"Santa Monica Popular," I reply as I slip into his seven-seater pickup truck.

Alejandro frowns. A family friend had pleaded with me to choose a dance school closer to where I'm staying because this one is close to the Autopista Sur, a highway dividing central from eastern Cali, which is home to some of its most dangerous neighborhoods. But I was determined to go to this school, and besides, I'd found a handy color-coded map online based on the number of active gang members per barrio, and this school is only on the border of the red zone.

In a city that has over two hundred dance schools, how had I concluded that this was the right one for me? While in Medellín I'd contacted a few other schools in addition to this one, but I hadn't been able to decide until

I'd asked Mayra—a Cali native and professional dancer—for advice.

"Combinación Rumbera," she'd said without hesitation. "It's the school where I chose to train. The director and teachers are such humble and generous people, and they're nothing less than champions."

Their slogan, "More than a group, but a way of life," confirmed I was making the right choice. Clearly the school and I share the same philosophy.

With drivers being regular sources of insight into local life during this Latin American journey, I ask Alejandro about his reaction.

"*¡Está todo jodido p'allá!*" (It's completely fucked up over there!) he tells me, shaking his head.

Slightly taken aback by his rather indelicate description, I reassure him that it's west of the autopista everyone warns about.

He nods his head toward a dodgy-looking shirtless man readjusting the rosary draped across his bare, tattooed chest as he walks past our car, and he tells me to be careful not to cross the autopista. I might end up in a barrio full of thieves.

I wonder why criminals in Latin America appear to be so religious, incorporating Catholic symbolism and motifs in their style. Are the rosaries meant to be protective? Prophylactic forgiveness for sins to come?

The car pulls up in front of a red building. The school stands just above a huge bakery displaying endless shelves of *pan de bono*, a corn- and cassava-based crumbly cheese bread that is one of Cali's signature delicacies.

Up the stairs I find a school that seems to be under renovation, and empty, but when I step into the first room I meet a charming Colombian woman. She's about my age, has a huge mane of curls and bright brown eyes, and introduces herself as Diana. She's been waiting for me and will be teaching me *estilo feminine* ("lady style") before my male teacher arrives. She gently leads me toward a large mirror in the studio where she takes me through the basic steps of Cali-style salsa.

She places her hands on my arms as she slowly guides me through the steps, and I feel that she genuinely wants to transmit everything she knows *con sentimiento* (with feeling). It seems easy enough to follow at first, but she slowly starts to increase the speed. Soon my brain can barely keep up with the pace of my knees and feet.

"Cali-style is all about tiptoes and flexed knees," she says. "If you thought cumbia killed your ass, Cali-style salsa will kill your calves."

My second teacher arrives, a handsome man dressed in sports clothes. He's muscular, with dark blond hair, hazel eyes, and long eyelashes. Diana introduces him as John Freddy, my teacher, not the John Freddy who is the school's director.

While John Freddy is not as gentle as Diana, and seems a bit more direct, he is no less professional or polite. As Diana and I dance together, he sits by the mirror, observing carefully, then walks away to practice some steps for a few minutes before returning. It's like he's putting together a puzzle.

After we finish showing him the steps I've learned, he asks me to sit down, which I find strange for a dance class. He pulls out a pen and paper and starts to draw different circles and arrows in all directions.

"This method is from a great teacher of salsa Caleña called Luz Aydé Moncayo Giraldo," he tells me as he continues to draw circles. "She found a way to explain the basic steps to foreigners so that they can visualize them. It helps them learn more, and in less time, and also helps the teachers get past the language barrier if they don't speak much English."

He hands me the paper covered in symbols, and they instantly start to make sense, with the arrows showing the different directions of the feet. We go through each of the steps a couple times, and he seems to be satisfied as I keep up with him through the various sequences.

"Now try to follow me," he says. He turns to face me and takes my hands in his, stretching my arms out to each side while keeping our elbows bent, until they're almost in a *V* shape. It's very different from the one-armed embrace common in other styles of salsa. He takes me through three sets of footwork, which, although seemingly complex, I'm surprisingly able to follow. We dance faster and faster, filling in every beat with our feet without any pause in movement.

It's easier for me to dance quickly than slowly. When I dance quickly, there's no time for hesitation that leads to mistakes. I wonder if most of my mistakes in dance, and maybe also in life, come from my thoughts rather than my ability. My feet speed up, transporting me into a sort of autopilot driven by instinct and musicality, not by fear or self-doubt.

After class, I stop by the bakery to pick up some pan de bono and try to process the euphoria I've just experienced. I haven't eaten all day, and three hours of dancing on my tiptoes and bouncing my knees has left me hungry. The friendly man behind the counter recommends a selection of items and hands them to me in a small paper bag.

"Are you new around here?"

"Yes, I just enrolled in the school upstairs," I say as I smile shyly.

"Well, there's nothing like pan de bono after dancing salsa!"

As the famous Cali-based salsa group Grupo Niche says: "*Esto es cuestión de pan de bono*"—this is a question of pan de bono (or of Caleño identity). I always find solace in practicing mundane activities in other countries, doing the things that locals do, to feel closer to other cultures in a way that is simple, honest, and authentic. As I stand on the corner of the autopista, eating pan de bono and shuffling to the sound of salsa coming from the school's window, I relish the feeling of belonging to a world that isn't my own.

ANOTHER DAY, ANOTHER Uber. This time my driver isn't as engaged as Alejandro and gets lost on the way to my school. I can tell he can sense my impatience as he peers at me in the rearview mirror. Maybe he's new in town and doesn't know his way around. Eventually I spot the red bakery on the other side of the autopista and direct him over.

I'm already late, and after greeting my new friend at the bakery, I fly up the stairs and into the dance studio, breathless.

"You're familiar with the clave, right?" asks Diana, clapping its beat with her hands. "In Cali-style, we step on every single beat. We never take a break."

I nod understandingly. Yesterday's class had given me insight into the sheer speed of the footwork, and it seems there wouldn't be time for a break. Maybe each country's style reflects its respective culture and way of life.

"You need to learn how to lock your elbows so that your partner will be able to hold your weight up while you do decorations with your feet. Look at this," she says, taking my hands. As I hold her up, she points one of her legs out to the side and then, at lightning speed, starts twisting it in and out and then back to the center before doing the same with the other leg. My eyes can barely follow—her legs almost resemble scissors. "Now you try."

Hesitantly, I place my hands in hers. This kind of move makes me conscious of how heavy I am. Though I'm not overweight, I'm not that light either. I worry that I'll topple over. As I do the move in slow motion, my muscle memory begins to kick in. I've done something similar before that my body seems to remember. Racking my brain, I find the answer: the *punta tacón*, or what they call *punta talón* here, the heel-and-toe step in Mexican folklore dancing. The two dances couldn't be more different from one another, but the sequence is strikingly similar.

I ask Diana how the punta talón made it from the traditional dances dating back hundreds of years in Mexico to 1970s Cali salsa, and she explains her theory that Colombians watched a lot of Mexican cinema and television series in the 1970s.[109] She says that Cali salsa dancers took some steps from the folklore dances they saw in telenovelas and adapted them, mixing them with other styles including *Pacifico* dances—dances from the Pacific region.

"You know," she says, "Cali salsa started off without any rules. Caleños never used to dance in time with the music and did all sorts of things with their feet. The only reason we started having rules, like counting the beat and things like that, was so that we could compete internationally."

I like this idea of not having rules and being free to dance in whatever way you want, even if others might consider it wrong. Who cares if it's wrong if it feels good?

"Let me show you another move. It's called *patinetas*." She stands behind me and holds my arms out to the side.

"Like skateboards?" I ask, amused at the name of the steps translated in English.

I quickly understand the connection. One foot makes a sweeping movement on the floor, similar to the foot movement that puts a skateboard in motion, and then there are tiny, fast steps before the next foot sweeps out to the other side. We practice this for a while and become so in tune with one another that we almost look like synchronized salsa twins.

When eventually I'm out of breath, we stop and rest by the mirror as we wait for John Freddy. Diana tells me that she's just returned to Colombia after having been out of the country for more than five years, working in Dubai, Oman, and other places in the Middle East. She has a Cuban boyfriend from a small village just outside of Havana.

"My dream is to travel to Cuba, Brazil, and all over Latin America," she says, her gaze drifting.

I'm not sure if she means that she wants to dance in all of these countries or just visit them, but I realize that I'm not only living my own dream but also the dream of many dancers along my path—like Teodora in New York, and now Diana, a champion dancer from Cali.

John Freddy walks in and seems to be a little stressed as his phone buzzes with notifications. He throws it into his bag and stands in front of me.

"Right, explain to me exactly what you've been doing with your dance project."

Now that I have it almost memorized in Spanish, I recite the whole story, including where I've danced and with whom.

"Griselle Ponce?" he asks with widening eyes. "She's one of the most well-known and acclaimed salseras in the world!"

Launching my journey with Griselle in New York was the most sparkling start one could ask for. At the time, my salsa ignorance meant I didn't know who she was, but now I understand why they call her the Mambo Diva. She'd been so sweet and humble, always telling me to never give up on my dreams. I took for granted that I had begun my journey under the auspices of a world-famous dance icon.

We start to talk about how dance pushes you to be determined and disciplined, and how it has so many unexpected effects on the brain. John Freddy asks if I've heard of Howard Gardner's theory of multiple intelligences.

This not only happens to have been one of the most important theories in my career, it was also a key reference in my work on happiness in schools. The theory argues that rather than there being one form of human intelligence, human intelligence encompasses several abilities. I can't help but be surprised that a salsa dancer in Cali is so well versed in a 1980s theory put forth by a Harvard professor. John Freddy begins to explain how dance, quite literally, requires a person to use multiple intelligences at the same time.

"We use visual-spatial intelligence because we need to recognize the movements, musical rhythmic intelligence because we connect with the rhythm of the music, bodily-kinesthetic intelligence because we feel that movement in our bodies, and logical-mathematical intelligence because we need to count and move ourselves within a limited space and time."

This lecture perfectly captures my motives for ending up here. I have a passion for learning these dances, yes, but my interest goes beyond the dances themselves. I want to learn the sources of joy. I want to develop a multitude of abilities and intelligences to guide me in my search for what it means to live a good life. Gaining knowledge of the dances themselves and a Rolodex of folkloric movement and salsa-infused steps would be nice, but it isn't everything. It is the *learning* to dance that calls me. Learning to cope with and navigate the multiple challenges that dance, just like life, provokes—that is the journey.

If Gardner is right, dance goes beyond just making you feel happy—it embraces all forms of intelligence and strengthens them. Creativity and education expert Sir Ken Robinson, whom I have deeply admired throughout my career, argued that schools should consider dance as important as traditional subjects and that it makes us better at those other subjects.[110] Surely it must be the same for adults. Perhaps dance should be compulsory in schools and also in the workplace.

"Dance isn't a talent," John Freddy continues. "It's something that can be developed through time and effort."

Clearly his statement relates to growth mindset, another powerful theory considered the key behind many people's success. Championed by Stanford psychologist Carol Dweck, the theory challenges fixed theories of intelligence and ability and posits that anything is possible through effort and resilience, which allow for greater levels of learning and success.[111] I'm impressed by John Freddy's knowledge and discourse. Beyond the technique, his discourse shows me that he digs deeper into the benefits of dance for personal growth.

John Freddy tells me that back in the day, the elite listened and danced to porro music and shunned salsa, which is what the lower classes danced to. Now Cali's identity is defined by salsa. He starts to write down a long list of books and movies for me to read and watch to learn more about Cali's salsa history.

I press him for more information about the history of dance in Cali, and he tells me that salsa hit its prime in the seventies when *la vieja guardia* (the old guard) would dance to *salsa de golpe*—a harder salsa style with "punch" that can be naturally punctuated by the Caleño fast feet. According to John Freddy, the nineties brought a slower and softer style—*salsa romantica*—and it led to an exodus of Cali's renowned *bailadores* (dancers) to foreign lands in search of opportunities that welcomed their frenetic, fast-paced style. But in the latter part of the 1990s and early 2000s, salsa de golpe made a comeback, leading to a revolution in Caleño style and local and national competitions.

"There are three types of dancers. First, the social dancer who goes out dancing just for fun and has the basics. Then you have the bailador, who isn't a professional dancer but highly skilled with a lot of moves. Finally, there's the *bailarín,* who dances professionally and competes—the best of the best." He takes a breath, contemplating me for a second. "I think for you, we're going to aim for bailador."

I can barely conceal my excitement. I'm flattered he thinks I can get there. Based on his knowledge and professionalism, there must be sincerity in his judgment. He's methodological in his approach to dance and teaching, has several technical diplomas, and has attended many workshops on arts education. He even teaches Latin dance at one of the local universities as part of a wellness program. It's one thing to be a good dancer, another to be a good teacher, and another to be a good choreographer, and John Freddy has mastered all three. Most of his dance pedagogy is self-taught, since dance classes are prohibitively expensive for most Colombians. They are very affordable for foreigners, like me.

He claps his hands and directs me to show him what I remember.

I slowly go through the many sequences I've learned in the past two days. John Freddy then teaches me a new step called *dinos* and tells me that one of the theories in Cali is that the step was named in honor of a dancer from la vieja guardia nicknamed *el Dinosaurio* (the Dinosaur), presumably in reference to his old age. The move involves marching while tapping the floor with pointed toes and launching into elevated but intricate mambo steps that lightly bounce our knees higher, causing a satisfying and reverberating movement in the hips.

After class, I pick up another bag of pan de bono and head home to meet Clarke. We plan to explore local life in the barrio for the rest of the day and start by stopping by a café for a special local juice, *jugo de lulo* (lulo juice). Its lulo fruit is only found in parts of Colombia and neighboring countries and looks like a tomato but tastes somewhere in between an orange, a passion fruit, and a guava. I later read unique descriptions of its taste, describing it as akin to everything from sherbet to Skittles. There couldn't be a more perfect drink to refresh with after three intense hours of salsa Caleña.

We finish our juice and head up the hills and onto a narrow cobblestone street, walking past rows of white colonial houses with large wooden doors. We stop by a tiny antiques shop manned by a centenarian and a young Caleña who appears to be his granddaughter and unsuccessfully tries to convince us to buy porcelain tea sets. As we continue walking, we find a small park on a hill leading up to one of the most iconic sights of the city: the San Antonio Church. One of the oldest churches in Cali, with a white brick facade topped by a small bell tower, it offers a panoramic view of the city. From there, I can see an orange haze that haunts the skyline. I'd like to think it's caused by the heat of hundreds of salsa steps happening all over town at this very moment.

I'M NOT THE first to be fascinated by the social and educational benefits of salsa Caleña, and dance in general. John Freddy tells me that he even worked with someone who came to take classes as part of an anthropological study.

"You know, we even have curriculum guidelines on artistic education in Colombia," he says seriously.

Columbia's Ministry of Education has realized how arts such as dance and theater can give students values and attributes that a purely traditional education cannot give, and even has striking tenets regarding this in its curriculum guidelines: "The arts offer a language that has written our history, our customs, our dreams and utopias, our love and heartbreak, and our successes and failures."[112] Such emotive language in a ministry document is possible only in a culture that is not afraid to feel. And beyond this dreamy vision are concrete competencies that the arts, especially dance, are capable of offering. From the text in this ministry document, I understand these as: healthy relationships; attention to detail; the understanding that a single problem has multiple solutions and that our path toward our goals may change during the journey; confident decision-making in the absence of rules; imagination as a fountain of creation; the pursuit of possibilities when faced by limitations; and an understanding of the world from a point of view of ethics and aesthetics.[113]

"There's a model of learning when it comes to dance," John Freddy tells me. "Phase one: *imitación* (imitation). You see someone dancing, observe them carefully, then try to imitate them. Then you have phase two: *indagnación*."

"Indignation?" I ask, wondering how anger and resentment could help someone learn to dance.

"No, no, no. *Indagnación*, not *indignación*. It means 'inquiry'. This is the creative phase."

We continue to talk about the importance of creativity in life, and in dance, and he tells me about an amazing soloist named Carlos Paz, who created his very own dance steps purely based on his own interpretation of the music.

"Salsa Caleña really gives a lot more freedom to interpret the music than other styles," he continues, "especially with our feet."

John Freddy tells me that before there were dance schools in Cali, the only way to learn how to dance was to pay fifty cents to get into a club, sit down, and watch other people dance, observing their feet and then trying to imitate. But over time, Cali's dance schools opened, and some even started developing signature steps. *Latinos*, for example, is a step with a kick and point that was created by El Mulato, the renowned founder of Swing Latino, Cali's most famous dance school. The school is known for having trained Jennifer Lopez and for winning many competitions. Today this step is pivotal, literally, for the repertoire of any salsa Caleña dancer.

I ask John Freddy if anyone ever tried to document all the different steps, wondering how all these intricate staccato sequences have been passed on from one generation to the next, and he tells me that Carlos Estacio, director of the Escuela de Baile Acrosalsa Latina, tried to do a codification of all the Caleño steps to keep a record of them and create a standard across the different schools. He tells me there's a book on it somewhere, and the University of Salsa also does work around this.

"The University of Salsa?" I ask, surprised at the nickname that many Colombians use for Universidad de San Buenaventura Cali.

He looks at his watch and quickly goes to put the music back on. We go through several of the Caleño steps together, and he carefully watches my feet.

"Right, now dance on your own," he says. "Do you know why I'm making you do that?" he continues, noticing my surprised face.

"So that I can internalize what I've learned?"

Thinking about it, it's the moments when I'm alone with the steps, usually with my eyes closed, that they become engraved in my mind. This is deliberate practice—repeating the same thing again and again until it becomes natural, as preached by Angela Duckworth.

He watches me for a while and then takes my hands in his and lifts my arms to steer them from side to side as we mirror each other's jaunty steps. He turns me a few times, each one igniting a short, explosive flame in my heart, before jumping back into fast footwork and a series of perfectly synchronized kicks. My movements are more fluid, more natural than before.

I am learning how to be a good follower—a critical milestone for any beginner. It's not so easy to allow yourself to be guided by someone else, to relinquish control and compel yourself to let go. And it is certainly not easy to do this while keeping your intuition engaged and reflexes sharp.

With a new sense of confidence, I finally feel like I'm ready to go dancing at one of Cali's most famous salsa clubs, Tin Tin Deo, and Clarke, always intrigued by the promise of a night out, offers to join me to check out the vibe.

We walk through the club's door, which is under an enormous neon sign, and make our way up a narrow stairway, hearing the sound of salsa grow increasingly louder as we near. As in almost all the salsa clubs I've visited on my journey, a large framed poster with the watchful gaze of Héctor Lavoe hangs on one wall, an image used on one of his record covers. I feel like Héctor Lavoe is following me along my journey. A large crowd fills the dance floor, and the frenetic energy of salsa Caleña can be felt en masse. The crowd is a mix of locals and foreigners, and we spot a peculiar gringo dancing by himself in his own eccentric style.

Clarke raises his eyebrows at the sight of him and turns to the bar. "Dios mío, I need a drink."

We sip our cocktails as I watch the crowd and eagerly wait for an invitation to dance. I get off the barstool and decide to stand instead, hoping that it might be a clearer indication to potential dance partners that I'm available and ready to dance. But nobody approaches me.

"We need to find you a dance partner, socio!" says Clarke encouragingly.

It's not easy to find a dance partner when we are out together. People inevitably assume that we are involved, putting off prospective partners. I take two large steps to the side away from the bar, leaving Clarke swaying to the music on his barstool. Finally, a timid German man approaches me, and though I've come here to dance with Caleños, I imagine he's as nervous as I am and that he too has come here to learn and practice. We dance at a very basic but enjoyable level. The grin on his face is a mirror of one I've seen on myself. He's also someone from a colder, less expressive culture who has come here to find the very opposite. As the song ends, I'm immediately picked up by my next dance partner, who proceeds to make me move in so many different directions that I can barely follow. The feeling of dread takes over once again, washing away my confidence that has taken so long to build.

Taking a break at the bar, I spot a woman with wild curls who is dressed in black. She seems familiar. Her name is Kathy, from Germany, and I recall that she had been taking classes with Felipe at the same school in Medellín immediately after mine. She seems elated, almost gravitating off the floor as she dances. I can tell that she's in that state of salsa flow—a level where you stop worrying how you dance and allow yourself to be carried away by the music. This is when salsa feels exquisite, almost like you're transported to heaven. El Gran Combo, one of the world's oldest salsa orchestras, caught on to that feeling long ago and captured it in the title of the song "Sin Salsa, No Hay Paraíso" (Without Salsa, There Is No Paradise).

I WAVE HELLO to my friend at the bakery and then rush up the stairs to the studio. I've now mastered Cali-style's basic step with fast diagonal kicks and cha-cha steps in between, propelling my vigorous hip movements. I've learned to create almost geometrical shapes by tapping the tips of my toes in strategic spots and scissoring my legs in the iconic punta talón. And today, I've set aside my fear of falling to make a small, graceful jump and land on John Freddy's thigh, which he then bends so my body leans to the side while my arm thrusts into the air to reach new heights.

We're advancing well in a choreography that I never could have imagined myself doing. But Diana and John Freddy have a way of breaking it down into small, achievable sequences, and the combination of Diana's encouragement and John Freddy's pedagogy is helping me learn faster than ever before. This kind of approach seems to be instilled in Combinación Rumbera's ethos, and they have no shortage of slogans to motivate their students.

"The slogan changes as the students progress," says John Freddy. "First we have 'We go like the elephant, slow but crushing,' because you have to learn slowly first. Then we have 'Always one step forward, and not a single one back.' And we have one for competitions." He gestures at a poster hanging on the wall with the words "Without the effort and struggle of rehearsal, it's impossible to achieve joy and victory."

In Combinación Rumbera, students work on a different value each day: friendship, respect, camaraderie, solidarity, dedication, and compromise. It's not compulsory for dance schools to champion specific values like these; this school chooses to do so because it works with vulnerable youth from barrios *populares*, socioeconomically disadvantaged or low-income neighborhoods. The school enrolls many students from Comuna 12, a group of barrios considered to be one of the poorest categories.[114] Since young people from the neighborhood started attending the school, there have been many positive changes in the community. Dancing at the school, especially with its emphasis on core ethical values, has helped the youth— some of whom had entered the school as former delinquents—to find an alternative to crime.

The work with disadvantaged youth is personal for John Freddy. He grew up in Barrio Paraíso, which is next to Barrio Santos—a very dangerous neighborhood. One of the teachers in his barrio was worried about the number of young people turning to crime, some of them even becoming *sicarios* (hit men) and trading drugs, so she consulted with the local church, the Parroquia Santa Ana, on what to do. They offered a small room for young people to use in their free time to stay out of trouble. But nobody really knew what to do with it, so she suggested they start a dance group there.

Combinación Rumbera was born out of this. It started to become known as La Catedral de la Salsa (The Cathedral of Salsa), and John Freddy the school's director (not John Freddy my dance teacher) would take charge at just seventeen years old. Over time, the group grew steadily.

My teacher John Freddy theorized to me that men started joining either because they wanted to learn to dance socially, to get girls, or were homosexual and wanted to be part of a group where they could be accepted without judgment. La Catedral de la Salsa allowed them to be themselves.

The story of Combinación Rumbera shows how the arts can contribute to the inclusion of people from all backgrounds—regardless of their race, gender, orientation, or socioeconomic situation.

"I'm grateful to this school for having trained me and given me a career in dance. Now I feel that I can give back to society."

We get back to the choreography. It's almost finished, missing only the ending.

"What song do you have in mind?" I ask him.

"'Cali Pachanguero,'" he replies affirmatively. "It's our anthem here."

We go through the routine again, but this time with the song. I have to move much faster than before, and it's exhilarating to feel the speed of my steps. Sunday morning, just a few days from now, we'll be wearing sparkling salsa costumes and performing this in front of a church.

On my way out I stop to pick up a new selection of pan de bono, but my friend suggests I try some different baked goods, including *pan de yuca,* a bread made from cassava starch and cheese, and the soft and squishy *almojábana,* a bread made from yuca flour and cheese, which turns out to be my favorite. I put in my headphones to listen to "Cali Pachanguero" as I wait for my car. Looking up at the window of the studio, I identify with their slogan even more than ever before. *"Más que un grupo, un estilo de vida"*—more than a group, but a way of life.

AFTER MY FINAL three hours of class, the choreography is done. Diana sits with me on one of the new red leather sofas in the reception area to chat. We're waiting for John Freddy and his fiancée, Zulma, to come back to the studio with a costume and professional flesh-colored fishnet tights for dancers.

When they arrive, they hand me a bag with a completely transparent bodysuit. It has an open back and dark blue sequins scattered strategically to provide minimal modesty.

"What kind of underwear do you even wear with this?" I ask.

"You don't wear any!" scoffs Zulma, amused by the horrified look on my face.

I put the costume on in the bathroom and then walk into the studio's hallway, where groups of students are hanging around. I feel naked, and embarrassed, with the bodysuit's tail of royal-blue sequins tucked between my legs. I squirm in my sequins, but the costume fits.

We'd considered a number of Cali's iconic spots as possible places to film the video, and ultimately we chose to film in front of one of the city's most iconic churches. Tomorrow is Sunday, and we'll meet at eight in the morning for the filming.

At home, I rehearse intensely. Thanks to my desire to do everything wholeheartedly, I need to feel that I've made the best possible effort to showcase my progress. When Clarke walks in, he slips into his room, nonplussed by my stomping and twirling. Eventually, I take a break to have dinner with him at a fancy-looking Pacífico-fusion restaurant on our street. It feels good to relax and enjoy dinner and a glass of wine. When in the final stages of memorizing a choreography before a performance, just like preparing for an exam, your brain reaches a level of saturation. The routine plays over and over in my head, and I try to unwind as I bite into my patacón.

"Do you know that they've named a salsa Caleña step after these?" I say to Clarke as I go in for a second patacón. "So many of these dance steps are named after aspects of local life like the *patacón pisado*—literally, trodden patacón. You step three times in a row with the same foot because when you make patacónes, you step on a bag full of mashed plantains to press them into flat slices."

"Dios mío! Well, they do love their plantains!" he replies.

We talk more about salsa and our shared hypothesis that it has the capacity to make anyone instantly happy. Feeling inspired, Clarke decides to venture out to the Topa Tolondra nightclub to find a sweet salsera who might invite him to dance, and while I'm dying to go out and join in the fun, I know it's wiser to go home and keep rehearsing.

After going through the choreography an additional four times, I finally feel like I'm starting to internalize it. Perhaps for once in this journey, I won't be clumsily stumbling through.

I go to bed early, determined to get enough rest, but "Cali Pachanguero" is playing on repeat in my head, and I keep envisioning my feet storming through the steps. After sleeping for about an hour, I suddenly wake up as light floods through my bedroom's wooden doorframe. I hear what sounds like Clarke stumbling home, but his movements sound off.

Paranoia takes over, and I start to wonder if it isn't Clarke but someone who has broken in. *What if they're armed?* My heart beats fast, my body tenses, and I'm now completely awake. But after the sound of bumping into furniture and kitchen cutlery, I finally hear his door shut, followed by silence. It was Clarke after all. I will find out the next day that we hadn't been robbed but that he had rushed home in an emergency after falling victim to a Red Bull overdose.

In a cruel twist of fate, I cannot fall back asleep. I manage to get in just one hour of sleep before the brutal sound of my alarm.

When it starts buzzing, it's six in the morning and I'm exhausted. Yesterday's rehearsals were intense, and my body feels stiff—the last thing an amateur dancer wants.

I take my time getting ready. The early morning hours always feel the longest. I battle with the fishnet tights, slip into the sheer bodysuit—which without underwear leaves me feeling particularly exposed—pin up my hair, and apply way more makeup than I would usually wear. It dawns on me that dolling myself up like this on a Sunday morning at the crack of dawn is ridiculous. I attempt to cover the bodysuit with a skirt and drape a shawl over my bare back, and then I head out.

The driver frowns as I slip into the front seat, my tail of sequins sneaking out from the back of my skirt.

"Iglesia la Ermita," I tell him, and his frown deepens further at the sight of a gringa heading to church in sequins at seven thirty on a Sunday morning.

Iglesia la Ermita looks like it's made out of intricate powder-blue lace. After it was almost completely destroyed by the 1925 earthquake, the only relic that survived was the eighteenth-century image of *El Señor de la Caña* (The Lord of the Sugarcane) that rests on a marble altar inside and is revered for causing many miracles (among them its own survival).[115]

I arrive early, and in front of the imposing church I timidly walk around, hoping to avoid being approached by anyone. At this time of day, the church grounds and neighboring park are mostly frequented by vagabonds and dog walkers. When the church bells ring at eight o'clock on the hour, I check my phone and see a message from Diana.

"Where are you? We're outside the church doors."

"I don't see you," I reply. "I'm outside the church too. I got here twenty minutes ago!" I walk around a few more times as I wait to hear back. Perhaps sensing the perfect moment to further test my patience, a rather dubious man starts to approach me. As I scamper away, my sequined tail sways under my skirt.

"What church are you at?" writes Diana.

"La Ermita! You?"

"San Antonio . . . "

My hands trembling, I pull out my phone and desperately try to get a car, but there aren't any in the vicinity. Another message comes through from Diana. They have a rehearsal in less than two hours. Finally, a driver appears on my screen, and I send the pickup request. But then I watch his car on the screen as it drives around the church three times.

I call him and almost shriek with desperation. "Where are you? I have an emergency!"

"Okay! I'm coming the back way, behind the church," he says, relenting to my sense of urgency.

I run to the parallel road and, recognizing the license plate, jump in front of his car and abruptly get into the front seat.

I cry in desperation for him to drive.

"What happened?" he asks politely after a few moments of silence, trying not to laugh at my bizarre attire—not really something you might wear to church.

I reluctantly tell him the situation. I know that filming a salsa video isn't an *emergency*, but this means the world to me. He smiles slightly, as if we have a silent understanding, and speeds across town to San Antonio.

When I reach the church, John Freddy is standing next to his motorbike in an open-chested royal-blue velvet salsa suit, along with Diana and Zulma. Apologizing breathlessly, I rustle through my bag with shaking hands to take out my salsa shoes and dramatically throw off my shawl and pull down my skirt. Zulma helps to sew the top of the costume together, while Diana reassures me that everything will be alright.

"Can we go through the choreography just once before filming?" I plead. Despite all the rehearsals, I want time to get back into the swing of the routine.

Taking a deep breath, I try to put the events of the morning behind me and stand tall, ready to go. But as I launch into my first patacón pisado step, my ankle twists, leading to an acute pain. There is an element I have to contend with that we hadn't considered: cobblestones. New elements and unforeseen events or circumstances can throw me off my game and rob me of my confidence, ultimately impacting the quality of my dancing. In this case, my metal heel keeps falling between the gaps in the cobblestones, making it impossible for me to dance fast and requiring me to dance on the tips of my toes to avoid stumbling over.

"Let's give it a try anyway," says John Freddy as he glances at his watch. We head over to the foot of the church steps while a helper sweeps around the entrance behind us. It's not ideal for the background, but I guess he'll have to be part of the decor. With our tripod and camera in place and the speaker ready, John Freddy and I stand tall in our revealing outfits.

"Cali Pachanguero" starts to play, and we launch into the routine. Everything seems to flow, until suddenly, the church bells start to ring. We burst out laughing but keep on dancing. We're not going to let this bother us.

"*¡Les faltan swing a esa gente!*" (These people have no swing!), mutters an old man as he hobbles along with his walking stick.

Diana and Zulma mutter something back, and we continue dancing. Nothing can stop us now—what more could possibly happen?

Behind us, one side of the double church doors opens and a head peers out to observe what's going on. A nun steps out from the other side.

"You can't be dancing outside my church!" she screams, waving her arms in protest.

We turn around in shock, and in an attempt to pursue dance diplomacy, John Freddy turns to reason with her. "*Nene,*" he says. *Wait, did he seriously call her baby?* "We are professionals! We're showcasing the best of Cali to the world!"

"I have mass at nine," she taps her finger on her watch. "You need to go!"

He looks down at his watch again and tries to reason with her.

"But *mami*, it's eight forty-five. Just give us five minutes?"

Can you seriously call a nun mami?

"No! Get away from my church!"

She shakes her finger menacingly as we back off and walk away in shock from our salsa-nun incident.

I sigh, taking my hands up to my head in disbelief.

But things don't end there. We face a litany of *Colombianadas*, as Zulma calls them—little, crazy things that could only happen here. As we go through different takes of the routine, we face obstacles from squat-jumping CrossFitters to dogs that interrupt. During our final take of the routine, filmed in front of a traditional colonial home, a taxi stops in front of us and the driver begins to loudly beep his horn. Diana throws herself in front of the taxi to allow us to slide into our final pose, in which I lean my body sideways against John Freddy's thigh and raise my twirling wrist into the air. (Diana had taught me that the elegance behind this move comes from pretending you're picking up an apple, eating it, and throwing it away—all in one sliding motion.)

We step back to let the taxi drive past, and as I breathe a sigh of relief, I turn around and accidentally kick John Freddy in the shin with my metallic heel.

While I apologize profusely, he bites his lip to conceal the pain. Then I turn around in shame and promptly trip over an avocado. A grand finale, if you will.

THERE'S ALWAYS A strange sense of emptiness after a big event, an anticlimax just like after exams or a birthday. I decide to take a walk and stroll along the riverbank to visit Cali's most renowned landmark after the monuments of Belalcázar and the Cristo Rey: *El Gato del Río* (The River Cat) and "His Girlfriends," an enormous bronze statue of a cat by Colombian artist Hernando Tejada Sáenz that is accompanied by slightly smaller bronze lady cats created by other artists as an homage. One of the female cats catches my eye. "La Cálida" (The Warm One), the sign reads. I take a step closer to read the description. Translated, it reads:

> I'm warm, just like our city and our people, and I represent the decision that we can and must fight for her.
>
> I'm a mulata, I have the beauty and sensuality of the Caleña woman, and I want everyone to see in me the colors of our landscapes and of our skin.

I admire the cat's long eyelashes, red lipstick, and elaborate hair and tail. She is the Caleña women's confidence, energy, and contagious happiness incarnate.

That night I drag Clarke out to discover more underground salsa venues, known as *viejotecas*. *Viejo* means old and, combined with *discoteca* or *salsateca,* conveys a "seniors' disco," intentionally drumming up the image of the age of the music played and the patrons. The viejotecas are one of the most authentic places to find la vieja guardia and watch them dance.

There's one place at the top of our list, Viejoteca Pardo Llada, and after some serious Googling, several phone calls, and driving around in circles through a quiet neighborhood, we finally find it. We pay what we assume is a gringo tax and then make our way down a narrow walkway leading to an open-air dance hall with a packed dance floor surrounded by plastic tables and chairs.

Clarke and I order a round of Club Colombia beers, grab seats at the plastic tables, and scan the crowd of salseros. I feel like we're watching a vintage film, observing a village ball, and not actually here. My eyes settle on a woman who is dancing with her eyes closed. Her connection to the rhythm seems almost transcendental. When the song ends, she is guided toward her next dance partner. Only after watching her for a few minutes do I realize she's blind. The world of la vieja guardia, and of salsa in general, seems socially inclusive in a way that other spaces are not; I have even seen a man in a wheelchair excel on the dance floor. I watch her dance in awe. There is a solidarity between her and her fellow salseros.

Two men curiously come over to say hello and ask what we're doing here—it must be obvious we're not regulars. One is wearing a white T-shirt with letters that spell out "Brazil" hovering above the image of a busty brunette in a bikini. He gives us an affirmative thumbs-up when we say we're here because we love salsa.

After we finish our drinks, we head to meet Diana to discover one of Cali's most legendary salsa institutions, home to the same bailadores who have been showing their best moves on the dance floor since the seventies. This time we find the club easily; its name glows in red neon lights: La Comadre (The Godmother). When Diana arrives a few minutes later, she finds us staring at the building in awe—the club seems enormous.

Inside we take one of the tables closest to the dance floor so we can have the best views. It isn't long before one of the regulars approaches Diana and asks her to dance. He's the ultimate bailador—dressed in a floating pistachio pantsuit, with a thick moustache and dazzling smile that make him seem like he has just emerged from 1979 to show us his moves. But he doesn't know what he signed up for by asking a champion to dance. Diana keeps up with his dramatic moves, his kicks and twists, and they put on a spectacular performance.

I dance with him also but can't keep up with his speed. I stumble my way through to the end of the song, with uncontrollable laughter, and then he suddenly pulls up my leg and dips me.

The other men I dance with stick to the basic steps, probably assuming that because I'm a gringa, I won't know much more. But I'm itching to do all the fancy footwork I've learned over the past week.

Diana picks up on my frustration and takes me to the dance floor with her, while Clarke happily sits with a glass of whisky, bopping his head from side to side with his eyes closed.

It feels incredible to dance to a whole song with so much intricate footwork—and just for fun. Being able to memorize a choreography in the studio and use it on the dance floor while spontaneously adapting the moves to a different song or because I'm inspired by an instrument feels good, feels right, and feels like freedom. In Diana I've found not only a teacher of the highest stature, but also a friend with a pure heart. She is a professional dancer who has won titles and tours the world but always has time for spreading the joy of salsa to everyone around her, including me: a girl with a dream to learn how to dance.

IT'S MY LAST morning in Cali and I'm dreading packing my suitcase again. After stopping by the supermarket to pick up some super glue—I'd accidently broken one of the tribal masks in the apartment—I head home and paste the pieces back together. It's an impromptu therapy session for my current lifestyle. Everything feels scattered, like my life is all over the place. With the traces of damage on the mask almost invisible, I place it back on the shelf where it had previously been. To the naked eye, no one will know it was once shattered.

Clarke walks in abruptly, in search of his backpack and computer, while I'm folding my clothes into my suitcase. It's time for me to head to the airport and he shifts awkwardly in the doorway.

"Bye, socio," he says, before heading out with his bag thrown over his shoulder.

I find Clarke's disdain for hugs peculiar given his love of Latin American culture—probably the most affectionate continent on the planet. He blames this on his professional training, as well as his plight as a human being.

When it's time for me to leave, Maycoll picks me up. On the way to the airport, we drive past the bronze trumpet monument dedicated to Grupo Niche and I'm hit with a sharp pang of nostalgia. "Cali Pachanguero" plays in my head as I gaze out the window.

Cali es Cali . . . lo demás es loma. (Cali is Cali . . . the rest is all mountains.) The phrase reflects Caleño pride that Cali is not only the best city but the only main city that stands in the plains when the rest are in the mountains.

BOGOTÁ

LANDING IN BOGOTÁ, where Juan grew up, I'm met with sunshine and a crisp cobalt-blue sky. I'd always heard that it was a gray and rainy city, but it seems a bit of Cali has come with me.

Juan greets me at Arrivals. His warm embrace makes me feel like I've come home. When we travel for so long, it's easy to underestimate how much it affects us not to hug someone we love. Outside, the bright sunshine and dry climate and altitude make me slightly dizzy. I open the door of Juan's Volkswagen and slip into the front seat. It's such a different scenario being with him in this capacity, seeing him drive a car like a grown-up, when in our previous lives we'd take the sky train or hop on the back of a motorcycle taxi.

The elevator opens straight into his living room, and we are greeted by his family's housekeeper, Celia. Juan invites me to sit at the dining room table and try what he calls the "house special." Celia brings over a tray with fresh pineapple and mint juice and two bowls of tomato soup and then brings another tray with several smaller bowls filled with toppings: tortilla chips, fresh avocado, cheese, and shredded chicken. She's also prepared a delicious banana and chocolate cake and coffee, which we will indulge in shamelessly before passing out.

AFTER A DEEP night's sleep, I don't want to emerge from the warm feather duvet. My dreams were filled with sequins, kicks, and twirls but also candles, frilly skirts, bicycles, and bouncy neon clothes—as I'd been on my dance journey through Colombia from cumbia to champeta.

I step into the living room, rubbing my eyes at the light, and find Juan making me a Colombian breakfast: scrambled eggs with onion and tomato, an arepa, and a cup of *tinto* (a black coffee). He tells me he wants me to feel at home. He knows how my nomadic lifestyle leaves me feeling completely

uprooted in many ways. Normal things start to feel like unique luxuries. To
see artwork, objects, and photos—signs that I'm in someone's home—is a
far cry from what I've seen in the countless Airbnbs, hostels, and hotels that
I've been staying in, which have been colder, designed for people in transit,
and often feel lifeless.

After breakfast we stay for a while stretched out on the sofa. Juan wraps
his arms around me in a warm embrace, and tears fill my eyes.

I HAVE ONE last item on my agenda to do in Colombia, a reason for stopping in Bogotá before the next destination on my dance journey. Juan had
long told me about his grandfather, his abuelito, whom he wanted me to
meet one day. His grandfather is Belisario Betancur, who served as president
of Colombia from 1982 to 1986. Despite an agenda full of engagements, he
has enthusiastically invited us to a luncheon on my last day. We drive up a
hillier part of town, the trunk bursting with my luggage ready to go to the
airport, and steer through a heavily militarized street where armed security
guards in refined suits and earpieces eye us suspiciously before escorting us
to an elevator ascending directly into a small waiting room with a large set
of wooden doors. An *empleada* (employee) wearing a white maid's uniform
greets us warmly.

"Buenos días," she says, ushering us inside. "El señor presidente is
waiting for you."

I have just enough time to catch a glimpse of the incredible city view
from the floor-to-ceiling windows and of colorful art pieces before we turn
left into the dining room. And then, there he is—the abuelito I've heard so
much about. Dressed in a crisp navy-blue suit and blue tie, he is seated at a
table and looking, well . . . very presidential. I'm not sure how I should greet
him, but I decide to be true to myself and give him a kiss on the cheek.

He asks about my name, and I explain how I was named after Aliénor of
Aquitaine—the twelfth-century queen of France and England—given my

French-English parentage. Aliénor of Aquitaine had loved music, dance, reading, and politics, just as I do.

"Ah! Leonor de Aquitania," he nods, dreamily. "She would have been my girlfriend!"

Juan explains that I'm on a journey to, quite literally, dance across Latin America, and his abuelito asks me to explain in detail what dances I've learned.

"An anthology!" he exclaims, impressed.

He tells us that he made his way around the dance floor back in his student days, when there were only men to dance with.

"There was one young man from a rich family. He was my dance partner. We used to dance together quite close . . . and I liked it!"

I ask him what he thinks of my belief that dance might be a path toward happiness, hoping my hypothesis will gain a presidential endorsement, and he concurs.

"Dancing is like learning the world. When I think back to my 'parejo,' my dance partner, I would allow myself to be carried by his invisible imprint. It's something quite beautiful. Dancing is a silent language, a silent conversation."

After lunch we tour the apartment. Its curated artwork, photos, and mementos make it seem like a time warp of the twentieth century—all accompanied by live commentary rather than an audio guide. There are medals awarded by various countries, and photographs with Pope John Paul II, Fidel Castro, and a Chinese chairman who grins with his eyes closed. Juan's abuelito recalls his lunch with the French luminary Albert Camus in Paris and shares memories of his inner circle, which included Gabriel García Márquez and Fernando Botero.

Before we leave, Juan hugs his grandfather, and as I go to say goodbye, I hesitate to give him one of my hugs from the heart and instead give him a normal hug.

"One more," he says, as if he was able to sense that I hadn't put all my feeling into it. This time I give him a sincere, powerful hug.

"Much better."

"Okay, a third one," I say, leaning in to give him another hug. I feel a pang in my heart. He may be a former president, but right now he just reminds me of my own grandfather.

He follows us out, and as we step into the elevator, I turn to see his face and decide to rush and give him one final hug. We wave as the elevator doors close, while he stands holding his cane and smiling at us.

I lost my grandfather—my first dance partner—exactly one year ago. I tell Juan to make the most of their time together while he can and to treasure his grandfather's stories to allow his memories to live. It doesn't matter if your grandfather was once a president, or a factory worker or sailor like mine were. They are all our abuelitos.

In the car we listen to Juan Luis Guerra's top bachata hits as we swerve on the curves of hilly Bogotá. I feel slightly brokenhearted to be leaving a country I've fallen in love with. I've enjoyed such a positive energy here and met people who are excited about moving toward a more peaceful and prosperous future. And with Juanito, a dear friend, I've felt at home. After months on the road, like a criminal on the run, it was incredible. I've also found that when people here dance, a kind of magical realism happens, transporting my heart to a lush realm at once essentially true and totally surreal.

9

BRAZIL

Samba No Pé, Forró, Samba de Gafieira, and the Lambada

"*Bom dia! É hora da sua refeição.*" (Good morning! It's time for your meal.)

I open my eyes and find myself wrapped in a thick duvet in a reclined airplane seat. Thanks to my air miles, I've managed to secure a flight from Bogotá to Rio in business class for just sixty-five dollars. I feel like an imposter living a life that I can't afford, or maybe it's just that I'm the protagonist of my own movie where anything is possible. Caipirinhas and machine guns. Copacabana and samba. I'm excited but also scared. In Colombia, I had developed a deep sense of attachment to Juan's family and to a country that in another life could have been my own, and now I'm headed somewhere new. A woman taps my arm and speaks to me in a language that I can barely understand.

"*Senhora? Peixe ou frango?*"

I think she's asking whether I want fish or chicken. In Brazil I'm going to have to learn a new language and a new culture. It's time to discover life as a Carioca, the demonym that identifies anything or anyone related to a city that, until now, I have only discovered in my dreams: Rio de Janeiro.

While I'm beyond excited, I've heard horror stories about Rio. My paranoia led me to arrange a safe taxi well ahead of my trip, a pick-up by a well-reputed driver turned entrepreneur named Anderson who accepted PayPal payments. But when I arrive, he is nowhere to be seen. I guard my suitcase with caution, looking around suspiciously for signs of danger. But instead I find an international airport like any other. This is the thing about places often depicted as extremely dangerous. You think the minute you land, you'll be surrounded by bandits in balaclavas. Instead, you find an ATM and Starbucks. But I'm not naive. I know that beneath this sleek surface is a country with a painful past, where deep inequality and desperation bred violence and crime along with one of the highest homicide rates in the world.[116]

My phone rings. It's Anderson and he says he's spotted me. I look around for what I assume will be a middle-aged man with a beer belly and mustache, but instead I find a handsome young man with muscles visible through his shirt. He takes my bags and with an elegant gait leads me toward his car.

We set off to Rio from Ilha do Governador (Governor's Island), which houses the Galeão International Airport. Huge glass panes with a dark reflective sheen line the side of the highway. I look into the rearview mirror to see if I can make eye contact with Anderson out of a reflex that comes from being briefed upon arrival. I want to ask him what the glass panes are, and so many other questions about Brazil, but I feel incapable of communicating even though I can understand most words. In other countries, my fluent Spanish enabled me to get the inside story on everything, including social issues. But now the words won't come.

I know I've read about the panes, but now I rack my brain to try to remember what I read about them. The "Wall of Shame"—that's what it was called. It had been built to hide the Maré favela, a shantytown, from the eyes of international visitors flying into Galeão for the Olympic games that had been held the previous year.[117] In the same way that urban planning can be used as a tool to bring opportunities, it can also be a weapon for division. Behind the glamorous face of the host city lie forced evictions, gentrification, and human rights abuses. Bus routes linking poorer areas to the tourist zone had been redirected to dissuade slum dwellers from stepping on the streets of Copacabana or Ipanema.[118] It is a sad state of affairs reflecting extreme social inequality.

There is an image I remember from school that was often used to depict inequality: a Brazilian apartment block with a swimming pool on each floor that stood next to a favela. Brazil faces an inequality crisis, where its six richest men possess the same wealth as the bottom half of the country's population.[119] It is this inequality, more than poverty itself, that breeds crime, violence, and insecurity and creates a culture where murder, kidnappings, and police brutality are daily realities. Despite this, I will discover an unlikely rebellion—joy, celebration, and an explosion of colors manifested through singing, dancing, and celebrating every second of life, knowing that it could be taken away at any moment.

We make a turn, and Anderson drives along the promenade of Copacabana, stretching onward to Ipanema Beach, which until now I have only seen in films but is just like I expected: a postcard of blue skies, white sands, and an immense ocean view, adorned by bronzed bodies and the twin peaks of the Morro Dois Irmãos (Two Brothers Hill) rock formation in the background. Soon, I imagine, I will be joining the beachgoers, playing beach volleyball and drinking caipirinhas—Brazil's national cocktail of cachaça (a spirit made from sugarcane), lime, and sugar—with new friends, soaking in the sun and embracing the life of the Girl from Ipanema, like in the famous song.

After all, I have a built-in best friend: a Brazilian roommate named Doris, thanks to accommodation arrangements made by my language school. She's in her mid-thirties, has a cat, and loves both yoga and dance.

What a perfect match, I think to myself, already warming to the incredible memories that we will share together, not to mention everything that I can learn from her by immersing myself in Carioca life. Yoga on the beach, dancing in the city's secret samba spots, deep conversations in Portuguese about life and love.

"*Chegamos ao seu destino*," says Anderson in a formal tone to inform me that we have arrived.

I peek out the window and see the street sign, Rua Barão da Torre, and search for my building's number. I start to strategically plan my exit so that I'm not targeted as a foreigner freshly arrived on the streets of Rio armed with all her belongings. Fortunately, Anderson helps me get to the right building. We ring the doorbell, and a woman emerges from the main door. She is in some ways both the epitome of Brazilian beauty and the fusion of its demographic diversity—smooth black hair, dark bronzed skin, an upturned nose with freckles sprinkled around her cheeks. She's dressed entirely in white, in a long, flowing skirt and a short crop top revealing her toned stomach.

"Eleonora!" she exclaims and embraces me in a warm hug.

Okay, this is my name in Brazil then, I think to myself, used to having a different adaptation of my name in every country. Switching names, languages, and now dance costumes has become an essential part of life on the run that allows me to be a different person in different places. She seems quite a bit older than mid-thirties, but she seems warm and fun nonetheless. I spot a huge surfboard and yoga mats in the living room, and I beam just thinking of all the activities we'll do together.

"*Minha princesa*" (My princess), she murmurs, picking up her cat, which she cradles in her arms. It seems her little princess is much more like a child than a pet for her and receives unconditional adoration.

The cat glares at me suspiciously, asserting her superiority.

Initially I was meant to live in the "mezzanine room," which sounded fancy but is nothing more than a bunk bed set up in the living room with a single, lone shelf for belongings. Instead, Doris takes me to a large, spacious double room, which, despite the lack of air-conditioning and cracked windows that won't even open, is decent.

"Re-beh-cka," Doris calls to our other roommate in the room next door.

A tall, tanned girl with platinum blond waves emerges. She's just twenty-two years old and strikes me as innocent, even vulnerable. We get to chatting, and she tells me how she ended up here after breaking up with her Belgian-Brazilian boyfriend, whose heart she had sadly broken. She's from the tiny German-speaking minority in Belgium, a community of a few villages. She's been here for two weeks already and has had the chance to explore quite a few places, including Búzius, a beach resort outside of Rio known as Brazil's Saint-Tropez.

Doris rustles around in the kitchen, and I go to join her to set my things up. I open the fridge and find it completely full.

In broken Portuguese, I ask her where I can put my things.

"Are you going to cook?" she asks, her eyes shifting. "The students usually just eat out all the time. They don't cook at home."

I tell her that I like to cook and can't afford to be eating out all the time.

She lets out a growl and mutters something to herself in Portuguese. She is visibly annoyed, and I'm not sure why. She steps in front of me abruptly to open the fridge and angrily moves her things to leave me half a shelf of space. Then she turns around to face me and lists her house rules.

"When you cook, you need to clean everything up after you. *Absolutely everything*," she emphasizes in a coarse voice. The contrast of her tone with the zen music playing through the apartment sends chills up my spine. "You need to wash your dishes immediately and dry the surface after. I don't want to see even a drop of water on the counter!"

She leaves me feeling cold. I'm confused by her sudden shift in behavior. She seems like a different person than the one who had welcomed me just minutes before.

I put my worries aside for the moment and follow her out to go buy a SIM card and find the supermarket. She takes me to her favorite local places, introducing me to everyone she knows in the neighborhood. Though I don't yet speak Portuguese, we can somehow communicate. I can make out quite a few of the words, using both French and Spanish to orient myself, and then reply in Spanish, which seems to be enough for us to talk about everything from yoga to fashion and dancing.

We head to Visconde de Pirajà, the main shopping street in Ipanema, where boutiques burst with colorful clothing, açai bars abound, and men with bronzed bodies and women with regal statures strut in Havaianas flip flops and stilettos, respectively. Within a week, strolling down this avenue will be a daily occurrence for me—a cup of açai in one hand and my Portuguese language books in the other.

MY CLASSES AT the language school start on Monday, but I've signed up for their signature Friday afternoon tour, which explores a new part of the city every week. This week it's Vidigal, a "pacified favela" considered safe enough for foreigners to visit.

I arrive at the meeting point—Posto 9 on Ipanema Beach—and meet my fellow classmates, who are mostly in their early twenties and from various European countries. I spot a handsome Dutch-Turkish guy who reminds me of Cristián, a skinny Swiss guy with braces, and a cheerful Italian girl who eagerly tells me all the languages she can speak and that her goal is to become fluent in Portuguese in just two months. A young man with a soft face glances over at me, and, charmed, I begin talking with him. His name is Andreas. He's from Oslo and twenty-two—eight years younger than me. Even though he's Scandinavian, he has darker features, and his eyes reveal a certain fragility—as I've been told my own do. It turns out that over the last few months we have been in the same place at the same time. He had been an intern at the Norwegian Embassy in Havana and has just finished a semester in Medellín—but clearly destiny wanted us to meet in Rio.

We take the public bus, snaking through the Leblon neighborhood until we reach the foot of the Morro Dois Irmãos. From there, it's a steep uphill walk. I'm engrossed in conversation with Andreas the whole time; in addition to the other things we have in common, he also has a background in political science. I get so caught up in our conversation that I almost feel like it's just the two of us. We talk about everything from geopolitics to our shared love of the reggaetonero Nicky Jam.

But then the Italian girl interrupts our conversation, joining in to sing along to Nicky Jam's hit song "Travesuras" (Mischief). "*Hola, bebé, la la la . . .*"

I welcome the distraction to take in my surroundings. We're certainly walking through a favela, but it feels relaxed, with vibrant street art painting the social struggles and celebrations of its residents, portraying subjects from a struggling water supply to division and diversity.

We arrive at the top of the hill, where we enter a fancy-looking cocktail bar. As we walk through, I'm submerged in the sound of soft samba—a breezy style resembling bossa nova, a jazz-inspired adaptation of samba that emerged as the "new wave" in the 1950s and 1960s. Guided by the melody and slow, gentle beats of softa samba, I reach an open terrace that reveals a breathtaking view.

The Morro Dois Irmãos towers over a thin stretch of land that separates the ocean from the lake and shows how white pearly beaches form a protective curve along the coastline. I turn to look at Lagoa, an almost heart-shaped lake, and my eyes scan the horizon, eventually landing on the Corcovado (Hunchback) mountain and the *Cristo Redentor* (Christ the Redeemer) statue—an imposing statue of Jesus Christ stretching his arms to embrace the city—atop it.

Andreas joins me and we take in the view together, with a shared silent moment of reflection, before the rest of the group joins us for the inevitable group photo. A huge table has been set aside for us to enjoy rounds of caipirinhas. I feel young and alive, submerged in sun and the samba music filling the bar.

We leave the bar with the sound of samba spilling out onto the streets. Andreas takes my hand and we begin to dance salsa. It doesn't matter that it's not the right dance for the music—when you find the rhythm, you can dance anything to it.

"Hey, guys! We need to go now," a coordinator calls to us.

I slowly detach my gaze from Andreas and find the rest of the students staring blankly at us, waiting. Laughing, we head downhill behind the group and back onto the bus.

MY LANGUAGE SCHOOL has organized a weekend trip to the beach-studded peninsula of Búzios, a little over one hundred miles outside Rio.

I meet Edson, the school driver, a tall and skinny man with Bob-length braids who winks at me with a gleaming smile. He's from the infamous favela of Santa Marta, where Michael Jackson filmed the music video to "They Don't Care About Us" and stands immortalized as a bronze statue looking out at a picturesque view of Rio. (More than two decades later, tour groups come to have a "favela experience" and pay tribute to the King of Pop. They don't know that at the time of Jackson's filming, he inadvertently caused a diplomatic scandal by choosing narco-traffickers for personal security instead of Rio's police force.[120])

The others show up—first a sunburned Australian surfer dude with big muscles and a "Brazil" T-shirt who's "doing" Latin America, then a middle-aged Russian man who goes by the name Sergio and a young Syrian refugee who has resettled in Brazil (she tells me that one of the most striking aspects of her culture shock was transitioning from a war zone to a land where everyone hugs). We head to Cabo Frio, known for its cold water and large sand dunes. The soft, fine white sand feels like powdered cream, the bay stretches out into infinity, and a line of tiny surfers bobs in the distance.

As we set up camp, I'm introduced to the *sunga*, stretchy Brazilian Speedo-style swim briefs popularized in the sixties that are high-cut enough to allow for a perfect thigh tan.[121] Edson has opted for a rather explicit white number that leaves little to the imagination.

I turn onto my stomach, looking away. I don't dare to swim in the blustering wind, and I'm not sure if it's a result of Edson's crazy driving or my first site of a sunga, but I prefer to withdraw and read my book.

Later we head to Búzios, a picturesque fishing village with cobblestone streets, golden sand, and translucent azure water. I try to be more sociable, chatting with the rest of the group. But when the others go swimming, I decide I'd rather have more alone time and hold back. Edson stays too and flashes me a smile from time to time. I don't know how to react to him, so I go back to lying on my stomach and looking away. The sun's golden rays caress my back, and I fall into a deep sleep.

A loud shaking sound abruptly ends my serenity. Someone is right beside me, and for the umpteenth time on my journey, I feel my personal space being invaded. I suspiciously open one eye and there's Edson, kneeling next to me and flashing a smile as white as his sunga.

"Caipirinha?" he asks while shaking a cup and grinning at me audaciously.

I am as frozen as the caipirinha that he hands me. This feels like too much of a cliché to be real. I cautiously take a sip while observing Edson in disbelief as he remains kneeled in front of me, smiling.

"*Eu vou dormir agora*" (I'm going to sleep now), I tell him, putting together the few Portuguese words I have. Edson nods agreeably and goes off to swim in the sea.

Before we head back to Rio, I go for a solitary walk to explore the bay. I come across a bronze statue of Brigitte Bardot dressed in casual jeans and a Breton-style striped top and looking out toward the sea. She was always the epitome of beauty for me, and on the few occasions that I have been told I resemble her, it has always been the greatest of compliments. Her 1956 film *And God Created Woman* left me breathless and in some ways may have instigated my desire to escape and dance. Her character in the movie, Juliette, cares little for societal norms and, tormented, runs away from her loving husband only to find a group of musicians in a bar. She dances barefoot by them, tapping her feet to the pulsating beat of the drum and swaying her hips to the swishing sound of maracas. In my case, I wasn't escaping life as a 1950s housewife. I was a burned-out millennial escaping screen time and searching for authentic meaning in the world.

"Do you know of a country where people think only of dancing and laughter?" Juliette asks Eric Carradine, her much older and mega-wealthy suitor in the film. Brazil is one of those countries.

IN THE LIVING room, Doris wears a tank top and a G-string revealing a perfect Brazilian posterior. She strokes her cat while having an animated conversation with one of the neighbors through the window. It's like a creepy Carioca version of *Breakfast at Tiffany's*.

I dodge past her to slip into the bathroom unnoticed. Today is my first day of language class, and despite being thirty (or probably because I am thirty), I relish this "back to school" feeling. They've placed me in a special "pre-intermediate" group for Spanish-speakers, which hopefully will accelerate my learning. Languages are like dances. They are a form of communication built upon social codes, ideas, and norms, and learning them stimulates our senses, forcing us beyond our usual boundaries.

Rebecca and I walk to school together, and as we stroll through the hallways my eyes catch the gaze of Andreas.

"Hola, bebé," I sing to him in the words of Nicky Jam. My head turns to look back at him, almost in slow motion, and he smiles coyly. I feel like a teenager again. I found my crush.

Our teacher, Natalia, is young and elegant, with tanned skin, freckles, and an accent that leaves me hypnotized. She distributes our textbooks and worksheets and starts us off on some typical daily words before introducing us to the Rio accent. Their *t*s and *d*s sound fudgy to my ears, and they seem to add a *y* sound onto the end of many words. I appreciate classroom camaraderie even more as an adult. Whether it's while studying dances or languages, learning and advancing as a group is a uniting feeling.

During our coffee break, I bump into Sergio, who had been on the Búzios trip. He invites me to the *padaria* (bakery) next door to grab a coffee and a bag of *pão de queijo*, Brazil's signature squishy cheese bread. Originally from Moscow, Sergio had moved to London and found a lucrative career receiving Russian delegates for conferences, involving the suspicious laundering of rubles, and then dabbled in investment banking and finance before retiring from the working world at just forty years old. He has a certain innocence about him, seeming more like a middle-aged man completely enchanted with the sights and sounds that surround him than a mobster from the Russian Bratva. He's only slightly taller than me and lean, with a bald head and a kind face that lights up in awe as he expresses his love for Brazil, its people, and its culture.

"Brazil opens your heart, and you can never close it," he tells me and then asks if I dance *forró*.

I've been told that forró is by far the most popular dance in Brazil, but its style isn't clear to me. Based on a few YouTube videos that I had watched, it seems like a partner dance that incorporates twists and glides. Its music, with its bouncy beat, dry-tuned accordions, and twinkling pulse from a metal triangle, is unlike anything I've heard before.

Sergio invites me to check out a forró bar tonight on Rua Barão da Torre with him and his Polish friend Karolina, and I jump at the chance. I've come here to focus on samba, but why not check out another dance?

We decide to meet at Exit A of General Osório Station, the most central meeting point in Ipanema. I've seen an entrance to the station on my street, and I walk down from my apartment. On the dark, narrow pavement, I try to avoid the few people who cross my path; one man makes intense eye contact.

Something doesn't feel right, and I can't see the exit anywhere. I pull out my phone, discreetly, to quickly tap the station into Google Maps. I can feel the blue light glowing against my face, making it visible to all around. Another man walks past me, this time looking at me in disbelief. *What am I doing?*

I start to panic but continue walking straight and try to appear confident. It feels like I've entered a darker, shadier side of Ipanema. A group of people congregate outside a corner shop, next to an alleyway leading up to the hills of a favela. They stare at me with empty eyes.

Suddenly I spot the entrance to the station, but Sergio isn't there. I find a street cleaner with a broomstick, and using the little Portuguese that I know, I manage to ask for help. He lets me past the gate, and I run down through the station to get to the right exit.

"There you are, princess!" Sergio calls out to me. He's been waiting patiently for over twenty minutes on the main square. He tells me that Karolina should be here soon.

Sergio is extremely punctual, even though in Rio, like most places in Latin America, foreigners tend to adapt to the local time, myself included.

With time to kill, I ask Sergio what led him to Rio and why he has a Brazilian name.

"My real name is Sergei," he explains, rolling a thick Russian *r* to show the proper pronunciation. "But at some point I stopped connecting with it. I switched to 'Serge' because it sounded French, you know. It's cool, innit?" he asks, using London slang for "isn't it." "And then I discovered Brazil," he sighs dreamily. "So I thought, why not become Sergio?"

Like me, he seems to be rootless, switching identity and name in different lands far from his own.

"There's Karolina!"

Sergio points to a woman with choppy blond hair who appears to be in her mid-thirties. She has one foot out of a car and is in an animated conversation in Portuguese with her driver. She seems like the kind of woman who knows exactly where she's going and what she wants. She motions us into the back of the car and takes her place in the front, which doesn't surprise me at all. I ask Karolina about her experience living in Rio and with the people here.

"Have you been with a Brazilian man yet?" she asks, almost holding back her breath.

I shake my head. "No, well, not yet."

"Just please, don't fall in love with one," she pleads, looking at me with eyes that reveal pain, regret, and, most of all, a warning.

AFTER PAYING A cover fee, we walk up the stairs of an old crumbling building in Lapa, a bohemian party district in the center of Rio, taking one step after another. I've become hooked on the anticipation of these moments, when I'm about to step into a new venue flooded with music, sparkling stage lights, and people dancing their hearts out.

Inside, the band's set is upbeat—a silver triangle chimes against the sounds of a deep, rotund accordion and the heavy beat of a bass drum. Forró reminds me of country music in how joyful it is—a quality typical of Brazilian music.

Onstage, men wear what look like pirate hats in the shape of a wide half-moon framing their foreheads. The hats are adorned with embroidery, ribbons, and small mirrors. Ignorantly, I ask Karolina if it's costume night.

She laughs and explains that the hat is typical attire of *nordestinos*, people from the northeast, in the country's dusty and desert-like *sertão* (hinterland). Forró had long been considered the dance of the countryside, while in the cosmopolitan cities of Rio and São Paulo, samba and bossa nova reigned.

I ask Karolina about the dance's history while admiring the dancers' impressive ability to bounce and glide in one single motion. As with almost every dance's history, there are two versions of the story. It either comes from *forrobodó*, which means "a really fun party," or it is a derivative of the English words "for all."[122] The latter theory is romantic, denoting

all-inclusive balls for locals and English engineers working on Brazil's Great
Western Railway in the early 1900s, but that was unlikely—forró had been
around before then.[123]

A young hipster approaches us and asks Karolina for her hand. On the
dance floor, they face each other and lock into an intimate embrace, her
temple touching his. The way their bodies coalesce and glide forward and
backward reminds me of tango; but then, suddenly, she starts to twist her
knees from side to side, causing her dress to rustle suggestively, and then
begins spinning. The dance is a confusing mix of the gliding elegance and
connection of tango with the bouncy beat of cumbia and the circular spins
of Cuban salsa.

When a man approaches me to dance, I turn to look at Sergio, who until
now has been patiently watching our table and drinks. He motions at me
with his hand in approval, as if he is the guardian of my initiation to forró.

I'm not sure how to step and my instinct is to dance salsa, but I remember the key to any dance is to listen to the music and find its rhythm. I allow
my body to glide and bounce along to the beat, and I let myself be carried
away. For so long, my body had struggled to tackle new dances or follow a
dance partner. Now I feel like I am flowing within minutes of taking my
first steps in a new dance. Until now, it wasn't my body that struggled, it
was my mind. I have been blocked by my own limiting beliefs: *I won't be
able to follow, I don't know, I just can't.* But when you allow yourself to be
transported by your environment—whether that means the music, your
dance partner, or the atmosphere—and take that first step, you will find
that anything is possible.

I'm settling into my Girl from Ipanema lifestyle, enjoying it more
each day, and pleased with how my Portuguese is progressing. English
is my work language, tailored to an external audience and suited for my

professional persona; French is the language of my heritage, my family
and childhood; Spanish is where I can allow my personality to shine and
effectively be myself, socialize, and express my emotions freely. Brazilian
Portuguese affects me on a different level. It has a certain softness that
doesn't exist in other languages, and when I speak it I find myself almost
purring in a softer, more feminine version of myself.

I adore my daily routine: language classes in the morning, homework on Ipanema Beach in the afternoons (a fresh coconut or caipirinha
optional), walks back home via Visconde de Pirajá to window-shop, and
stops to pick up a cup of açai or a bag of *coxinhas de frango*—tear-shaped
Brazilian chicken fritters that have fast become my favorite snack.

Spending time outside where the locals are has given me fascinating
insight into body image in Brazil. With all the six-packs and sungas I've
seen, I've come to think that perhaps in Brazil—in contrast to other parts
of the world—men face more pressure than women to have perfect bodies.
Their bronzed muscular bodies remind me of Greek gods and are the result
of Brazil's multibillion-dollar gym industry. Gyms seem to be springing
up everywhere in Rio, and it comes as no surprise that the fitness market
in Brazil ranks second worldwide, after the United States.[124] Women here
also seem to move about with pride. Watching voluptuous women strolling confidently in crop tops and hot pants has been—as it was in Puerto
Rico—empowering and has led me to purchase skimpy Carioca beach
outfits that I wear without shame.

Cariocas seem comfortable in their skin and unfazed by revealing flesh.
The first time I saw a Carioca strutting down Visconde de Pirajá wearing
nothing more than a sunga, I couldn't believe it. Now I walk along that
same street in a bikini covered by a sheer wrap. Along with much of my
clothing, I have shed many of my complexes. I've mostly stopped caring
for restrictive societal norms or what others may think, and it makes me
feel liberated.

THIS EVENING WE'RE attending a rehearsal at a samba school. I've heard so much about these and have been dreaming of going to a school's *quadra* (training ground) to see the dancers rehearsing in the lead-up to a competition.

We take the metro to Cidade Nova (New City), a central part of town; most schools have their quadra far on the outskirts. It's nice to be introduced to samba with other people from my school. I didn't know what to expect in terms of safety when venturing to a quadra, and my Portuguese is still limited, so I'm relieved not to be going alone. I'm also glad I'm going with other students who are as immersed in Brazil as I am, not just tourists passing through.

We arrive at the São Clemente Samba School and then pass through an entrance decked out in its colors, yellow and black, which I soon see everywhere. I'm surprised to see the quadra filled with dancers of all ages. While the female *passistas* (dancers) in their scintillating samba outfits shine on the training ground, a crowd spanning from the oldest generations to the youngest surrounds them. Together they form not only part of a school but also a community. I'm also struck by how the passistas are of all shapes and sizes—a contrast to the idea that they all have perfect, curvaceous bodies. It seems like there are also very skinny and overweight passistas on the front line.

A young girl dances under the watchful eye of one of the main passistas; a group of older women with white foulards on their heads twirl; the flag bearer spins across the training ground; a prominent passista enrobed in diamonds struts along the front line displaying both power and grace. The dancers all have sparkling costumes, and as they stomp their stiletto heels, their skin glistens from sweat.

When a man, presumably the manager or producer, gets on the microphone and gives some sort of motivational speech, the dancers look at him full of hope. Some of their eyes glisten with tears. I can tell they really want to win the Rio Carnival parade—where the city's best samba schools compete for the crown of champion school. No matter who they are up against, they will pour their hearts into it.

Everyone cheers to the same song that repeats over and over again as its singer tirelessly sings from a balcony on the second floor of the school, hurling his soul into the microphone. The dancers give it everything they have as they follow his pace, their samba adapting to the pauses in rhythm and the renewed emphasis as he starts a new phrase.

"Do you think they're on drugs?" asks a fellow student.

They are definitely intoxicated, swept up in the unrestricted expression of emotion, connected to music and community, but no, they're not on drugs.

I'VE HEARD GREAT things about Bruno, my language school's resident samba teacher, who teaches a beginner class once a week. When I arrive for my first lesson, I find chairs stacked on tables to make space and a man looking up dance videos on YouTube on an old desktop.

"Bruno?" I ask, lightly knocking on the door.

He turns around and flashes a friendly smile. He's tall and slim, with short hair and a tan complexion. He enthusiastically asks me to tell him about my project and nods thoughtfully while I do. He shares my perception that dance is a language—a unique form of communication.

"Right, let's just give it a go." He gestures for me to stand in the middle of the room and takes me through the basic samba step—a seemingly simple concept, but a difficult movement to execute. At first it feels like simply stepping back on one foot, lifting the other to step only on tiptoes, and then dragging the back foot forward. But it looks awkward when I do it. I watch Bruno and try to understand what makes his movement so much more graceful than mine. I mean, after all, it is just like walking, except stepping backward then forward again.

"Just imagine that you're waiting for the bus," he says, receptive to my frustration.

What does waiting for the bus have to do with samba? What do I even look like when waiting for the bus? I take a deep breath, close my eyes, and imagine myself quite literally waiting for the bus. My hips instinctively shift to one side, my weight pushing into my left leg to leave it tall and strong, while my right knee bends and my foot rests on its tiptoes.

Learning new steps, after my struggles and failures in previous dances, has gone from being torturous to enjoyable—my body is untrained, unable to move in a certain way until it is hit by the magic of muscle memory. Sometimes it takes just one small detail or one small moment of imagination to unlock a curious movement.

"There! That's it! Now do the same thing with the other leg."

I shift my weight to my right side, as if changing my mind to catch the bus from the other side of the road.

"Now when you step, step just slightly back," he says, as if we're on the brink of something.

We start slowly and then gradually increase the speed of the music until I feel like my feet are the masters of the powerful percussion in the song. I dance faster and faster, with speed and strength, while maintaining a posture that makes me feel regal, confident, and fearless—like a true Carnival queen. My soul is awakened, enlightened by enchanting melodies as the drums drive my determination. This is not just a dance. It is an internal embodiment of a state of being, an affirmation of presence.

After we finish my first class, Bruno and I discuss my samba plans for the rest of the month. He offers to take me to some samba parties, and I've also come across a two-day workshop at a famous dance school. And then, there's the once-in-a-lifetime experience and the very foundation of this trip: taking part in the Rio Carnival parade. I've already bought a costume—the ticket to participation—to parade with the Beija-Flor samba school. It turns out that you don't necessarily need to be a professional samba dancer to take part in Carnival. You just need to purchase a costume, which allows you to take part in a special section for nonprofessional dancers. My school is famed for having won the Rio Carnival parade over a dozen times, but it is most famous for its singer, who has performed at every Carnival since 1976 and even changed his name to match the school's name, becoming Neguinho da Beija-Flor.

As usual I'm in a rush, and I quickly put the espresso maker on the stove while multitasking to gather my Portuguese books and prepare my bag. I've been trying to fit so many things into my Brazilian experience that it's become crammed. Suddenly I hear a shriek coming from the kitchen. It's Doris yelling. I can't make out what she's so alarmed about until I find her flapping her arms around and angrily pointing toward the espresso maker as steam erupts from the top, indicating it's ready for pouring.

"You're going to burn my espresso maker! Do you know how much this machine costs? If you burn it, you're going to have to replace it!"

I stand frozen, not knowing how to explain myself. The old rusty machine isn't even burned. *Why is she so upset?* I leave Doris angrily muttering to herself and slip quietly out the door.

I get to class a few minutes late, and I'm behind on my homework. Natalia glances at me curiously but not judgmentally. My phone rings during the coffee break, and it's Renata, a Brazilian woman from a useful concierge service who had helped me arrange my participation with Beija-Flor directly with Ana, my *presidente de ala*—the person in charge of a specific *ala,* the wings that make up the components of the parade.

"Aliénor! I've spoken with Ana and she says that she can get you an interview with Neguinho da Beija-Flor—in his house!" She's bursting with excitement. Neguinho is a national treasure. How on earth has she managed this? And how will I interview him in Portuguese? I run the logistics through my head.

"When would the interview be?"

"This afternoon," she says. "He's only got one interview slot left."

I FRANTICALLY RUN to the school reception, and with the help of Mel, the school manager, I manage to secure a Brazilian Portuguese interpreter within two hours. His name is Tomazo, and although he's not a professional interpreter, his English is apparently excellent.

I get back home to find Doris in the kitchen, boiling apples with the mantra music still playing in the background. Rebecca is sick due to a suspicious ice cube in her caipirinha earlier today. She's barely able to move or eat anything. "Boiled apples are what she needs," Doris tells me affirmatively.

I knock softly on Rebecca's bedroom door and walk in. She lies limply on her bed, her face pale.

"Doris told me that you're not allowed to use the coffee machine anymore," she says with a giggle, before dropping her head in exhaustion.

Doris summons us for lunch, and Rebecca walks weakly to the table and stares blankly at her boiled apples. Meanwhile, I'm going through my phone, responding to last-minute details in preparation for my interview with Neguinho.

"You need to learn to live in the moment," says Doris. "Put away your phone now."

I look at her in shock. The only person allowed to give me orders like that is my ninety-year-old grandmother.

"Doris, it's really important," I reply dryly. This is starting to feel more like a boarding school than a co-living experience.

"This is a shared moment at the table together—you shouldn't be on your phone." She looks at me judgmentally.

I turn to look at Rebecca, who is still staring at her apples, barely conscious enough to be affected by Doris.

"Doris," I say firmly, "I'm going to interview Neguinho."

She drops her knife and fork, and I worry for a second at the kind of reaction that this might provoke.

"Neguinho!" she howls. "Do you know that I'm originally from Nilópolis, where the Beija-Flor quadra is?" she shrieks.

I sit stoically and smile awkwardly, disturbed by her sudden mood changes that are as unpredictable as they are extreme.

"Oh, how I love Neguinho. And Beija-Flor is my school. My school since I was nine years old!" She puts her hand on her heart then shows me her arm, now covered in goose bumps.

Bate no peito, eu sou Beija-Flor. Beat your chest. I am Beija-Flor.

TOMAZO IS WEARING aviator sunglasses and a shiny black suit when we meet. On our way to Neguinho's beachfront home, he tells me how Neguinho is *the* most famous samba singer in Brazil. ("Like, if you say samba school, his name is the first thing that comes to mind.") It's thrilling to hear this but also nerve-racking. Thus far it has been my ignorance of these incredible characters that has enabled me to keep calm in my encounters with them.

Originally, my plan had been to study with a school called Mangueira and stay in their community, but I was told it would be too dangerous. Then I had tried to obtain a costume with Salguerio samba school, but they had sold out. Then while I was looking at the catalog of Carnival costumes, one stood out to my eye—a delicate white lace outfit embroidered in gold, with a floating skirt split on each side. That's when I decided to choose Beija-Flor. The costume had sold out online, so I'd tried to contact a "Carnival agency" that arranged costume sales, but it was to no avail. Thanks to Renata, however, I ended up getting straight through the school to the presidente herself, who was eager to introduce me to the school's icons. If things hadn't gone wrong—three times—I wouldn't be showing up on the doorstep of Neguinho da Beija-Flor. *Trust in the universe*, I think to myself. *It always has much better plans for you.*

Tomazo squirms in his suit when we arrive. It has a plastic, synthetic quality to it, and he looks like he's about to break into a sweat.

"Are you okay?" I ask.

"I'm a bit nervous," he says, adjusting his collar "I mean, it's Neguinho."

As we approach the seventh floor, we can hear the sound of samba gradually get louder and louder. Tomazo and I look at each other—this must be it.

A woman, presumably Neguinho's wife, opens the door. She stands with their young daughter and another woman. They are all dressed very casually, and even though the apartment is vast and in the heart of Copacabana, it is simple and modest—two qualities that Neguinho is known for. The home has large colorful paintings, including a few of tropical birds, and one of them stands out to me. It's a painting of two hummingbirds—the symbol of Beija-Flor, whose name, made up of the words for "kiss" and "flower," translates to "hummingbird."

We find Neguinho sitting in front of the TV in a T-shirt and Adidas tracksuit bottoms. His wife asks if we plan to take photos, and when we nod yes, she sends Neguinho into his room to get changed. He emerges dressed in a tropical sparkling top, with the Adidas track bottoms, clearly nonnegotiable, still covering his bottom half.

We begin to talk about samba's evolution from when he first started singing at nine years old until today.

"Samba has evolved, just like everything in life," he tells me as I record on my iPhone.

As a child in the late 1950s or early 1960s, Neguinho would watch people parading in cowhides from makeshift bleachers roped off by the Brazilian navy—a far cry from watching the sparkling nylon and feather-filled parades from the grand VIP booths of the sambadrome today. Carnival organizers started paying international stars like the French actor Alain Delon and American actress Raquel Welch to fly into Rio and attend Carnival to give it prestige. Today celebrities call three months in advance and pay a fortune for a box. Sixty or seventy years ago, singing samba could get you arrested for being a bum. Today, it's the heart of the biggest show on earth. Members of high society dream of participating, and international models compete for the role of *la rainha da bateria* (the queen of the drums).

"Samba has reached such a level—thank God that I caught it in this phase." He starts to sing a phrase from a song: "*O samba já foi marginalizado. Há bem pouco tempo passado, cantar samba era pecado capital. Mas hoje até a sociedade despida em sua vaidade, canta samba quando chega o carnaval.*"

"What does it mean?" I ask Tomazo. Nobody has ever sung an answer to me in an interview before, and seeing Neguinho's face so full of emotion sends a shiver down my spine.

Tomazo translates: "Samba was marginalized. Not so long ago, singing samba was a capital sin. But today society has said farewell to its vanity and sings samba when they arrive at Carnival."

I ask Neguinho if the music and dancing have also evolved since he was a child, and he tells me that they're much faster than before. The parade now allocates less time for each samba school to compete, so they need to parade through the sambadrome at a faster pace, whereas before it was unstructured and would last for hours. The current time limit is one hour and twenty minutes—if you exceed it you lose points or risk elimination—so the number of people passing through the sambadrome in time has been slashed from nine thousand to three thousand.

"The emotion I feel after all these years is still like it's the first time," Neguinho tells me. Despite the rigorous rehearsals, the sacrifice, and the responsibility of holding that one hour and twenty minutes in his hands—or microphone, rather, as the spokesperson for the greatest show on earth—performing is a feeling of bliss so bewildering that he doesn't even notice the size of his audience, sometimes focusing on just the ten or twenty people in front of him.

"Sometimes I ask God if I deserve all this happiness. I don't think there's any money in the world that can buy that moment."

His philosophy as a performer inspires me. While I've come to enjoy the rush of adrenaline, the blinding lights, and that first deep breath before launching into a keynote speech or presentation, my experiences dancing onstage have more often left me debilitated by absolute mortification and anxiety. I hope that I will get to experience this bliss he speaks of, to manifest the swelling energy of the audience as I parade down the sambadrome in less than two weeks.

Neguinho has been singing with Beija-Flor for forty years. He sang through a devastating cancer diagnosis and even married his wife on top of a float during the parade. Beija-Flor is his family, his food, his mother, his daughter. His world. And now it is his name.

"Nobody knows who Luiz Antônio Feliciano Marcondes is. They know Neguinho da Beija-Flor!"

But Neguinho sees the power of samba beyond his own story, a power that imbues society with an energy so powerful it inspires hope.

"It is magic, infectious, and makes people interact. You cannot distinguish a samba that is rich or that is poor. Unless you notice a different appearance, better treated skin, or better brushed hair. But samba has that power. There are people playing on the drums that you wouldn't make much of, and it turns out they are a colonel, a commander, an industrialist, or a millionaire. That person is there because they like it, and they're taking orders from someone who doesn't even have the most basic level of schooling. Samba manages to make people of different races, social classes, or purchasing power equal."

Neguinho leans in toward me to reach his arm out and place it alongside mine, showing the contrast between the colors of our skin. "Black and white, you see the difference?" he says to me, smiling.

"But we both love samba," I reply, my eyes gleaming.

He takes my hand and kisses it gently.

RENATA HAS SOMEHOW also managed to arrange my visit to Beija-Flor's rehearsal at their quadra tomorrow evening. It's all the way out in Nilópolis, a small municipality northwest of Rio that's about an hour's drive out of town. It hadn't occurred to me that taking such a long trip on my own, into the suburbs of Rio, might be putting my life at risk.

Once my driver exits the city, we pass through a highway that looks almost like a periphery, and he tells me he's going to drive faster now—that this neighborhood is dangerous.

With my limited Portuguese, I try to ask him what he means. "Why are we in a dangerous place and what are the risks?"

He raises his hand as if he's pointing a gun. "Pow!"

I don't ask any more questions and instead lean back into my seat and wait silently for us to pass the red zone that we are apparently traversing.

We pass through the territory of Comando Vermelho (the Red Command), one of the city's most violent gangs, known for arms trafficking, money laundering, bank robberies, and murders, but when we make it to the school on a downhill street that has a warm, community feel, I don't feel unsafe.

After waiting over an hour for anyone else to show, the quadra begins to fill up with people. The *bateria* (drummers) set up their drums and passistas emerge in sparkling two-pieces and stiletto heels bearing the school's colors: blue and white. Some dancers wear official school shirts, while others dress in varying levels of formal and flamboyant outfits that seem to indicate some sort of hierarchy. A crowd of older dancers forms one square, while a tribe from an indigenous group forms another.

I ask Alex, the school's interpreter, who everyone is. It seems like there are distinct roles and hierarchies in the parade. He tells me that everyone has a role and that some players are more important than others. First up: *la rainha da bateria*. Considered the godmother of the school, the rainha presents the percussion section, made up of 250 to 300 drummers, to the crowd and keeps morale high throughout the parade.

Alex tells me that a lot of models and celebrities compete for the role, as Raissa de Oliveira, the rainha of Beija-Flor, walks by. Alex waves, and she flashes us a dazzling smile before flipping her glossy black hair and shimmying across the quadra.

He introduces me to various "official" types, such as the school's president and members of the organizing committee, and then motions for me to walk up the stairs to a small box where a serious-looking man watches over the quadra with an authoritative glare.

"That's Laíla," he whispers. "He's the school's manager. He actually just got out of the hospital. He has seriously high blood pressure and the doctors told him to avoid all stress. We thought he wouldn't be able to make it this year, but he pulled through." He introduces me to Laíla, who firmly shakes my hand and exchanges a few polite words before getting back to work.

It seems like people will not miss Carnival at any cost—the love for an annual event that builds community and a sense of belonging can surpass even the most difficult and pressing issues—blood pressure in Laíla's case and cancer in Neguinho's—and make them come second.

Alex then introduces me to the flag-bearing queen with a stunning smile, who goes by the name Selminha Sorriso (the last name means smile!). Selminha took this role in 1996, after being "acquired" from another school—much the same way that a football team acquires star players. He invites me to pose for a photo with her.

We are joined by Claudinho, a buoyant man in a sumptuous bright blue suit who is the *mestre-sala* (master of the room) whose job it is to accompany the flag-bearer. He asks me if I know how to samba. When I slowly start to show him the basic step that I learned with Bruno, he takes my hand to dance. But instead I jump clumsily, shifting my weight from one foot to the other. We speed up to keep pace with the percussionists, who are pounding into their drums as they walk in to join us in the outdoor parking lot of the quadra. My heart beats quickly, conjoining with the drums.

Claudinho didn't need to take the time to dance with me, but like so many people I have come across in my journey, he is charming, friendly, and generous with his time. It is like he feels a responsibility as an ambassador to sweep me into his world and make me feel what he feels: a love of samba so powerful that it is all-consuming and radiates from his very core. After dancing, he gives me a kiss on the cheek and waltzes off to catch up with Selminha, who has begun to spin across the quadra armed with the school's flag.

In the runup to the parade, it is customary to pledge allegiance and give your blessing by kissing the school's flag ahead of the big day. A row of people in official shirts stand at the side of the quadra's main dancing area, and Selminha spins toward them before pausing to bow before them and offer them the flag. An elderly man grips on to his cane as he leans down to kiss it. It's like nothing would stop him from pledging his allegiance to Beija-Flor.

"May I?" I shyly ask a woman holding another flag on the sidelines.

She's a tall, sculptural black woman whose regal stature is a little intimidating, but she holds out the flag and towers over me as if giving me her blessing, and I lean in to give it a kiss.

There are young children dancing samba around me, and a group of adults who march in a straight line, presumably rehearsing their walk down the sambadrome. The school's flags twirl, and the passistas samba relentlessly. Some wear headdresses adorned with blue feathers that resemble those of Brazil's indigenous peoples, and Alex tells me that every year, each samba school has an *enredo*—a theme that it will embrace for the entire parade, showcasing it with costumes, floats, and song lyrics. Beija-Flor's theme this year is Iracema: A Virgem dos Lábios de Mel (Iracema: The Virgin of Honeyed Lips), based on the classic 1865 romance novel by José de Alencar and subsequent film adaptations.

The novel tells the tale of Iracema, a young indigenous girl from Ceará in northeastern Brazil who falls in love with Martim, a Portuguese colonist. Together they have a son named Moacir (meaning "son of pain") before

Martim abandons them in the name of war and patriotism. Moacir is considered the first true Brazilian in Ceará, bringing together two different worlds in a fusion born from agony. *Iracema* is an anagram for America. Through her story, de Alencar tells the origin of the Brazilian nation.

My Carnival parade costume represents the intricate laces brought over to colonial Ceará centuries ago. Samba—just like Brazil, just like Moacir— was born out of this heavy past. But now it represents joy, celebration, and the greatest show on earth.

MY EYES ARE red with exhaustion, and I try to keep sitting up straight to avoid falling asleep while working through my language book. My Portuguese could be so much better, but dance has to be my main focus. I had underestimated how much my dance journey would actually be a full-on project, leaving me with little time to lounge on Ipanema Beach, study, or even keep up with the school's social calendar. My dance classes, rehearsals, and nocturnal outings are exhilarating and rewarding, but they require diligent research and planning. Luckily, each experience always brings me a welcome, spontaneous surprise.

Today's class is structured around the theme of "Who will you be in Carnival?" Natalia has prepared not one but four costumes to wear during the *bloco* parties—pre-Carnival street festivities—including costumes for a mermaid and a famous murderer from the northeast. She has a wide range of equipment to create her costumes, including sequins and a glue gun. This is serious stuff. I text Rebecca: "We need to go Carnival costume shopping after class!"

After class, I find Rebecca outside looking slightly solemn.

"What happened?"

"It's Doris," she sighs, looking down. "Today she banned me from using her pans."

This is another blow. We also haven't been allowed to use the laundry or change our linens. I feel a responsibility to protect Rebecca; she seems so fragile, and we are clearly being ripped off. I had been warned of this—it isn't uncommon for Cariocas to overcharge foreigners in any way they can.

"That's it. We've got to do something," I say. I'm not going to let this situation continue any more.

We head to General Osório Station to take the metro toward one of the city's most important markets while debating how to approach Doris. We start to draft a message in Portuguese, wondering how to tackle it in a way that doesn't bring on one of her episodes.

We emerge from the metro station in the middle of the market, where we find a multitude of Brazilian flags, multicolored sungas, and an array of things that you don't know you need until you see them. We each buy a beach sarong with the Brazilian flag—a must for any temporary Carioca—and I pick up a neon crop top before proceeding toward the costume aisle.

It's a never-ending labyrinth, complete with a rainbow of wigs, glitter, sequins, and feather boas on display, every kind of plastic fruit imaginable, accessories, and ready-made costumes. I'd promised Andreas that I would help him with his costume and decide to get him a Zorro cape and hat, while Rebecca and I pick up various accessories for ourselves—from a Carmen Miranda fruit headpiece to a princess tiara—and various shades of glitter. We plan to share everything and alternate who wears what. The Cariocas around us are on a serious mission to complete their outfits, and we seem like amateurs next to them—but as long as we're covered in glitter, we can't really go wrong. I look at the time.

"We need to go!"

The technical rehearsal is tonight, and all the samba schools will get the chance to rehearse their parade in the sacred Sambódromo Marquês de Sapucaí.

I'D SEEN THE sambadrome in documentaries about Carnival, and it was always filled with sequin-clad revelers and grandiose floats. But nothing captured the immensity of the place. Designed by Brazilian architect Oscar Neimeyer and inaugurated in 1984, it's a far cry from the naval ropes and temporary bleachers of the 1960s that Neguinho had described. It's a full-on stadium that stretches almost half a mile in length and has the capacity to host ninety thousand spectators plus the thousands of people who parade from each school.

Rebecca and I meet our friends and head inside. Elderly women dressed in white with beads around their necks chant and slowly shimmy down the sambadrome. They are practitioners of Candomblé and Umbanda, Afro-Brazilian syncretic religions that developed among enslaved Africans under the Portuguese Empire and are sister religions of Santería. They aren't here just for the last technical rehearsal but also for the *lavagem do sambódromo* (cleansing of the sambadrome), a traditional purification ceremony to bless the sambadrome ahead of the parade.

After the practitioners stream past in what feels like an ocean of white, the schools start to parade, each bearing its colors and flag. The passistas scream the lyrics of the school's songs, and as the hundreds of percussionists pass us, night starts to fall, as if they had pounded the sun out of the sky, leaving instead a haze of blush and indigo clouds above us, and a collective emotional aura of hope, apprehension, determination, and desire.

I ARRIVE THE first morning of a two-day samba workshop at the famed Carlinhos de Jesus dance school—starving. I've barely been eating, and with samba's grueling pace, I've lost so much weight that my clothes are starting to fall off me. There's no food around except for packets of dry biscuits for sale along with instant coffee. I push myself to power through. After all, this is what I've been doing the whole time—I'm not the type to give up or miss out on these incredible experiences and opportunities, even if it is a little risky for my health.

Have I reached an unhealthy level of grit? Has my determination led me to force myself to extremes that are against the very nature of this journey? Maybe. But at the same time, the extremes are exhilarating and rewarding. When I get a moment to sit down and rest after hours of dance training and look into the studio mirror, my reflection shows me what I have become—a person who is stronger and more confident than before.

Our first teacher is not just good but really good, which helps push me onward. He starts us off with the basic samba step, instructing us to gently bend one knee and then let it rebound lightly, followed by the other. We step one foot back, keeping one leg perfectly straight while bending the other knee to step forward and then drag the back foot forward to meet it. Three tiny steps, just inches apart. After we've covered the fundamental bases, we shift from one knee to the other to a slow, relaxing samba beat. It sounds simple, but in Carnival samba—the fastest of all sambas—these tiny steps gain speed, sending the hips into a tremendous fury.

Today, things start off mellow; our teacher allows us to syncopate our movements and keep at ease. People often have the misconception that the harder the class, the better it is. But learning at a slower pace allows us to comprehend the material fully, rather than cramming in a bunch of rapid-fire sequences.[125] This journey has taught me so far that when given the time to learn slowly, I can reach new heights; when rushed, I remain an eternal failure.

As we progress, the music starts to speed up and continues to do so until our samba is fast and fearless. But because the teacher started us off slowly, I can keep up. He had given us time to mentally grasp the steps as one single ensemble. In the mirror, I see my hips slowly undulating above my fast feet. I can't help but smile, and this sense of ease allows me to open up my arms, almost as a benevolent offering to my own reflection.

At the end of the class, we have a group photo taken with the teacher, and then everyone rushes to have their selfie taken with him.

"Who is he?" I ask Melina, a fellow student.

She looks at me in shock that I don't know. "It's Carlinhos!"

I was completely ignorant about the fact that Carlinhos is one of Brazil's most important dancers and choreographers—the school had even been named after him. He has worked for some of Rio's biggest samba schools, from Mangueira to Beija-Flor and Portela, dancing, choreographing, and directing theater, cinema, and, of course, Carnival.[126] *To think that I got to take a class with him!* I should be ashamed of my ignorance, but in a way there is something special about not knowing how special or famous someone is. It means that you can form an authentic judgment based on the person's qualities and attitude toward others, especially as a teacher. It also means that instead of frantically looking for my phone to capture the moment, I was fully living it.

After a brief lunch of biscuit crumbs from the crumpled packet in my bag, I walk back into the studio with my head held high, determined to give it all I have. A curvaceous woman with fluttering eyelashes and a wide smile greets me in the doorway. She's sporting blue-and-white striped leggings, threateningly long acrylic nail extensions, and an impressive mane of hair, and she speaks in a coarse accent that I find difficult to understand. She is none other than Nilce Fran, a veteran passista who rose through the samba ranks to *porta-bandeira* (flag bearer) and then rainha da bateria, and is now director of Passistas of Portela, one of Rio's most prestigious schools. This year, 2017, will be her thirty-eighth Carnival, and she is considered a leader in shaping the samba talents of Rio's Carnival.[127]

We start with a slower, simpler alternative to a full samba step.

"When you feel too tired to samba, just alternate your weight from one knee to the other. The key is in your posture and the arms so that it's always lovely." She creates a delicate shape with her fingertips and circles it into her chest while stretching her other arm out gracefully to one side, her gaze following its flowing movement. She then alternates her arms, creating an almost birdlike, floating movement. As the music speeds up, her arms go faster and faster.

I try to keep up, but as with any new dance step or decoration, until fully mastered, the movement loses its beauty if you speed it up too fast too soon. I've experienced this time and again throughout this journey. Everything is mastered through repetition, allowing oneself to make mistakes, and understanding the concept of a movement in slow-motion before you can speed it up. My arms on autopilot, I hear Nilce shouting instructions in the distance of my daydream. Her voice seems to have changed in tone. She's talking to me. I stop dancing, and she starts to speak at me while the others giggle.

I feel humiliated. What did I do wrong? Why am I being singled out in front of the others?

One of my fellow students, a striking woman with green eyes and a passion for belly dancing, interjects. "She doesn't speak Portuguese very well," she says to our teacher before turning to me to talk to me in English: "She's explaining that in a samba party you have to reduce the size of your arms so you don't hit anyone in the face, and you will if you're stretching your arms out wide."

Nilce covers her face with her hands. "*O, meu amor!*" (Oh, my love!)

She walks toward me and takes me into her arms before affectionately stroking my face with her slender, acrylic-tipped fingers.

THE NEXT DAY we embark on *samba de gafieira*, a type of samba danced in pairs that became a *dança de salão* (ballroom dance). The instructors have brought in an entire troupe of young male dancers to accompany us (as is sadly quite common with these events, more women show up than men). I'm pleasantly surprised at how much I like it, and it somehow feels natural despite being a dance that I have never danced before. It seems to be an interesting fusion of samba and salsa, with a touch of tango. As is true of all partner dances, the ability to follow, be guided by your intuition, and make snap decisions is important, and the dance has a language of its own. The teacher keeps repeating the name of one of the steps, *balanço*, a direction for us to swing from side to side, and it's becoming one of my favorite new movements.

I make a mental note to ask Bruno if we can practice this dance more, before diving into traditional dances from the northeast of the country that have a heavier Afro-Brazilian influence. In flower-patterned cotton skirts, we hit two large wooden sticks against each other while chanting. I'm slightly confused and unable to really follow what's going on. But as always, I go with it and participate as best as I can.

And then, the cherry on the cake: a flag-bearing class with the porta-bandeira and mestre-sala of Unidos da Tijuca, another important samba school whose colors are blue and yellow. It turns out there is an entire technique for holding the flag properly. You must position it against your hip and hold your posture so that you can spin graciously while ensuring the flag is held high.

Experiencing what it's like to be a porta-bandeira, even if for just a moment, allows me to live one of the integral parts of Carnival. The flag is much heavier than I had imagined, and I rest its mast carefully against my hip and take a deep breath before stepping out that first pointed foot that symbolizes the beginning of another dimension of this journey. I slowly start to spin and, in awe of its prestige, history, and meaning, use all my strength to keep the embroidered, shimmering flag held high.

My visit to Beija-Flor left me enchanted. I have no obligation to rehearse ahead of the big day, but I want to go to their last rehearsal before the parade, and this time I want to dance. Ana has already told me that a group of young passistas will dance with me. Watching all the samba school's characters had been an experience itself, but to live samba, to live Carnival, I have to actually dance it.

I go to school dressed in my quadra rehearsal outfit: white shorts, my new Beija-Flor tank top displaying the face of Iracema, and blue stiletto heels. Andreas crosses my path in the corridor, and we exchange a few words. He stares at me in a way that might be capable of burning through my clothes. In a world where you can swipe through your options, where sex is available on demand and a person can be tossed away, it has become rare to feel such intensity, especially through one single glance. A tap on my shoulder brings me back to my thoughts, almost causing me to spill my extra-strong coffee. It's Sergio.

"Hello, princess. Any more samba fun?" he asks, observing my outfit with approval.

I tell him about the rehearsal and invite him as well as Helene, a French girl from the school who's overheard our conversation, to join me.

"You guys realize this place is really far, right?" I ask cautiously, not wanting to be responsible should anything happen to them.

But they nod, seemingly unfazed. For Sergio, the magic of his retired life lies in waking up without knowing where the day will take him or how his night will end.

When we arrive at Beija-Flor, the quadra is once again empty, and this time the gates are locked so we can't even wait inside. We soak up the local atmosphere and imagine what it might be like if it were our own, watching the sun slowly set above the downhill street. The shops display merchandise and memorabilia in Beija-Flor's colors, and this year's song blares out of the speakers. We approach a makeshift bar, where people sit on plastic stools while watching a football game on a huge flat-screen television. We take a seat and order a round of beers.

When I hear the sounds of metal blinds lifting and chains clinking, signaling the opening of the gates, we head over and I march inside, determined to dance. Ana greets me with a hug and then heads to look for the passistas. I hand my bag to Sergio before conducting a quick site analysis to see where we could dance.

"You walked in like you own the place," whispers Sergio, with a mix of fear and admiration.

I would usually feel intimidated and vulnerable walking into a huge place like this, especially when I barely speak the language or know anyone. *What's changed?* I ask myself, and the answer comes readily. Samba is a dance made for Carnival queens to parade down the sambadrome with charisma and splendor, and it has taught me how to carry myself with confidence, to develop a powerful presence, and to embody a sparkling strut. The effect has transformed my way of walking: my arms now float by my sides, my head is high, my legs lengthen with each step.

Ana comes back over to us, this time with the passistas. At barely seventeen years old, they are already the front-line dancers of the parade. Today everyone wears relaxed clothing, not the shimmering training outfits that they had on last time.

We start to warm up together and then one at a time step to the front to samba.

Each dancer is different. One muscular, ebony-skinned girl with long braids has incredible thighs that add strength to her samba; another girl has a head topped in caramel curls and makes feminine, delicate arm movements; one with terra-cotta skin glides effortlessly in her transitions with a mesmerizing moonwalk movement; another has skin that is ivory white, long, straight blond hair, and hip movements so sharp that they could cut glass. They each might appear different, but they are united in their love of samba and Beija-Flor.

I'm the last to go, and they cheer me on to take my turn and samba. I hesitate but force myself to give it everything, stampeding with my feet to the speed of the song. We join together to dance different steps, including new ones that I've never danced before. They don't judge my sometimes clumsy efforts to follow them but instead encourage me. While many seventeen-year-olds in other parts of the world might laugh at an "older" woman of thirty trying to dance with them, these girls take an almost pedagogical approach, wanting to share what they know and love with me. Dance has shaped their character and provided maturity; it has equipped them with respect, perseverance, understanding, and kindness.

We skip across the quadra and toward the outdoor parking lot to join the bateria and continue to samba until I can barely stand. If you had told me months ago that I would be dancing samba with a group of teenagers in an outdoor parking lot in a distant suburb of Rio de Janeiro, I wouldn't have believed you. But the beat of a drum has brought us together despite age, background, and language.

ANDREAS HAS INVITED Rebecca and me to join him and his roommates in the Flamengo neighborhood for a bloco celebrating the LGBTQ community. Just a few days ago we experienced our first full-on bloco in Santa Teresa since the official start of carnival; it was dedicated to the Carmelites but inspired less than saintly behavior. Rebecca and I both dodged kisses from Edson, who was dressed in a giant diaper and awaited the students walking through the bloco's main route. Meanwhile, the tension with Andreas, who proudly sports his new Zorro outfit, has reached a boiling point.

Today Rebecca and I make our way to our go-to meeting point outside General Osório Station. Andreas, dressed as Zorro once again, introduces us to his roommates, who today are a rainbow unicorn and Che Guevara, accompanied by a Roman god and a clown with a multicolor wig. Andreas seems more distant today, but I can still feel the tension that has been accumulating between us. Perhaps he's holding back because he's with his friends. Rebecca has been fully briefed on my teenage crush and carefully observes the situation.

We take the metro, crammed with people in colorful costumes. The guy in jeans and a white T-shirt is the odd one out compared to us covered in a myriad of colors and leaving a trail of glitter behind as we walk through the metro's underground tunnels. When we emerge, it's into a huge park filled with people. I scan my horizons to check out the costumes—my favorite bloco activity. I've been to quite a few more casual blocos since my arrival. This has the most exceptional costumes that I have ever seen.

I walk past a row of Smurfs, one of them staring at me intensely with blood-spattered contact lenses and a malicious grin. We continue through the crowd of angels, fairies, and pirates and are stopped by a handsome young man in tight white shorts and gold epaulettes who resembles something between a cheerleader and the Nutcracker and insists on having his photo taken with me. A male trio of Hercules, a Playboy bunny, and Cleopatra then asks for one as well.

It's rare to stand in one place for too long in these blocos. You typically keep walking, or parading, giving high fives, admiring costumes, and occasionally getting your face devoured by anonymous Cariocas. In this bloco, however, I feel much safer than in others. None of the men are interested in me here, so rather than being on the defensive, I enjoy my role as a casual observer. However, I did neglect the fact that my crush, Andreas, is a prime victim here, and as we approach the main concert stand, a man grabs his face for a kiss. He does not entirely reciprocate, but he doesn't pull away either. *Is there something that I've missed? Or maybe he likes both men and women?* He turns back toward me. "I've kind of gotten used to it by now," he says helplessly, smiling at me.

I'm determined to make it happen with him. It's clear that we have a connection, we're in a bloco, and the beer is free-flowing. What could possibly go wrong? I find the courage to flirt a little more strongly, our gaze now almost unbreakable each time he glances back at me.

Suddenly a bold Brazilian girl emerges from the sidelines: "*Você é tão fofinho!*" she exclaims, clutching his jaw. She proceeds to speak in English to ensure his consent.

"You are so cute I want to kiss you," she says, and then, since he doesn't run away, devours his face, leaving me mortified.

Seriously? How did she just swoop in and completely kill my moment? I've had a connection with him for weeks, and she manages to get him just like that? I hate to admit to myself what the real problem is here: I've never had the guts (or confidence) to act on my crush. Instead, I have timidly hinted without acting, waiting and hoping that he might kiss me. How wrong I was! What I needed was to take a cue from the Brazilians: to grab the face of the guy I like and kiss him.

I start walking around in distress and Rebecca follows me supportively but isn't sure how to help. Then, all of a sudden, another boisterous Brazilian woman appears, and this time the woman presses her lips against Rebecca's, who stands limply, unsure what to do.

I wade my way through an ocean of mermen and Tritons with tridents. I feel lost and scan my surroundings for a way out. A sailor in a blue tutu with six-pack abs and a glittery beard approaches me: "Darling," he says in a soft Brazilian accent, "what is wrong?"

"I liked this guy . . ." I blubber helplessly, "and then he kissed someone else."

The sailor leans in to kiss me passionately, softly at first, and then more intensely. It may be one of the best kisses of my life.

I pull back, confused. "But you're gay!"

"Darling," he says with a shrug, "it's Carnival!"

As I arrive at the sambadrome for the big event, the magnitude hits me. I will be fulfilling a lifelong dream by parading through the Sambódromo Marquês de Supucaí to a crowd of almost one hundred thousand people. Our school is the last to go through, and we've been asked to arrive at one in the morning and begin parading at 3:30 a.m. If the sambadrome had seemed colossal when I saw it during the technical rehearsal, it now seems to be of a proportion beyond what I imagined. The thousands of people from each of the six schools wait for their turn to enter the sambadrome, lining up alongside their floats on a closed-off dual carriage way.

I hadn't realized just how high-stakes this competition was. Forty judges spread over ten categories determine the winners based on a wide range of criteria: the drums section and its ability to keep rhythm throughout the parade, the themed samba music, the harmony of the parade—whether visual, acoustic, or musical—the theme of the parade as reflected in its floats and costumes, its evolution through movement and dance, allegories and themes expressed through props and costumes, the vanguard commission that opens the parade, the porta-bandeira and mestre-sala, and the most subjective category of all, accomplishment and the school's overall impact.[128]

And this is just the judges' role. There must be scores of people involved in the organization and running of this event, between the light and sound technicians, ushers, cooks, cleaners, and other workers. Some universities even run graduate programs in samba school management as part of parade organization efforts. Carnival is a multimillion-dollar business that generates hundreds of thousands of jobs. This year alone, an estimated 1.5 million tourists have come to Rio for the Carnival celebrations.[129]

I've been waiting for an hour, so I stroll to check out the next ala for a little distraction to help the time pass. Enormous growling jaguars guard the front of a float, protecting entire tribes of dancers with giant feather headpieces. At the very top, a passista with glossy long straight hair and body paint waits patiently, perched on what appears to be a giant nest.

After some time watching in awe, I head back to our ala, which is filled with a lavish wave of dancers in white and gold. From the ground it's impressive to see an entire block of people dressed the same—I can only imagine how striking it looks from above. There are other foreigners in this ala too, though I hadn't seen any at the rehearsals. Maybe they had their costumes delivered through one of those Carnival agencies.

By three o'clock we still haven't started getting into position. I ask a friend what's going on, and it turns out there has been a tragic accident.

A float crashed into the fence separating the pavement from the stands, injuring at least twenty people. The first school to parade—Paraíso do Tuiuti—had run various tests to check the safety of the floats, but with the drizzling rain and wet pavement, the driver of the three-ton truck carrying forty dancers lost control and reversed, causing the float to sway before running over several people and crashing into the fence. Even as paramedics rushed victims to the hospital, the decision was made to carry on. In Rio, not even a tragedy can stop the Carnival parade.

I start to feel apprehensive. The floats seem so wide and heavy. A small maneuver could be perilous. And there are tens of thousands of people in one confined space. What if I fall under a float? Or get trampled by the crowd? I jump at the sound of a sonic boom and turn to see sparkling bursts overtake the sky. The fireworks have gone off and Neguinho has started to sing. It's time.

Ana marches up and down to put us into neat ornamental rows of white and gold, dressing the pavement like layers of lace. We begin to march, keeping a steady, harmonious pace. I can't see much around me because a flock of feathers is obstructing my field of vision—but I can vaguely see big boxes filled with people and cameras, one filled with a particularly observant group of people. *Those must be the judges*, I think to myself, holding my breath. I hold myself high, performing my best samba strut and flashing my happiest smile as we parade past them.

I expected this to be a euphoric experience, but my body feels overcome by exhaustion and the feathers from the row in front of me keep poking my eyes. Only the pounding beat of samba can keep me going, and as we reach the end of the sambadrome, the elderly man with a cane, the president of Beija-Flor, awaits us. He gives me a proud smile, holding on to his cane as he bounces to the samba, and shakes my hand. I am not from Nilópolis, a Carioca, or Brazilian—I am not even an experienced passista—but I feel an incredible sense of belonging. I am a part of Beija-Flor, and it has become part of me.

DORIS HAS GONE out of town for the Carnival weekend, to a mystical mountain retreat with her yogi friends, and Rebecca, our new Argentine roommate—Hernán—and I are overjoyed at having the house to ourselves. We can use the kitchen whenever we want, without being followed around or reprimanded for our every move.

Tonight Juan's family is in town for Carnival and to visit Adriana—another cousin, who is studying here. I'm thrilled to meet up with them and watch the final day of the parade together—it feels like I haven't spoken Spanish in forever. We arrive at the sambadrome to a heaving atmosphere with crowds of people. This time I get to go inside the viewing area, which is bustling with counters selling everything from caipirinhas to coxinhas. From our seats high up, we have a wide view of the sambadrome, including a huge replica of Christ the Redeemer and cardboard cutouts of samba dancers. People have come with homemade signs and flags to cheer on their samba school, while others sport their school's official T-shirt or wear its colors. One man wears a captain's hat with pink tulle wrapped around it to match his green-and-pink striped top—the colors of Mangueira. A couple has come in matching blue-and-white striped outfits, ready to support Portela.

The drums start to play, and the first Carnival queens in sparkling bodysuits and enormous feather headdresses arrive onto the track, towering in their stiletto heels. Even from far away, an iridescent ray of light catches on each sequin to capture every shimmer of their samba.

What fascinates me most is how this composition of colors and costumes, dancers, music, and props all comes together to represent one theme. How it can tell a story, potentially one that can touch people's hearts and minds, and challenge their ideas and behaviors for societal change—and all this in a parade of over three thousand people. Carnival isn't just a chance for schools to compete for the most prestigious samba prizes but a way to express societal discontent and tell the stories that form Brazil's history, culture, and legends.

Key to this is the *enredo* (plot)—the story that each school seeks to tell. União da Ilha shares the legend of Angola's king Kitembo Nzara Ndembu, the Senhor Tempo, in homage to Brazil's African roots. Mocidade has an enchanting Scheherazade theme telling the tales of *One Thousand and One Nights* through its glittering floats representing genies and magic carpets, and a colorful seahorse float that leaves me mesmerized. It's one of my favorite floats so far, a gleaming pale turquoise with each iridescent fin made up of a different passista, fluttering with each samba step. Some dance more enthusiastically than others, creating texture in the seahorse's movement.

São Clemente has chosen the theme of Louis XIV's Versailles and, more specifically, the tale of his finance minister, Nicolas Fouquet, who built the stunning Chateau Vaux-le-Vicomte and invited the King Louis XIV, the "Sun King," there for a night of iridescent splendor. But the magnificence of the chateau outraged the king, who was swayed by a brewing plot in his court to scheme Fouquet's demise, and had him convicted of embezzlement while building himself a grander replica that would become France's iconic palace of Versailles.[130] Each golden float reflects a different aspect of exuberance and excess: couples in white wigs dancing, an enormous gold structure of the sun drawn by a troupe of horses, Versailles's perfectly manicured gardens (with passistas making up different flowers and shrubs), and cascading fountains topped with marble statues of mythological gods. The theme is a dig at the greed, jealousy, and vengeance among those who rule, hinting at the latest corruption scandals and violence in Rio[131] and its neighboring state of Espiritu Santo.[132]

Unidos de Tijuca, which has also suffered a terrible accident tonight, has chosen a theme of American music, with one entire ala dedicated to Beyoncé and another to Michael Jackson's "Thriller," while passistas dressed as Justin Bieber and Nicki Minaj cheer on the crowd.

Portela has gone with a theme of rivers, playing on the relationship between water and human life. Entire alas reflect different textures of water, with every detail of the passistas' costumes in different shades of blues contrasting against thin trails of sea foam. The sambadrome has become flooded with a sea of blue feathers, each of them representing one drop of water in the ocean, and they transport me to a mythical aquatic underworld. Suddenly, a brown float approaches, depicting a fisherman crying out in despair, spoiling the ultramarine and turquoise stream that had until now enchanted my seascape.

"Why did the parade suddenly change tone?" I ask Adriana, hoping that her fluent Portuguese and knowledge of the local context will enable her to provide me an explanation.

"It's a reference to the 2015 Mariana dam disaster. It was named as a mining tragedy. The collapse of the dam sent a sea of mud into the Doce River, killing all fish and aquatic life for hundreds of miles."[133]

"Foi um rio que passou em minha vida, e meu coração se deixou levar" is the official name of Portela's theme and means "It was a river that passed in my life, and my heart let itself be carried away."

In the years before I took off on this journey, before I wound up in the sambadrome with a caipirinha, I held certain ideas about my life. I sought fulfillment from my achievements. I needed status, a high income, a world built of possessions. But I denied myself the most precious resources: pure and meaningful connections with myself, others, and the world. These are simple things. But simple things—as in the case of Portela's theme, water— are the most pertinent to our existence.

THE NEXT MORNING, I walk into the kitchen, rubbing my eyes with fatigue, and find Doris, who has unexpectedly returned home four days early from her vacation, in a cheerful mood.

"Thank you for taking such good care of my princess!" she squeals, before shimmying around the living room. It turns out that she had gotten into a fight with fellow yogis during a fire ritual, and suffice it to say that she had been banished and sent back to Rio.

I don't ask questions and tread with caution. Her good mood could change at any moment, but maybe this is a good time to ask her about the lambada—the forbidden dance. I remember sitting at four years old in my grandparents' veranda in France, watching the music video of Kaoma's iconic 1989 song "Lambada"—a worldwide phenomenon until today.[134] Though it is often considered one of the most iconic Brazilian songs, it was produced by Kaoma—a French record label created by Olivier Lamotte d'Incamps, who had previously bought the rights to over three hundred lambada songs.[135] This particular song, also known as "Chorando Se Foi," was an unauthorized adaption of Bolivian group Los Kjarkas's "Llorando se Fue" (She Left Crying).[136]

Still, the music is Brazilian in tone, and the music video features smiling people with maracas happily dancing down along the shore until they reach a beachside shack, the women dressed in crop tops and colorful skirts and the men donning vibrant shirts. Loalwa Braz, Kaoma's lead singer, embraces a rhythmic beat and a nostalgic tone rich with yearning.

In the video, a young blond girl dances the lambada, radiant and smiling, her body swaying from side to side in tight syncopated steps. Much to the dismay of her father—who disapproves of the dance and even slaps her in the face—she continues to dance the lambada into the sunset. Watching this music video as a child indelibly marked my own fascination with dance. Like the girl in the video, I also felt an unshakable desire to be myself—regardless of what was deemed appropriate. Hearing the song now, I can't help but experience it with the same childlike wonder, innocence, and desire for individuality that I experienced as a child.

What happened to the lambada as a genre? I haven't heard this type of music anywhere since arriving in Brazil. In a dark twist, it turns out that Loalwa Braz was brutally murdered mere weeks ago, at the age of sixty-three. Her body was found charred in a burnt-out car forty-five miles east of Rio de Janeiro, and it's thought that she was killed in the course of a burglary gone wrong.[137] It's a shocking discovery on its own, but the revelation of Braz's recent death feels all the more unsettling given the childhood innocence with which I first fell in love with her music.

"When I was young it was all you could listen to," Doris tells me, her wide eyes full of emotion. "They played it everywhere in the streets, and then one day, it just disappeared."

DESPITE HOURS OF research, calls, and texts, I struggle to find a lambada teacher. Bruno theorizes that its disappearance is likely due to Kaoma's monopoly over the lambada market, which allowed the record label to accumulate royalties at the expense of local producers. He believes the DJs and radio hosts who dominated the pre-streaming world thumbed their noses at the French executives and made a secret pact: they would stop playing lambada music altogether.

He tells me that almost overnight, the music disappeared from the airwaves. And when the music suddenly vanished, all the lambada instructors had to retrain. They looked for something similar that they could dance to and found a home in the French Caribbean dance style of zouk, which has a similar rhythm. To the zouk rhythm, the lambaderos added lambada steps, incorporating hints of Angolan kizomba to create a slower, and perhaps more sensual, dance. Soon, they began writing zouk songs in Portuguese, and from their efforts emerged a new hybrid form called the zouk-lambada or lamba-zouk.

"But what if I want to learn the lambada as it was danced in 1989?" I ask Bruno, determined to honor my nostalgia.

"It's not going to be easy," he tells me. "But I'll help you."

I FINALLY MANAGE to find a lambada teacher who's willing to teach me: Renato Dias, who started dancing lambada in 1990 and even wrote a thesis on the dance. In 1993, Dias invented "lambada 3," where a man leads two women who dance different movements at the same time. He has opened a cultural dance center, launched the Rio Dance Congress, and spent almost twenty years traveling the world to teach his technique. I'm in the hands of a true master.

Renato is well over six feet tall and has waist-length curls tied up in a bun and an enormous smile that reveals transparent braces. He seems like a gentle giant and reminds me of a benevolent version of Jaws from *James Bond*. He's wearing a baggy T-shirt and shorts and opens the gate, taking me through a tunnel of tropical trees that leads to an expansive wooden house with a large, rustic dance floor at its core.

"We're going to start by learning how to walk," he says, taking my hand and leading me to one side of the room.

I'm surprised. *Why would I have come all the way here to learn how to walk?* I want to be swaying and spinning to lambada.

"I don't think you will realize just how important this is until much later," he says as if he has read my mind. "Just trust me."

I start walking normally, but Renato corrects me. It's almost like I need to glide instead of walk, with my foot pointed and arched and my posture straight. Ironically, it requires huge concentration and some discomfort to look natural and effortless.

He then guides me to the middle of the room and has me sit on an exercise ball. He holds a wooden stick in his hand, which scares me slightly.

"Look," he says, holding the stick with the tip of his finger. "When the stick leans forward, backward, or to the side, it doesn't bend. It falls. I want you to do the same."

I stand up hesitantly. This feels strange. I lean all my weight forward, then to the right, to the back, and to the front. Even leaning the tiniest bit makes me feel uneasy.

"Lean more," says Renato reassuringly.

"I can't," I insist. It really feels like I'm going to fall. I try to push myself. I can manage forward and to the sides, even if slightly losing my balance and stumbling to catch my step, but leaning backward makes me feel afraid he won't be able to catch me if I fall.

"Again," says Renato. We continue to repeat this exercise, along with walking, for another hour, and I struggle to hide my frustration. I just want to dance! What I don't realize is that identifying my axis—my point of balance—stands at the very core of bodily awareness. This new, conscious way of walking will give me the superpowers to step and pivot as I please.

We take a break in his kitchen, and he kindly offers me a glass of grape juice. I take a seat at the kitchen table, entertained by the strange combination of lambada and grape juice. He slowly opens a cabinet to retrieve a bottle of Absolut Vodka, which he then pours generously into his own glass of grape juice. It's before noon, but he seems unfazed.

"Now we're going to get into the lambada."

We launch into the steps, which feel similar to salsa, but much faster. We start to incorporate some neck rolls, which create the dramatic hair-whipping effect that I have always sought to emulate. It's a round, sensual movement, and I develop an innate trust as he dips me backward—my entire balance depends on him. He flips me from side to side, my hair flying through the air. It feels liberating; never before have I allowed myself to make these kinds of movements. It is so beyond my comfort zone, and foreign to my body.

Suddenly I start to feel sick, and nausea takes over, flushing from my forehead to my shoulders. I think I'm going to vomit.

It's an unpleasant break from a fleeting feeling of elation. But I have no choice other than to lie down on his sofa, my head leaning backward, while trying to contain a fit of hiccups.

Poor Renato stands by helpless, wondering what to do as I lie down, my body jerking with each hiccup. I ask if he has Coca-Cola—this seems to help whenever I feel sick—and after a few sips, my hiccups start to slow down and eventually disappear. The neck rolls made me seasick—almost as if being flipped from side to side was like sailing through a stormy sea.

We continue to dance, but a wave of nausea hits again and I burst into another fit of hiccups. This feeling is so bizarre; I simply don't understand why the lambada makes me feel sick. Several breaks and three cans of Coca-Cola later, we rehearse to the actual lambada song, omitting any rolls or dips for the time being. The song never seemed that fast to me, but to fit three steps in between the two beats makes it feel almost like a shuffle. Eventually I let myself go, allowing my body to wave to the song of my childhood, my head rolling and hair flipping. For just a few minutes, nothing else exists in the world except for a feeling of total exhilaration. The earth has stopped spinning. I launch into orbit.

I RETURN HOME to find that Doris's cheerfulness from earlier in the day has dissipated. She's roaming in my room with a feather duster and turns to look at me, annoyed, as I walk in. She barely mutters a *bom dia* (good morning) before throwing a pair of my shoes on the floor. Having lived in Asia, I'm shocked. Any action involving shoes, or feet in general, is considered insulting, especially when combined with the action of throwing things abruptly. Considering her aspiration to become a master yogi and her interest in Buddhism, I imagine how she would be immediately ruled out for this behavior alone.

She starts to tell me off for not having taken out the trash in the bedrooms and in the bathroom that I share with her. Rebecca, alarmed at Doris's grunting, walks out of her room and looks at me inquisitively.

"I was supposed to be traveling and taking a break, but instead I have to clean! Can you imagine?"

Rebecca and I remain stoic, wondering how to react to this spectacle.

"I am so fragile, so fragile . . ." she whimpers, her voice trailing as she walks out of the kitchen and into the living room to find her cat.

Her outburst bewilders us. Here we are paying the cost of an entire apartment in Europe for a non-air-conditioned room that comes with a neurotic roommate. Hernán, our Argentine roommate, had taken her "mezzanine room," the improvised bunkbed that she rents to tourists while sleeping on the sofa with her cat. What was sold to us as a chance to live with a local had ended up being nothing more than a slot in a flophouse built to rip off foreign students.

Rebecca and I head out to avoid the tension and enjoy a delicious set of sushi rolls at a nearby Ipanema restaurant with friends from our language school. It's a welcome break from Doris. Then Hernán sends me a message: "Be careful coming home. Something's happening on our street."

We head home cautiously. It's strange to be on a main avenue bustling with people, full of shops and restaurants, all the while aware that danger lurks, literally, around the corner. As we approach the corner of our street, our friends offer to walk us home to make sure we make it back. We only have one block to walk, but you never know.

As we turn the corner onto Rua Barão da Torre, a man runs toward us, his face covered in blood. Two girls follow him, screaming.

I grab Rebecca and head right in the direction of the madness, toward home. With my key in hand, I'm ready to open the gate as fast as possible, but suddenly my eyes and nose start to itch, a feeling that then turns into a burning sensation. We've been hit by tear gas.

"Help us!"

I turn around to see a young couple behind us.

"Just let us in through your gate so we can hide," the man pleads, his eyes red from the gas.

I'm torn. In Brazil, where I am constantly warned to keep my wits about me and where shootouts and robberies occur every day, it feels ludicrous to allow strangers to walk in through my gate. At the same time, I feel responsible for keeping them safe. I let them in and quickly lock the gate behind me. They crouch behind the gate to hide themselves from the rest of the street, and Rebecca and I run inside.

It's hard to understand what has gone down. Doris has gone out to see friends—after, we see, finding the time to prepare handwritten signs, taping them to the walls in the kitchen and bathroom, reminding us to clean and take out the trash. We get the scoop from Hernán, who tells us that people from the favela farther down the road had set themselves up on a corner and were robbing people one by one at gunpoint. The police arrived and ended up in a shoot-out with whoever was in their way and ultimately blasted tear gas throughout the street.

THE WINNERS OF the Rio Carnival Parade have been announced. Beija-Flor ranked in sixth place this year, below most people's expectations. From what I understand, the result had something to do with the way that certain figures had been spread across sectors to be more reflective of indigenous tribes, rather than separated in alas, as is traditionally done. The intention was to better tell the story, but it did not bode well with the judges, causing our school to lose points. Portela has won, and having seen their entire parade, it's well deserved. Although Portela is the school that has most often won the title—twenty-two times including this year, 2017—it hadn't won since 1984.[138]

The good news is that the top six schools will parade down the sambadrome one more time for the Desfile das Campeãs (Champions' Parade) tonight.

At the sambadrome, I insist on a cold beer to beat the Rio heat; before, when we had been competing, drinking was forbidden as it could reflect poorly on the school. But this time we are celebrating—I should be allowed just one.

As we prepare to put ourselves into position, a man in an official Beija-Flor T-shirt hovers around, looking at the various groups gathered chatting as we wait. He looks me in the eye and walks over to me.

"*Você quer subir no carro?*" he says, asking if I would like to go up onto the float.

I blink in disbelief. "*Sério?*" I ask. *Seriously? Me? On the float?*

He sighs, seemingly losing patience.

"*Sim, quero subir*" (Yes, I want to go up), I say and nod affirmatively before he changes his mind. To be up on the float is a prime and prestigious position usually kept for the principal passistas. They get to wear skimpy outfits compared to those below, who need to wear enormous costumes for the visual effect.

He looks suspiciously at my beer. "How many did you drink?" he asks, raising an eyebrow.

"Not even one," I say and show him that the can is still three-quarters full. I really don't understand why this is such a big deal.

"Okay, fine—go to the left of that float over there." He points to a majestic float that depicts a theater stage. "Someone will be waiting for you there."

I walk over to the float, and a man there guides me toward a ladder that can't be wider than my thirteen-inch laptop. He motions for me to climb up the ladder.

"*Tenho medo*," I whimper, telling him that I'm scared.

"Everyone else got up here!" cries a man from the top of the float. He's waiting for me on one of the podiums. "Now you come up here to the top!"

How on earth will I climb this tiny ladder in my oversized costume? It barely gives me much movement on firm ground. I take a deep breath. Looking up at the ladder, I take the first step. It's only about twenty feet tall, but the ladder is shaky and I can feel a wave of vertigo. *What if it falls backward?* I push through and continue climbing with determination, looking up at the man whose hand reaches out to mine. Just two steps more, I tell myself, repressing the filmstrip that loops in my head of me falling off a Carnival float. The top step is so close now, I know that I can make it. I reach out my trembling hand, which grazes the man's fingers. The ladder wobbles. I push myself up and manage to clasp his hand as he pulls me up onto the top of the float.

"This is your podium," he says, before hopping from my podium to another to deal with someone else.

Unreal. I can't believe that I have my very own passista podium on the top of one of Beija-Flor's floats—one of Rio's most prestigious samba schools.

The other passistas on my float wear skimpy sparkling outfits, while I feel frumpy in my oversized lace. A majestic woman in a crown of white feathers stands at the front as queen of the float, which represents the stage of a famous theater in the state of Ceará.

The wait is wrenching. Our float isn't even moving yet, but I can feel that I'm unstable. When watching the parade, I had wondered why the passistas held on to what looked like an integrated cane on their podiums, swaying from side to side rather than dancing a full samba step. But now I realize that there is no way to balance up here. If not for these canes, we would topple over.

The queen passista's podium starts to rise higher and higher, along with those of two other prominent passistas. The fireworks go off, and we begin to maneuver. I grip the handle to steady myself and take a moment to take in the faces around me. Neguinho's voice echoes from half a mile away to reach us. I turn my gaze to focus on what's ahead of me, and the float suddenly jerks forward. I'm terrified. I block my mind from the accidents that happened earlier this week and tense all the muscles in my body to stand as straight as possible.

There are things that you notice from above that you wouldn't see while parading on the ground or watching from the stands. From up here, I can see the stars, the Cristo Redentor gleaming from the top of Mount Corcovado, and the favelas glittering in the distance. The sambadrome's round arcs lie before me and people cheer from below. Just before the entrance lie makeshift rows with plastic seats, free seating for those who can't afford tickets. Some of them wear Beija-Flor T-shirts and sing all the lyrics of the song with indomitable faith in their school. One woman with tears in her eyes looks up at me; her arms are reached out like she's trying to touch me, and she's screaming the lyrics so fervently it seems they might leap out of her chest. Her face radiates hope, loyalty, and utter devotion. I look into her eyes and smile, doing my best to pronounce the lyrics. I feel a pang in my chest, like she has sent emotion from her heart to mine, but I feel uncomfortable that I am not Brazilian, undeserving of the blessing that she transmits through her gaze.

We approach the arc of the packed sambadrome, filled with the most people I've ever seen gathered together in my life. Now I need to dance (as much as gravity will allow me to) before them. The crowd is a sea of blue, cheering and singing, taking pictures, and waving with such fervor that I feel I can't just stay gripping the podium handle. I carefully lift one hand and then the other, slowly bringing out my arms to each side as if spreading my wings, and start to slowly dance a basic samba step, leading them to scream. The atmosphere is incredible and infectious. But despite the immensity of this place, it's the energy of each person fused together that nearly knocks me off of my feet.

I transcend into a collective roar, one that reverberates in the tens, possibly hundreds, of thousands of hearts fervently pounding to the beat of the samba drums. I am proud to be part of Beija-Flor. It's my school now, and to see the respect and love reflected in people's faces as I walk past them in my costume reveals that tonight is about something much deeper than just a dance parade. It is about identity, integrity, and inspiration to embody the spirit of samba.

THE ORIGINS OF any genre are always disputed among different countries, cities, and neighborhoods, but it's widely accepted that in Rio, Pedra do Sal (Rock of Salt) is one of the places where samba has its roots. I'd come here with Bruno and Helene just days before for a daytime practice of samba de gafieira—a style I've come to really enjoy, with its buoyant balanços and alluring leg movements that make it known as Brazilian tango with a twist.

This evening, one of my last in Brazil, Bruno and I share a car with Sergio and his comrade Tatiana to Rio's Saúde neighborhood, close to the port. After having been immersed in Carnival samba, I'm excited to explore the roots of this sacred dance and attend one of Saúde's iconic samba parties that take place every Monday and Friday.

"What's the story behind Pedra do Sal?" I ask Bruno in what has now become a customary car-ride briefing before I reach a dance destination.

He explains that Pedra do Sal is a special place for samba in Rio. Known locally as Little Africa, it was a quilombo settlement of Bahian migrants and escaped slaves who sought work in the nineteenth century—including dragging huge sacks of salt (which is what led to the name)—in the Saúde neighborhood's port.[139] To celebrate their culture, they would gather to sing and dance samba. And those samba parties have lasted over hundreds of years.[140]

To some historians, the neighborhood, which has been an officially recognized quilombo village since 2005[141] (a government-bestowed status that confers land titles and legal protection to the community),[142] still bears remnants of an oppressive past afflicted by racism, inequality, and intolerance. Pedra do Sal isn't just another stop on the tourist route but an opportunity to witness a tradition, to pay homage to a place's historical significance, and to see how a painful past led to celebrations of joy and life.

We arrive at the party and are greeted by a seemingly endless crowd bursting with a cacophony of musical styles. Some revelers sing samba and play drums, while others dance a routine to funk blasting out from a speaker. I've been so engrossed in samba that I've had little time to explore funk—the Brazilian reggaeton pronounced as "funky"—other than in Carnival blocos and clubs. Raquel had told me to add a funk rave in a favela to my dance bucket list, but that will have to wait for another trip. I join in the routine, with easy movements to follow along to, with Sergio, who, as always, seeks to embrace as many new experiences as possible.

It's a casual affair, with street vendors selling snacks and caipirinhas to Carioca and tourist samba revelers alike. We walk up the rock and take in an impressive view of the crowd.

"Look at these steps," says Bruno. "The freed slaves carved them into the rock to help them carry huge sacks of salt on their backs."

It's humbling, but also confusing. This place exudes pain and joy, past and present. I don't know whether I should be solemn or instead celebrate the resilience that created hope in the face of adversity.

THE FOLLOWING YEAR, Beija-Flor will win the Carnival parade with the theme "*Monstro é aquele que não sabe amar*" (the monster is the one who does not know how to love), comparing Brazil's corruption and violence to the story of Frankenstein. Superstar drag queen Pabllo Vittar will perform as the school's Carnival queen in a show of support for the LGBTQ community, while floats will depict scenes of favelas with shootings, kidnappings, corrupt politicians, and the body of a dead child in a coffin labeled "another bit of hope lost."[143]

Samba is so much more than a musical genre. It is a form of resistance and political protest—a cry of despair in the fight for equality. It tells the tale of a complex country that faces division, violence, and injustice, and yet it is made up of an incredible diversity that was able to create a new sound—one that supports alternative communities, pushes social boundaries, and, eventually, defines the identity of the nation.

10

ARGENTINA

Tango and La Chacarera

Emma, my dear friend from university, has flown in from London and is waiting in a café just beyond the Arrivals gate. There's something comforting about ending this journey reunited with someone who has known me my entire adult life. I had seen her shortly before embarking on my trip, and she had highly approved of my dance odyssey, immediately offering to join me for the last leg in Argentina. Several years ago, when I first left England, embarking on my international career to work in Mongolia, she had sat with me in a London restaurant and helped me overcome my fears. I was so anxious and scared that I almost pulled out. Now she is well accustomed to my pursuit of new adventures to chase my never-ending dreams across the globe. She always encourages me to tap into an indomitable spirit, happily joining my colorful world of cultural and culinary outings. Now she is going to share part of this journey with me to see just how magical life can be when you step into a world of music and dance.

I spot her sitting quietly reading a book and rush over to collapse into her arms.

"Pookie," she says, stroking my hair and calling me the affectionate nickname she gave me when I was eighteen.

Emma has always wanted to visit Argentina, so we had planned a scenic itinerary to explore the country. But first, our mission is to get to know Buenos Aires as the spiritual home of tango.

We get into a taxi and head to our first residence in San Telmo, the city's historical neighborhood, filled with cobblestone streets, tango salons, and narrow alleyways. Home to the city's first colonial mansions (which were abandoned by the elite)[144] and later to the country's African population (both freed and enslaved), San Telmo evolved into an industrial bastion that stored the city's exports of wool, hides, and leathers.[145] The African population drastically declined as a result of wars and epidemics, while the demand for workers drew waves of European migrants to Argentina between 1880 and 1950.[146] Those empty colonial mansions, split up to become the first *conventillos* (urban tenements), are commonly acknowledged as the birthplace of tango.[147]

In these tenements, families from different backgrounds inhabited one room, often sharing cramped and unsanitary conditions. They found release and diversion in communal spaces. Shared patios became a place of longing and nostalgia for the old countries, a place where settlers could express their misery and decry the harshness of their living and working conditions. They would become the place to play instruments, sing, and of course, dance tango.[148] The patios were also frequented by *guapos*—knife fighters who would become the male archetype of tango—who characterized the sound of the conventillo, a "harmony of a concerto of knives."[149] Their sharp metallic sound is a reminder of the depravity, crime, and gang violence that reigned in the streets of Buenos Aires.

AFTER WE ARRIVE at our converted conventillo—a polished Airbnb with a patio that could not deny its own history—we head out to explore Plaza Dorrego, famed for its antique flea market and tango. A couple dances on the main square surrounded by terraces of curious tourists and locals. The woman dons a black velvet dress, her skin pale and her expression forming a solemn pout. (I will later discover that what appears to be sadness is actually concentration and inner connection.) The man's hair is gelled back, and braces hold up his wide-legged pants. He twirls the woman fervently before sliding her body toward the ground, her leg stretching out behind her, in an iconic tango pose. We watch them in silence, captivated.

We continue on through the flea market, stopping to eat *alfajores*— Argentine sandwich cookies filled with layers of dulce de leche and dipped in chocolate—and then head to the end of the square where we reach a small set of stairs leading down to a dedicated section where people dance tango. It is Plaza Dorrego's Sunday evening *milonga*—the word used to describe events for social tango dancing. But the word "milonga" has more than one meaning; it's also the word for a more animated and staccato dance considered to have contributed to the development of tango that dominated Argentina, Uruguay, and southern Brazil in the 1870s.[150]

In nineteenth-century Argentina, gauchos, local cowboys, would gather together to organize *payadas*, gatherings where they would compete in improvising lyrical melodies with their guitars.[151] Enslaved Africans would often attend these payadas but wouldn't understand what was being said. They called the events *milongas*—meaning "many words" in Kimbundu.[152] Mostly of Bantu origin, these enslaved Africans had brought over the drumming and dancing style of *candombé*, in which the term *tangó* referred to their gathering spot, percussion, and the dance itself.[153] It turns out that tango—a dance strongly associated with European origins and immigration to the Rio del Plata region—actually has its roots in Africa.[154]

Emma and I watch the dancers in the milonga under the final rays of sunlight. The emotion in people's faces reveals a fragile bliss—eyes closed and lips trembling—as they cautiously glide over the cobblestones. The dancers span all ages: I spot an older man with white combed-back hair, an elegant jacket, and a silk ascot wrapped around his neck. He's dancing with a young woman, visibly a foreigner, and takes great enthusiasm in sharing his culture with her. To see such a multitude of characters dancing in the open air, and at a free event, reminds me that we don't need an elite club with disco balls or a grandiose ballroom with chandeliers. We just need an open space and a speaker—atmosphere comes from within.

I WOKE UP this morning feeling calm and profoundly happy. I can't remember the last time I've slept so well, and it's the first time in a while that nobody wants anything from me. There's no Doris, no blocos to go to, no dance classes to organize. Today I'm turning thirty-one, and everything feels wildly different than it did a year ago, when I was months away from leaving Bangkok. On the cusp of turning thirty, I experienced a range of dread and stress—the fear of losing my youth, the pressure to throw the biggest and most outrageous tropical-themed party, the anxiety of who would show up and whether they would have a good time.

I stretch out my arms in bed and pause to reflect. This year my birthday will be a little more low-key. My mother entrusted Emma with an envelope containing cash and instructions for the two of us to do something fabulous. Without any hesitation, I've booked us tickets to the most glamorous tango show in Buenos Aires—and therefore in the world.

I'm now six months into my journey and have reached the last of the eight countries on my dance itinerary. *How can I already be reaching the end? It feels like I'm just getting started.* Concerned, I check my phone and send a message to Clarke, who responds almost immediately.

"Happy birthday! Maybe this isn't the end, socio. Maybe this is just the beginning. . ."

And this is how I will be ending my journey—in a country that seven years ago, before I accepted a job offer in Asia, I had dreamed of moving to. Hannah, whom I had been reunited with in New York, had even gifted me a city guide for Buenos Aires on my twenty-fourth birthday. Now my life as a *porteña* (a common demonym for someone from Buenos Aires) has begun. I have made it all the way here, after a six-month journey through a whirlwind of colors, sounds, and emotions that has shown me that anything is possible.

And what will my future look like? Will I settle here and marry a gaucho or, better yet, a polo player? Will I end up working with the UN again, perhaps in its regional offices across the border in Chile? Or will I return to Mexico or Colombia, the two countries that stole my heart? I surrender my future to *el destino* (destiny). Not having to be on email, attend meetings, or live an office-based life has opened my eyes to new possibilities and helped me develop some trust in the universe. No plan, no commitments, and no obligations. Freedom.

TONIGHT WE WILL be going to the show *Rojo Tango* (Red Tango) in the opulent and luxurious Faena Hotel. It's the same dance troupe and directors as at Café de los Angelitos—the city's most traditional tango show—but it is set in a smaller, more intimate, edgy, and exclusive venue with fine dining and a limited audience. Given the occasion, I put on my favorite red silk dress, which has become a trademark of my journey, and twirl for Emma as I step out of my room. She smiles at me in an amused but caring, sisterly way.

We arrive at the Faena Hotel and find a simple firebrick wall with a small, unassuming door. *Are we in the right place?* A man in a cape greets us and opens a small door to an outdoor patio lit with candles that leads to a narrow hallway made of polished wood with high ceilings. We pass through a cascading silk curtain and then descend into a mysterious world of red velvet that houses fewer than a dozen tables draped in crimson tablecloths and topped with red roses. My dress melts into the setting, and I'm entranced by the slow electro-tango that's playing softly in the background. There are no glaring stage lights, just dimly lit crystal chandeliers and the soft glow of candles that reveal a piano on one side of the room and a small, circular platform on the other side.

A svelte woman with a long ponytail and a pencil skirt takes our names and guides us to a table directly in front of the stage. She hands us delicate menu cards and adjusts our opulent cutlery and scarlet-and-gold enamel-rimmed plates.

"Champagne?"

Emma and I look at each other. Of course!

We indulge in the exquisite menu—a shrimp appetizer followed by beef tenderloin with truffled mashed potatoes and then a decadent chocolate marquise dessert. The meal is accompanied by a selection of fine Argentine wines.

Suddenly, I hear the sounds of piano keys and the plucking of a cello from behind me. I turn around to see a quartet made up of a pianist, cellist, and two *bandoneonistas* (players of the bandoneon, the smaller accordion used in tango) dressed in maroon velvet suits. They break into a nostalgic tango that leaves me yearning for a time I never knew, while the dancers begin to appear from various parts of the room—grazing our tables, on the bar, on the stage, and all around us. They take us on a journey through the decades of tango from its earliest days until today—from the glitz of the 1920s flapper years in sparkling dresses to the dark 1940s of gangster mobs in fedoras. With each new act, we don't know which decade we will be in or from where the dancers will appear. The tango steps are tantalizing, with pivots that twirl like a hurricane. The beauty, the passion, and the glamour leave us gasping.

Emma and I walk out entranced, both by the experience and the unlimited champagne and Malbec that were offered. I feel so inspired and walk confidently down the red velvet corridor in my silk dress. As we walk past the elegant woman who welcomed us, I cannot resist asking her who is in charge of the show.

"The director is actually just behind you," she says, smiling.

I turn around and see a refined man in what I'd guess is an Armani suit. His slightly long white hair is drawn to one side and he looks at me with pale blue eyes as he extends his hand.

"Antonio, director of *Rojo Tango*," he says.

Struck by this surprise, I pull myself together and then introduce myself. I also share my project and tell him that I dream of learning tango. He maintains his gaze and purses his lips before eventually reaching into his pocket and handing me a luxurious scarlet-embossed card. "Get in touch," he says, and then whisks off outside and slips into a sleek silver convertible.

I stand in disbelief, looking down at the card in my hands. Antonio fascinates me. He seems like a real dandy, the kind of suave gentleman that you only see in vintage films.

I KEEP ANTONIO'S card preciously tucked in my purse during my travels in Argentina. From the purple vineyards of the Malbec region to crushed diamond glaciers, hikes up staggering snowcapped peaks that reveal hidden turquoise lakes, and horse rides through Patagonia's grassy steppe, Emma and I witness the most incredible landscapes that we have seen in our lifetime.

On our return to Buenos Aires and for Emma's final night in Argentina, we indulge in pan-Latin fine dining followed by a Carlos Vives concert— the cultural ambassador of Colombia whom I have so far only been able to track down in street performer impersonations and over supermarket speakers. I want Emma to savor the Latin flavors and sounds that I have discovered on my journey. The concert paints a resplendent illustration of musical diplomacy—introducing us to the tribes and regions of Colombia but also paying homage to other artists from across Latin America.

When Emma's taxi arrives to take her to the airport, I feel a sudden pang in my chest. There was something significant about being here with Emma, having her bear witness to my dreams and bearing witness to hers.

"Alright, Pookie," she says, taking me into her arms. We both start to cry. Despite the fact that we have lived a thirteen-hour flight away from each other for several years now, our friendship has never changed and our affection never shifted. Our tears are celebratory, honoring an unbreakable friendship capable of traversing the world.

I PACK MY things and head to a hostel in my new neighborhood of Palermo Soho—a hipster barrio equivalent to Brooklyn in New York or Shoreditch in London—to socialize and make friends. Walking with my suitcase, I come across a house whose facade is covered in paintings. *This must be the right place.*

After checking in, I head up to my room and start to put my most precious belongings in my locker. A handsome young man walks in and puts his bag on the bunk opposite mine. He has a four-leaf clover tattoo on his chest—perhaps a reference to Irish ancestors, an important group of immigrants in Argentina. He introduces himself as Facundo and shakes my hand with a friendly smile.

We exchange the usual questions. He seems very warm, friendly, and polite—not the exact stereotype of a porteño. It turns out he's from a town near Córdoba, a student hub and a city known for its friendliness.

I explain to him that I'm looking for more dance experiences.

"Ah, well in that case you should go to Córdoba for *cuarteto*!"

"Cuarteto?" I ask, wondering if he means a classical music quartet or something different, and he jumps into telling his cuarteto stories. I've barely started my life as a porteña here in Buenos Aires, but I feel like I'm already discovering a wealth of dance styles beyond tango. Cuarteto and the local cumbia, *cumbia villera*, named after the villas—favelas—on the outskirts of town, he tells me, are more contemporary and representative of Argentina. Of course tango shaped Argentina's culture and has an important role in its history, but Facundo claims that outside Buenos Aires, cuarteto and cumbia are what inspire people to socialize, drink, and have fun.

Argentinians have suffered through economic crises, inflation, and hunger. But dance, Facundo tells me, could never be taken away.

I can identify with what he's saying. Despite tragedy and hardship, resilience and joy come alive through dance. My journey so far has confirmed this. We don't need all that much, just each other and the ability to authentically express ourselves. Modern life's insatiable appetite to consume—news, social media, alcohol, food, and material things—has left us addicted and estranged from who we really are, instead feeling empty, disenchanted, and unfulfilled. Instead of searching for outward distractions, we must learn to tune in to ourselves.

In *Before Happiness*, Shawn Achor invites his readers to see the world through a positive lens, choosing the best of multiple perspectives or realities to any given situation. Our perspectives are the stories and scenarios we create for ourselves, and it's up to us to choose the ones that serve us best. A positive outlook on life is not just an attitude but also a choice. For me, the choice to live joyfully and the choice to dance are the same.

Dance also offers those nascent conceptions of love and physical intimacy. According to Facundo, teenagers dance cuarteto in nightclubs, winding sensually to songs that describe the first throes of passion and romance.

"So where can I dance cuarteto or cumbia here in Buenos Aires?" I ask, having already added those styles to my list. But he warns me not to search them out here.

"The only places you will find them here are really dangerous. I don't recommend that you go there. But you know what's crazy? If you go to Córdoba, cuarteto will be played in the poshest of places. It's almost like they represent a different social class in each city."

This seems to be a recurring theme, where dances mirror different social strata and are experienced differently among cultures, eras, and places. But one thing is clear: the most celebrated Latin dances today—whether salsa, bachata, samba, or tango—were all once shunned by the elite as the dances of the poor.

AFTER A FEW days of hostel life, where I befriend fellow travelers, go on free street art tours, and explore my new neighborhood, I have my first, short-lived, Argentine romance. I fall victim to *chamuyo*—seductive smooth-talking where carefully crafted words make you believe there is nobody as beautiful in the world as you, and that you are the moon that makes *the chamuyero* feel he can touch the stars. I am entranced by tales of a chamuyero's tango tours in Europe as a bandoneon player in a prestigious orchestra. Empty words and false promises, an overall red flag. Beware of the chamuyeros—they are the world champions of sweet talk and bullshit.

I am now prepared to check into my new life as a porteña, or at least to my new Airbnb, and push my suitcase on a ten-minute walk through the streets of Buenos Aires, my backpack digging into my shoulders as I scan the house numbers on the street. I stop in front of a modern cream-and-gray building and ring the bell.

A male voice answers in an Argentine accent with a British note. "Coming down!" he says cheerfully. He dramatically opens the door and offers his hand for a polite handshake. His name is Matty, and in a theatrically posh accent he tells me that he is not any ordinary Airbnb manager, but a singer, musician, yoga teacher, and dancer. Like many Argentinians who have grappled with economic hardship, he is a multi-hyphenate, creative as a means of survival. He offers to introduce me to his friend Mariano Botindari, the winning coach of *Bailando por un Sueño* (*Dancing for a Dream*), Argentina's equivalent of *Dancing with the Stars*. His friend apparently offers "modern jazz classes that aren't really modern jazz" that he says I need to attend to understand.

How do I always end up coming across these messengers, these connectors that appear out of nowhere to guide me along this journey? I tell him how thrilled I am to have met him, but for him it's not a coincidence—we were meant to meet.

"You know, Aliénor, when you take that first step and you choose to follow your heart, everything in the universe will start lining up for you to take the path that will lead you to your destiny." He takes a dramatic pause, shifting his weight to cross one leg in front of the other. "And then the world just . . . " He places his hand on his heart and takes a deep bow.

It's like I've manifested Paulo Coelho in the form of a Shakespearean Argentine who performs ukulele concerts by night and does Airbnb check-ins by day.

The apartment is a short walk from DNI Tango, a foreigner-friendly school, which according to their website offers the first group class for free. I had signed up immediately.

To get there I walk through leafy residential streets before reaching a white building with intricate Art Deco window grills. I show the reception-ist my email coupon, and she sends me upstairs, where I find a large group of mostly foreigners waiting for class.

"*¡Empezamos, chicos!*" (Let's get started, guys!), says a woman with a slight French accent. (I will later discover that there is a large community of French tango dancers living in Buenos Aires to fulfill their porteño dreams.) We gather inside in a circle while she and an Argentine man give instructions in English and Spanish, through simultaneous interpretation. It will be a ninety-minute bilingual class where we go over the very basics with a small routine.

We will start by learning the Tango 8—the eight fundamental steps of tango that form the basis of the dance. They divide the group so that women are on one side and men are on the other side, and then we begin. Mirroring the man in front of me, I take a step forward (one), glide to the right (two), take two long steps back (three, four), and cross my left foot over my right foot (five). My toes close and ankles touching, I proceed to step back with my right foot (six), out to the left (seven), and then close my feet together to shift my weight (eight).

I wonder, *Was that it?* But of course it isn't that simple. This was simply a blueprint for the intricate architecture of this complicated dance.

In pairs we try more complex pivots and turns that feel foreign to my body. I have become so used to moving my hips and shimmying my shoulders in other dances, and now I have to stand straight, able to rotate only from side to side. Tango is slow, with lingering pauses that make me feel like I'm losing balance and about to fall.

My partners are the typical variety that you might expect to find in a beginner class: the guy who steps on your feet, those who make you stumble because they can't lead you smoothly and then blame it on you by sighing heavily and telling you that you aren't doing the steps right, and the sweet beginner who can't dance very well but is humble and willing to learn. I greatly prefer, and consider myself to be, the last type. Today, when I'm paired with a man whose style I like, I cling to him, hoping that they don't make us rotate again.

"Don't lean back so much," says the French instructor, supporting my back with her hand to make me lean forward into the front part of my foot. This causes my torso to face my partner's.

"You want to imagine that you have a lightning bolt connecting your heart to his," she says, touching an imaginary tunnel of light as if it could burn the tips of her fingers.

I proceed to dance with my partner, with the basic steps that we've learned, and as I focus on the connection, I feel a beam of light penetrate my chest.

After class, our teacher invites us all to a milonga she's performing in tonight just a few blocks away, and I join the group going. After all, if I've survived my first tango class, perhaps I can also survive my first tango milonga.

We enter a dark room with tables forming a horseshoe shape around the room. A spotlight targets the center of the empty dance floor. After we take our seats and order drinks, I scan the crowd. Some people wear typical tango attire, like sparkling shoes and asymmetrical fishtail skirts, while others are dressed like hipsters or hippies or have come straight from the office wearing their work clothes.

The music quiets, and the French instructor takes to the stage in a midnight-blue dress. We are kept in a moment of suspense before a piano introduces a song instantly recognizable to all: "La Foule" (French for "The Crowd") by Edith Piaf.

I had grown up listening to this song with my grandmother—she was from the generation of ardent Edith Piaf fans—but had never imagined that tango could be danced to it. However, with each dance I've learned, I've discovered that you can dance to literally anything by adapting your steps to each song. It is like the rest of life: you just have to show up and use what you've learned. If you can adapt, you can move to the rhythm of life, embracing any dance, any genre. This song has known so many genres. I will later find out that it was originally composed by Ángel Cabral with lyrics by Enrique Dizeo—both Argentine—as a Peruvian waltz in 1936. Almost two decades later, Piaf heard a 1953 recording of the song during her Latin American tour, and recorded a French version that became famous worldwide.[155] I also danced quite a bit to a cumbia version of the song, "Amor de Mis Amores" (Love of My Loves) by Colombian band La Sonora Dinamita when I was in Mexico.

On the dance floor, the instructor pivots from turn to turn, the skirt of her dress swirling as she turns faster and faster. My heart beats heavily as I watch her connection with her partner grow with such raw intensity that I'm in suspense as I wait for each step. The bandoneon's rich, reedy sound starts to swell and continues until its pitch reaches a peak and then the song suddenly ends. Overwhelmed by emotion, the dancer collapses into her partner's arms and starts to cry.

THERE'S BEEN A strange shift in the weather, and I've been finding it hard to leave the house the last few days. It's almost like because I've reached the end of this journey, I just want to rest at home.

A notification pops up on my phone. It's Matty, my spiritual guide and Airbnb host.

"Is it too early for a contemporary jazz class this morning? At the risk of seeming pushy, you should really go."

I hesitate but decide to see this as a signal from the universe that I should get dressed and out of the house.

When I get to the studio I hesitantly ask if I've arrived at the right place for Mariano's dance class. It's taken me forty-five minutes to find the building.

"It is! And you're lucky. It's the last class he's giving before he leaves for Europe."

Inside I spot Mariano instantly, not because I've seen his photo but because of the students crowding eagerly around him.

I introduce myself as Matty's friend and wave shyly as I creep in.

He instantly makes the connection and walks over to give me a kiss on the cheek and tell me to choose whatever spot I prefer. He seems friendly and humble, which I like. The other students are much younger than me, and as I watch them stretch, they strike me as being very advanced. We start the class with gentle yoga postures, and I start to feel fire building inside my core. The sun floods through the window, just like in my yoga classes in Bangkok, and I allow its rays to fuel my movements. Then Mariano tells us to lie quietly in Savasana, also known as the corpse pose, which is usually performed at the end of a yoga class to allow for total relaxation—but our class has just started.

We take a moment in it, and then he puts on flowing new-age electronic music and asks us to rise to our feet while keeping our eyes closed and to then move in any way we want.

What? I panic. I'm used to dance styles where I have specific steps and movements to follow. *Now I have to improvise completely? No choreography, no steps to master, no partner to hide behind.* I feel awkward and ashamed, and I peel open one eye to see what everyone else is doing. Some people are on the floor rolling from side to side, while others are performing pirouettes across the room. One girl clings to the legs of a guy standing up.

My heart is beating furiously, and I begin to feel light-headed. *What if I look stupid?* I start to panic, and Mariano notices. He comes over to ask if I'm okay and gently holds my arms, encouraging me to make larger movements. He slowly stretches me out, almost like a Thai masseuse, elongating my body to reach higher and stretch wider. When he slowly steps back, I can feel his energy still supporting me. This helps me to get out of my head and let my body guide me. My movements may be small, but aided by the rays of sunshine stroking my skin, I allow myself to float. As the music speeds up, I follow its growing intensity. This is it. No more flights to catch. No next country on the list. I can move wherever and however I want. *And I must.* I am running out of dances on my list. Running out of time to master new choreographies. Running out of partners to hide behind. I turn to face the window, my back to the rest of the studio, and tears start streaming down my cheeks.

When class wraps up, I try to process my experience. I can't understand what I felt, but I'm emotionally knocked out. I hesitate whether to approach him to discuss it and his techniques, but I am put off by his groupies and instead shyly thank him from afar and slip out, cursing myself for not having taken the opportunity to talk with him. I start to walk the forty-five minutes back and chide myself for my shyness—a part of me not often seen by others, suppressed to give way to my exuberant, extroverted side.

Near my studio, I stop by a tiny café to buy a salad and juice and then head back out with my head hanging low and my gaze down. I walk right into a man on the street—Mariano. *Maybe the universe really wanted us to have that conversation after class.*

"Ah, it's you! Are you going that way?" he asks, pointing right ahead. I nod yes and we begin to walk together.

"So how did you end up here in Buenos Aires?"

I tell him my story, the dances I have learned and the countries I have danced in.

"Why are you doing it? Why dance?"

"Dance was the most palpable form of liberating myself from my desk," I say with a sigh, as if exorcising a knot I've kept locked in my throat. I have never put it in those words before. It just came out that way.

What I've said resonates with him. He tells me how after ten years of working on *Bailando por un Sueño*, he's decided to leave it all behind for an adventure to discover Europe. This year, the tenth season of the show, he won the title of winning coach, and people expect him to fight in the eleventh season to defend his title. He's famous, successful, and in demand, but he feels called to leave his success behind him, to dive into a new, unknown life and live new experiences.

I too used to have the job that I had always dreamed of—but occasionally we need to let go of some dreams to make way for new ones.

"Are you scared?" he asks. "Or are you happy? Having no plan. Not knowing where you will go next."

"I'm happy this way!" I reply, reflecting on my conversation with his friend Matty. "My future . . . I will leave it to *el destino*."

As PART OF my tango research, I had searched for other free introductory tango classes and milongas. The city's Centro Cultural Kirchner (Kirchner Cultural Center)—also known as the CCK—is the largest cultural center in Latin America and one of the largest in the world, and it offers a free tango class every week with rotating instructors.

The Uber driver who takes me there is a man named Daniel. He has glasses and a gray beard and appears to be in his sixties. After the usual pleasantries, he asks the inevitable question: "So what are you doing here in Buenos Aires?"

I tell him about my dance adventures and the many ideas I have to share the beauty of dance with the world. "But I don't make a living from this project," I say and shrug, as if to clarify my intentions. My savings are starting to run out, and financial anxieties are beginning to sink in, but my heart is determined to keep this project alive.

"But you are *living*, aren't you? That's what really matters. When God wants something, he puts the right people along the path to guide you. I'm not a religious man, but it's happened to me so many times. The problem today is that people don't talk to each other. In life there are always—and this is for all human beings—opportunities that surround us. But we don't see them. We don't know how to read the signs."

It seems Paulo Coelho has come to pay me a visit again, this time manifested as an Uber driver, but I soon learn that Daniel has been very involved in the art world and is the director of a well-respected classical theater in Buenos Aires. He lived for his art, but unfortunately his art couldn't bring him a living. Working part-time as a driver allows him to keep living his dream.

When we arrive, Daniel tells me to wait a minute and scribbles something onto a piece of paper. As he hands it over he tells me it's the phone number of Liliana Belfiore, one of the most important classical ballerinas of all time. He tells me she's like a sister to him and to tell her that Daniel gave me her number. My jaw drops as I take the paper and slowly step out of the car. He smiles through the window and speeds away.

The CCK is an imposing, eclectic building constructed in the style of the French Second Empire. Its nine floors contain fifty-one exhibition halls, sixteen rehearsal rooms, eighteen foyers, and an enormous concert hall named La Ballena Azul (The Blue Whale).[156] The grand stature of the space and the generous programming offered within match the national priorities; after all, according to Teresa Parodi, a singer and songwriter who is the former minister of culture, Argentinians "consider culture to be a right."[157]

The building's exterior is bathed in deep purple lights, echoing the jacaranda blossoms that paint the city in spring, and as I walk inside I am greeted by a huge blue sphere in the entrance. It is composed of more than three thousand pieces of acrylic and supported by invisible strings that gently sway in the light breeze that flows in.[158]

After walking up a marble staircase, I find myself in a large, futuristic hall coated in a violet sheen. There must be at least one hundred people here—and just like at the other class, there are a variety of characters: students, investment bankers, artists, and more. I watch a man with a mustache in a navy-blue suit tighten his tie, a couple in seventies-style bell-bottoms, and a man who appears to be in his sixties wearing a tweed suit and aviators; the little hair he has left is gelled back into a skinny ponytail at the nape of his neck.

We gather around the instructors, who call for us to walk in rows from one side to the other. It almost looks like they are preparing space cadets rather than dancers. Aware of my tendency to bounce, quite like an astronaut, I try to keep my head level with a fixed point in front of me—the "visual line" that I had learned from Yosnel in Cuba. We walk like this for half an hour, and then the instructors give new directions. Some of their words I've never even heard before, but I understand when they tell us to hold our *panza* (belly) in when we dance.

We are put into pairs to practice the usual combination of basic steps and a short routine, before rotating to the next partner. I dance with a Venezuelan named Rodolfo, who like me suffers from relentlessly moving hips, and I find comfort in our shared struggle. Then there's a short and skinny middle-aged man with dark-rimmed glasses and a rugged face. He leads me abruptly and out of tempo and is impossible to follow.

"You need to look at the man when he's dancing with you," he croaks in a menacing voice that implies he's smoked far too many cigarettes. While he's been leering at me intently, I've been trying, politely, to look elsewhere.

"I know, I'm ugly," he tells me, "*¡Es así!*" (That's how it is!)

My body in the grip of a machista is without a doubt the most painful dance to have to endure for the length of a song.

Next up: a friendly but rather intense middle-aged man whose face is plastered with a permanent grin and gives almost constant eye contact. He has terrible breath, which I try my best to ignore. And lastly, a frail man in his late seventies who approaches me hesitantly at the next rotation. His hands are shaking quite badly, but as I dance in his trembling embrace, I stand strong, ready to support his weight as we shift and pivot from side to side.

"I have Parkinson's," he says, quivering. He seems ashamed.

"It's okay," I reply, having guessed as much.

I had heard of a project for tango therapy in Buenos Aires that supports those suffering from Parkinson's disease or other illnesses or disabilities.

He trembles throughout our tango. When the song ends, he tells me, sounding defeated, to go and dance with someone else. "Someone your own age."

I firmly tell him no, that I want to dance with him, and his face softens with my words. With the reassurance, his embrace seems to improve and he seems to better stabilize.

Dance is not only a form of socialization, it is therapeutic and healing. If this journey has taught me anything, it's how powerful dance can be in making us more accepting of others. Tango, I've come to realize, is especially intimate and forces a deep, vulnerable connection. When partners connect, it is almost like one would not be able to breathe without the other, without their balance—their *abrazo* (embrace).

IT HAS TAKEN me a while to find the courage to email Antonio, the director of Rojo Tango. When I finally do, he, much to my surprise, puts me in touch with his production manager, Marisa, who tells me that one of their dancers might be interested in dancing with me.

"Are there any others?" I ask, almost concerned that one option might not be enough. I had contacted various tango schools and been greeted with little enthusiasm, leading me to become pessimistic.

"Try this one first," she says, and tells me the instructor's name is Ramiro Izurieta.

I send Ramiro a message, expecting nothing. I tell him the usual: that I left everything behind to learn to dance and am looking for people to share this journey with me. I can't help but write it in a short and almost abrupt way because I doubt he will be interested.

"Of course I'm interested!" he replies, to my surprise. He suggests that we meet up at a terrace restaurant in a nearby plaza, Plaza Armenia, to discuss the project in more detail.

I arrive at the agreed-upon spot dressed in a colorful floral dress and blue-lensed Ray-Bans, but I don't see him immediately. His profile photo was an artistic sketch of his face, so I'm worried he'll be hard recognize, but after scanning the people around me, my eyes settle on a man with pale skin and a sharp, rectangular jaw. He's dressed in black, wearing dark sunglasses, and sits engrossed in a book. His short, silvery hair wields an almost metallic allure and embodies tango's origin from the banks of the Río de la Plata (Silver River). He seems shrouded in mystery. *It must be him.*

"Ramiro?" I ask. It's him, and he gives me a kiss on the cheek then invites me to take a seat opposite him at the table.

I explain my journey through the various countries that have led me to Argentina, what I hope to learn from dance, and from him. I can't really tell what his reaction is. His face is not very expressive, but not necessarily in a bad way. He seems like a stoic, silver statue. I wait through a moment of silence before he reacts.

"Well, first of all, I think your journey is very noble. The world of tango, unfortunately, can be very elitist and driven by money. Why do you think they gave you my number?"

I have no idea and tell him so.

"They know that I'm not motivated only by money."

His slightly cold and distant exterior seems to be concealing a great sensitivity—a delicate heart wrapped in a steel sheath.

"Tell me," he says. "What do you know about the history of tango?"

I tell him I have a general idea but haven't started investigating much yet and that I'd rather hear his insight. He indulges my request and launches into a comprehensive overview, beginning with the great wave of immigration in 1880 when a rising (heavily male) population popularized brothels. Women were in short supply and started being lured over from Europe with the promise of a loving husband, only to be forced into prostitution by a vast network of organized crime, especially the famous mob Zwi Migdal.

"So wait, this was basically nineteenth-century human trafficking?"

"Yes, exactly. There were long lines to get into these brothels as men waited for their 'turn.' So they put out small orchestras to entertain them, usually composed of a guitar, a violin, and a flute."

Ramiro tells me that the musicians played European melodies, eventually mixing different genres, and that while the men waited in line they began to dance the earliest forms of tango. The high society of Buenos Aires originally rejected tango, given its association with prostitutes, brothels, and guapos, but when Paris fell in love with tango in the early twentieth century, the Argentinian upper crust could not resist its newly fashionable allure.

"Argentines seem to be fascinated by Europe," I muse. I'm reminded of how European interest in samba was seen in Brazil as a sort of endorsement.

"We have an inferiority complex when it comes to Europe," Ramiro concedes. "There is a popular phrase that says, 'An Argentine is an Italian who is poor, born in Argentina, believes he is French, but would like to be English.'"

The saying reminds me of my two nationalities and confused identity. *What do I want to be?*

Ramiro goes on to tell me how the newfound acceptance of tango led to *la época de oro* (the golden age) in the 1940s, when tango orchestras, clubs, dance academies, and singers thrived. But after the coup d'état of 1955 that overthrew President Juan Domingo Perón, a series of dictatorships sought to choke and censor tango. He asks me to write down the names of two people: Astor Piazzolla, an innovative composer sometimes considered the Picasso of tango, and Carlos Gardel, the singer who gave tango a voice and who died, I recall, in Medellín.

In the 1960s and 1970s, tango shows and performances became popular, pioneered by the iconic couple Juan Carlos Copes and María Nieves. By the 1990s, tango was not a sideshow, a hidden or obscured art form, or an artifact of the Bohemian past; it was the main event. It may have taken a century for tango to evolve into the refined and captivating dance that it embodies today, but now, he tells me, huge groups of people show up to dance tango: dancers, teachers, performers, and students. With so many people learning and dancing tango, there is a wide range of expressions and practices. Each dancer's style is very individual; often, the same step will never be danced in exactly the same way.

"What is your personal style like?" I ask, intrigued.

"My personal style is universal. I like to keep tango pure so that everyone can appreciate it. In many ways, I am quite orthodox when it comes to tango, because I avoid bringing any fashion or trends into the dance. It must have as much softness as it has strength."

I feel like learning tango with him would be a transcendent journey through an array of emotions, not to mention the last 120 years of Argentine history.

"Sometimes I wonder if what I'm doing is stupid," says Ramiro pensively. "Dancing in these shows onstage every night, what am I really contributing to the world? Does it even have any meaning?"

"Dance," I tell him, placing my fist on the table, "is the epitome of human connection. You have to hold your partner in your arms and feel their steps as you move together as one. You have to look into each other's eyes. Even if for just a moment, dance allows two souls to touch."

His face freezes as he takes in my words.

"Now tell me, what isn't meaningful in that?" I ask, surprising myself by my outburst.

Ramiro needs to rush off to another appointment, so I get up to say goodbye and give him a kiss on the cheek. But right before he gets up, he pauses, taking off his sunglasses. I follow his lead and place my glasses on the table. We hadn't until now seen each other's eyes. I meet his gaze, which is feathered with shades of silver, matching his hair.

Eye contact is our first form of communication at birth, and yet we often turn to look the other way—to avoid awkwardness and anxiety, but also judgment and criticism. Locking eyes with another sparks engagement and empathy, recognition and respect.

TODAY IS MY first class with Ramiro. My apartment will be our studio, and as I wait for him I find myself pacing, anxiously wondering what kind of teacher he'll be. *Will he say what he thinks, or will he be more reserved?* He seems like he's going to be strict, the type to correct me openly, and quite demanding, but I also have a sense he's going to extract something deep out of me that other teachers cannot.

The doorbell rings. He's here.

I invite Ramiro inside, and he takes a panoramic gaze across the living room and then starts to redesign it, moving the chairs and then asking me to help him move the table. The redesign creates a big, open space.

"There. Now we can get started," he says.

We start by practicing the basic 8. The silence and concentration on his face make me paranoid, and my body feels stiff and awkward. This dance feels unnatural to me. It requires a specific kind of balance, as if there is a string suspended from the ceiling to the crown of the head.

"There's something key to tango," says Ramiro, gently letting go of my hands. "It's the *eje*—the axis. You need to find your eje."

My eje. I had read that it takes three to tango: the follower, the leader, and the eje. I'm not sure what this means exactly, but the reason I feel unstable is that I'm missing something—the invisible string that will carry my weight to glide effortlessly without wobbling from side to side. Renato Dias's balancing-stick exercise immediately comes to mind. I need to find my axis, my balance.

"Tango is all about physics. First there's disassociation—the ability to separate the different parts of your body: the knees, waist, and shoulders." He demonstrates how a body can turn in three separate parts while the other parts stay completely still. "This is going to be really crucial to the follower's pivots," he explains.

I try to practice separating the different parts of my body, almost like a twisted cloth that slowly unravels. First I turn my head with the impulse of my shoulder blades, followed by my torso, my hips, and my knees. I finish with a final pivot on the ball of one foot while the other steps gently next to it. I feel stiff, like my body doesn't want to follow the directions I send it from my brain.

"Then we have potential energy and kinetic energy. Potential energy in tango is the energy one has within them relative to where they stand compared to their partner."

I try to think of an example and find myself visualizing the pull of a bow and arrow just before its release, almost like a compression. Pushing weight into one foot might be what gives that potential energy to glide forward with the other.

"Kinetic energy," he continues, "is about the accumulation of force through movement that will allow you to go faster and slower." He demonstrates some intricate foot pivots and hooks that cause him to spin.

I watch, mesmerized. I had never been great in physics, but these definitions through tango make far more sense to me than anything I learned in school.

Ramiro leads me through more basic steps, trying to demonstrate these different concepts so that I can feel them in order to understand them. I feel like a whole new window of learning opportunities has opened itself to me. So far I have learned to recognize patterns and time, increased my visual and auditory memory, improved my problem-solving, enhanced my creativity, and become a more tolerant and empathetic person—and now I'm finally understanding physics!

"Let's practice walking together," says Ramiro, guiding me to the back of the room. He places my hand on his chest, and we rock side to side until I find my eje, a discreet point in the balls of my feet that pulls through my hips and up through my body. It starts to feel relaxing, and I can feel the equilibrium between our steps. I start to zone out, completely engrossed by this meditative state. I feel his heart pounding against my palm, and my own heart starts to swell gradually until it reaches the point that it might burst.

As I follow his movement, pushing forward as I step backward, I stare only at his chest. I'm so engrossed in the movement that I don't even dare to make eye contact with him anymore. For all the joy and excitement that I've felt in all the dances that I've learned, I have never felt something so intense.

"Your homework," Ramiro interjects, "is to learn to embody the women who danced tango at its peak. Watch a film called *Naked Tango*. I want you to identify with the main character—feel her pain, her desire, and passion when she dances. I want you to feel fear at the dangers of knife-fighting gangs and sexual slavery that threaten your very existence. Your only ability to breathe—is tango."

I watch the film that night and it gives me shivers. The protagonist falls into the clutches of a famed trafficking ring and enters the 1920s tango underworld. But she's fierce and unshakable. She kills the first man who forces himself upon her. She also develops an unlikely romance with one of her captors, who teaches her to tango.

The next day I rush back from a nearby café and arrive home just five minutes before class. Ramiro is already waiting outside. I don't know what to say to him about the movie. It was intense, erotic, and dark. I almost feel ashamed to embody these emotions while dancing with him.

"I have news," he says, his tone serious. I brace myself as we step into my building's elevator. Then again, he's always serious.

"I need to travel to Spain in a few weeks, the weekend we plan to finalize our choreography."

As we start to discuss the various options for our classes together in the coming weeks, Ramiro looks at his watch. "We should probably get started now," he says. We are already five minutes into our class.

I learn a few new steps to the choreography. One is called *Americanos* and is a waltz-like movement across the room that involves another step in which we seem to almost create a square before crossing one foot behind the other. Finally, there's a step that challenges my blockages with sensuality. For the movement, we stand side by side, my hand in his, and both step outward. I summon my potential energy to fold into him, sweeping my foot across the floor and then bringing my knee up to his chest, while he turns his head toward mine, almost like a kiss.

It feels simultaneously terrifying, exhilarating, and earth-shattering. It is so beyond my comfort zone to dance like this—to act out seduction and desire with my partner. But Ramiro shakes his head slightly, almost in disappointment.

"No, Aliénor, this movement needs to be much more sensual. You can't just abruptly lift your leg like that. You need to graze your toe along the floor and then lift your knee up to my rib—the higher the better."

I'm crushed. For me just being able to do this step felt like an impossible achievement. I try it a few more times, feeling ungraceful and inept, but to my relief, he sees improvement and says we can move on to the next step. For that he holds me in an embrace, and I can feel his lead pushing me toward the ground. I take one step back and bend my knee to lower myself into a lunge, while the other leg stretches out and slides away. It is our embrace—our intense and powerful connection—that keeps me from falling.

I feel like I'm starting to understand this dance. As with languages, I just needed to change the chip in my head. Sure, my technique needs to improve to make the movements more graceful and effortless, but I can feel progress.

"You feel very heavy, Aliénor," sighs Ramiro.

His words are a striking reminder of how my recent indulgences in

Malbec wine and dulce de leche have led me to put on ten pounds, and now I just feel like an elephant trying to be a swan. The shame hits fast, and hard. *Maybe my body isn't made for tango.* I also have a strange pain in my shoulders, and my body feels extremely hard, making it difficult to lift my arms.

We continue to pivot through a step called *ochos* (eights). With my lower body, I trace figures of eight on the ground to each side of Ramiro, keeping my upper body connected to his through an invisible beam of light, while isolating my waist, hips, and feet—dissociating them by performing each movement one by one, propelled by the strength of the muscles in my back.

We then try more turns, but I feel very stiff in my ochos and stumpy in my turns. I feel like I just can't get them right. To be able to dance tango, I need to not just learn the steps but embody this dance with elegance and grace.

FOR OUR NEXT lesson, Ramiro, early as usual, waits for me outside a studio on Junín Street in the Congreso neighborhood, where we've come to utilize a large mirror. I'm a visual learner, so even though mirrors can make me self-conscious, I'm hopeful it will help me improve. When we arrive, a professional tango couple has just finished rehearsing and steps out to leave us the space.

We start with our usual exercise, and I place my palm over his heart as we walk backward and forward across the room. It has become our meditative routine, one that helps me forget the outside world and enter the underworld of tango. These steps allow me to transform myself into a pivoting, turning, and gliding creature, guided by my eje and connection with Ramiro.

"*¡Muy bien*, Aliénor!" he says. "Have you been practicing at home? Right now the width of your steps is of an acceptable size."

I try to hide the beaming smile on my face. It's quite rare for Ramiro to give positive feedback like this, so when I get it, I really know that I'm progressing.

We continue to go through my ochos and turns, and I try to stay focused in my tango zone so I can try to make these movements in a feminine and more sensual way. But every now and then, my concentration breaks. When I get lost like this it's because my brain is confused or distracted.

I share my frustrations with Ramiro. Moments of insecurity and hesitation always lead me to make mistakes. I wish I could control my mind—my thoughts can be the enemy of my progress. Now I feel like I'm learning the alphabet for the first time, or learning to forget it altogether.

"The worst thing you can do onstage, when you feel a step didn't work out as you thought it would, is to dwell on it afterward," Ramiro tells me, sharing from his own experience. "Otherwise it will ruin the next steps. I can see this in you, but it's very common. You make one small mistake and then the next steps come out all wrong. This is what I do when it happens to me," he says, demonstrating a sudden pause between two steps, then adding an elaborate leg movement and strengthening his gaze. "I make a bold movement to show my confidence; it helps to make up for the error and start again. So if you make a mistake, forget it immediately and do something that makes you feel more confident."

This strategy could work in many contexts—in any kind of performance, but also public speaking or even when a conversation turns awkward. Maybe all we need is a short phrase—whether it is danced, spoken, or sung—that we use when we make mistakes and need to bounce back into our confidence.

I used to play the piano as a child, and during my first performance I made a mistake—one wrong note out of hundreds. I was mortified and humiliated, and the whole performance was ruined, not from my error but from my reaction: my sudden hesitancy, my sudden inescapable shame. Confidence is worth more than accuracy. Some people make mistakes all the time, but they are so confident that we don't even notice. They don't stop themselves from moving forward based on one small hesitation. But that small moment of hesitation conjures many negative emotions and causes self-judgment, criticism, and disappointment. We need to turn our self-doubt into the confidence to make a bold move, even when we want to cower.

I WAKE UP from an amazing night's sleep thanks to my arduous tango training and walking throughout Buenos Aires on foot, and I consider my plans for the day. Today I have tango class again, and I am also determined to reach Liliana Belfiore. I had tried calling her to no avail, although I did reach her assistant, Fernando, who told me to just walk in. I resolve to call Liliana Belfiore's studio one more time before I go there in person.

A woman with a chirpy voice answers, and I ask to speak to Liliana.

"That's me!"

I do the usual introduction, explaining how I have left everything behind to dance, and she asks me my star sign.

"*¡Bárbaro!*" she exclaims, which translates to "barbaric" but is an Argentinian expression for when something is really great. "Only a Pisces, a great *romántica*, would do such a thing."

"I'm interviewing different people who dance, from the most famous to those not famous at all. Would you be interested in sharing your story with me?"

"Of course! Come by the studio."

It's only nine in the morning, and I have managed to get an interview with Liliana Belfiore—one of the most important prima ballerinas in history and a former partner of Rudolf Nureyev while dancing for the London Festival Ballet (which later became the English National Ballet).

Today's lesson with Ramiro will be at my place since the studio isn't available. It's Monday, the first of May, Labor Day in Argentina (and many parts of the world) and a public holiday. Everything in Buenos Aires is closed, and apart from a few people walking around, the city is like a ghost town.

When Ramiro arrives, we immediately get to work. We start with our usual meditative walking exercise and then practice ochos and turns. I can tell that I'm really improving in my walking and equilibrium throughout the choreography. And Ramiro seems happy with the improvement in my turns, which I've found to be the most challenging, as they involve a sequence of pivots and side steps.

"*Very* good, Aliénor!" he exclaims to my surprise, as he's been quiet.

His emphasis on "very" makes me so proud that I can feel my cheeks flush. There is an inevitable reward system between the learner and the teacher, and when you work so hard and are finally told you did something right, it has an enormous impact.

"I just have one correction," he says. "You know how puppets move in those puppet shows?

"You mean like marionettes? The puppets suspended and controlled by strings?"

"No, not at all. Hand puppets. One comes in to surprise the other, and the other puppet jumps, turns around, jumps again, and then runs away. Each of their movements is separate. They are done one at a time within one single sequence."

I had no idea where he was going with this, but now it's starting to make sense. Instead of merging all the movements in tango, I need to execute each step individually.

"So you need to make sure that your movements are in sequences rather than overlapping."

It's true that I often take the next step before I'm done pivoting. It's like I don't have the patience to finish one thing before starting the next. Maybe I'm too used to modern life requiring this—a rush from one task to the next, fueling a lack of mental engagement, and a resulting lack of fulfillment.

As usual, Ramiro arrives first for our 10:00 a.m. class at the studio in Junín, even though I arrive a whole three minutes early. I believe that people in the dance world are generally more punctual and disciplined and that this is because of dance. Discipline is at the heart of dance. Not only does it require immense self-regulation and control—whether it be tied to trying to isolate one part of the body or to rehearsing a sequence a thousand times—it requires showing up for rehearsals and performances that won't wait for you to arrive.

Today is our final class before Ramiro jets off, and I ask him about his performance in Spain. It sounds like something really special, and I'm curious to know more about his work.

"It's a very exclusive culinary function," he says. "Different countries will be represented including Argentina. We've been asked to prepare something very high-level for the event."

Wow, so both dance and food play diplomatic roles in representing a country and culture, I think to myself.

He tells me how his dance partner, Raquel, suffered from several foot operations and injuries, a sad reality for professional dancers, and that he's hoping she will recover in time. "You know, we were selected out of thirteen couples for this event," he says seriously.

We start our class and then go through the entire choreography that I have been slowly building with him over the last few weeks.

"You're lucky," says Ramiro, "your legs form an *X*." I have no idea what he means, so he explains that he's referring to a deformation called genu valgum, or knocked-knee. I don't think I am clinically knock-kneed, but I can see what he means, and he assures me that it is good for dancers. In tango, for example, you need to squeeze your inner thighs together while creating space between your ankles to glide, and my *X* legs, luckily, make this second nature.

We go through the choreography again and again. It's incredible how much progress one can make within the space of a few minutes. I can feel that I've reached a breakthrough. Gone are my stumpy steps, and I dance fluidly to an entire tango song. I'm pivoting and turning, my body gliding across the dance floor. I've danced well today. Really well. And Ramiro tells me as much. It's not always the case that we feel the same about my performance, but this time we do.

"I could tell that you were really concentrating," he adds.

The choreography is complete, and I feel confident dancing it. All we're missing is a dramatic tango ending and a dramatic tango dress. To address the latter, I step through the vintage glass door of Naranjo en Flor, a tango-wear boutique nearby, and find racks of tango dresses and skirts. Their colors range from onyx black to deep red, with sequins sparkling as they catch the light from the glimmering crystal chandelier, and ultrasoft fabrics from thick velvets to shimmering satins, as well as delicate laces sprinkled with sequins. I fall in love with a midnight-blue velvet pencil skirt, its fabric ruched at the back to look like the shape of a heart, and an asymmetric black lace skirt with a few blue sequins scattered in delicate layers.

I also try on a traditional black velvet dress with translucent mesh sleeves and a cluster of sequins creating a flower pattern by my shoulder blade. With the velvet dress draped over my skin, I feel like I have begun to embody tango in a new way. I look at my reflection in the mirror and don't recognize the silhouette in front of me—a woman who looks as if she would have been at home on a 1920s tango dance floor.

That night I send a photo of the dress to Ramiro, who approves of my choice.

I HAVE RELEASED myself from fear. I'm finally starting to take pleasure in dancing tango, and I've even danced in an intermediate class, summoning everything within me to focus on the nuance, precision, and creativity that tango requires. While I've taken to the large, sweeping steps welcomed in stage tango, dancing in tight milonga rooms requires a keen awareness of space and profound intuition to tune into each new dance partner. Tonight I'm going to a milonga called La Discépolo, named after the tango legend Enrique Santos Discépolo, in the nearby neighborhood of Villa Crespo.

I arrive early and order a glass of Malbec from the bar. This seems to have become a ritual, and appropriately so, because if tango were a drink, it would definitely be red wine.

We start with a beginner/intermediate class with a teacher who looks strikingly like Shakira. Her name is Florencia Daluisio, Flor for short, and she's warm, friendly, and open. I have a feeling she's from somewhere else, but I can't pinpoint her origin. There aren't enough men for all the women to have a male partner, so she partners with me. Her energy feels like it's burning through my skin. It's so powerful that my temple falls to touch hers as we glide around the room.

At the end of the class, she hugs me warmly and, noticing that I've come alone, invites me to join her and her friends at their table while the advanced class is in progress. I happily accept and we get to chatting about life and love, sharing romantic misadventures that lead us to laugh so uncontrollably that the teacher of the advanced class comes over to complain that our noise is disrupting his class.

We switch to a whisper but continue to tell our stories, with some of the girls going into graphic detail, only to discover that a tape recorder, presumably intended to record the class, was placed on the table the entire time.

WHILE RAMIRO WAS away in Spain, I'd tried to make the most of the different dance experiences and opportunities, starting by finally going to Liliana Belfiore's studio. She wasn't there, but I did meet her assistant, Fernando, whom I'd spoken with on the phone. He is tall and handsome with thick black hair and green eyes. We got to talking about the magic of dance, and he made intense eye contact as we spoke. He then suggested we go out dancing some time and asked for my number.

When I'd told him that I would be going out to La Discépolo tonight, he had suggested that he might stop by. I'm nervous about his intentions and expectations but can't help but feel intrigued by the idea of dancing with him. Now, after several flattering messages and pouting selfies, he's leading me to the dance floor.

Another Fernando. I should know better by now.

We sway gently from side to side looking for our shared balance. I can feel my body tremble in his embrace out of uncertainty that I may give the wrong impression. But as the song starts, he locks me into a secure *abrazo* (embrace) and we set off, gliding slowly around the room, our temples touching and our eyes closed in deep concentration. I can feel the lightning bolt between my heart and his, almost burning through my chest. As it grows in intensity, I face him, pivoting side to side in my ochos, and his embrace tightens. Through his silent, invisible signals, I feel myself lifted, my weight resting into my left leg as my right knee bends to lift the tip of my right foot up behind me. He turns me to pivot in this pose, the tip of my toes pointing upward to draw an imaginary circle in the air. A harpist teases a melody and the notes quiver in the air—flickering, taunting, and pressing against the palpable density of the room.

The song ends with the vibrating strings of a violin, followed by silence. My heart pounding, I freeze, not knowing what to do next. Fernando gazes at me before leaning in toward me, but terrified by the emotions I'm feeling, I turn my head to the side to decline his kiss.

I just experienced what some people call a "tangasm"—a powerful connection and bracing intimacy comparable in pleasure to an orgasm, but not derived from a sexual encounter. This felt different—it was a level of intimacy that I have rarely felt before, an ephemeral feeling of my feet floating up from the floor and my body temporarily transporting to another world. This is why tango is known as a three-minute romance. You can fall helplessly and desperately in love for the length of a song.

I WALK UP the staircase in Junín to the studio and find Ramiro pacing back and forth. This makes me nervous. The last class had been such a breakthrough, and now I fear that I'm a little rusty.

We start to go through the routine, and my fears are confirmed. I keep blocking in certain places—both in my body and in parts of the routine. Ramiro remains stoic, his gaze focused just over my head. I'm hoping that he doesn't say anything harsh. I feel too vulnerable right now. But he can tell that I'm upset and instead keeps silent.

"Why is this happening?" I ask him at the end of the class as I remove my tango shoes. "I felt like I progressed so much last time, and now it's like it's all gone!"

His face softens from its usual frostiness. "But you can never go backward, always remember that."

After class we head to Café de los Angelitos, just a few steps away. Ramiro performs there as well as Rojo Tango, since both their shows are by the same group. But Café de los Angelitos is not only home to the most traditional tango show in town; it's a legendary café where all the greatest dancers and singers have graced the stage, even Carlos Gardel.

The café's well-polished wood and powder-blue walls invite us inside, and as we walk in, I'm struck by the nostalgic beauty of the place and admire the gold-stained glass and luminous chandelier. With the sound of clinking glasses and shuffling waiters dressed in black and white, the restaurant resembles a refined Parisian bistro from another time. I imagine the motley crew of characters who must have frequented it—musicians, poets, guapo knife fighters, and more.

The maître d' lights up as we walk in. "Ramiro!"

Everyone here knows Ramiro, and thanks to him, I might get the chance to dance on this stage like so many of the greats have done.

An older gentleman in a gray suit gets up from one of the tables when he sees Ramiro and greets him with a firm handshake. He's obviously someone important, and I wonder if he's the café's manager. Ramiro introduces me to him, referring to me as "*la niña*" (little girl), which I find a bit disturbing, and asks if we could use the stage to dance next week. Despite my pride and all the confidence I have worked so hard to bolster, I find myself devolving into a disempowering stereotype. I play along and look at him wide-eyed, hoping it will convince him to let me dance. He agrees immediately, quite to my surprise.

Red velvet curtains embellished with gold patterns line the stage. Above, an intricate gold-and-white ceiling draws my attention. To think that I will dance on this very stage—it's like something out of a dream. A small voice in my head tells me that this is ridiculous. *What would I, a slightly chubby and clumsy dancer who always makes mistakes, look like dancing on the same stage as the best dancers in tango history?*

We walk out, past a huge framed poster of their current tango show and its star dancers. One of them is Ramiro. What had started off as a day of sadness and disappointment is ending with triumph and hope. Feeling inspired, I decide to complete my full tango agenda for the day by attending a lecture on its history followed by a milonga.

THE ALLIANCE FRANÇAISE is hosting a series of lectures on tango history by the Instituto Argentino del Tango (Argentine Institute of Tango), and I'd signed up immediately when I heard about them, eager to learn more about this perplexing dance.

I arrive a few minutes late to the first lecture and slip into the auditorium. The main speaker—prominent tango historian Marcelo Castelo—is sitting at a table on the side of a stage, with a huge projection screen beside him. He plays a silent video clip from the early 1900s and then invites professional tango dancers to come onstage for a live demonstration. It's the most active historical lecture I've ever attended.

Marcelo talks animatedly as he transports us back to the nineteenth century and doles out aphorisms ("Respectable people don't go to *pulperías!*"—a reference to the grocery stores where one can also grab a drink) and key context about the conservative Argentine society of the 1800s, which railed against everything from pulperías to pointed shoes, women and men bathing near each other, and maté—the caffeine-rich drink beloved in Argentina. Everything was a sin. And so was dancing, an activity associated with prostitution and decried by the Catholic Church as a perilous path to hell. But unlike what I had learned from Ramiro, Marcelo suggests that tango was not born in the brothels but, rather, that the prostitution angle helps to sell its appeal.

"People did not dance pelvis to pelvis *at all*," he says, causing some members of the audience to nod and others to gasp. He projects a photo from around 1850 that shows women dressed in wide hooped skirts supported by crinoline petticoats, which would have made it impossible for them to dance close to their male partners. He then screens various black-and-white clips of *tango primitivo* (primitive tango) and different types of waltz. He points out the embrace of waltz, its aesthetic resembling that of tango, and how it evolved over time from the dancers holding each other's arms to the man gradually placing one hand on the woman's waist. One clip from 1902 shows a rapid waltz with lots of surprisingly modern turns and dips.

It is a failing of archives that they typically document only the waltz of the higher classes, and not *la valsa popular* (the popular waltz). But Marcelo presents an alternative source of evidence: Impressionist painter Pierre-Auguste Renoir's 1876 painting depicting a dance scene at the Parisian institution the Moulin de la Galette, a former windmill converted into an open-air dance hall and café at the height of La Belle Époque.[159] It shows couples in different kinds of embrace—some very close, the woman's arm either above the man's shoulder or below it. Among lower classes, it wasn't such a big deal if people danced close together, or if the man kissed the woman on the cheek, but it would have been considered indecent among the elite.

Based on the timestamps of the images, Marcelo argues that the higher classes in Buenos Aires accepted tango long before it hit big in

1920s Paris, once again challenging what I'd thought to be the case. And those who rejected tango before the Paris era were not so easily swayed by its popularity, continuing to reject it even after it had met its cultural moment abroad.

Tango's roots are not unlike those of the other dances I've learned. The dance emerged from a unique fusion of dances, cultures, and classes and was shaped, finessed, and molded by its travels across the world. Tango, in its conception, is a great equalizer, influenced in equal measure by African slaves, immigrants, sailors, and wealthy Argentines returning from their annual European voyages.

I FEEL VERY tired during my final class with Ramiro, and it's affecting my dancing. We start to run through the entire choreography. But suddenly I make a mistake that causes him to stop.

"No," he sighs, before going over to the speaker to switch off the music and start again.

I find this so frustrating, the same frustration I felt with Yosnel in Cuba. I would much rather continue dancing through the routine, and through my mistakes, than be abruptly stopped. It completely shatters my confidence, making me feel helpless and inept. *Does he realize how harsh he can be sometimes?*

During the next run-through, I'm hit by a wave of tiredness. I then get lost during a turn and end up skipping a couple steps.

He stops me again, this time pushing me away in what feels like the ultimate rejection.

"No." He shakes his head in disappointment and goes back to switch off the music.

Do I really dance so poorly? I feel absolutely terrible about myself.

"I don't understand, Ramiro. It's not like I'm deliberately trying to do it wrong. For some reason my brain just can't handle the routine today."

His face softens. He can tell that I'm miserable and fed up. "You know, what you're learning isn't easy."

I look up at him in unexpected hope, and then he says, "Actually, this choreography is almost professional level."

Boom. This makes me feel so much better and lifts an enormous weight off of me. What a journey this has been, learning with great professionals in legendary dance destinations in eight different countries. I've come so far— and while I'm struggling, I've evolved from battling beginner-level errors to now working toward an almost professional level. Instead of feeling sadness, I should acknowledge this with pride. Ramiro demands a lot from me, but my immense progress with him in such a short time is undeniable.

We go through the routine another time, and this time I feel better. Despite a few errors, I can finally dance my way through the whole thing. I'm having trouble with the ending, though—a dramatic spin after the final turns. Ramiro decides to remove it.

"It's too difficult and not necessary."

I can't help but feel like he's robbed me of the climactic moment, but I bow my head and nod in acquiescence.

I STOP ONE of the elegant waiters at the Café de los Angelitos and order a glass of wine to help calm my nerves. It's only just turned midday, and I would never usually drink at this time, but I'm about to have my last dance with Ramiro, and I feel a mix of apprehension, relief, and sadness all at the same time. I've worked so hard to learn the routine. Tango felt so unnatural to my body at first, but I eventually learned to handle its twists and turns, and now it has unlocked something deep inside of me—a fragility and vulnerability more tantalizing than they are terrifying. When you know you will do something for the last time, you feel a certain sense of pressure, but also a nostalgia and the clinging on to a feeling that you may never feel again.

Ramiro walks through the doors and scans the room until his gaze rests on me at a table right ahead of him.

"Oh! You look great!"

He had asked me to look up tutorials on YouTube to learn how to do a tango hairstyle and makeup. The result wasn't bad at all—dark cat eyes with sharp cheekbones and blood-red lipstick, my hair pinned up into a loose bun with twirled strands of hair framing my face.

We greet the manager, who wears the same gray suit, and head to the back of the room, where I pass through the velvet curtains and go down the stairs to the bathroom to change.

This is the first time I wear my tango dress, and the soft velvet caresses my skin as I slip it on. I adjust the transparent mesh sleeves and the thigh-high slit on my left leg, ensuring that the jeweled black flowers embroidered onto the dress form a perfect trail on my right collarbone. I top up my red lips with a sensual scarlet hue.

I slip on my champagne-colored tango shoes and take a deep breath before heading back up the stairs, where I find Ramiro in a traditional tango suit with almost slouchy straight-cut pants, a shirt, and suspenders that reflect another time. His face is solemn. He rests his cool, metallic gaze on an empty space as he adjusts the collar of his shirt.

We walk up onto the stage, and the red velvet curtains open slowly as we pose in a powerful embrace—my weight lowered onto one bent knee while my other leg stretches out behind me with only the tips of my toes touching the polished wooden floor. Although only my friend filming and a few waiters are watching, the grand stage makes me feel we're performing for a vast audience.

The music starts. "La Yumba" by Osvaldo Pugliese—a 1946 instrumental tune inspired by the sound of metalwork. The title is said to have been chosen by Pugliese for its onomatopoeic effect,[160] which alludes to the gasping sound of the bandoneon. Its opening creates a sense of mystery as the striking of sharp chords turns to magic, notes delicately plucked from a violin before eventually melting into a smooth vibration from the breathing of the bandoneon.

We begin to dance, and for the first time I allow myself to truly feel the song, my body tracing the music, whether with tiny staccato steps or sweeping circular leg movements. The song ignites a blazing fire that grows larger and wilder as we pivot and turn, abruptly pausing for intense moments of stillness as I allow my leg to slide out behind me and let my weight sink to the ground, or suddenly rise up to wrap my leg around Ramiro's waist. This ferocious energy continues to grow into a powerful force as it culminates in the end of the song. Ramiro then unexpectedly forces me into a powerful double spin, firmly shifting me into a final embrace as my weight leans into my front leg, leaving my heart palpitating as we share a final flaming gaze.

I FEEL EMPTY. It's like I reached a climax with tango and now it's over. Well, my time with Ramiro at least. Last night, to avoid sitting at home in solitude and solace, I joined Bettiana, an Argentine friend from Bangkok who had moved back home, trading the opulence of tango for a rough, neon-lit billiard bar in Congreso to experience the depths of cumbia villera. We danced until dawn to the genre's rebellious and synthesized sound, narrowly escaping a twitchy character in a cap who complimented my villera moves before trying to bite my ear. Today, I'm back on track with a more dignified tango agenda and going to see a renowned tango dancer named Yanina Erramouspe.

"You have to go to her lecture," Flor had told me. "If you want to understand the emotional significance of tango, then you could really learn a lot from her."

I'm not sure what to expect, but the venue is only a ten-minute walk from my apartment, and I'm intrigued. When I step inside, I find that before the lecture even starts, we have to dance. This throws me, but fortunately I brought my tango shoes with me, just in case. I quickly put them on, fasten their straps, and join the group. The dancers are already standing in pairs in a circle, and the famous Yanina stands in the center. In traditional milonga style, we will all dance counterclockwise around the room. The one man left on his own opens his hand toward me, and I enter his embrace to find our eje. I'm okay at first, gliding through my basic 8, but then I start to block, unable to recognize his cues. I became so used to Ramiro that I could read him as if he had his own unique language. But I don't really know how to dance with someone else, and this new man seems quite advanced. I just can't follow him. *Is it my lack of skill? Or is it just that we don't speak the same language?*

I sit the next song out, feeling disheartened, before braving the third.

"See that couple over there," whispers my new dance partner, inclining his head to his right. "They're from Colombia—finalists in the Mundial!"

He's visibly starstruck—the Mundial de Tango is the world tango dance tournament, crowning champions every August.

No wonder I feel out of place—world finalists come here to dance. This realization makes me feel better, and I relax into the song, allowing myself to glide across the room. When the music ends, we gather around Yanina. She appears to be in her mid-forties, and she wears a short modern dress not usually seen in the tango world that reveals her incredibly toned and tanned legs. Her shoulder-length platinum blond hair bounces as she talks animatedly, introducing herself and her talk for the evening.

I take a seat and order a glass of red wine, eagerly waiting to hear her story and perspective.

"I've been dancing for twenty-three years," she starts, looking at the floor briefly as if to collect her thoughts, "and tango is going through an evolution. I'm an anti-traditionalist myself. People say that tango isn't what it used to be." She pauses to scan the room. "Well, no, it isn't. But that's not a bad thing. Tango came back in the 1980s, and by the 1990s people thought it would die again. Just like everything, it has to die and be born again. It's a cycle."

She changes the subject to talk about the *viejitos*—the old men she used to dance with who would carry her away in one dance. "Obviously it's not like I was going to hook up with them, but in just one song I could fall in love. It's hard for me to find that feeling in a dance these days."

I completely identify with this. I've managed to feel more with some of the viejitos I've danced with than with some men I've dated.

"Tango is not sexual," she warns. "It's intimate—and this is what makes it even more terrifying."

Tango undresses us to reveal our emotional nudity. This is the magic of tango—the ability to strip us of our socially constructed defenses and barriers to allow our hearts to lay bare in front of a stranger, to be vulnerable.

"The role of women has changed a lot too," she notes. "We have become more independent, and you can feel that in the way we dance."

I wonder if she considers the modernization of tango to give more of a lead role to the woman. In my case, my extreme independence is what makes tango challenging for me—to have to trust another person with my balance and my body, trying to decipher their cues while decorating the floor with my feet.

Her speech ends with a final word of advice. "Listen to tango, go to milongas—and not necessarily to dance, but to watch. I dance very little when I go out. It's about quality over quantity. I don't choose ten ordinary dances—I save myself for that one precious dance."

I'VE SPENT A quiet Sunday afternoon listening to Piazzolla. I'd taken Yanina's advice seriously, and I can already tell how listening to the music at home helps me understand the structure of the music and its instruments but also how I would dance it in my mind.

I've been in touch with a Colombian man named Carlos, and a Brazilian woman named Cecilia, who goes by Ceci, whom I had met at a milonga in the Teatro Mandril theater a few weeks ago. Ceci has invited me to join her at her two favorite Sunday milongas. The first is the outdoor milonga in Plaza Dorrego in San Telmo, the one that I'd seen on my first night and dreamed of dancing in. The second is La Maldita Milonga (The Damned Milonga).

We meet up just off the square and go to a nearby bar for empanadas before the first milonga starts, and we get to chatting about her life. Born in Rio de Janeiro, Ceci studied linguistics in Brasília, Brazil's capital, and is fluent in multiple languages. She grew up dancing bolero and samba de gafieira, even studying at the famous Jaime Arôxa dance school, until she fell in love with tango. She and Carlos taught tango lessons together in Brasília.

"Are you and Carlos together?" I ask.

"No, not at all," she says. "He has a girlfriend in Colombia now. But . . . it's happened a few times that we end up kissing at the end of a tango song."

"So you share a connection then?" I ask, curious to understand their dynamic. Maybe it's the same kind of feeling that I'd had after dancing with Fernando, something so powerful that it leaves you breathless.

"It's not so much us. It's tango," she replies. "Sometimes you just feel so much in a tango that it takes over you."

After eating, we walk to Plaza Dorrego, where I spot the older man with white combed-back hair I'd seen on my first night. He sports the same elegant jacket and silk ascot. It seems he's one of the organizers, as he's talking with two young people and motioning for them to check the speaker.

I've been in Buenos Aires for almost three months now, and I still haven't been able to dance comfortably in a milonga. It's been a struggle— whether physically, mentally, or emotionally—but the rare moments I've been able to flow in this complicated dance have been nothing short of entrancing.

"What are you doing?" asks Ceci, noticing me lurking in the back behind the crowd, contemplating the dancers gliding effortlessly across the cobblestones.

"I'm just going to watch for a bit," I say and shrug helplessly.

"No!" she exclaims. "*Bailar se aprende bailando.*" (Dance is learned by dancing!)

I had planned to take Yanina's advice to just watch—especially since it fits neatly with my dance shyness and fear of being reprimanded by my partners for mistakes. But Ceci is right. Beginners need to practice a lot at first. Classes can teach the fundamentals, but it takes social dancing with various partners to truly advance, to be able to interpret the music and improvise with a partner.

"Why don't you put your tango shoes on?" she asks. "That usually works to show people that you're not here to watch, you're here to dance!"

I sit down on one of the cobblestone steps and slip my shoes on. My struggle isn't always only the dance; sometimes it's also getting an invitation to dance. Traditionally, a man would ask a woman with a *cabeceo*, a slight nod of the head, which could either be accepted by a reciprocal head movement and locking eye contact or refused by the woman looking away. Only the most traditional milongas maintain the tradition of the cabeceo; more modern milongas encourage women to ask men to dance instead. While I love this tango feminism, I have battled a shyness my whole life when it comes to approaching men. Asking them to dance puts me in danger of vulnerability, where I could face being hurt, rejected, or abandoned.

Luckily, a man approaches me within minutes of my fastening the shoe straps around my ankles. Ceci was right! Apart from the stench of cigarettes from my chain-smoking dance partner, the dance is smooth and I begin to feel that this is not as impossible as I had thought. The blockage was in my mind; I had convinced myself that I couldn't do this. After a few gentle glides, I manage to start pivoting, as much as the cobblestones allow, and making turns that make me feel grounded and almost spiraling from my core. I end up dancing a full *tanda* with the man—a turn of dancing usually made up of three to five songs played in a row by the same orchestra before a short intermission plays a different style of music. As the tanda comes to an end, I spot Ceci out of the corner of my eye, her waif-like body sitting on her partner's bent thigh before bouncing off as he dips her backward into his arms for a dramatic embrace.

As the tango music starts again with the shrill sound of a violin, I turn around to find the old man with white hair inviting me to dance. I've been wanting to dance with him all night, in the hope of experiencing a nostalgia for a time I never knew. He must have experienced the final years of tango's golden age before dictatorships caused its decline. By dancing with him, I almost feel like I am transported to a time when Pugliese was composing his innovations and tango orchestras were at their height. Our dance triggers a generational exchange, where the viejito transmits his knowledge, experience, and skills to me during the length of a song. What I find remarkable is that these older gentlemen not only have a lifetime of tango knowledge but they're also kind, humble, and generous. A young, professional tango dancer might scoff at the prospect of wasting time dancing with a beginner, but the viejitos delight at the chance to share their time and knowledge with one.

I couldn't have imagined a better way to celebrate having marked a milestone in my pursuit of tango. On my first night I had stood silently watching others dance, hoping that one day I could be one of them. And now I am.

When Ceci and I head out, we take a short walk up Calle Perú to make our way to the Maldita Milonga. There, we enter a dark underworld. Its black walls and draped red curtains create an undeniable intensity, while the smoky stage and orchestra feel otherworldly. We choose a high table that gives us a side view of both the dance floor and the stage.

Ceci says she'll be right back and grabs her backpack. "I'm just going to the bathroom."

She reappears transformed. We'd met dressed casually, but now she's traded her tight skinny jeans for a high-waisted pencil skirt with a slit and has dramatically made-up eyes, red lipstick, and a discreet jeweled barrette in her hair. She looks timeless.

A man standing to our left nods his head as he looks at her, and she reciprocates. I end up watching her on and off the whole night, finding the fragility of her movements both touching and exhilarating, her feet almost caressing the polished wooden dance floor.

At one point a Japanese couple emerges, dancing enigmatically around the dance floor in luxurious tango attire. The woman wears a white ensemble embellished with silver embroidery that contrasts against her shiny black hair. The tail of her asymmetric skirt leaves a shimmering trail of light as she spins in the darkness with her partner—a man in a pin-striped tango suit whose hair is neatly gelled to one side. I've heard that tango is popular in Japan[161] and that Tokyo is considered a tango capital. People travel from the other end of the world to be able to experience tango there, and Japanese dancers have even won the Mundial. My understanding of Japanese culture has led me to believe that establishing personal space and keeping a distance is primordial, so I wonder if tango is valued as an opportunity to embrace closeness in a way that doesn't violate social codes.

As our world becomes touch deprived,[162] as people wrap their hands around their phones rather than each other, tango reminds us that physical touch is the fundamental basis of our humanity. Touch is our first sense,[163] developed in the womb to accompany our physical and mental development and strengthen our immune system, reduce pain and risk of disease, and regulate our nervous system for the rest of our lives.[164] Touch is a sacred connection between the mind and spirit and has multidimensional effects, even at cognitive and behavioral levels.[165]

Dancing with a partner allows us to embrace the divine power of human touch in a connection that is pure—physically, emotionally, and spiritually. It begs us to share balance and breath in a resplendent meditation that is centered on one single, soulful moment.

I'VE BEEN LUCKY to spend time with incredible people who've come from all around the world to dance tango in Buenos Aires—people from Brasília to Singapore who want to experience this esoteric dance in its spiritual home. But I've also had the chance to spend time with porteño tango dancers thanks to Flor, my tango angel who has taken me under her wing since I met her for the first time at La Discépolo in Villa Crespo.

A renowned tango dancer and aspiring champion, Flor will later dominate the headlines for having fought machismo by dancing with a woman in the Mundial—countering stereotypes that only a man can lead. In a whirl of controversy, assumptions will be made about their sexuality, accusing them of "lesbian propaganda," when in fact, Flor and her partner, Cynthia, are childhood friends. In an interview they will say that tango reflects society and that today it must reflect the very different role that women have within it.[166]

Tonight I'm attending Flor's performance at Milonga a la Parrilla. At the VIP table where I sit with her and her friends—all professional tango dancers—I feel like I've been let into a secret, an intimidating world of tango intrigue. Being the star of the show doesn't hamper Flor's sensitivity and awareness; she makes me feel welcome and included, even noticing my bewilderment at the slang that everyone's firing off.

"They're speaking Lunfardo," she tells me, referring to a slang that came out of the immigrant communities in Buenos Aires. It's apparently used a lot in tango lyrics, with words from all sorts of languages. It used to be that it was the jargon of criminals and the working class, but now, Flor tells me, everyone uses it.

Lunfardo—drawn from the word "Lombardo," referring to the inhabitants of the Italian region of Lombardy—is rich with words that give insight into the world of tango at the turn of the twentieth century.[167] Most of the words come from Italian or French, but many are from indigenous languages like that of the Guaraní or Angolan Bantu.

"Uff, it's a real *quilombo* in here," says one of Flor's friends while looking around at the scattered tables full of people. She's using a word that comes from the Bantu dialect of Kimbundu, which would have been spoken by the Afro-Argentine community to refer to their settlements, just like the quilombos of the liberated slaves in Brazil. But in Lunfardo, the term has been adapted to mean a commotion (as is the case tonight), a mess, or even a brothel.[168] Some say that it was actually in some of the quilombos of Buenos Aires that the earliest forms of tango were born.

Flor will be dancing to "Tormenta" tonight—a 1939 song by Francisco Canaro with lyrics that condemn God for pain and injustice and reveal a loss of faith in religion and in the world. I find her voice captivating and am enamored by her soft Argentine accent. Her eyes shine and her face illuminates with a sense of wonder and amazement at every word someone says to her, and she carefully articulates each word of her response.

When it's time for Flor's performance, she goes to the center of the room, and she and her partner embrace and gently sway from side to side, searching for their eje. Her right foot gently caresses the floor while making circular movements, and then they go on to glide, stepping to the song's almost march-like pace. Flor slides her foot up her own leg to a lingering strike of the violin and then taps her foot to mark staccato piano notes. As the song intensifies, its fury is reflected in Flor's face. Her eyes are fastened shut in concentration, and she and her partner are turning with torment.

Before gracing us with a second dance, she rushes back to the table to quickly pick up her champagne flute and take a quick sip. She then deliberately spills champagne on the floor and rubs the soles of her tango shoes into the puddle to add a coat of friction. "¡Se me patina!" (I was slipping!) she says before rushing back to the dance floor.

I will later ask her how she came to dance the way that she does. Although I've seen more famous professional dancers using stunts and adornments, there's something about her style that is honest and deep, seeping into my emotions in a genuine and profound way.

She will tell me that dance found her when she was very young, when she'd first started with ballet as a child and later trained in tango as a teenager. Her current teacher is eighty-nine years old, a man who has seen everything. He has told her about how he's seen the entire social construct of tango change from something you danced so you might turn a romantic prospect into your girlfriend, to something you dance so you can dance well. He, she will claim, is the secret behind the authenticity of her tango and self-expression.

SALTA

WITHIN TWO WEEKS, I board a flight to Salta, the heart of Argentine folklore culture. The city is nestled in Lerma Valley, in the northwest, almost equidistant between Argentina's Chilean, Bolivian, and Paraguayan borders. It's a typical Criollo city that blends Spanish and indigenous influences through its music and dances, and it is also said to resemble Texas in its contrasting blend of country folk and conservative elites.

I've already tallied seventeen dance styles during my journey, and that's only counting those that I took classes in and can dance an entire song to—not the many more styles I've watched and dabbled in. *La chacarera* will be my final dance in this odyssey that has led me to reevaluate everything. It wasn't on my initial dance itinerary, but an Uber driver had pleaded that if tango was Buenos Aires, then la chacarera was Argentina, and I couldn't leave the country without learning it.

I'd asked Ramiro if he knew anything about chacarera dance and music, and he'd put me in touch with a trusted dance contact who has already set me up with an authentic gaucho dance partner named Fabio.

I step out of the plane to find a dry and dusty climate, very different from the cold and humid winter creeping up on Buenos Aires. I scan my surroundings as I walk down the steps to the tarmac at Martín Miguel de

Güemes International Airport, named after the Salta native and national hero of the Argentine War of Independence against Spain, and can see the Andes mountain range and cactus-filled deserts on the horizon.

Each year, festivities commemorate Güemes, and I've arrived just in time for the *fogones* tonight, traditional singing and dancing around camp-fires on the eve of the anniversary of his death—a particularly brutal affair in which he was shot in the back by pro-Spanish forces.[169]

After I check into my hotel, a charming but creepy colonial house cur-rently occupied by a colony of cats, I take a brief walk around the historical center, encountering an architectural scheme unlike anything I've seen so far in Argentina. The neoclassical cathedral, home to Güemes's ashes, looks almost like a dessert, painted in pale pink with intricate yellow decorations like icing on a cake. As I take a seat on a bench in the Plaza 9 de Julio to admire its confectionary beauty, a small troupe of gauchos passes by on horseback, proudly but solemnly sitting up on their saddles, bolstered by the clip-clop of hooves. It is the Cabalgata de la Agonía (Cavalcade of Agony), held the day before the anniversary of Güemes's death and representing the culmination of the ten days of agony that he suffered between the moment he was shot and his painful death.

Back in my room, I put on a warm jacket and slip on my boots. The fogones don't get started until 10:00 p.m. and are a trek away, but the owner of the guest house has told me it's much safer here than in Buenos Aires. I lock the door with a large bronze key, which I quickly put back in my pocket, and slip out into the night.

I walk past the cathedral again, and then the church of San Francisco, which is lit up in an impressive jeweled glow. I make my way to a big ave-nue filled with bars, making me momentarily sad, wishing I had a group of friends to go out with tonight. Avenida Belgrano gives way to Paseo Güemes, lined by vast houses with peaceful patios and brightly colored tiles—typical features of the Moorish architecture found in Andalusian homes. Ahead of me is the statue of Güemes, illuminated in scarlet and violet lights and standing at the foot of the San Bernardo Hill, where all the action is tonight.

I find a spot near the statue while a ceremony takes place with speeches from local leaders. Military men are guarding the area. This event is a vigil, a wake of insomnia, to watch over Güemes in his final hours.

I start to trek up the hill through the pine trees and find groups of gauchos gathering around campfires, draped in deep red ponchos and tawny felt hats. Some gaucho troubadours have even turned this tradition into a verb, *fogonear*, a favorite activity of the *paisanos*, country people. They play classical guitars and sing harmonic pitches accompanied by the somber beat of the *bombo legüero*, a hollowed tree-trunk drum covered with sheepskin. Some couples dance, facing each other while stomping the ground, clapping their hands, and snapping their fingers up in the air.

The fire warms my cheeks on this cold desert night; fifteen hundred guachos gather around the glowing campfires, basking in the warmth from the flames and a nostalgic pride for their history, for their heritage. While people peer at me curiously, I feel like I'm almost not there and instead watching a scene from two centuries ago.

I hadn't planned to come to Salta during the Güemes commemoration; it was pure coincidence. But the timing couldn't be more perfect to experience Salta's folklore scene at its best.

TODAY, FOR THE official anniversary of Güemes's death, there will be a civil-military parade in which folklore dancers, youth groups, and five thousand gauchos on horseback pay homage to their city's fallen hero.

I make the long walk through the historical center and dodge horses on my way up Avenue Belgrano and Paseo Güemes, finding a spot that offers me a prime view of the parade, marshaled by a young and handsome governor draped in a red-and-black poncho (the patriotic colors representing Güemes's blood and his mourning) and wearing a white neckerchief.

Revelers carry textile banners, and the cavalry of gauchos arrive on horseback in cowhides and capes. Women wear full skirts, their hair either braided to one side, in two braids, or let loose, while men wear bombachas—wide, almost floaty gaucho pants tied at the ankle—tucked into heavy leather boots. They both wear the wide-brimmed and flat-topped felt hat of *gauchos norteños* (gauchos of the north).

The next block features a regiment of camouflaged commandos. They proudly display their machine guns and are accompanied by yeti-like snipers in gillie suits covered in fake grass to resemble foliage. Following them is a solemn procession that carries an enormous vertical flag with a number of islands embroidered on it. The MC announces an homage to the heroes of the Guerra de las Malvinas (Falklands War)—a territorial dispute over a group of islands in the South Atlantic that culminated in a ten-week war in 1982 and remains very much alive in the minds of Argentine citizens. Next are regiments of youth cadets who proudly don their uniforms, and another block dressed entirely in red ponchos and hats that resemble sleeping caps, folded over to one side of their heads and adorned with a pom-pom.

After, Andean beauty queens offer regal waves to adoring crowds, and folklore dancers in traditional dress appear to dance zamba, a national folklore dance with indigenous, Criollo, and African roots, where partners tease each other by twirling their handkerchiefs. It's considered a slow, gentle, and romantic dance with lyrics that often evoke love and longing.

TONIGHT I'LL BE meeting Fabio Pérez—gaucho and professional folklore dancer who has toured Europe as part of a dance troupe to represent Argentinian culture. He'd sent me a message asking if I'd spotted him in the parade. I'd managed to identify a man with long, black curly hair accompanied by a child on a pony (he'd told me he would be parading with his nephew), but I send him the photo and he tells me it isn't him. With almost five thousand gauchos having paraded today, my chances of getting it right were slim.

We haven't found a dance studio, so we'll be rehearsing on his patio in a neighborhood a short drive away. I'm excited to learn la chacarera, and even though the dance is originally from the neighboring province of Santiago del Estero, I'll be learning it in Argentina's folklore capital. Its popularity has spread through the country and it is frequently used to spread a romanticized notion of national identity.

My taxi pulls up in front of a gated, square house. I ring the doorbell, and Fabio emerges, his long, black hair pulled back in a ponytail under a black beret that contrasts against his striking green-hazel eyes. He's with his teenage cousin, who shyly greets me on his way out, and a woman named Olga, who also loves to dance folklore.

"You don't mind if she joins the class, right?" he asks. "She's excited to be part of this—teaching a foreigner la chacarera." Olga looks at me, her eyes gleaming. I can see the reflection of her Inca ancestors in her features as she shyly twists her hair to one side.

Fabio's patio is scattered with saddles, cowhides, and a roughed-up pair of boots, and it abounds with flourishing blooms of bougainvillea.

"Let's get started," he says and walks over to pick up his laptop placed on top of a giant speaker next to a *parilla*—the traditional Argentine barbecue. He opens his laptop to reveal a screen saver of horses in a field.

Fabio has a gold pin on his beret that looks like the same archipelago that I'd seen at the parade. As he puts on the music, I tell him that I recognize the sound from the fogones—the same romantic tones and soft, bouncy notes. He smiles, happy with my observation, and then hands me a piece of paper with a drawing of the steps of the dance in the shape of a star and tells me what to expect with la chacarera. I will start the song by clapping with my palms as I stand in position, perform a simple zapateo with my feet to complete the basic step, and then snap my fingers in the air as I move toward my partner in various angles, creating a star shape. He demonstrates the dance with Olga. It looks just like what I'd seen people do around the fogones last night, but with a noticeable flair and precision found only in professionals. He motions for me to stand in one corner of the patio, facing him diagonally.

I lift my hands to the right of my face, my palms clasped together. With a nod of the head, he invites me to start clapping together in *palmas*—a similar clapping style to that used in flamenco to emphasize the beat of the song. He then comes to stand by my side and shows me the basic zapateo: three small, waltz-like steps with a strong accent marked by the first step. It's similar to the basic step in Mexican folklore, and I practice it several times around the patio. I get the hang of it quickly, finding it much easier than the Mexican zapateo. I'm not sure if the step is objectively easier or it's easier because I've strengthened my muscle memory and can more readily analyze and configure new patterns.

"Okay, now you're ready to try dancing it with me. But first, let's take a break," he says, noticing my pink face puffing for breath. "Do you drink maté?"

I'd seen the sacred maté ritual several times in Buenos Aires: people sitting in a group passing each other a gourd with a silver straw known as a bombilla. The herb has a bitter taste, but there's something satisfying about this caffeine-rich drink.

Fabio prepares the maté, stacking the *yerba*, or herb, into his silver-encrusted gourd and then using the bombilla to push it to one side to carefully pour hot water from his thermos. He hands the gourd over to me. The first serving tastes the most bitter, but I don't want to refuse. I take a couple of brutal sips; it's so pungent that I'm unable to finish.

"*Gracias*," I say as I hand it back to him.

"No," says Olga, "you can't say thank you if you don't finish the whole serving." She's caught me breaking one of the many rules that come with the strict social codes in a maté-drinking ceremony. I take the gourd back and continue sipping on the bombilla to correct my maté faux pas while Fabio heads inside to refill his thermos.

THE NEXT DAY, I'm back on Fabio's patio. This time he's brought his bombachas and boots to demonstrate his footwork. We go over the zapateo again, and he teaches me how to hold up my arms and make a snapping sound with my fingers. When he tells me that I'm ready to dance the whole sequence, I stand in position, facing him diagonally, and make my way through the entire dance on my first try. I've never managed to get the hang of a routine so fast, and I'm really enjoying snapping my fingers. It's strangely satisfying.

"Not bad," says Fabio. "You're smiling enough but you need to engage with me more. When you turn around, you need to keep your head facing me. Keep eye contact as long as possible."

I've finally reached the point where I can dance and smile at the same time. But he's picked up on my weak point—my fear of flirting with my dance partner and, more generally, with men. But Fabio feels safe and nonthreatening, and armed with my growing dance confidence, I give it another go.

The eye contact, smiling, and suggestive head movements not only give my dancing an actual aesthetic but feel liberating. It's like I'm allowing myself to show a side of my femininity that I often repress. As I step out to his side, twirling to gaze at him suggestively, he launches into his fancy footwork, with jumps, kicks, and an intricate zapateo made even more impressive in his heavy boots.

"I think you've got it already!" he says and smiles. It seems that I've made an impression on Fabio, and he's not alone. He calls out his father, Rubén, who emerges from the shadows. Fabio had told me that his father had lived and performed in France and was dying to meet me so he could practice his French. Now Rubén greets me timidly in French and asks to take me out dancing.

Rubén rubs his hands together to warm up in the cold and then tells me, "You haven't really lived Argentina's folklore if you haven't been to our *peñas* (taverns). They are the heart of our folk singing and dancing."

MY TAXI PULLS up on Balcarce Street and I can see Rubén's shadow. He's waiting with his hands in the pockets of his jacket, this time in a different doorway. It feels like what Tinder would have been in olden times, meeting someone whom you already know at a specific place and time. While the sentiment in this case is purely platonic, it also runs deeper. In Rubén I have once again seen the reflection of a father figure—something I have found in strangers along this journey, as if the universe is trying to fulfill an unmet childhood need.

I had felt the absence of a full-time father figure keenly, casting shadows of reticence and doubt on my relationships with men. I could rarely approach them directly or dare to show my interest, due to an immense fear of being rejected, ignored, neglected, or abandoned. This has made partner dancing in social settings a huge challenge for me. But during this journey, I've learned that this is a fear that time and effort can help me overcome.

Rubén's face brightens as I slip out of the car and go to greet him with one kiss on the cheek. He seems almost nervous, shifting from side to side with his hands in his pockets. There's a softness in his voice, and his eyes crinkle when he smiles.

A singer, songwriter, and poet, Rubén Pérez is a local personality. Born in the south of Salta Province in a small town called El Tala, at only fourteen years old he composed a zamba titled "Mi Taleñita" about his hometown crush that has become a classic of Argentinian folklore. Now he leads me into a small, rowdy peña packed to the brim.

"Rubén!" A man who appears to be the owner rushes over to us and hugs Rubén enthusiastically. Rubén introduces me, proud to have a foreign guest. A group of folklore musicians play vigorously, the singer red in the face from relentless singing. Upon seeing us arrive, they stop mid-song.

"Ladies and gentlemen! We have someone very special here tonight. A round of applause for one of the figures of our folklore—Rubén Pérez!"

The crowd starts to cheer, looking at us, while Rubén laughs gently, almost shrugging off the attention with modesty. The band breaks into song, this time playing "Mi Taleñita" in honor of Rubén.

The song is as gentle as Rubén himself, and the lyrics speak of an innocent love perhaps only possible to imagine at fourteen years old. The band barely gets through an entire verse before they call Rubén up onto the stage. He touches my arm as if to ask permission and I motion for him to go ahead. He walks up onto the stage and faces the audience.

"I'd like to dedicate this song to a beautiful young woman from France," he says, his eyes crinkling as he gestures toward me.

My jaw drops. *Do men like this even still exist? Why aren't they part of my own generation?* Nobody has ever dedicated a song to me before. I can't hold back a beaming smile.

The crowd roars as he starts to sing, swaying in their seats with some resorting to twirling napkins from their tables in the absence of hand-kerchiefs, which feature in the lyrics of the song. People of all ages sing their hearts out to this soft, romantic song. It seems that folklore traverses generations, forming part of customs that run deep in their history and identity.

The song ends, and Rubén turns to whisper to the musicians. He turns back, smiling at me, and starts to sing one of the most emblematic songs of my childhood, one that transports me back to the summers with my grandparents in the rugged coastal region of Brittany: "La Bohème" (The Bohemian), a worldwide hit by French singer Charles Aznavour about a painter in Montmarte—the bohemian village in the heart of Paris—who despite his hunger finds happiness in art and love.

I sing along from the crowd, and to my surprise many of the locals join in. For me this song also evokes the nostalgia for a time I never knew, but in my own culture. To hear this song—this theme of my culture, my home, and my family—in the gaucho heartland of northwestern Argentina feels surreal, like after ten months of searching, traveling, and yearning abroad, I have arrived at exactly where I need to be.

The audience cheers when the song ends, and Rubén gives a timid bow before raising his hands in thanks and then walking back to me. I hug him tightly.

We head back out, strolling up Balcarce, and enter a large tavern, much larger than the others. Miraculously, it isn't jam-packed, so we grab a large table by the side of the stage. Fabio and Olga also show up, and I once again feel an incredible sense of belonging in a community and culture that aren't my own. Dancers perform various genres from zamba to la chacarera. They invite Fabio onstage and he launches into a masculine *malambo*—a style with intricate footwork traditionally danced by men and usually performed by a lone gaucho to instrumental music. I'd heard of malambo because of the dance troupe Malevo, which gained international recognition on *America's Got Talent* for bringing a fiercely modern twist to the dance filled with both virility and voracity, and embodying the iconic persona of the "sexy gaucho,"[170] with wet hair, black leather jackets, and skinny jeans.

Fabio continues with his ferocious footwork on stage for an ecstatic audience that joins in by stomping their feet at their tables and waving their napkins in a way that makes them part of the show, not just silent observers. In Latin America, the audience takes part in the performance. Because what's the alternative? To watch from the sidelines, passively letting life slip away? No, I choose to get up and join the dance.

THE CULMINATION OF my final day in Salta will be the ultimate folklore experience—dancing la chacarera in full costume with Fabio. I'd spent the whole morning searching for a place to find a costume that includes the full, ruffled skirt and a blouse with a fitted bodice. I hadn't found the glamorous version that I'd dreamed of, but I did find a simpler blue-and-white cotton combination that suits me well.

I arrive at Fabio's place and greet him, Olga, and Rubén with a kiss on each cheek. We quickly go through the whole routine and then I head inside to get changed. There's something very special about being graced with the privilege of wearing a culture's traditional clothes. Different cultures are not fun costumes to try on, or roles to slip into. But learning experientially by eating new foods, dancing to different styles of music, and appreciating traditional artisan crafts allows me to gain insight into their nuances, histories, and values. I am honored by the opportunity to appreciate the cultural expression that this dress offers—feeling the texture of the fabric and admiring the details of the adornments.

I come back out, and Olga hands me a pair of leather shoes with a low but sturdy heel that make a satisfying stomp, and she then goes to deal with my hair.

"Traditionally we wear either one braid to the side or one on each side, and then add a flower. What do you like the most?"

"One braid on the side," I reply decisively.

She puts on the final touches, stroking the braid to one side of my face while slipping the flower onto the other side, almost tucked behind my ear.

"Ah, you look like a *verdadera paisana*!" exclaims Fabio, applauding me with the widest smile I've seen yet for looking like a "true countrywoman."

The bright blue skies are crisp, and the sun beams onto the bougainvillea that gleam in the light, its rays warming my face. The horse saddle is still there, and a bombo legüero draped in Salta's traditional poncho is placed decoratively in the corner of the patio for the occasion.

Fabio wears a blue checkered shirt with a traditional white neckerchief, a beige hat, and his black poufy bombachas tucked into his boots.

I take my position in one corner of the patio, trying not to squint at the sun in my eyes. I raise my hands, gently clasp them to the right of my face, and start to clap while looking at Fabio. We launch into a bouncy, joyful dance as I take my synchronized zapateo steps toward him, while raising my arms and snapping my fingers with a beaming smile on my face. I feel a sense of liberation in my expressions, which have led to an unrestrained feeling of pure joy and connection.

As the song draws to an end, we shift from a star shape and move toward each other. As he takes my hand for a final twirl, I meet his gaze. This time it doesn't feel uncomfortable. I look into his eyes and smile with ease.

When we finish the dance, the sun has already started to set. I go back inside to get changed into my normal clothes. My use of the chacarera dress has been short-lived, and I will miss it. It carries so much history, craftsmanship, and culture.

Fabio asks if I would like to stay for a maté with them, and then he and Rubén set up a table and various metal tins with interesting patterns. "We can have my best maté—I save it for special occasions."

We gather together, and Fabio starts to prepare his best yerba in his gourd, while Rubén fetches his guitar. He graces us with an acoustic rendition of "Mi Taleñita." I discreetly glance at Olga's face brimming with excitement, her hands almost trembling as she films him on her phone. He gently strums his guitar as he sings softly, and Fabio and Olga join in. Having now heard it enough times, I do too.

I consciously try to memorize each detail of this moment of togetherness at dusk, drinking maté and singing folklore on a gaucho patio under pink skies. How did I end up here? It wasn't a planned part of my itinerary. But the most consequential parts of any journey are the detours—if you decide to follow them.

"THERE YOU ARE!"

Even though she's never met me before, Liliana Belfiore hugs me tightly in a way that is both generous and genuine, before motioning me toward the changing rooms.

With just a few days left in Buenos Aires, and after several landline phone calls and message exchanges with Fernando, I finally have the opportunity to meet the legendary ballerina and attend one of her classes.

I'd brought a pair of pale pink ballet shoes with me on my journey, without knowing if I would ever use them, and now I'm grateful for that. I'm already dressed in my black bodysuit and leggings, and I slip on the shoes before going into the studio. I've dabbled with a couple of ballet classes as an adult, but to be able to take a class with one of the most important prima ballerinas of the twentieth century is something that I couldn't have even imagined.

We start with some exercises at the barre, my childhood reflexes coming back to me—until we need to perform an incredibly wide lunge that makes me feel like I'm hanging off the barre rather than holding on to it, trying not to topple over. In the same vein I struggle with lifting my pointed foot over the barre—these are stretches and movements that I haven't done in the other dances, but if I can master them, they will enhance any dance style. We stand at one side of the classroom and take turns leaping across the room in a jeté. I don't want to participate, fearing that I won't be able to leap very high, but Liliana encourages me, telling me that a small leap is worth as much as a big leap as long as I give it my best. We end by dancing a gentle *pas de valse* (waltz step) performed either individually and decorated with a port de bras, where you round your arms in front of you, or with a partner. I enjoy this movement, a classical take on steps that feel close to the dances that I have been learning on my journey.

After the class, I manage to get a moment alone with Liliana. We go back down to the lobby and sit together at one of the tables, where I launch into my questions about her life and the meaning of dance.

"All human beings," she begins, "have innate gifts. Dance for me is a link with God. It's a profound necessity that comes from within. It's about revealing your inner emotions to the outside, to share your feelings with another."

"What do you think was behind your success?" I ask, turning on my phone's recorder and readying my pen and notepad.

"It's work. It's passion. It's obsession. It's desire. You need to believe that when you do it, you imagine yourself doing it in the best way possible—and for that you need to really work a lot. It's a search for beauty, perfection. But what is perfection? Perfection is beauty within the movement, within the expression. It's being a painter of the music—the dancer is the palette of the music because the music is invisible. You have dancers who are really skilled, almost acrobats, but they're not great artists, because they don't have the ability to hear, the sensitivity that impels them to be transmitters of musical phrases, or ideas."

She tells me that classical dance is a compendium of things—reflecting both historical points in time and the magical worlds of myths and legends. For Liliana, dancing is authentic and real if it endeavors to transform the audience from a group of spectators into an affected, engaged body. A dancer, she says, must interpret and express emotions in a way that makes the audience feel those emotions and be drawn into the show, not just sitting and observing.

"Classical dancers defy gravity to leap so high that they can reach the magnitude of beauty, truth, and in certain ways the divine," she concludes, her eyes twinkling.

I ask her how she would describe the magic of dance to someone who doesn't dance, and she tells me that it lies in surrender—the giving of oneself to another. The surrender of your emotions, thoughts, and body through music, movement, and expression. That's why, she claims, dance is an inherently social modality—the first artistic form of human communication along with song. She compares the feeling of joy and accomplishment after performing ballet onstage to dancing tango in a social context.

"If you dance tango with someone that you don't like or with whom you don't feel that there's communication, it feels uncomfortable and there can be no happiness. That's why tango is so difficult, because it's something close and intimate."

I found a sense of safety in my choreographies, preparing for the stage or camera in perpetual search of that joy and accomplishment. Their structure allowed me to anticipate each step, sheltered within a familiar embrace. But when I danced socially, I was vulnerable. There was always the risk that I would be surrendering myself to someone who could bring me either immense joy or distress. I feel there's something deeper to this, and the researcher in me can't resist diving into social inquiry.

"What do you think dance can contribute to society, culture, and humanity?"

I'd formed some of my own convictions, but I wanted to hear it from a leading dance figure to see if my intuition was right.

"If everyone danced, there would be no wars," Liliana states. "Because to dance with another person, you need to show love, respect, recognition as an individual. That's why there are so many types of dance in the world that represent different cultures."

I feel that we're living in a world of over-information, where we are over-connected on our phones and disconnected from one another. During my journey I've frequently thought that dance could allow us to regain our humanity. I ask if she agrees.

"Dance is a form of contemplating and valuing others—to look into their eyes, to be in their embrace, to give a smile—whether you open up your arms, offering yourself in a chacarera, or glance at your partner while presenting a port de bras. The essence of the dancer lies in that gaze."

I ended this journey with the dance that, ironically, I had started with at four years old. My dance journey—just like history and life itself—has been a cycle returning me to my roots. Ballet, the mother of all dances, and Liliana's insights through her vast repertoire confirmed so much of what I've discovered along this journey, including my perhaps not-so-crazy conviction that dance brings peace, love, and happiness into the world.

I HAVE A bittersweet relationship with this city of silver and purple lights. I have been sad here at times, waiting for my destiny to pluck me from the sidelines and lead me to dance floor. It has been hard to accept the weather growing cold and the hostile attitudes of some porteños, but it is even harder to accept that this journey has come to an end, and in my last few days I cram in all the final things I want to do before leaving.

I go to some hipster underground milongas that have a more liberal and welcoming approach to dancing tango. Some are hidden in old conventillos of San Telmo, with people dancing on their terrace patios, while others are in tiny wine bars with multicolored balloons and signs banning the cabeceo, as a means of encouraging women to invite men to dance. In one of those I spot Fernando, and inspired by the code of conduct, I invite him for one last dance.

I also take a zumba class filled with middle-aged women that is taught by a huge bearded man who has us perform a Beyoncé-inspired catwalk strut. Seeing the women pop their hips to reggaeton moves and feeling good in their own skin—sexy, feminine, and confident no matter what their age—makes me feel that dance can make us shine forever.

I visit El Ateneo Grand Splendid, a former theater converted into a bookshop that is both grand and splendid, where I sit in what used to be a balcony box and read. Dancing and writing, my two great passions in life, are similar in many ways: both have a message to transmit, both inspire, and both transport us into another world.

Encouraged by my time with Liliana Belfiore, I manage to get last-minute tickets to a matinée performance of *Swan Lake* at the Teatro Colón. I don't know who the prima ballerina is, but in my mind all I can picture is Liliana and imagine what she must have felt while performing. I have seen *Swan Lake* dozens of times before, but I see it with new eyes in Buenos Aires.

At Café Tortoni, an iconic Parisian-style institution haunted by cultural figures from Carlos Gardel to Argentina's national writer Jorge Luis Borges, I drink hot chocolate and eat alfajores before leaving to visit the World Tango Museum, whose founder, Horacio Ferrer, describes the history of tango as "a century and a half of dreams, nights, encounters, corners, and solitudes, of apogee and of crisis."[171]

AT EZEIZA INTERNATIONAL Airport, still tipsy and joyful from my going-away party, I browse through the photos and videos of my time in Buenos Aires with a sense of melancholy. I come across the clip of me dancing tango with Ramiro on the stage of Café de los Angelitos, my leg stretched out in an alluring lunge as the heavy red velvet curtains draw to a close. I sigh, my nostalgia evoking a song by Jorge Luis Borges and Astor Piazzolla:[172]

> *Buenos Aires no te olvida*
> *Tango que fuiste y serás*
>
> (Buenos Aires does not forget you
> Tango that you were and will be).

In tango, each song usually ends with two strikes of the violin, but the occasional song ends with just one. It leaves you hanging in suspense, your heart both pining and palpitating, stuck somewhere between reality and the imaginary. This is how my journey ends, with a sense that I've only struck one chord on the violin and that I have a lifetime to live with this feeling until the second chord strikes.

AFTERWORD

— —

I arrive back in England penniless, having spent my life savings and maxed out my credit card, but armed with a new definition of success, seeing it now as the ability to find new meaning in the simplest things. I may have landed far from financially rich, but I have never been so rich emotionally. I have found a new way of living in a world full of distractions, one that engages all my senses and emotions to bring joy, freedom, and connection. I have found my rhythm.

I am determined to share what I've found with the world, to put the life-changing power of the people and places but also the vivid colors, sounds, and movements into words. Unfortunately, there will be weeks of no dancing for me, at least for a while. Mr. Geng, the fortune-teller I'd consulted with in Bangkok, would prove to be right when he told me to watch out for my hip. I'd dislocated a small joint in my pelvis, causing a painful imbalance and preventing me from dancing for four weeks.

One month after my return, I take the train to London, desperate for a weekend of Latin music and dance. I've managed to get tickets to see Havana D'Primera in concert, but with my tiny budget I end up sleeping in a makeshift hostel on top of a pub manned by a surprisingly angry Rastafarian who threatens me with his broom when I tell him someone has stolen my bunk.

The next day Sergio invites me to his friend's house for a *feijoada*—a black bean stew that is a traditional Brazilian dish served in buffets and social settings. I meet him and Fabiana—a fellow dance lover who is from northeastern Brazil—outside the station, carrying an overnight bag.

We enter a London living room effortlessly brought to life by a group of buoyant Brazilians. It feels good to hear the sound of Brazilian Portuguese, and Caco Barros, a renowned Brazilian musician living in London, serenades us with a soft samba that brightens up the gray Sunday afternoon.

"Let's do a *roda*!" says Roberta, a Carioca woman who organizes cultural events for the Anglo-Brazilian Society.

Everyone takes off their shoes and gathers in the center of the living room for a *roda de samba*—a tradition of gathering in a "dance circle" filled with improvisation and imitation that was brought to Brazil by Bantu slaves but now represents freedom, liberation, and joy.

"Sergio, I'm embarrassed," I whisper, pointing down at the holes in my stockings, which, along with my having shown up with my overnight bag, have probably given the impression that I am completely destitute.

"But it's beautiful!" he exclaims in his Russian brogue, his eyes gleaming. "It means that you care about things that are so much more important now." He puts his arm around me and motions me toward the circle.

We start to dance a basic samba step, one that's softer and more casual than in Carnival, while clapping and cheering in an explosion of joy that I haven't felt in weeks.

"Let's have this girl show us some of the dances she's learned!" says Sergio, motioning me inside the circle.

He's taken me by surprise. My weeks in isolation have made me uncharacteristically shy and withdrawn. But this is my chance to bring everything—my journey, my very self—back to life. Caco Barros, our designated DJ, invites me to select the music. I take a deep breath, and the first song, "Amor de Mis Amores" (Love of My Loves) by La Sonora Dinamita, begins to play. I lift my arms up into a *V* and make tiny shifts with my hips.

We enter a realm of different styles, dancing everything from Colombian cumbia to reggaeton, Cuban salsa, and cha-cha-cha. Then I switch the music to a forró, dragging Sergio into the middle circle with me as the rest of the group claps. I haven't danced with anyone in so long—the connection, especially with a dear friend, is healing. As he twirls and shuffles me, I don't even try to conceal the beaming smile on my face. We end by playing "La Gozadera" (The Party) by Gente de Zona and Marc Anthony, an ode to Latin America and its philosophy of enjoyment, not just in dance but also in life. So many of the dances I've learned on my journey have been relived within just one circle.

DANCE GIVES US hope in a world where we have become starved of human connection to the point that we have forgotten how to interact, let alone forge intimacy. In dance, we can be held in a warm embrace, if only for the duration of a song or an evening.

Dance has the divine ability to turn pain into joy—with so many dances created to overcome and provide a living record of some of the greatest hardships in human history, from colonization to slavery. It is a reflection of the human experience, with each style recreating scenes of the past, evoking different emotions, and carrying a unique value system. Dance, like painting and literature, is the expression of history and heritage. But dance, more so than any other art form, requires human interaction; the medium of dance, after all, is people. With dance, I have found a way to reconnect to my basic human needs—making eye contact and holding strangers—and it leaves me with feelings of compassion and connection.

But learning to dance is not unlike learning to walk, and when we are adults this learning curve can be frustrating; after all, everything nowadays is available on demand. But we need to accept the discomfort of learning if we want to progress. We should embrace the things that we are not good at, or at least not shut the door on them altogether. While of course it's great to enhance our talents and gifts, it's also good to challenge ourselves with something out of our comfort zone. You don't have to be good at something in order to do it—it just needs to make you happy. Learning something new will always be full of mistakes and failures. Both are crucial and necessary for our growth—teaching us resilience, perseverance, and grit. There is no success without effort.

Every dance style can unlock different tools and shape different aspects of your character. People often ask me what my favorite dance is. My simplified response is: "Cali-style salsa for my extrovert, tango for my introvert, and forró for something in between." But the truth is much deeper than that—each dance reflects a different facet of who we are and want to become. The array of Latin dances illuminates a range of weaknesses we can work on and strengths we can build.

Liliana Belfiore told me that she felt a unique emotion in each ballet, that she was a different version of herself in *Romeo and Juliet* than she was in *Giselle* or *Swan Lake*. I had discovered that each style had something unique that it could bring me: Cuban salsa makes me feel soft and feminine, Cali-style salsa makes me feel euphoric and motivated, while New York style makes me feel elegant and timeless. Samba makes me feel like a queen, bringing me a unique confidence that is both powerful and majestic, while tango forces me to embrace my vulnerability through a shared meditative connection that makes my heart feel naked and my toes like they are floating off the ground.

And this vulnerability is strength, not weakness. After all, aren't we born with the capacity to feel for a reason? Why repress the ability to see, hear, and feel beauty everywhere around us, from embracing the smile of a stranger to watching a bird resting on a branch? My renewed sensitivity has led me to feel so much through dance, to the point that I can sometimes feel my heart fluttering like the wings of a hummingbird, or a tingling sensation running through my body like the calm, cascading melody of a harp.

I was kicked out of ballet school at ten years old for being both too round and too rebellious, but today I dance because it brings me joy. I'm a slow learner, but one who seeks to understand dance, to dig deeper to discover its meaning and reveal its stories, its socio-emotional benefits, and its incredible ability to help us realize our full potential. I may not have the perfect technique, poise, or precision, but in the end, does that really matter?

I didn't embark on my journey with the desire to become a professional dancer—I embarked with the desire to find simplicity and sincerity. Along the way I discovered that I need to dance in order to feel alive. I've since started dancing in the streets and the supermarket and at home as I cook or clean dishes. I don't care what anybody thinks—I continue to live my ultimate dream every day. Now it's time to live yours. All you need is the courage to take that first step.

ACKNOWLEDGMENTS

This book wouldn't have been possible without the many people who formed part of my journey, each of them acting as a signpost on my path that guided and inspired every dance step and word on the page.

Thank you to Naoko Enomoto for asking me a question that led me to reevaluate my life, envision a different future, and define my dream. I am also immensely grateful to Arianna Flores Corral for her enthusiasm when designing my dance itinerary and insisting that I should write about it, as well as to travel writer Joe Cummings, who told me that this should become a book and mentored me in the process.

My heart is full of gratitude to the friends who encouraged me to write this book and who reviewed the very first pages and extracts along the way: Kathleen Sullivan for her strategic insight and love of alliteration; my socio Clarke, for cackling to my excerpts and telling me to "keep at it"; Emma Beard for her unconditional love and friendship; Rosie Morle for her wisdom and humor; Raquel Ream for sharing her dance-travel knowledge;

and Rachel McCarthy for helping me realize that this is what I was meant to do with my life. Thank you to my besties, Lauranne Beernaert and Emily Cholette, for cheering me on since this story first began, to Manus McCaffery for fueling my "giichiiness," and to my accountability buddies, Laurie Vaquer and Charlotte Terouanne, for keeping me motivated in moments when I was full of doubt and about to give up.

Writing a book is one of the most challenging things I have ever done, and even more so was getting it published. I am deeply grateful to Fergal O'Gorman for his advice from the very beginning to help me get started and to Damien Cozette for introducing me to my agent, Gregory Messina, who took on an unknown writer. Gregory, thank you for being there for me, believing in me, and guiding me with kindness, encouragement, and humorous email exchanges. Thank you to my editor, Margaret Kaplan, for making lockdown a time of escape and emotions by working with the beauty of words to tell my story, and to my publisher, Julia Abramoff, for her determination to make this book shine.

My immense gratitude goes to all those who were part of my journey: to Hannah Bennett, Fahrünnisa Bellak, and Juan Camilo Gaviria Betancur for hosting me in their homes and to the many wonderful friends I made along the way who are mentioned in this book. And above all, words cannot express my thanks to the incredible dancers who taught me, the dance schools that welcomed me, the directors, historians, artists, messengers, and Uber drivers who guided me, and the cultural figures and dance icons who agreed to be interviewed to share their stories with me.

To all of my dance partners who took a chance on a beginner, thank you for dancing with me when I didn't know how.

NOTES

1   Juliet McMains, *Spinning Mambo into Salsa: Caribbean Dance in Global Commerce* (New York: Oxford University Press, 2015).

2   Ibid.

3   Lise Waxer, "Of Mambo Kings and Songs of Love: Dance Music in Havana and New York from the 1930s to the 1950s," *Latin American Music Review / Revista de Música Latinoamericana* 15, no. 2 (Autumn–Winter, 1994): 139–176.

4   Raquel Laneri, "How New Yorkers' Obsession with Cuba Gave Rise to Salsa," *New York Post*, June 14, 2017, https://nypost.com/2017/06/14/how-new-yorkers-obsession-with-cuba-gave-rise-to-salsa/.

5   Jonathan Goldman, "Fania at Fifty," *The Paris Review*, October 9, 2014, https://www.theparisreview.org/blog/2014/10/09/cha-cha-with-a-backbeat/.

6   Juliet McMains, "Palladium Ballroom," Palladium Era Mambo Dancers Keeping the History Alive, 2012, accessed July 30, 2020, http://palladium-mambo.com/ballroom.shtml.

7   Ibid.

8   Goldman.

9   Jon Pareles, "'Rhythm & Power': A Little Bling, a Little Politics, a Lot of Salsa," *New York Times*, June 15, 2017, https://www.nytimes.com/2017/06/15/arts/design/rhythm-power-salsa-in-new-york-exhibition.html.

10   Griselle Ponce, "Exclusive Interview with Griselle Ponce," interview by Aliénor Salmon, Bailando Journey, October 21, 2017, https://bailandojourney.com/2017/10/21/exclusive-interview-with-griselle-ponce/.

11   Juliet McMains, *Spinning Mambo into Salsa: Caribbean Dance in Global Commerce*, 366–7.

12   Julie Bloom, "Salsa Spins Beyond Its Roots," *New York Times*, July 29, 2007, https://www.nytimes.com/2007/07/29/arts/dance/29bloo.html.

13   "Grito de Dolores," *Encyclopaedia Britannica*, September 28, 2018, https://www.britannica.com/event/Grito-de-Dolores.

14   "Jarabe Tapatio," Don Quijote, accessed July 25, 2020, https://www.donquijote.org/mexican-culture/traditions/hat-dance-jarabe-tapatio/.

15   Judith Matloff, "The Tale of New York and Neza York," Al Jazeera America, January 18, 2014, http://america.aljazeera.com/features/2014/1/the-tale-of-new-yorkandnezayork.html.

16   Brian Resnick, "The 10,000-Hour Rule Was Debunked Again. That's a Relief." Vox, August 23, 2019, https://www.vox.com/science-and-health/2019/8/23/20828597/the-10000-hour-rule-debunked.

17   "Women Travelers," Cuba in Detail, Lonely Planet, accessed July 24, 2020, https://www.lonelyplanet.com/cuba/narratives/practical-information/directory/women-travelers.

18   Ibid.

19   Eli Rosenberg, "The Y's and Wherefores of How Cubans Name Their Children," *New York Times*, June 1, 2016, https://www.nytimes.com/2016/06/02/world/what-in-the-world/the-ys-and-wherefores-of-how-cubans-name-their-children.html.

20   Angela Duckworth, *Grit: The Power of Passion and Perseverance* (New York: Scribner, 2016).

21   Joseph M. Murphy, "Santería," *Encyclopaedia Britannica*, accessed October 2, 2020, https://www.britannica.com/topic/Santeria.

22 Paxtyn Merten, "In Cuba, Santería Flourishes Nearly Two Decades After Ban Was Lifted," The GroundTruth Project, July 31, 2018, https://thegroundtruthproject.org/cuba-santeria-catholicism-flourish -two-decades-freedom-granted/.

23 Julie Schwietert Collazo, "The Goddess Who Moves Like the Waves," *Hakai Magazine*, March 10, 2017, https://www.hakaimagazine.com/article-short/ goddess-who-moves-waves/.

24 Valerie Mesa, "How to Invoke Oshun, the Yoruba Goddess of Sensuality and Prosperity," Vice, April 20, 2018, https://www.vice.com/en_us/article/3kjepv/ how-to-invoke-oshun-yoruba-goddess-orisha.

25 Rogelio Manuel Diaz Moreno, "Cuba's Divisive CDR Defense Committees," *Havana Times*, September 26, 2014, https://havanatimes.org/opinion/ cubas-divisive-cdr-defense-committees/.

26 CNN Wire Staff, "Fidel Castro Marks 50 Years of Neighborhood Watch Group," CNN, September 28, 2010, https://web.archive.org/web/20110409001629/ http://articles.cnn.com/2010-09-28/world/ cuba.castro_1_raul-castro-fidel-castro-marks?_s=PM:WORLD.

27 Osmel Ramirez Alvarez, "Do Cuba's CDRs Still Exist?" *Havana Times*, October 2, 2019, https://havanatimes.org/diaries/osmelramirez/ do-cubas-cdrs-still-exist/.

28 Yoani Sanchez, "Fidel's 'Revolutionary Collective Surveillance,' Neighborhood Spies Create Social Violence and Hatred," Huffington Post, September 28, 2012, https://bit.ly/39KFIEf.

29 Ibid.

30 Ramirez.

31 Ashwin Rodrigues, "Our Brains Are Being Overloaded with Push Notifications About Nothing," Vice, June 19, 2018, https://www.vice.com/en/article/a3a848/ facebook-notification-overload.

32 Janna Anderson and Lee Rainie, "Stories from Experts about the Impact of Digital Life," Pew Research Center (June 2018): http://www.elon.edu/docs/ e-web/imagining/surveys/2018_survey/Elon_Pew_Report_Digital_Life_ Anecdotes_7-3-18.pdf.

33   Jane E. Brody, "Hooked on our Smartphones," *New York Times*, January 9, 2017,
      https://www.nytimes.com/2017/01/09/well/live/hooked-on-our
      -smartphones.html.

34   Umi Vaughan, "Shades of Race in Contemporary Cuba," *The Journal of the
      International Institute* 12, no. 2 (Winter 2005):
      https://quod.lib.umich.edu/j/jii/4750978.0012.211/--shades-of-race-in
      -contemporary-cuba?rgn=main;view=fulltext.

35   Khang Duong, "Music History – Cuban Son," CP Salsa, accessed July 30, 2020,
      https://www.cpsalsa.com/archives/music-history-son.

36   Michael Slezak, "Supermoon Science: November 2016 Moon Biggest
      and Brightest in 60 years," *The Guardian*, November 10, 2016,
      https://www.theguardian.com/science/2016/nov/10/the-science-of
      -supermoons-the-lunar-lowdown-on-the-biggest-and-brightest-in-60-years.

37   Cordelia Hebblethwaite, "Who, What, Why: In Which Countries Is Coca-Cola
      Not Sold?" BBC, September 11, 2012, https://www.bbc.com/news/
      magazine-19550067.

38   "125 Years of Sharing Happiness: A Short History of the Coca-Cola Company,"
      The Coca-Cola Company (2011): https://www.coca-colacompany.com/
      content/dam/journey/us/en/our-company/history/coca-cola-a-short
      -hisotry-125-years-booklet.pdf.

39   Delfín Xiqués Cutiño, "La Ceiba del Templete de La Habana Perduró 131 Años
      (+ Fotos)," Granma, March 18, 2018, http://www.granma.cu/hoy-en-la-
      historia/2018-03-18/
      la-ceiba-del-templete-de-la-habana-perduro-131-anos-18-03-2018-17-03-53.

40   Jack Anderson, "Alicia Alonso, Star of Cuba's National Ballet, Dies at 98," *New
      York Times,* October 17, 2019, https://www.nytimes.com/2019/10/17/arts/
      dance/alicia-alonso-dead.html.

41   Ibid.

42   Ibid.

43   Ibid.

44   "Cuba Ballet Legend Alicia Alonso Dead at 98," *Bangkok Post*, October 18,
      2019, https://www.bangkokpost.com/world/1774264/
      cuban-ballet-legend-alicia-alonso-dead-at-98.

45 Jasmine Garsd, "Romeo Santos: Taking Bachata Mainstream," NPR Music, NPR, November 18, 2011, https://www.npr.org/2011/11/19/142514062/romeo-santos-taking-bachata-mainstream?t=1599157612223.

46 Deborah Pacini Hernandez, "Dominican Bachata: Moving from el Campo to the Garden," *ReVista: Harvard Review of Latin America* (Winter 2016): https://revista.drclas.harvard.edu/book/dominican-bachata.

47 "The Humble Roots of Old-School Bachata," NPR Music, NPR, July 31, 2008, https://www.npr.org/templates/story/story.php?storyId=93140350.

48 Antonino Cusenza, "Bachata History," Corazon Latino Family, September 25, 2016, https://www.bachatabrno.com/fr/history/.

49 Frances Robles, "Behind Closed Doors: 'Colorism' in the Caribbean," NPR, July 16, 2007, https://www.npr.org/templates/story/story.php?storyId=12001750&t=1601804563921.

50 Michael Deibert, "Dominican Republic: George Floyd Protests Spark Reckoning with Race as Elections Loom," *The Guardian*, June 15, 2020, https://www.theguardian.com/world/2020/jun/15/dominican-republic-haiti-racism-election-protest.

51 Jim Wyss, "Dominican Republic Becomes Latest Country to Close Its Doors to Venezuelan Migrants," *Miami Herald*, December 10, 2019, https://www.miamiherald.com/article238221649.html#storylink=cpy.

52 "Solidaridad con los Venezolanos en República Dominicana," Acento, August 8, 2017, https://acento.com.do/editorial/solidaridad-los-venezolanos-republica-dominicana-8481079.html.

53 Robles.

54 Abby Phillip, "The Bloody Origins of the Dominican Republic's Ethnic 'Cleansing' of Haitians," *Washington Post*, June 17, 2015, https://www.washingtonpost.com/news/worldviews/wp/2015/06/16/the-bloody-origins-of-the-dominican-republics-ethnic-cleansing-of-haitians/.

55 "Colonial City of Santo Domingo," UNESCO, accessed October 7, 2020, https://whc.unesco.org/en/list/526/.

56 Shimon Braithwaite, "A Brief History of the Dominican Republic's Cathedral of Santa Maria la Menor," Culture Trip, May 6, 2017, https://theculturetrip.com/caribbean/articles/a-brief-history-of-the-dominican-republics-cathedral-of-santa-maria-la-menor/.

57   "Petit Futé's Opinion on Catedral Santa María La Menor Primada De América," Petit Futé, accessed October 7, 2020, https://www.petitfute.co.uk/v37158-santo-domingo/c1173-visites-points-d-interet/c925-edifice-religieux/4593-catedral-santa-maria-la-menor-primada-de-america.html.

58   Valerie I. J. Flint, "Christopher Columbus," *Encyclopaedia Britannica*, May 16, 2020, https://www.britannica.com/biography/Christopher-Columbus/The-first-voyage.

59   "Sir Francis Drake," Guide to the Colonial Zone and Dominican Republic, accessed October 7, 2020, https://www.colonialzone-dr.com/drake/.

60   Braithwaite.

61   Ben Johnson, "Sir Francis Drake," Historic UK, accessed July 29, 2020, https://www.historic-uk.com/HistoryUK/HistoryofEngland/Sir-Francis-Drake/.

62   Peter Hess, "Francis Drake's Sack of Santo Domingo: A Case of Terrorism?" Cultures Contexts, University of Texas Austin, March 28, 2014, https://sites.utexas.edu/culturescontexts/2014/03/28/francis-drakes-sack-of-santo-domingo-a-case-of-terrorism/.

63   The Editors of the *Encyclopaedia Britannica*, "Diego Columbus," *Encyclopaedia Britannica*, February 19, 2020, https://www.britannica.com/biography/Diego-Columbus.

64   "Museo de las Casas Reales," Casa Dominicana de Cultura, accessed October 7, 2020, https://casadominicanadecultura.com/museo-de-las-casas-reales/.

65   Kathleen Squires, "Hotel El Convento: A Former Convent Transformed," *Condé Nast Traveler*, accessed October 7, 2020, https://www.cntraveler.com/hotels/san-juan/hotel-el-convento-san-juan.

66   Christopher Klein, "The Birth of the Piña Colada," History, June 16, 2015, https://www.history.com/news/the-birth-of-the-pina-colada.

67   Ivan Roman, "Senator Wants To Slap Leash on Spicy 'Perreo' Dance," *Orlando Sentinel*, May 26, 2002, https://www.orlandosentinel.com/news/os-xpm-2002-05-26-0205260105-story.html.

68   Jesus Trivino, "The Best Salsa Singers of All Time," *Latina* magazine, February 3, 2016, http://www.latina.com/entertainment/music/best-salsa-singers.

69   "Anthony, Marc," Encyclopedia.com, updated September 1, 2020, https://www.encyclopedia.com/people/history/ancient-history-rome-biographies/marc-anthony.

70   Pável M. Gaona, "Soy Feminista y Me Encanta el Perreo," Chilango,
      June 8, 2017, https://www.chilango.com/ciudad/soy-feminista-y-me
      -encanta-el-perreo/.

71   "Tourists Seeking Despacito Discover Puerto Rico's La Perla," *The National*,
      July 31, 2017, https://www.thenational.ae/arts-culture/music/
      tourists-seeking-despacito-discover-puerto-rico-s-la-perla-1.615712.

72   Ibid.

73   "Everything you need to know about Cumbia," Colombia Co, accessed
      October 7, 2020, https://www.colombia.co/en/colombia-culture/dance/
      everything-need-know-cumbia/.

74   Ibid.

75   Jasmine Garsd, "Cumbia: The Musical Backbone of Latina America," NPR
      Music, NPR, February 18, 2015, https://www.npr.org/sections/
      altlatino/2013/09/30/227834004/
      cumbia-the-musical-backbone-of-latin-america.

76   Gerhard Straussmann Masur, "Simón Bolívar," *Encyclopaedia Britannica*, July 20,
      2020, https://www.britannica.com/biography/Simon-Bolivar.

77   Nayanika Mukherjee, "What Are the Afro-Colombian Dances Shakira
      Brought to the Super Bowl," Outlook Traveller, February 7, 2020,
      https://www.outlookindia.com/outlooktraveller/explore/story/70223/
      champeta-mapale-shakira-afro-colombian-pride-at-the-super-bowl-halftime-show.

78   Nicholas Sea, "The Story Inside the Rhythm: Mapalé," Sounds and Colours,
      January 16, 2012, https://soundsandcolours.com/columns/street-sounds/
      the-story-inside-the-rhythm-mapale-16448/.

79   Ibid.

80   Ibid.

81   Juan D. Montoya Alzate, "Champeta's Heritage: Diasporic Music and
      Racial Struggle in the Colombian Caribbean," *Transposition* 8 (2019):
      https://journals.openedition.org/transposition/3254.

82   Danielle Dorsey, "Everything You Wanted To Know About Champeta,"
      The Culture Trip, June 24, 2020, https://theculturetrip.com/south-america/
      colombia/articles/an-introduction-to-champeta-colombias-biggest
      -dance-craze/.

83 Ari Shapiro, "In Colombia, Preserving Songs That Tell Stories," NPR Music, NPR, July 7, 2016, https://www.npr.org/transcripts/484944084.

84 Angela Posada-Swafford, "Romancing the Stones," *The Boston Globe*, November 16, 2003, http://archive.boston.com/travel/articles/2003/11/16/romancing_the_stones/?page=full.

85 "The City of Cartagena de Indias in Colombia Honours Its African Legacy," UNESCO, May 31, 2016, http://www.unesco.org/new/en/member-states/single-view/news/the_city_of_cartagena_de_indias_in_colombia_honours_its_afri/.

86 John Otis, "Miss Universe Snub Is No Laughing Matter in Colombia," *Time* magazine, December 23, 2015, https://time.com/4160554/colombia-miss-world-response-ariadna-gutierrez/.

87 Jack O'Keefe, "The Former Miss Colombia Has Been Up to a Lot," Bustle, January 29, 2017, https://www.bustle.com/p/where-is-miss-colombia-now-ariadna-gutierrez-knows-that-living-well-is-the-best-revenge-33463.

88 Diana Marti, "Carlos Vives Premieres Music Video for 'Al Filo de Tu Amor' Featuring Ariadna Gutiérrez," E! Online, January 24, 2017, https://www.eonline.com/uk/news/823896/carlos-vives-premieres-music-video-for-al-filo-de-tu-amor-featuring-ariadna-gutierrez.

89 Thomas Lewis, "Transatlantic Slave Trade," *Encyclopaedia Britannica*, April 6, 2020, https://www.britannica.com/topic/transatlantic-slave-trade.

90 Dr. Alan Rice, "Legacies of Slavery: Dance," Revealing Histories, accessed July 29, 2020, http://revealinghistories.org.uk/legacies-stereotypes-racism-and-the-civil-rights-movement/articles/legacies-of-slavery-dance.html.

91 Ibid.

92 Barbara Wanjala, "African Echoes in Champeta," Fundación Gabo, Fellowship 2017, https://fundaciongabo.org/es/node/5296.

93 April Clare Walsh, "Champeta Is Liberation: The Indestructible Sound System Culture of Afro-Colombia," *Fact* magazine, August 21, 2016, https://www.factmag.com/2016/08/21/champeta-colombia-sound-system-music-lucas-silva-palenque/.

94 Aylish O'Driscoll, "Caribbean Coast Celebrates the Legend of the Cayman," Colombia Reports, January 18, 2012, https://colombiareports.com/caribbean-celebrates-the-legend-of-the-cayman/.

95   "The Trouble with Miracles," *The Economist*, June 7, 2014, https://www.economist.com/the-americas/2014/06/07/the-trouble-with-miracles.

96   "Everything you need to know about Cumbia," Colombia Co, accessed October 7, 2020, https://www.colombia.co/en/colombia-culture/dance/everything-need-know-cumbia/.

97   Nicholas Sea, "The Story Inside the Rhythm: Cumbia," Sounds and Colours, February 12, 2012, https://soundsandcolours.com/columns/street-sounds/the-story-inside-the-rhythm-cumbia-18391/.

98   Stanley Stewart, "How Medellin Went from Murder Capital to Hipster Holiday Destination," *The Telegraph*, January 4, 2018, https://www.telegraph.co.uk/travel/destinations/south-america/colombia/articles/medellin-murder-capital-to-hipster-destination/.

99   Stephanie Eckardt, "At 84, Artist Fernando Botero Is Keeping Things Supersized," *W* magazine, November 16, 2016, https://www.wmagazine.com/story/at-84-artist-fernando-botero-is-keeping-things-supersized/.

100 Mimi Yagoub, "Narco-aesthetics: How Colombia's Drug Trade Constructed Female 'Beauty,'" Colombia Reports, February 5, 2014, https://colombiareports.com/amp/narco-aesthetics-colombias-drug-trade-constructed-female-beauty/.

101 Lyra Bartell, "Colombia To Ban Cosmetic Plastic Surgery for Minors," Colombia Reports, June 8, 2016, https://colombiareports.com/colombia-outlaw-boob-jobs-minors/.

102 "Women Dying in Colombia After 'Garage Clinic' Cosmetic Surgeries," NPR, May 7, 2017, https://www.npr.org/2017/05/07/527250417/women-dying-in-colombia-after-garage-clinic-cosmetic-surgeries.

103 Manuela Henao, "Teen Liposuction and Busty Pinatas: Narcoaesthetics in Colombia – In Pictures," *The Guardian,* April 23, 2015, https://www.theguardian.com/artanddesign/gallery/2015/apr/23/teen-liposuction-busty-pinatas-narcoaesthetics-in-colombia-in-pictures.

104 Seth Kugel, "Once Colombia's 'Deadliest City,' Buenaventura Is Coming Back," *New York Times*, July 9, 2018, https://www.nytimes.com/2018/07/09/travel/buenaventura-colombia-pacific-coast.html.

105 Elaine Shannon Washington, "Cover Stories: New Kings of Coke," *Time* magazine, June 24, 2001, http://content.time.com/time/magazine/article/0,9171,157350,00.html.

106 Ian Neubauer, "Colombia's Buzzing Comeback City," BBC Travel, July 24, 2019, http://www.bbc.com/travel/story/20190723-colombias-buzzing -comeback-city.

107 Will Worley, "World's 50 Most Dangerous Cities Revealed," *The Independent*, January 27, 2016, https://www.independent.co.uk/news/world/world-s-50 -most-dangerous-cities-revealed-a6836416.html.

108 Hugh Thomson, "Rhythm Nation – How Cali Became Salsa Capital of the World," *Financial Times*, January 11, 2019, https://www.ft.com/ content/9dc0ba04-126d-11e9-a168-d45595ad076d.

109 Juan Pablo Acevedo, "Cali Salsa: A History of Slaves, Cuban Bands and Mexican Cinema," Colombia Reports, December 12, 2014, https://colombiareports.com/ how-salsa-came-to-cali-colombia/.

110 Ken Robinson and Lou Aronica, "Why Dance Is Just as Important as Math in School," TED Ideas, March 21, 2018, https://ideas.ted.com/ why-dance-is-just-as-important-as-math-in-school/.

111 Lisa Trei, "New Study Yields Instructive Results on How Mindset Affects Learning," *Stanford News*, February 7, 2007, https://news.stanford.edu/ news/2007/february7/dweck-020707.html.

112 María Nohora Coronado de Chavarro, "La Voz de una Educadora," Educación Artistíca, accessed July 28, 2020, https://www.mineducacion.gov.co/1621/ articles-339975_recurso_4.pdf.

113 Ibid.

114 "Caracterización Socioeconómica de la Comuna 12," Universidad ICESI, accessed October 7, 2020, https://repository.icesi.edu.co/biblioteca_digital/ bitstream/10906/65178/1/comuna_doce.pdf.

115 "Iglesia De La Ermita," Organización Colparques, accessed July 28, 2020, http://www.colparques.net/ERMITA.

116 Robert Muggah, "Brazil's Murder Rate Finally Fell—and by a Lot," *Foreign Policy*, April 22, 2019, https://foreignpolicy.com/2019/04/22/ brazils-murder-rate-finally-fell-and-by-a-lot/.

117 Donna Bowater, "Rio's 'Wall of Shame' Between Its Ghettos and Shiny Olympic Image," *The Telegraph*, July 23, 2016, https://www.telegraph.co.uk/ news/2016/07/23/rios-wall-of-shame-between-its-ghettos-and-shiny -olympic-image/.

118 Aaron Gordon, "Rio's Olympic Legacy Bus System Is Leaving Poor and Working Class Residents Behind," Vice, August 10, 2016, https://www.vice.com/en_uk/ article/aeb33e/rio39s-olympic-legacy-bus-system-is-leaving-poor-and -working-class-residents-behind-uk-translation.

119 "Brazil: Extreme Inequality in Numbers," Oxfam International, accessed July 25, 2020, https://www.oxfam.org/en/brazil-extreme-inequality-numbers.

120 "A Visit to the Brazilian Favela Where Michael Jackson Filmed," ABC7NY, June 29, 2014, https://abc7ny.com/world-cup-michael-jackson-santa-marta -they-dont-care-about-us/147460/.

121 Paul Kiernan, "Locals Are Showing Off Their Sungas on Rio's Beaches," Wall Street Journal, August 8, 2016, https://www.wsj.com/articles/ locals-are-showing-off-their-sungas-on-rios-beaches-1470670582.

122 Megwen Loveless, "Bodies That Sing: Forro Music in a Traditional Setting," Harvard Review of Latin America, Dance! (Fall 2007): https://revista.drclas.harvard.edu/book/bodies-sing.

123 Ibid.

124 Laura Dibiase, "Economies of the Fittest: Brazil Leading Latin America's Fitness Revolution," Latin America Business Stories, February 26, 2019, https://labsnews.com/en/articles/ecommerce/economies-of-the-fittest-brazil -leading-latin-americas-fitness-revolution/.

125 Study International Staff, "Slow Down Your Learning, It Could Speed Up Your Understanding," Study International, February 2, 2018, https://www.studyinternational.com/news/low-learning-speed-understanding/.

126 "Carlinhos de Jesus," Carlinhos de Jesus, accessed October 7, 2020, http://carlinhosdejesus.com.br/carlinhos.php.

127 "Nilce Fran: Damas Do Samba," EBC TV Brasil, September 30, 2015, https://tvbrasil.ebc.com.br/damas-do-samba/bastidores/nilce-fran.

128 "The Parades: How the Parades Are Judged," Rio Carnival, accessed October 7, 2020, https://www.rio-carnival.net/en/samba-parade.

129 "Rio Urges Carnival Visitors to Stick to Urban Areas," VOA, January 30, 2018, https://www.voanews.com/americas/rio-urges-carnival-visitors-stick-urban-areas.

130 William Cook, "Royal Revenge: Why the 'Real' Versailles Outraged the Sun King," BBC Arts, June 3, 2018, https://www.bbc.co.uk/programmes/ articles/286GzwDLSZfYV6j9cqzLNdQ/royal-revenge-why-the-real -versailles-outraged-the-sun-king.

131 Andres Schipani and Joe Leahy, "Brazil's Rio State Ex-Governor Sentenced to 14 Years in Prison," *Financial Times*, June 14, 2017, https://www.ft.com/ content/deaf3d80-507f-11e7-bfb8-997009366969.

132 "Brazil To Boost Troop Deployment in Troubled State," Al Jazeera, February 11, 2017, https://www.aljazeera.com/news/2017/02/brazil-deploy-forces-espirito -santo-violence-170209190912082.html.

133 Dom Phillips, "Brazil's Mining Tragedy: Was It a Preventable Disaster?" *The Guardian*, November 25, 2015, https://www.theguardian.com/sustainable -business/2015/nov/25/brazils-mining-tragedy-dam-preventable-disaster -samarco-vale-bhp-billiton.

134 Marcos Hassan, "Here Is the Wild as Hell Story Behind 'Lambada,' a Cultural Shift Forgotten in Time," Remezcla, September 3, 2020, https://remezcla.com/ features/music/ponlo-en-repeat-30-years-ago-lambada/.

135 Kim Rottier, "What Is Brazilian Zouk," Zouk New York, accessed July 29, 2020, https://www.zouknewyork.com/?page_id=389.

136 Alan Riding, "Brazilian Wonder Turns Out Bolivian," *New York Times*, July 4, 1990, https://www.nytimes.com/1990/07/04/arts/brazilian-wonder-turns -out-bolivian.html.

137 Billboard Staff, "'Lambada' Singer Loalwa Braz Murdered in Brazil," *Billboard*, January 20, 2017, https://www.billboard.com/articles/columns/latin/ 7662436/lambada-singer-loalwa-braz-murdered-in-brazil.

138 AP/AFP, "Portela Samba School Wins Rio Carnival with Political Message," Deutsche Welle, March 2, 2017, https://www.dw.com/en/portela-samba -school-wins-rio-carnival-with-political-message/a-37775138.

139 Sarah Pruitt, "A Port Where a Million Slaves Were Trafficked Is Now a World Heritage Site," History, August 22, 2018, https://www.history.com/ news/a-port-where-a-million-slaves-were-trafficked-is-now-a-world-heritage-site.

140 Mariah Barber and Rhona Mackay, "The Little-Known History of Little Africa in Rio de Janeiro's Port Zone," RioOnWatch, June 3, 2016, https://www.rioonwatch.org/?p=29191.

141 Ibid.

142 "Understanding Brazil's Present Day Quilombos: A Small Term for a Big Reality," Yale Gilder Lehrman Center, End Slavery Now, October 23, 2014, https://endslaverynow.org/blog/articles/understanding-brazil-s-present-day -quilombos-a-small-term-for-a-big-reality.

143 "Rio Carnival: Samba School Wins with Anti-Corruption Message," BBC, February 15, 2018, https://www.bbc.com/news/world-latin-america-43067679.

144 "San Telmo: Stories Behind an Amazing Place," Pie y Pata, accessed October 8, 2020, https://www.pieypata.com/en/san-telmo-buenos-aires-2/.

145 Vicente Pinilla and Agustina Reyes, "How Argentina Became a Super-Exporter of Agricultural and Food Products during the First Globalisation (1880–1929)," *Cliometrica* 13 (September 2019): 443–469, https://link.springer.com/ article/10.1007/s11698-018-0178-0?shared-article-renderer.

146 Michael T. Luongo, "Argentina Rediscovers Its African Roots," *New York Times*, September 12, 2014, https://www.nytimes.com/2014/09/14/travel/ argentina-rediscovers-its-african-roots.html.

147 "Tango in Argentina," Welcome Argentina, accessed July 28, 2020, https://www.welcomeargentina.com/tango/history.html.

148 Sherelle Jacobs, "The Day I Tangled with Tango in Buenos Aires," *The Telegraph*, March 1, 2016, https://www.telegraph.co.uk/travel/destinations/south-america/ argentina/buenos-aires/articles/the-day-i-tangled-with-tango-in-buenos-aires/.

149 Edmundo Rivero, "El Conventillo," track 3 on *En Lunfardo,* Phillips, 1966.

150 Treva Bedinghaus, "What Is Milonga?" LiveAbout, February 25, 2019, https://www.liveabout.com/what-is-a-milonga-1007415.

151 "Evolution of the Milonga," Milonga History, Very Tango Store, accessed July 28, 2020, http://www.verytangostore.com/tango-milonga.html.

152 Ibid.

153 Ibid.

154 Romin Puga, "Candombe: Afro-Uruguayan Drums and the Roots of Tango," ABC News, April 10, 2013, https://abcnews.go.com/ABC_Univision/ Entertainment/candombe-dummer-daniel-tatita-mrquez-uruguay-plays-live/ story?id=18926610.

155 Eduardo Frajman, "Classics of Latin Music: 'Que Nadie Sepa Mi Sufrir' by Hugo de Carril and Many Others," LemonWire, March 31, 2017, https://lemonwire.com/2017/03/31/classics-of-latin-music-que-nadie-sepa-mi-sufrir-by-hugo-de-carril-and-many-others/.

156 "Cristina Kirchner Inaugura el Centro Cultural que Costó Casi el Triple de su Presupuesto Inicial," *La Nacion*, May 21, 2015, https://www.lanacion.com.ar/politica/cristina-kirchner-inaugura-el-centro-cultural-que-costo-casi-el-triple-de-su-presupuesto-inicial-nid1794642/.

157 Bob Mondello, "In Argentina, Where Culture Is 'A Right,' A Free New Art Center Opens," NPR, October 3, 2015, https://www.npr.org/2015/10/03/442664722/in-argentina-where-culture-is-a-right-a-free-new-arts-center-opens?t=1595591772637.

158 "CCK: The Landmark Former Central Post Office Transformed into Latin America's Largest Cultural Centre," BA, accessed October 8, 2020, https://turismo.buenosaires.gob.ar/en/otros-establecimientos/cck.

159 Kelly Richman-Abdou, "The Story Behind Renoir's 'Bal du moulin de la Galette,'" My Modern Met, February 16, 2020, https://mymodernmet.com/renoir-bal-du-moulin-de-la-galette/.

160 Ed Loomis, "A Guide to Tango Terminology," Tejas Tango, December 13, 2005, https://www.tejastango.com/terminology.html#Y.

161 Alfred Romann, "Asia: World Tango Capital?" Huffington Post, June 3, 2015, https://www.huffpost.com/entry/asia-tango_n_7505828?guccounter=1.

162 Paula Cocozza, "No Hugging: Are We Living Through a Crisis of Touch?" *The Guardian*, March 7, 2018, https://www.theguardian.com/society/2018/mar/07/crisis-touch-hugging-mental-health-strokes-cuddles.

163 Matthew Fulkerstone, "Touch," *Stanford Encyclopedia of Philosophy*, May 6, 2020, https://plato.stanford.edu/entries/touch/.

164 Jonathan Jones, "Why Physical Touch Matters for Your Well-Being," *Greater Good Magazine*, November 16, 2018, https://greatergood.berkeley.edu/article/item/why_physical_touch_matters_for_your_well_being.

165 Maria Konnikova, "The Power of Touch," *The New Yorker*, March 4, 2015, https://www.newyorker.com/science/maria-konnikova/power-touch.

166 "Dos Colonenses Bailarán Juntas en el Mundial de Tango," Primera Plana,
     August 10, 2018, http://primeraplana.com.ar/dos-colonenses-bailaran
     -juntas-en-el-mundial-de-tango/.

167 Bridget Gleeson, "How Italians Influenced a South American Dialect," BBC,
     October 2, 2017 http://www.bbc.com/travel/story/20171001-how-italians
     -influenced-a-south-american-dialect.

168 Ramiro Barreiro, "¿Por Qué para los Argentinos Todo Es un 'Quilombo'?" *El
     País*, May 14, 2017, https://elpais.com/cultura/2017/05/11/
     actualidad/1494529191_436778.html.

169 "Biografía de Martín Miguel de Güemes," Gobierno del Salta, accessed July 27,
     2020, http://www.salta.gov.ar/contenidos/biografia-de-martin-miguel
     -de-guemes/8.

170 Paula Soler, "La Historia de Malevo: el Verdadero detrás de Escena de Su Llegada
     a America's Got Talent," *La Nacion*, December 22, 2016,
     https://www.lanacion.com.ar/espectaculos/la-historia-de-malevo-el
     -verdadero-detras-de-escena-de-su-llegada-a-americas-got-talent-nid1966895.

171 "Dancing through Time: The World Tango Museum," Wander Argentina,
     accessed July 30, 2020, https://wander-argentina.com/world-tango-museum/.

172 Jose Luis Borges and Astor Piazzolla, "Alguien le Dice al Tango," 1965,
     El Tango, Phonogram S.A.I.C.

7/7/21